MW00988992

The Greek Revolution and the Violent Birth of Nationalism

The Greek Revolution and the Violent Birth of Nationalism

YANNI KOTSONIS

PRINCETON UNIVERSITY PRESS
Princeton & Oxford

Published by Princeton University Press
41 William Street, Princeton, New Jersey 08540
99 Banbury Road, Oxford OX2 6JX

press.princeton.edu

Library of Congress Cataloging-in-Publication Data

Names: Kotsonis, Yanni, 1962– author.
Title: The Greek Revolution and the violent birth of nationalism / Yanni Kotsonis.
Description: Princeton : Princeton University Press, [2025] | Includes
    bibliographical references and index.
Identifiers: LCCN 2024007474 (print) | LCCN 2024007475 (ebook) |
    ISBN 9780691215266 (hardback) | ISBN 9780691263618 (ebook)
Subjects: LCSH: Greece—History—War of Independence, 1821–1829. |
    Europe—History—1815–1848.
Classification: LCC DF805 .K678 2025 (print) | LCC DF805 (ebook) |
    DDC 949.5/06—dc23/eng/20240229
LC record available at https://lccn.loc.gov/2024007474
LC ebook record available at https://lccn.loc.gov/2024007475

British Library Cataloging-in-Publication Data is available

Editorial: Priya Nelson and Emma Wagh
Production Editorial: Ali Parrington
Text and Jacket Design: Heather Hansen
Production: Danielle Amatucci
Publicity: Alyssa Sanford
Copyeditor: Tash Siddiqui

Jacket image: *Histoire Picturale de la Guerre de l'Independance Hellénique par le Général Yannis Makriyannis*, (Geneva, Éditions de l'Art; Paris, Jean Budry & Cie) 1926; 24 plates after scenes of the Greek War of Independence by Panagiotis Zographos. © The Trustees of the British Museum.

This book has been composed in Arno Pro with The Future

Printed in the United States of America

10 9 8 7 6 5 4 3 2 1

For My Trinity

Dionyssios Maximillian

Mathilda Persephone

James Galen

Independence Indeed

If you can look into the seeds of time,
And say which grain will grow and which will not

—Shakespeare, *Macbeth*

Contents

List of Maps

Transliteration, Names, and Dates

THERE IS NO satisfying way to render Greek words into English. In the endnotes and bibliography I keep to the system of the Library of Congress, with some simplification, because it is necessary in order to locate a source in a catalogue. This is not a complete solution: Dimitris Dimitropoulos writing in English is also Demetres Demetropoulos writing in Greek.

But in the text the formally transliterated words would become unpronounceable, mispronounced, and often harder to look up. How would anyone in any language pronounce the word for prisoners, "aichmalotoi"? (It is echmaloti.) The words for "Friendly Society," Philikē Hetaireia? (Filiki Eteria.) For identity, "tautoteta"? (Taftotita.) In modern Greek, holding over from ancient and Byzantine Greek, there are five ways to write what is pronounced as ē (as in "beet"), and two ways to write out what is pronounced as e (as in "elemental"). In the text I generally simplify them into i and e, respectively. Dēmētrēs is Dimitris, and Delēgiannēs is Deliyannis. Still there are adjustments based on common usage: the name Rigas is Righas, and the Phanariots remain Phanariots rather than Fanariots.

Common Ottoman-origin words that were assimilated into Greek are transliterated from Greek: aga rather than ağa, kotsabases rather than kocabaşı. Greek-speaking Muslims from the region are rendered in Greek, as they rendered themselves: Arnaoutoglou rather than Arnautoğlu. Ottoman words that are less associated with Greece and the Greeks are transliterated from Turkish: Küçük-Kaynarca, Çeşme, and Hurşid.

Place names are even more complicated and interesting. A single place could have several names and pronunciations. This variety was part of the cultural fabric of the time and place: Greek, Ottoman (now Turkish), Albanian, Slavic, and Vlach, not to mention the Italian, French, Russian, and English. The town of Nauplion is spoken Nafplio, and it was also Anapli, Napoli di Romagna, Naples de Romagne, Mora Yenişehir, and Anaboli. Places had ancient, medieval, early modern, and modern names: Peiraias is pronounced Pireas today, and usually rendered Piraeus, and it was also Porto Draco, Porto Leone, and Aslan Liman, and before that it was Peiraieus. After independence and into the current century place names were changed again in order to reclaim a Classical past or a Christian present, and remove a Turkish, Albanian, or Slavic heritage. I have opted for the current Greek names since it makes it easier to locate them on a map. I lose the cultural richness but gain practicability. Again there are exceptions. If one were to search for today's Tripoli, one might not make the connection to the bloody events of Tripolitsa in 1821; here and elsewhere I adopt the current Demotic Greek spelling (Tripolitsa) rather than the Romaic spelling of the time, Tripolitza, or for that matter the Slavic Drobolicha. I keep to Morea because a quick search will land the reader more readily in the era in question than the current name, Peloponnese. As a rule I adopt standard usage in English, when there is one: Athens rather than Athēna or Athēnai, Corfu rather than Kerkyra, Hydra rather than Ydra, Missolonghi rather than Messolongi, Mani rather than Manē. Agios (Saint) is more commonly Aghios.

Greek alphabetical numerations, usually in catalogues, periodicals, and dating, are rendered Arabic: Catalogue H' in the Vlachogiannes Collection is Catalogue 8.

Ukrainian and Russian transliteration are standardized by the Library of Congress, unless the words are published in a different language: Arsh in Russian is also Arš in French and Ars in Greek. Turkish, French, German, Italian, and Romanian are straightforward.

Dates are in the Gregorian calendar (New Style) unless the Julian calendar (Old Style, twelve days behind in the nineteenth century) is specified. Sometimes it is not clear which calendar is in use and I opt for months without dates or make it plain that I am guessing.

Notes of Thanks

IN THE COURSE of researching and writing this book I have watched my children become adults and they noticed my absences as I traveled across Europe. I was thankful when they came with me, and I apologize for the times they did not. But watch I did, and I am proud of one unquestionably good thing I have done in my life. Dionyssios Maximillian became a young man, bright and with a sense of justice, and with his own mind. Mathilda Persephone is becoming the woman she wants to be, always a force of nature, and with her own mind. James Galen doubled in height, mastering what he wants to master with ease and talent, and with his own mind. I offer them my unqualified love, my admiration, and my cooking. Their mother, Kate Warren, migrated to New York when I was away; I am grateful to her for the support, as are our children.

I was lucky to spend part of the coronavirus lockdown with Sophie Lambroschini, not long after we discussed cocktails, Molotov cocktails, infinity, and Θ. Like me she is a child of many cultures and we can share in references in English, French, and Russian. I do my best to follow her fluent Berliner and Ukrainian and I take refuge in Greek. Cosmopolitans with multiple roots, she told me during a sojourn in one of many places from New York to Doğubayazıt, Paris to Izmail, Berlin to Ajaccio, Athens to London. She understands what I mean before I say it. She showed me her chapters and I showed her mine. She helped make my manuscript more daring and more reasonable, much like herself. She was and is *ma blonde*. Kostis Smyrlis opened his home and his good mind to me during my several stays in Athens. Along with Denise Klein, Nikolas, and Manos, we had warmth and cheer in the challenging months of the coronavirus lockdown.

I came to this topic during a stay at the EHESS in Paris in 2017, where Alessandro Stanziani proposed that I visit the French military archives in Vincennes because, he said, one never knows what one will find. Neither of us expected that I would find the Greeks and wonder who they were. He gave me fair warning about the dangers of writing about small countries (Greece for me, Naples for him), lest we fall into parochialism. I agreed and I hope we were wrong.

Soon after Ada Dialla became a colleague with an excellent mind and moral daring. A Russianist like myself, both of us inhabiting what remains of the Left, we sounded out ideas and exchanged references, and we challenged each other to think better. She let me know when I was being outrageous, which happened more than once, and naïve, which happened once. Her sense of the complexity of any historical topic helped me qualify the general statement, but I hope not too much.

Konstatina Zanou has been encouraging, challenging, and frank in many good ways. She and Michalis Sotiropoulos read the entire manuscript and I am glad they did not hold back on the criticism because they helped make this a better book. The incomparably capable and genial Athena Bozika gathered my images and permissions, a task which is time-consuming and requires patience. She has both. The wise and careful Alec Shea interrupted his own writing in order to produce a very good index on short notice.

Others helped in large and small ways but always in important ways. I hope I remember them all. Vasilis Panagiotopoulos, Stephen Kotkin, and Fred Cooper spoke with me about the conceptual stakes early in the research. Jane Burbank spoke to me about the importance of empires until I was forced to agree. Guy Ortolano read, understood, and drew me into the literature on national thinking and writing, on Britain in particular. Tova Benjamin tackled sections with sharp clarity. Alex Drace-Francis and Victor Taki advised me on matters Danubian. The late, great Evrydiki (Roura) Sifneou told me of ships, ports, and Odesa. Theophilus Prousis and Lucien Frary, both the products of an exceptional advisor, worked with me on the Russo-Greek nexus. Yusuf Karabiçak was a resource on anything Ottoman and Romaic Greek. Leslie Peirce helped me with Ottoman biographies and harems. Tassos Anastassiadis advised on religion and the churches. Elizabeth Fowden is a resource on Ottoman archeology. Thanasis Barlayannis advised on the outbreak of plague in the Morea, Dean Kostantaras on the outbreak of the Revolution. Giulio Salvati and his family helped me with Ionian version of Venetian dialect, and we compared East German spoons. Socrates Petmezas told me of property regimes. Anusha Rathi applied her skills to debt crises, and Nicolas Delalande told me of the sovereign debt of imaginary countries. Alexander Kitroeff advised on the Greeks of Egypt, Peter Hill on Greek soldiers in Egypt, Nikos Karapidakis on the French in Corfu, and Nikos Chrissides on just about anyone and anything. So did the diligent Dimitris Dimitropoulos. Michalis Festas read the draft and advised me on place names and demographics. Aristides Hatzis helped with matters constitutional as well as the rich biography of Nicole Papasoglou, and kindly invited me to discuss my research in a public forum.

I was invited to present materials by Cheryl Sterling at Pennsylvania State University, Michael Gomez at New York University, Nada Zečević at Goldsmiths, and the sorely missed Philippa Hetherington of the School of Slavonic and East European Studies. The collective of the Ottoman Political Economies seminar indulged me twice by considering chapters of the manuscript. At Princeton I was invited to present an early overview of the project.

On Corfu I had the excellent guidance and hospitality of Dimitris Zymaris and Perikles Pangratis, masters of the local past and present. Daria Koskorou kindly opened her home and the collection of her ancestor Ioannis Kapodistrias. They all helped make my stay with my father part of our last, monumental trip together as we followed the Ionian coast and its sundry forts and historical place names until we reached our hometown of Pyrgos: his Ithaca.

Sakis Trambadoros in Pyrgos has a command of people, places, and sources, and more than once helped with Romaic script. My friend and *koumbaros* (*synteknos* as they say in his homeland) Giorgos Mathioudakis, my schoolmate from Kifisia's B' Elementary School, was a constant resource on the current press, commemorations, and matters Philhellene, Ottoman, and of course Cretan. He tolerated my heterodox views on Greek history with smiling indulgence.

Various people in the villages of the Peloponnese steered me to sources and showed me the locations. They are generous, knowledgeable, and enthusiastic, talented in their ability to make the past a present.

I am grateful to all the personnel at the institutions where I researched, most of them anonymous. They work hard and should really be paid better. The archives include the Archives Nationales in Paris, the Service Historique de la Défense in Vincennes, the Archives Diplomatiques in Nantes, the Bibliothèque de Genève and its manuscript collection, the National Archives in London, the British Library Manuscripts and Archives, the IEEE in Athens, and the ELIA-MIET in Athens. I got to know some individuals. Nella Pantazi at the state archives (GAK) in Corfu with its spectacular collection was a marvel of efficiency and collegiality. I appreciated arriving in the mornings and passing between the two dogs that guard the building's entrance, usually asleep. Tasos Sakellaropoulos at the Benaki Archive was likewise efficient and friendly, as was his dog which warmed itself against me and snored gently as I read. In the state archives (GAK) in Athens a very good and cheerful group led by Amalia Pappa made my stay productive. The libraries included the Bibliothèque Nationale de France including the Arsenal, the Gennadius Library, and the library of NYU. Ilya Oehring at the American Academy of Berlin was impressively helpful and congenial; there was not a book or article he could not find. Indispensable in conditions of lockdown, and not only, was the Anemi Digital Library of Modern Greek Studies.

I received support and hospitality from the EHESS in Paris. A Fulbright fellowship in Athens was facilitated by the helpful Nicholas Tourides, and I was hosted by the good colleagues at the Athens School of Fine Arts who are an inventive group encouraging imagination. The Jordan Center for the Advanced Study of Russia financed research and hosted a conference, and when Josh Tucker replaced me as director his support was consistent, collegial, and unreserved. The European University Institute invited me as a Weber fellow and I regret that due to the pandemic I was not able to take full advantage. At the American Academy in Berlin I was the Gerhard Casper fellow and I was given incomparably good conditions to read and write in fall 2021: quiet, shelter, food, and a view of the lake. The Academy's *Berlin Journal* published my writings on the Battle of Dervenakia in issue 35 (2021–2) and some of that material appears here in chapter 11, with permission. It was a treat to be invited to work at the École Française d'Athènes in summer 2020: the grounds are special. The Global Research Initiatives of NYU, managed by Maya Jex, made additional stays in Athens and Paris possible and seamless.

I visited Ukraine in 2023 and I am grateful to the personnel of the Izmail Historical Regional Museum of the Danube for addressing my interests and receiving me in wartime conditions. An assortment of Izmail history lovers confirmed for me the places that were once Greek. The house where the Revolution was planned is gone, and any hope of locating the site was dashed the next day when Russia bombed the area. The staff of the Nizhyn Spaskiy Regional Museum likewise took out time from the war to volunteer information and original photographs which appear in chapter 8, including the history of the Nizhyn pickle. A pickled Bonaparte is memorialized on the island of Spetses and a photo appears in chapter 14, courtesy of Alexandra Manoli who volunteered her time and talent.

At Princeton University Press I had early conversations with Brigitta van Rheinberg while Eric Crahan explained how we might work together on this book. Priya Nelson worked with me in a sustained and encouraging way. I was blessed with the expert attentions of Morgan Spehar and the infinitely patient and capable Emma Wagh. Tash Siddiqui applied time and understanding to the copyediting. Ali Parrington coordinated people and departments.

If this book has merits, it owes a lot to this assortment of people—a family, *ma blonde*, a few friends, and the colleagues and professionals who breathe life into institutions and inspire me. Writing is solitary but it can only happen thanks to the constancy of a collective.

Greenwich Village,
December 2023

The Greek Revolution
and the Violent Birth
of Nationalism

The Greek Revolution and Our Modern World

Theodore Kolokotronis and the Arc of Modern Europe

THEODORE KOLOKOTRONIS IS not the subject of this book but he is a good way to introduce it. Kolokotronis was a commander of the Christian forces during the Greek Revolution, and today he is celebrated as a national hero. Rightly so: he was probably the most talented strategist of the Greek revolutionary era, rivaled only by his nemesis, Ibrahim pasha of Egypt. He lends his name to countless streets across Greece and his statue overlooks town squares. As a statue he is permanent and inevitable, like so many statues that oversee squares the world over. He has a determined frown. He knows where he is going, to Greek independence, and he points the way with an extended finger or sword, or leads with one foot forward. He was more interesting than that. He was all about motion, choices, uncertainties, and surprises to which he adjusted, until he made the final transformation: he abandoned the empires he had served most of his life and became a Greek in the nation-state of Greece. He was change itself.[1]

For most of his life Kolokotronis was known as Little Theodore (Thodorakis). Thodorakis is familiar and affectionate. It is a diminutive that captures something of the prerevolutionary setting of clans, friendships, loyalties, clientelism, loathing, and conspiracy that come from personal knowledge and intimacy. He was very much a man of the

Morea (today the Peloponnese), specifically its western coast. His friends and collaborators were both Christians and Muslims, and so were his enemies. In 1821 he used his networks of clan and region to carry out the Revolution and help create a nation-state that superseded the networks of clan and region and put an end to Islam in the region. From that time he became Theodore (Theodoros), the formal rendering of his name that befitted a man who would become a statue, the leader of a nation that seemed eternal as soon as it was created. And so he was fixed, as Theodore, in the history books, coins, stamps, coloring books, and board games. His life of choices and risks is lost; the circumstances and conjunctures that made Greece are also lost. This book aims to recover the uncertainty that preceded the Greek Revolution and made the Revolution, and Greece, a surprise.

Kolokotronis was born an Ottoman subject in 1770. Like his father and grandfather before him, Kolokotronis was a bandit for hire in the Ottoman Morea, working for Christians and Muslims alike. He was a man of his region and he was also an imperial creature, traveling easily from employer to employer. This was an age of empires, and there was no shame or treason in changing patrons. It was, at worst, a breach of contract.

Kolokotronis fought on many sides of the small-scale civil wars in the Ottoman Morea and worked with all sides of the Napoleonic Wars. Around 1800 he was hired by Christian landowners in the Morea to protect them against bandits like himself. When the anarchy was too much for the Christian landowners, when they were losing out on the economic boom that was the Napoleonic Wars, the Christians joined with Muslim landowners, Orthodox priests, monks, and Christian peasants to hunt him down. He escaped to the Ionian Islands in 1806 and left behind the corpses of many of his relatives and followers.

The Ionian Islands were only a boat ride away, a day or less in favorable winds. But the islands were in a different empire. They had been Venetian territory, from 1797 they were French and in 1806 they were Russian. The Napoleonic Wars had arrived in the region and opportunity beckoned. Kolokotronis became a corsair flying the Russian flag until he was arrested for attacking the wrong places. The order to arrest him came from Count Giovanni Capo d'Istria, later known as Ivan Kapodistriia the Russian statesman, Jean Capodistrias the European diplomat, and finally Ioannis Kapodistrias the first governor of Greece. (Given his evolutions, in places we will call him simply the Count, the one stability in his varied life.) But in 1807 the Count was an Ionian Islander in Russian service, and Thodorakis was an Ottoman Morean mercenary who had breached his contract. Thodorakis apologized and asked for his back wages. The Count released him, an act of *noblesse oblige.*

Undeterred, Kolokotronis returned to the Morea when he was hired by a Muslim notable named Ali Farmaki. Ali was his blood brother, a Muslim and a Greek speaker, and together they fought against the Morean pasha, also a Muslim and also a Greek speaker. When the two were defeated they again fled to the Ionian Islands. Now the islands were French again, and the conspirators asked to go to France to meet Napoleon; relations should be personal. They did not meet Napoleon but their proposal was transmitted up the army hierarchy. They wanted France to invade their homeland and end the rule of the sultan in the Morea. Under France, Muslim and Christian notables would share power and continue their pitiless exploitation of the peasantry. But just then the British were invading the islands and evicting the French, so Thodorakis abandoned the French plan and joined the British to fight the French. He attacked other Ottoman Christians and Ionian Islanders who were fighting on the side of the French, and he became an officer in the Duke of York's Greek Light Infantry. He affirmed his loyalty to "my king," George III of Great Britain.

It was here that the British gifted him the famous helmet that he wore through the revolutionary decade. It was the helmet of a dragoon, and dragoon helmets at the time were modeled on ancient Greek designs.[2] The British no doubt wished to honor his Greek heritage. Kolokotronis appreciated the symbol of British imperial might. Decades later, when the helmet was put on display in the National Historical Museum in Athens, his helmet became a symbol of modern Greece. In front of the museum is the equine statue of Kolokotronis in that same helmet, a good resting place for pigeons. What the British thought he should be,

FIGURE 0.1. Statue of Theodore Kolokotronis in Front of the National Historical Museum, Athens. Sculpted by Lazaros Sochos, 1895. Photograph by Paschalis Basios, 2023. *This is the most known of the Kolokotronis statues that adorn
squares in Greece.*

why he valued the helmet, how he is remembered, and the indifference of the pigeons are all captured nicely in this one artefact.

With the end of the Napoleonic Wars in the region, in 1814, he was discharged and unemployed. He stayed on the Ionian Islands under British rule and became a butcher—not figuratively, but literally, a purveyor of beef—as well as a grocer and a moneylender. His life under the British in Zante (today Zakynthos) was secure if boring and predictable, and his records from the time are ledgers and IOUs. As an Ottoman subject and a professional warrior, he had lost most of his relatives and his homeland. On the Ionian Islands he lost court cases. When the authorities discovered that he was using a house in town to keep his sheep and goats, which was against local ordinances, they did not extort him or loot the premises, they asked him to move his livestock. His neighbors were all Christians, like himself. Could the stability of the European empires since 1815 be recreated in his homeland in the Morea, with Orthodox Christians in charge? Was the Christian predominance in Europe, the relative homogeneity of the population, the source of European stability and power?

During his stays on the Ionian Islands he learned of the French Revolution, of nations, and of the mass mobilizations of the revolutionary era. He learned of the Greeks past and present, and read stories that were not in ancient Greek or church Greek. They were in a vernacular that was close to his own. The books were financed and shipped by a network of Greek merchants from around the Mediterranean and Black seas who were promoting an idea of Greekness that they were just learning about themselves. He identified with the people in the histories and identified with the people bringing the books. They were all part of an ancient continuum and a current community. He had not met all the Greeks and they were not on intimate terms, but they existed in his thoughts and in his books. Greece was an abstraction but it was acted out in a new solidarity. And soon the abstraction was armed.

From Greek merchants hailing from Russia he learned of a secret society formed in Odesa that recruited Orthodox members in the eastern Mediterranean. Its goal was to overthrow the sultan and create a Christian Greece. He joined. It matters that that the merchants were from Russia and he was in exile: nationalism sometimes flourishes when it incubates abroad, where unimaginable radicalisms can be imagined. At a meeting in Izmail (then in the Russian Empire, today in Ukraine) the members were told that there would be an uprising in March 1821. Word reached Kolokotronis on Zakynthos. He settled his business, boarded a boat, met up with his kin and comrades, and took the region of Kalamata from the Ottoman Muslims.

In his memoirs he was proud and careful to describe the flags he created and took into each campaign, including a flag with the cross and the crescent. In the 1820s he flew only the cross. In 1821 he and his men scoured the countryside and killed Muslims, and they persuaded and intimidated the Christian villagers to join them in a mass assault on all Muslims. As the commander of the Greek Christian forces, he oversaw the siege of the Morean capital Tripolitsa and witnessed its storming. He rode over some of the fifteen thousand corpses of men, women, and children that his men left behind. At the battle of Dervenakia in 1822, he commanded the forces that annihilated an Ottoman army and secured a purely Christian peninsula. He was at the head of not only a band of men but a national mass mobilization. This was new and it explains how the Christians, now united as Greeks, overcame the armies of the sultan. It was the *levée en masse* and he had learned it from the French. It was to put a bloody end to the chaotic violence that was the Ottoman regime in the region.

It was a demographic solution to a political problem. It was the mass mobilization of people into one category (the Greeks) in order to create another (the Turks) and make it disappear. Like any revolution that deserves the name, it was a great reorganization of people, territory, and allegiances. The same Kolokotronis who killed Christians and Muslims alike for most of his life, and who fought alongside Christians and Muslims alike, would now kill Muslims and refrain from killing Christians if possible. The Christians who would have gladly killed Kolokotronis in 1806 refrained from killing him when they fell out in the 1820s. They put him in prison. Muslim adversaries received no quarter, or they were enslaved, or they were ransomed, or they converted to Orthodoxy, or they went into permanent exile. Cohabitation was no longer an option.

Kolokotronis learned from the empires. He merged revolutionary enlightenment with Ottoman confessional governance, the brotherhood of citizens with the exclusivity of a nation, his long experience in warfare with a national cause. Absolute national belonging informed notions of total war where entire peoples were thrown at other peoples in a final confrontation. All in all, Kolokotronis had learned that people rather than only land and things were a source power that could function as a new weapon. By the same token, people rather than only generals and rulers were his enemy. His tactical innovation was the *levée en masse*. His strategy was the nation itself. His greatest discovery was popular sovereignty.

Kolokotronis died of old age in 1843 and became a statue. It is a monument to the nation that had recently come into being, soon styled eternal and unchanging. I hope we can look at the statue and recall the many things that he had been that made him interesting, and the many things that Greece might have been and might yet be.

The Empires that Made the Nation

National heroes like Kolokotronis were the children of empires,[3] and what would become Greece was an imperial crossroads. Most of the people who would become Greeks were subjects of the Ottoman sultan. Like so many empires—Russia, for example—the Ottoman Empire was organized around religion, and confessional institutions were a part of Ottoman governance. In theory each religion was protected.[4] It became common after the Greek Revolution to propose that the Ottoman Muslims persecuted the Christians as Christians but we know that this is untrue. Before the Revolution schools teaching Greek and Orthodoxy flourished and were patronized by regional Muslim rulers. The Orthodox patriarch in Istanbul was appointed by the sultan and the church was a part of the Ottoman administration. The problem lay in the inability of the Ottoman old regime to deliver on its promises of protection and security, and people of all religions suffered from official theft, arbitrariness, banditry, and each other. Ottomans of all religions fought each other in small rebellions and civil wars. Poverty was deep and endemic, with layers of Christian and Muslim notables, and Christian merchants and moneylenders, feeding on a mass of impoverished peasants.

Violence and poverty alone do not make revolutions. Were that the case, revolutions would be happening every day. Solidarity within the elite, in this case the Christian and Muslim elite, ensured that peasant disaffection would not go beyond small acts of resistance, banditry, and migration. Revolutions occur when it becomes possible to imagine something better, when expectations are higher, unrealized, and dashed.[5] These possibilities arose when new empires entered the region with different models of statehood, of law and order, and of security that made daily existence in the Ottoman regime seem retrograde, unacceptable, and brittle enough to overthrow. These ideas infected the Christian elite in particular because the European empires entering the region sought out the Christians as their natural allies. The encounter produced a rupture with their Muslim counterparts. People may rebel as they often did, but a crisis in the elite can land a rebel in a revolution.

The first outside incursion was Russian. Russia's victories on a broad front from the Danubian region (roughly today's Romania and Moldova) to the Caucasus (Azerbaijan, Armenia, and Georgia) from 1768 stripped the sultan of the entire northern coast of the Black Sea. The fighting spilled southward through what is today called the Balkans (roughly Romania to Greece). Russian expeditions stirred up rebellions as far south as the Morea and the Aegean Archipelago. Locals could see a more powerful army and state in action as it defeated the Ottoman armies in wars that erupted regularly. Balkan Christians, some uprooted, most in search of wealth and careers, streamed northward and settled the new cities of the Black Sea with Odesa at its center. It was in Russia that the hodgepodge of Balkan Christians consolidated their sense of Greekness, it was in imperial Odesa (today Ukraine) that the conspiracy that sparked the Revolution was hatched, and it was in Izmail (Ukraine) that the insurrection was planned.

The Napoleonic Wars further changed regional politics, as they changed politics around the world. Three empires entered the region through the Ionian Sea in the west. The Venetian Empire was overthrown by France in 1797 and France took the Ionian Islands. From that time the Ionian Islands were taken successively by the Russians, the French again, and finally the British in 1814. From the Ionian Islands one could gaze at the Ottoman mainland across the narrow channels, at the Morean Peninsula and Epirus centered in Yanena (Yanya in Ottoman, Ioannina in formal Greek). From the Ionian Islands the European powers intervened in the politics of the Ottoman Balkans. Invasion seemed possible, sometimes imminent.

The Balkan Ottomans gazed back. Muslims as well as Christians conspired with these powers and entertained offers of collaboration. One can understand why. The new empires in the region represented alternative models of stability and discipline, and it was their stability and discipline that impressed the Ottoman notables who ruled locally. The arriving empires may have been liberal, autocratic, or constitutional, they may have been Catholic, Protestant, or Orthodox, but they were all regularized states. To be sure, the European empires were hugely violent: what else could one call two decades of almost constant war, from Moscow to Madrid, from Germany to Italy, from Haiti to Cairo, from Spain to India? But the violence of the European empires was organized in a different way. It was largely predictable, it was in pursuit of a shared policy, the soldiers more or less followed orders, and they fought toward a strategic goal. They privileged the Christians.

The empires were also better paymasters and they offered careers to the aspiring mercenary. Tens of thousands of armed men from the Ottoman mainland worked for these empires. The people loosely called Greeks by the Europeans (they meant the Orthodox Christians) could pick and choose their empires. Familiar local wars were globalized, Ottoman Christians marched in all the imperial armies, and they sailed the seas under a dizzying variety of flags. Merchants and landowners sold their goods to all the armies and navies as they capitalized on a war boom.

The arrival of the new empires was a threat to Ottoman sovereignty. Different sultans reacted with efforts to direct more resources to a single imperial policy and defend the realm from outside incursions. The more the sultan tried to mobilize his subjects to defend the realm, the more intense the local violence and warfare. Local people pushed back and they conspired to seize resources from each other. In the long run Ottoman reform could produce system, predictability, and security, but in the short run the vestiges of the old regime competed even harder to carve out or maintain wealth and influence.[6] The most dangerous time for a weak regime is when it tries to reform itself.[7]

With the wars in the region over in 1814, tens of thousands of Greek mercenaries were unemployed, as were tens of thousands of soldiers across Europe. Some of the merchants and notables who had done so well off the wars saw their revenues shrink, and the incomes of craftsmen fell. Sailors were unemployed.[8] For many others trade continued to yield huge fortunes, and the dashed expectations of some were joined by the rising expectations of others. But there was not yet a good reason to suppose that there was to be a revolution, let alone a national one that pitted one confession against another. Christian notables could complain of their lost affluence or chronic insecurity, but so could the Muslims. Peasants could complain of their enduring poverty, but this was not new.

It took something more to make Ottoman multiconfessionalism into national exclusiveness, and that something was Europe—both the Enlightened version that produced the French Revolution, and the reactionary version that gathered in Vienna from 1815 to assert that Europe was Christian.

The Greeks of 1821 drew on both versions of Europe: they mass mobilized, and they created a nation of Christians.

Which Europe? The Greek Revolution as a European Event[9]

For some decades handfuls of Orthodox intellectuals had been exploring the European Enlightenment as a way to address the character of the would-be Greeks inhabiting the sundry empires. Some adopted the liberal creed. In the 1820s, in the midst of the Revolution, they wrote constitutions and laws. Quite a lot has been written about these intellectuals but these were a few people who wrote quite a lot.[10] In the history books they overwhelm the people who actually did the fighting in 1821–2. And yet the basic concept that was at stake in these writings was popular sovereignty, and this was acted out and practiced during the mass mobilization that gripped the southern Balkans. The tens of thousands of fighters did not read documents—most could not read— but for a brief moment they took control of their lives and went into action. They were entitled and empowered. Some concepts filtered to them and gave them an idiom and a direction, legitimizing and shaping what they were doing. The distinction between Muslim and Christian became an absolute binary opposition. The very term that the revolutionaries used to describe themselves changed rapidly in 1821: people who called themselves some variation on Christian revived the ancient term for a Greek: *Ellinas* or Hellene. It is what the Greeks call themselves today, living in land called Hellas. Armed in a new national whole, the Greeks mobilized.

Mass mobilization was the most important idea that the Greeks learned from the revolutionary and Napoleonic era: the peasant soldiers learned it from the warlords; the warlords had learned it in the European armies; the privileged Christian notables feared it but were forced to accept and use it. Without mass mobilization a Greek victory was unimaginable. Popular sovereignty was very much at issue for the peasant warrior but it was not always a matter of pristine liberty, and it was not bound by the legalistics of the sundry constitutions. It empowered people to march, kill, loot, enslave, and burn, and it gave the victors and survivors a basis to demand a better life. An imperial subject could supplicate and negotiate with a distant authority; a citizen was a member of the nation and could demand.

The revolutionaries spoke and acted the ideas of rights and sovereignty, but in this time and place these ideas, once a matter of the rights of man, were being particularized as the rights of the nation. The new nation was exclusive and limited to the Christians. In this regard the Greeks were appealing to a different kind of Europe, where liberalism was on the retreat. The imperial and royal courts and cabinets were part of the Congress System and the Holy Alliance, that system of monarchial domination that was established in Vienna in 1815 and continued to oversee European affairs into the 1820s. Led by Russia, the European cabinets were responding to the upheaval of the revolutionary and Napoleonic wars with a heightened sense of hierarchy, superordinate power, and Christianity. There were liberal elements in this system, to be sure, but not much of this was left by the time of the Greek Revolution in 1821.[11] At that moment the European powers were in the midst of a full-blown reaction and putting down revolutions in Italy. The Spanish Revolution was put down by French troops in 1823. Even Britain, which fancied itself aloof of the continental patterns, was reacting to revolutions with retrenched hierarchy authority.[12] The Greeks who rose up in 1821 sought European support and they were rebuffed because they seemed like one more conspiracy against established authority. It was exactly the wrong time for a revolution of the Greeks, and the European powers quietly hoped that the sultan would do to the Greeks what they themselves were doing to the Italians and Spaniards.

The Greeks adjusted to appear less liberal and not even revolutionary. Theirs was a war of separate peoples, Greeks and Turks, and the Turks were not compatriots and neighbors but foreign occupiers; what happened in Spain and Italy were civil wars among Christians. Contemporaries said all this at every opportunity and we need to listen more carefully. The Greek Revolution was exceptional, they held, not on a continuum with 1789 or the revolutions of Spain and Italy that erupted in 1819 and 1820. (Or even 1776: "banish the thought," *alimono*, wrote the notable Sisinis when writing about the connection between the American and Greek revolutions.) It was religious, a Christian war against the sultan and Islam. Liberty would apply to the nation only, and that nation was Christian. The movement of Philhellenes—the friends of the Greeks—came into existence across Europe to support the Greeks as Christians. They covered the whole spectrum from ultra-royalism and autocracy to liberalism and republicanism, but as Christians defending Christians they could find common cause. Many called their support for the Greeks a crusade and religious language permeated their appeals.

The Greeks and their supporters fused the two Europes into a new kind of nation. The talk and performance of liberty and rights, the stuff of the Enlightenment and the Age of Revolutions, were real and persistent, but these ideas were encased in a limited and exclusive nation. The background to the entire revolutionary decade, the setting in which liberty was understood, was exclusively Christian, and the axis of confrontation was religion. It was a historic compromise between the rights of man and the Romantic essence of a nation.[13] Greece was Christian. Others would have to convert, leave, or die.

European diplomats began to listen, though for their own reasons. They were impatient and alarmed by the regional instability that was a breeding ground for piracy along a major trading route. They had given the sultan five years to settle the matter, in the way that they themselves had settled matters in Spain and Italy. In 1826 and 1827 three powers (Russia, Britain, and France) warmed to the Greek cause because, they could now argue, it was not even a revolution. It was a Christian war of liberation from an alien, Oriental power. It was a war of nations. It was a War of Independence. The powers intervened. By 1830, with the Revolution redefined as something other than revolutionary, the European powers decreed a Greece with full independence for one reason in particular: it had a majority Christian population, it had been ruled by Muslims, and it was in Europe. French troops arrived to evacuate the last Muslims. The process that made Greece into a homogeneous space was begun on the ground in 1821 and blessed and completed by Europe around 1830.

There is a quiet paradox underlying the whole sequence leading to Greek independence and it requires more attention that is usually receives. It concerns Russia. For well over a century historians have worked mightily to associate the Revolution with Europe to the west, not to the north. And yet anti-revolutionary Russia incubated the nationalist movement that would produce the Greek Revolution. Autocratic Russia led the way to recognizing popular sovereignty insofar as it recognized the nation, in Greece to begin with but more generally in European diplomacy and finally worldwide. Multiconfessional Russia had agreed that a new nation be recognized with only one official religion. Russia had opened a Pandora's Box, mostly unwittingly.

The Demographic Revolution

The decade 1821–30 saw a thoroughgoing demographic revolution. This aspect of the Greek Revolution, its novel and shocking violence visited on towns, villages, households, families, and persons, as it sought out and destroyed an entire category of population, is too often missed because it is subordinated to words like "victory" in battle, the "fall" of a given town, and the "liberation" of a region. Some allowances are made to cast the massacres as the unfortunate side-effects of war. But this targeted and categorical violence was not an unintended consequence; it was the goal of the warfare. Contemporaries said as much as they attacked their neighbors, and we should listen more carefully. Muslims should not inhabit the land and they should never return. Popular sovereignty made all people in some way significant—significant enough to be empowered and to make demands, or significant enough to be worth killing.[14] The creation of modern totalizing categories can be the prehistory of their destruction.[15] In this time and place, the creation of two antagonistic demographic categories—Christian against Muslim, Greek against Turk—made the violence total and final.

It is easy to call this "ethnic cleansing," a term coined in the 1990s for Yugoslavia, but this does not capture the process that not only removed the Muslims but also made the myriad Christians into Greeks. It is better called simplification: the creation of two new national totalities, the one unified for the first time, the other erased. The disappearance of Islam is remarkable, and so is the merger of such a diverse patchwork of languages, dialects, regions, and localities into a single Greek nation. Nations destroy and nations create; they efface and they empower.

It was a great realignment. People loved and loathed in new ways, they marched with people they had recently fought, and they killed people who had recently been their comrades and neighbors. The new binary of Greek and Turk was absolute, and the myriad ethnicities of the region were simplified into two. The Muslims may have spoken Greek, Turkish, Albanian, or Roma, but henceforth they would be Turks and they belonged in Asia, not Europe. Christians also spoke Greek, Albanian, Turkish, and Roma, as well as Vlach and Italian. They could stay, and they would now be Greeks in Europe. Later they would be taught a standardized Greek language. Out of a mix of cultures emerged a totalizing binary, a war of total destruction, and a new kind of total unity. Changing masters was no longer normal; it was treason.

The empires converged on this place to create modern Greece. It was recognizably French in its totalizing tendencies and its capacity to mobilize the masses, Ottoman in its assumption that populations were defined by confession, and European in its heightened sense of Christian exclusivity, its civilizational superiority. Together these tendencies produced a demographic engineering of geography. They produced the national state.

And yet Muslims were and are indigenous to Europe.[16] Muslims were in Europe at the very time that a geopolitical Europe came into being in 1648. Writing them out of the history books was part and parcel of a new Christianization of Europe. To be sure, Muslims had been pushed out of the continent before, most notoriously in Spain from the eighth to the fifteenth centuries. But those expulsions were carried out by sovereign kings, not a mass movement; in warfare between kingdoms, not peoples; and did not leave in their wake a nation. It was also piecemeal, and it was only termed a single process after the fact, in the nineteenth century when nations were new and real, and historians began to term it a Reconquista and a national movement.[17] The Greek Revolution was thoroughly modern: it entailed mass mobilization, it rested on popular sovereignty, and it put in place a new kind of belonging that was national.

The Greek model spread. Since the 1820s new Balkan states have been systematically removing the traces of Islam, both the people and the landmarks.[18] The Yugoslav War of the 1990s is only the most recent instalment. The outward trickle of Muslims from Bulgaria is ongoing. Bosnia and Kosovo persist as precarious islands of Islam in a decidedly Christian sea. Europe as a whole has worked concertedly into the present day to keep Muslim migrants out of the continent. The front line of the continent was established by the European powers in 1830 and is patrolled into the present day: Greece, a cartographic, diplomatic, and demographic fact.

The Congress System had made Europe absolutely Christian. The granting of Greek independence made the Balkan Christians absolutely European. Both the land and the population would be the eastern boundary of Europe and of European civilization. 1821 was the start of the Balkan Century as more Ottoman peoples claimed nationhood based on their Christianity. The final act came a century later, in 1923, when the remains of the Ottoman Empire were overthrown by the Muslims who now called themselves Turks. The population of the Republic of Turkey was homogenized using the same axis as the Greeks of 1821, but in mirror-image. Now it was the Christians who had to leave, and Turkey made its way to becoming absolutely Muslim.

Writing the Nation: The Making of an Eternity

Explaining how Greeks became Greek is important. Historical actors become people facing circumstances and making choices rather than characters following a script written by Cleo.

We have a veritable sea of histories of the Revolution of 1821, which around the bicentenary became an ocean. In the buildup to 2021 the Greek press dutifully reported each new publication with a detectable groan and good humor. Most of this literature is in Greek and it can be very good. There are accessible overviews that synthesize large bodies of research and are good reads.[19] We have revealing and suggestive case studies that delve into specific topics, question the factual basis of the existing narrative, and put on display excellent research and methodologies.[20] The Russian-language scholarship, much of it from Soviet times, is expert and compelling.[21] In English there are some beautifully written books, from William St. Clair on the Philhellenes to the biographies written by C. M. Woodhouse.[22]

The Greeks rose up, then, but how did the Greeks become Greek? How did an imperial existence produce a national state? The usual answer is that the nation already existed but this is problematic because the Greeks had been imperial creatures, like most of the world. Historians of Greece have worked to extract from an imperial mosaic a discrete and homogeneous people. This is not unusual and much the same was done by historians of Britain, for example, from the nineteenth century: a certain race or people was pulled out of the fluidity of global empire, and a nation existed, untouched, despite revolutionary changes that gripped every facet and level of the polity.[23] Someone describing the American Revolution as the work of lifelong patriots is at odds with the historian of colonial America where those same patriots were loyal subjects of the king; George Washington fought for George III before he fought against him.

We all, collectively, tend to assume the existence of the nation and we project it backward, onto a time when there was no such thing. Professional history writing and national states emerged at the same time, in the nineteenth century, and historians have tended to assume and often identify with the nation. Writing history becomes part of an ongoing national project, not a study in national projects.[24] With history written in, for, and about the nation, it is a way to affirm and reaffirm the timeless reality of the nation, often traveling from some sort of darkness (the nation under a foreign yoke or absolute monarch) to some sort of light (national liberation, popular sovereignty, and the current nation-state).

But there was no nation until there was, and this is something worth writing about. For Greece, Konstantina Zanou began a rethinking in her study of the Ionian Islands in the revolutionary era, as a variety of people were faced with the new and simple choice, to decide whether they were Italian or Greek. One's sense of self was up for grabs, and this is a good way to think of the Greek Revolution as a whole. Anta (Ada) Dialla tells of Russian imperial ambition in the Mediterranean and points out that before 1821 Russians could not say for sure if the Aegean Archipelago and the eastern Mediterranean were Europe, Asia, or Africa. The ambiguity did not go away. Christine Philliou looks at the matter from the Ottoman perspective after 1821, when many of the people called Greeks remained in the Ottoman Empire and led imperial, not national, lives. In Greek Kostis Papagiorges tells of the tumult and violence of the Greek mainland from Yanena to Athens in the 1820s, and shows that national belonging was new, and for very many it was optional. Dionysis Tzakis shows the same in revealing case studies. Roderick Beaton enriches the story of Byron and breathes savvy life into Philhellenism as a quest for purpose on the part of men like Byron who was always ambiguous about the Greeks to whom he was, in the last few years of his life, committed.[25]

Outside of these studies it is something of an orthodoxy that a Greece and the Greeks have always existed. Like any nation, it claims to be eternal, which means that a revolution is a natural and perhaps inevitable event: a preexisting people finally pulls the trigger on a foreign conqueror and occupier. In fact no state called Greece had ever existed before. Loose references to Greece as a place around 1800 located it in any number of places. Revolutionaries thought that Greece might include today's Romania, which is in fact where the uprising of 1821 began, or that it might include the rest of the Balkans, Constantinople, and Anatolia. Some maps called the same places Macedonia, Turkey, Illyria, Serbia, Albania, and a host of local designations.

As for the people, it is a consensus, implicit or explicit, that there have always been Greeks who trace a line to Classical times, to Byzantium, or to both. By that reckoning they were persistently Greek, and three centuries of Ottoman and Venetian rule were a veneer. The Revolution was the proof. But the people whom others called Greek, and who called themselves Greek from 1821, called themselves a variety of things before 1821, and Greek was not one of them. Most often they were the Christians, what the Ottomans called the Rum, derived from Romans. In Greek it was Romios (plural Romiï), and colloquially it still is. They were the descendants of the Eastern Roman Empire and latterly the subjects of the sultan. But by that standard all Orthodox peoples from Trabzon to Bucharest, from Damascus to Athens, from Romanians and Serbs to Arabs and everyone in between, were Greek because they were all heirs to Byzantium. The Roma (Gypsies) claimed the same heritage.

Language does not narrow the field. Very many Muslims spoke Greek. People who spoke Greek and practiced Orthodoxy were distinct from the Ottoman Christians if they lived in lands to the west or north of the Balkan mainland, in Italy and Russia. They were Graiki (singular Graikos). Nor did all Greeks in 1821 speak Greek at home. Very many of the leaders of the Revolution spoke Greek but swore and sang in Albanian: Botsaris, Tzavellas, Androutsos, Karaiskakis, Miaoulis, Kanaris, and Bouboulina, to name only a few. The Greek revolutionary Righas Velestinlis was Vlach. The native language of the first governor of Greece was Italian and his Greek was halting. And yet somehow this Tower of Babel became the Greeks, and a Greek nation became very real.

Nations happen. With this truism in mind, Greece becomes a study in national formation, not national awakening. Since just about any Greek of 1820 was an imperial subject, the empires become the spaces where Greek nationalism was produced, not simply the regimes that held it back. This book tells the story of the many things that people could be, until the Revolution, quite suddenly, produced only two: Greek and Turk, though the Turks did not yet know it. Lost in the re-sorting were the Albanians, Catholics, Vlachs, Jews, and Roma who had to choose one or the other side—there was no third way—or leave.[26]

This story will tell of the many other things that the regional Christians were (chapters 1–6), suggest how this was changing by looking at one man (chapter 7), and consider where and how the Greeks arrived at their Greekness in their new settlements in Russia (chapter 8). It will remain to explain how a nation was consolidated from 1821 onward, how imperial complaint congealed into a national movement during the Revolution itself (chapters 9–14). The Greek nation was very nearly quashed by an Egyptian invasion that the Greeks could neither resist nor understand (chapter 15), and saved by a European mobilization of public opinion, diplomacy, armies, and navies (chapter 16). The independence that followed was ambiguous: a tiny country visited periodically by the gunboats of the empires and burdened by foreign loans, it anticipated a world of nation-states, governed and disciplined by sovereign debt (Epilogue).

The Crooked Line to 1821

The point of this book is to depart from the straight-line narrative and make the line to 1821 and 1830 crooked.[27] We should not be concerned with the coherence of the narrative, because at the time events seemed incoherent and the narrative seemed to lead in multiple directions. We should not follow our actors to their destination because they themselves did not know where they were going. The individual stories and microhistories that follow illustrate these many possibilities. Nor will it do to fit all the pieces into their place because contemporaries did not know what that place would be. We should remind ourselves that Greece and its Revolution were a novelty to all, including most of the revolutionaries. We should not recognize the Greek Revolution but encounter it. Cliché should be replaced by marvel and curiosity. But the same is true of any historical event and the story of Greece is a case study in something universal. It is a way of approaching what seems normal and natural and then doubting it, recovering its newborn glow. The world should be made strange[28] and once again interesting. We should marvel at its novelty.

The Archival Remains of the Empires

We will visit the less-known characters that are languishing in archives and old books, in Paris, Nantes, London, Geneva, Athens, and Corfu. The Greeks in 1820 were all subjects of the empires and a few kingdoms, and there was no Greek state to organize their lives into archives. Greek archivists have done an excellent job gathering together personal collections and scattered documents. But many of the stories surrounding the Greek Revolution are to be found in the archival remains of the empires. During my visits to Paris, Nantes, and London, I was in the company of north Africans, west Africans, south Asians, and southeast Asians investigating their national pasts and family genealogies, who by their very presence affirmed that our pasts are also imperial. Similarly, the magnificent archive of Corfu is in fact the records of successive imperial masters, the Venetians, French, Russians, and British.

I do not read Ottoman. I do read the main Ottoman language of the Balkans in that period, Romaic Greek. (Romaic is only partly legible to users of today's Demotic Greek.) Otherwise I rely on my colleagues who have begun the work of translating the Ottoman documents of Istanbul, and on one erudite historian who mastered the necessary

Ottoman, Arabic, and Persian alongside the Greek.[29] Russia is an important part of this book but visits to the archives of Moscow and St. Petersburg were postponed due to the coronavirus pandemic, and I had no desire to go following Russia's renewed assault on Ukraine in 2022. Luckily there is a long Russian and Soviet tradition of publishing documents as well as the excellent work of Soviet and post-Soviet historians. By reading them in a different way I make a point about the centrality of Russia to the story.

1821 as a Current Event

Greeks have a remarkable historical awareness of the Revolution. Just about any town and many villages have an amateur historian or two, people who gather documents, locate the sites they describe, trace lineages, and willingly and enthusiastically share their knowledge. One need only go to the café in the main square and ask, and it is worth listening to them. They make the landscape come alive, they have knowledge, and they connect a past to a present. More than once I found these encounters revealing, about the issues and about myself. Each chapter begins with an account of my visits to the sites and persons in question and conversations with locals, specialists, or fellow-travelers about events that happened two hundred years ago, give or take, and these introduce the historical account. These vignettes help me open questions and beckon toward the stakes, in a personal way that may be lost in the standard historical narrative.

It is common for locals to tell of historical events as if they are happening now, as if they witnessed them, and to narrate in the "we." At times they intimate that the goals of 1821 were not attained, that Greek independence and the social revolution were only ever partial. The Revolution is still with us and there are new stories to be told.

Chapter 1

The Ottoman Crisis in the Southern Balkans

Prologue

OVER AN EASTER *meal in the Peloponnese in 2018, my hosts describe a massacre of Muslims by Christians almost two hundred years ago as if it were yesterday. They speak of Thodorakis Kolokotronis and Ibrahim pasha as if they know them, of beheadings and enslavement as if it were still happening around them. As for the massacre, they know that the victims included men, women, and children, and recall from the memoir literature, oral traditions, and folk songs that the bodies clogged the alleyways and forced riders to steer their horses over the corpses. Somehow they agree that the Turks (meaning Muslims) are barbarians. "How else could you deal with such people?" My hosts then turn to signing songs of elopement, love, and nature.*

Back then and in that place, I think to myself, they were all barbarians, if by barbarian we mean carriers of disordered violence and unpredictable death and destruction. The Ottoman Empire was a regime that let Muslims and Christians share in the violence as both victims and perpetrators. The local landowners, Christian and Muslim, competed with each other for land and taxes and worked with moneylenders in systems of credit that always left the peasants dependent and destitute.

It won't do to wax nostalgic about the empires that were destroyed by the nations: both were extremely violent. But before the nation, people killed for different reasons. The notables, moneylenders, merchants, and armed men

who became Greeks had been the Ottoman Rum, tasked with governing a
place that was becoming ungovernable.

The Vampire, Vanishing Towns, and other Stories of Ottoman Crisis

Roumeli was the name for the region that stretched north from the
Gulf of Corinth. Depending on the time and the mapmaker, it reached
as far as today's Romania, so that Roumeli encompassed what today
we call the Balkans. For our purposes it was a band of territory that was
bracketed by the Ionian Sea to the west and the Aegean Sea to the east.
To the south is the Peloponnesian peninsula, what at the time was
called the Morea. The name Roumeli was Ottoman, meaning the land
of the Rum—the people of the Eastern Roman Empire.

This is a land of mountains and sheer cliffs overlooking valleys, lush
in winter and arid in summer. Pine is interspersed with plane where the
water is sufficient. Flowers explode everywhere in spring. In past centuries marginal lands in the mountains were given to intensive crops like
grapes, almonds, walnuts, and figs. Valleys produced wheat. Sheep
grazed around the pastures. Layers of peasants, landowners, tax farmers,
moneylenders, merchants, and administrators lived off that land. The
intensely blue sea was an outlet for trade and piracy and a source of fish.

There was and is a town on the southern coast of Roumeli named
Galaxidi, known today as a place for weekend escapes for Athenians. It
looks southward across Gulf of Corinth to the Peloponnese. At the start
of the eighteenth century it was a strategic trading town and pirate base.
Like many towns in the Ottoman Balkans, Galaxidi was run by Christian notables-cum-warlords, and from some point in the early 1700s the
Christian in charge was a man named Katsonis.[1] He was from a nearby
mountain village and moved about the region in search of opportunities, and Galaxidi was a prize. Like any notable, Christian or Muslim,
his job was to keep the peace and gather the taxes, rents, and tariffs at
the port, all of which he shared with a hierarchy of other notables.

Formally Katsonis and all Christians were *reaya*, the Ottoman term
for a herd of animals. It designated non-Muslims who lacked the

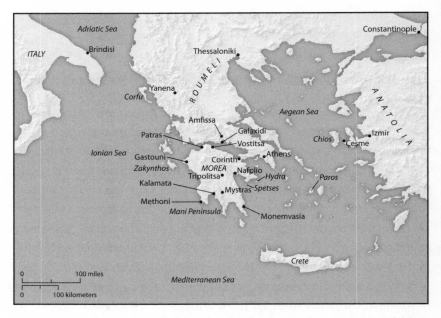

FIGURE 1.1. The Morea and Roumeli around 1800. Credit to Rob McCalebb.

privileges of a Muslim and were liable to certain taxes.[2] And it is true that a good share of the notables in towns and districts were Muslims, generically termed ayans, often with the title aga, as was a sizable minority of the population of this region. Higher levels of power—the beys, the pashas, and the viziers who ruled whole regions—were near-monopolies of Muslims.

But the reaya were also *zimmi*—non-Muslims who enjoyed the sultan's protection of their persons, families, properties, and religion. And with many towns and villages overwhelmingly Christian, Christian notables carved out a village or town in order to exploit the local peasants and traders, keep the peace, keep bandits at bay (or monopolize the banditry), and make a decent living off taxes and rents. Some of them were also captains, meaning warlords, mercenaries, and bandits. The notables and the captains were the privileged among the underprivileged and they could be quite powerful. They had some status and it was recognized by Muslim notables with whom they cooperated and competed. Be they warlords in command of a region or a populated estate, elders in charge of a town or village, or landowners and tax collectors in charge of a larger region, such Christians were a part of Ottoman governance. Their services were needed and they could benefit from the arrangement.[3]

But no position was secure in Roumeli in the eighteenth century, for Muslims any more than Christians. Wealth and status could be fleeting. In 1705 or so, an Ottoman armed detachment entered Katsonis's town and the commander billeted his home. When Katsonis was away the commander attacked his wife, may or may not have raped her, and certainly murdered her. When the unarmed Katsonis returned home he attacked the commander with his hands, and with his teeth he ripped out the commander's jugular. He then rang the church bell to call together the townsfolk to explain why they were now at war with the Ottoman detachment and any neighboring town that might come to punish them. He appeared with blood streaming from his mouth and down his clothing. It was common in the Balkans to believe in vampires, and the villagers made the obvious connection: their notable was a vampire who drank the blood of his enemies. Now commanding their fear and respect, they followed him into battle and killed the rest of the Ottoman detachment. They were motivated by the probability that official retribution would fall on all of them as a collective.

In the next months punitive forces were sent from nearby Salona (today's Amfissa), and two hundred Ottomans were slaughtered by a hundred men under Katsonis. Katsonis—now the Vampire—marched on Salona to attack the notables, Muslims and Christians alike. To calm him they offered him command of more villages and towns and the revenues that went with them. But he continued to loot their territories and he destroyed more punitive forces, until they made him commander of a still larger territory, if only he would agree to not burn their properties and not to kill them. The disorder was such that the sultan weighed in from Constantinople and agreed that in lieu of taxes the Vampire would owe his sovereign a tribute of one falcon a year. It was a sure sign that the sultan had lost control and would settle for a temporary restoration of peace and a token of submission.

The Vampire died peacefully, around 1740, and another local war ensued when his relatives fought over his lands. The Vampire's brother-in-law Kostas Zacharias (nom de guerre: Kostantaras) won the day as he eliminated his relatives and neighbors. The regional pashas and agas marched against him to claim his territories and revenues, and they captured his villages and tortured and killed the inhabitants. Kostantaras counterattacked and he burned their towns and olive trees, tortured the captives—men, women, and children—and took slaves and ransomed hostages. He displayed heads on pikes. He roasted the enemy commander Tahir Katsa on a spit. He ended up with even more territory and tax revenues, impressive ransoms, and payments from the surrounding notables to let them live in peace or simply let them live. At his death in 1755, he was in possession of a wide swath of territory. Muslim notables were paying taxes to a lowly reaya, and the Ottoman regime seemed upside down.

Meanwhile his nephew Lambros—one of the marginalized relatives—remained out of reach in nearby Livadia, until he too was forced to flee. His fortunes changed in 1768 when Russia invaded the Ottoman Empire from the north and he joined the invaders as a soldier, then a corsair under the Russian flag, and then as a pirate working on his own account. In Mani, the mountainous peninsula in the southern Morea that was a pirate haven, he did battle with other pirates and was evicted by the Christian notable. He made his way to Russia and was sent as an emissary to Persia. He was made a Russian officer and settled down on an estate in the Crimea that he was gifted for his services. He called it Livadiia in Russian, after his homeland. It later became a palace for the tsars and in Soviet times an insane asylum. Lambros's experience matters: whereas his uncle and grandfather were confined to Ottoman politics, Lambros was introduced to a new world of empires. The Russian presence changed everything, as would the French and British presence a few decades later. Local notables and warlords now had options that were global.[4]

The Vampire's story was not a Roumelian, Balkan, Greek, or Christian story; it was an Ottoman story. It was part of a general crisis of governance that took hold in the Ottoman Empire in the eighteenth

century. From Egypt and Syria to Anatolia and the Balkans, local powerful people became entrenched forces with which the sultan had to negotiate. In Roumeli what had once been a system of tenure in exchange
for military service collapsed. The holders of the estates began to see
their possessions as their private property and the revenues as their
own. Their estates were populated by dependent and tenant peasants.
What had once been a command from the sultan to provide armies and
funds was to them the start of a negotiation—a demand that more
towns be brought under their control, local taxes shared in a different
way, the territory of a neighboring notable added to their own, the tariffs
of a port or trading town handed over, or a fish farm added to their
revenues. Whole regions, such as Vidin (Bulgaria) under the warlord
Osman Pazvantoğlu in the 1790s, could be in open rebellion and at war
with a coalition of neighboring notables.[5]

The sultan did not have a standing army. He managed as best he
could to play the notables against each other, secure better revenues or
a military force in times of war, or make some trade routes safe.[6] In
Roumeli the trade routes mattered because these were regions through
which goods flowed in a west–east direction, and some of that commerce was the grain that fed Constantinople. Decrees required that the
harvest be sold to the capital. Every little war threatened that flow, and
small bands of thieves, notables, and merchants acquired new leverage.
They could and did redirect grain meant for the capital to markets to the
west.[7] Hence the importance of a notable guarding the passes and
routes (*dervenagas, derbent-ağa*). The Vampire and his successor targeted these agas systematically as a way to exert pressure on the regional
pashas responsible for the grain supply. The Vampire also targeted the
Christian notables who were responsible for securing and moving the
harvest, and for the credits that made the entire process of planting,
harvesting, and transporting possible. The more the Vampire disrupted
the trade routes, the more concessions he extracted.

But the price of any accommodation was a persistent violence that
ended with some patchwork of alliances and privileges that was fleeting.
A generalized unpredictability afflicted a hierarchy stretching from the
sultan who was desperate for soldiers, bread, and gold, to the peasant

farmer who fell prey to notables, moneylenders, warlords, and bandits. For the local notables, the price of defeat could be severe: a loss of territory and the attendant revenues, a loss of property to confiscation by the sultan or someone claiming to be acting for the sultan, beheading or strangulation, and collective punishment visited on whole villages and towns.[8]

It was common to change service away from the sultan to foreign powers and in this the Ottomans were not unique. European armies also comprised mercenaries, very often recruited from other empires (think British Hessians and Swiss Guards). In the Balkans these transfers of loyalties could be large. Migrants moved to other sovereign territories *en masse*, and local warlords and notables swore new oaths depending on what was on offer. What today might be considered treason was at that time a change of paymasters. Westward to the Ionian coast, warlords might fight for the regional pasha, for Venice which possessed the Ionian Islands, later for Russia and Austria which were pushing into the region, and still later for France and Britain. The examples of cross-imperial allegiances, shifting local alliances, and wholesale migration are legion.[9]

Even places could appear and disappear in short order. Moschopolis (today Voskopojë in Albania) had been a collection of sheep-herding villages and hamlets that formed into a township. By the 1730s or so, it was thriving by exporting wool to Austria and importing manufactures bound for Constantinople. The sultan and the pashas gave it privileges in return for taxes and tariffs and for keeping the goods moving. But Moschopolis was surrounded by bands of brigands, Albanian speakers who might be Orthodox, Catholic, or Muslim and were destitute enough to fight for a living. They sometimes worked for a notable and sometimes not, and they might sign up for faraway missions such as the Morea during the rebellion in the 1770s, Egypt after 1800, and Naples from 1815.[10]

In the 1760s such bands made the highways around Moschopolis unsafe. Traveling merchants were relieved of their profits, goods were looted, and notables and merchants were killed or ransomed.[11] The sultan took an interest and the local bey was able to defeat the brigands in a pitched battle. He sent their heads to the sultan as a trophy and the proof that his mission was accomplished. (On the gathering of body parts as trophies, see chapter 4.) But most of the time, the townspeople had to pay off the brigands to prevent more attacks. In 1769 the brigands had a shot at the ultimate prize. Russia invaded the Ottoman Empire on a wide front, including the Balkans, and the townsfolk were accused of helping the enemy. The townspeople saw what was coming, packed their valuables, and left. The town was looted and burned by the Albanian irregulars. The townsfolk relocated to the Austrian Empire. Some returned, but in the 1780s Moschopolis was caught in a different war, a civil one between Ali pasha of Yanena and his rival Ibrahim pasha. In 1789 Ali's forces (also Albanian speakers, like Ali himself) took the town and looted it again, and the last inhabitants left for good.[12]

In the next two centuries historians treated Balkan violence as national encounters but these were pre-national times. Greek histories enumerate the many Christians who lost their heads; the Ottoman and Turkish histories enumerate the many Muslim notables who lost their heads; Albanian historians have their own catalogue of heads lost. It's safe to say that no one's head was safe.[13] Any major fighting was likely to involve Muslims and Christians on both sides. When the Muslim Pazvantoğlu rebelled, the sultan sent the Christian Nikolaos Mavrogenis to fight him.[14]

The problem, then, was not that Christians and Muslims had a deep enmity. Christians had the formal protection of the sultan, and Christian and Muslim notables worked together in their shared enterprise of living off trade and exploiting peasants. The problem was that the sultan could not make good on his promise to protect them, be they Christians or Muslims, Jews or Roma, notables, peasants, or merchants. The taking of slaves illegally was a case in point. Sincere and detailed bans on the enslavement of loyal Ottoman Christians were regularly ignored by the soldiers who took them in times of civil strife, and by the sailors and merchants (usually Christians) who took them to market. Ottoman officials struggled after the fact to secure their release. Muslims were not to be enslaved at all, but we know that this happened, too.[15]

Nor can we speak of these events as part of a Greek cause, and the term "Greek" was not the local term of reference for an Orthodox

Christian. To be sure, outsiders from the west and north referred to the Christian populations as Greeks in English, grecs in French, greci (singular greco) in Italian, and greki (singular grek) in Russian. But in Ottoman parlance an Orthodox Christian was a Rum, in local dialect a Romios. It meant Roman, the heirs to the Eastern Roman or Byzantine Empire. The Ottoman regime organized them loosely into a community that they called a *millet*, a confessional designation that was not ethnically homogeneous.[16] At that time the Rum of the Balkans spoke myriad languages: forms of Greek, Albanian, Vlach, Romanian, Turkish, Bulgarian, Serbian and scattered local variations on any of these languages. Gypsies who were Orthodox also traced their lineage to Byzantium and could term themselves a variation on Eastern Roman: the Roma.[17] The term Graiki was used, in Greek, but it referred to the Orthodox who lived in lands to the west of the Balkans from the Ionian Islands to Italy and beyond, and north of the Balkans in the Russian Empire. To the Ottoman Christians they could be outsiders on par with the Franks (the Catholics). Some of these Orthodox spoke only Italian. The ancient term "Hellene" (Ellinas) was a literary flourish among limited groups of philologists and most often referred to Classical times, not their own day.[18]

By the same token, Moschopolis was not a Greek city in the modern sense of the word and it was not destroyed as a Greek place and people. It was attacked as a town of merchants with money. These merchants were in fact Vlach speakers who learned Greek as a language of regional commerce, as did all merchants of the Balkans and many Muslims who interacted with them (see chapter 8). It was also the language of learning and administration in parts of the Balkans. But to call them Greeks as Greek historians tend to do, or Romanians as Romanian historians do because Vlach is close to Romanian, or even Albanians because the town was in today's Albania, is to miss the point. Belongings were not total and one could be many things at the same time: Vlach, Roman, Ottoman, and Moschopolitan. Arriving in Austria in 1769, the refugees declared themselves to be Macedonians—a common designation of their geographic region and not at all an ethnic one.[19]

Or consider the case of Gardiki near Argyrokastro (Kardhiq and Gjirokastër in Albania). It was destroyed in 1812 and its inhabitants were

killed or sold into slavery on the orders of Ali pasha of Yanena. It is catalogued as one more example of Muslim barbarity toward Christians, but
the perpetrators were Muslims and Christians, and Ali's commander on
the scene was a Christian named Thanasis Vagias. The victims were a
mix of Christians and Muslims, speakers of Albanian, Greek, and Vlach,
and the slaves were of all religions. The town of Berat was also sacked,
in 1810, its Muslim population killed by Ali's gathering of Albanian mercenaries who were Muslim, Orthodox, and Catholic.[20]

A Muslim who might look askance at a Christian in a dispute over
privileges might look at the same Christian as a partner in the joint
venture of exploiting the peasants or selling goods or forming an armed
band, or as a compatriot because they both came from Salona. It would
be some decades—the year 1821, specifically—before the many ways to
describe belonging would be simplified into national ones, total and
exclusive.

The Morea and the Ottoman Crisis

The Morea lies to the south of Roumeli, across the Gulf of Corinth. This
was another land of forbidding cliffs and mountains that gave way to
valleys like Gastouni and Pyrgos in the west and Mystras (around
today's Sparta) and Molai in the east. The mountains encased the large
central plateau around the capital, Tripolitsa. Scorched, arid, and hot in
summer, the Morea was lush and green in winter and exploded with
vegetation in spring. Flocks of sheep grazed on the marginal lands. The
Mediterranean with its shades of blue surrounded the peninsula, and a
small strip of land around Corinth connected it to Roumeli and the
north. In Ottoman the Morea was called an island; it became so in the
1890s with the digging of the Corinth canal.

Here too the violence was endemic, a common tool to settle disputes.
And here too historians have narrated the violence as a national encounter of Christians ("Greeks") and Muslims ("Turks"). In fact the confessional axes were not yet decisive; the national ones were not to be seen
at all. The complaint of the Christian notable of arbitrariness and random violence was well-founded, but the Muslim aga had much the same

complaint—not to mention the peasant majority on whom all the notables fed. The question that will occupy succeeding chapters is this:
How did violence and belonging become reorganized as a clash of religions, when all the evidence points to a generalized political crisis and
a class division between rich and poor? How was disorderly violence
reordered into a conflict of nations?

On a map the Morea looks like a hand or a fig leaf. It appears coherent
and one might assume that the population was coherent as well. But
sheer cliffs and mountain ranges separated the regions from one another, so that travel among nearby towns was easier by ship or not easy
at all. Each finger and each gulf looked out at its own geographic vista.
A traveler from Gastouni in the west could reach Venetian Zakynthos
or even Italy more readily than Nafplio on the east coast. Populations
spoke variations of Romaic Greek, but no two regions spoke the same
dialect. The Maniot was unintelligible in Monemvasia, under 70 kilo-
meters away as the crow flies. The imprint of trade routes and invasions
over the centuries was to be heard in the idioms used into the twentieth
century. Slavic words and intonations around Mystras and Monemvasia
contrasted to the Albanian and Italian usage in the west. People identified themselves by their towns and localities more readily than as Moreans and were strangers to people in towns a few miles away.[21]

Rather than view the peninsula as a coherent whole, we should think
of it as they did, as sea systems.[22] There was the Ionian Sea system in
the west that included the coastal ports of Patras, Glarentza (today
Kyllini), Neokastro (Pylos), Koroni, Modon (Methoni), and Kalamata, and funneled goods from the hinterland. A useful map encompassed that coast, the Ionian Islands, and the heel of Italy. Frankish
place names were common, and waves of influence and events from
the west were felt most strongly here. And there was the Aegean Sea
(what at the time was called the White Sea or the Archipelago), centered on the ports of Nafplio and Monemvasia. This coast sent goods
east, and a map would encompass the islands of the Aegean and reach
the Anatolian coast with its ports of Izmir and Constantinople.

The region was unified by administrative practice. It was its own
pashalik, with the pasha appointed from Constantinople. He held court

in Tripolitsa. Morean politics and administration were organized around control of those crops which fed the population, other Ottoman regions, and European markets. Any notable was keen to get his hands on the Corinthian grapes from Vostitsa (today's Aigio) and Gastouni.[23] This small variety of grape (the English sailors corrupted "Corinthian" into "currant") was especially aromatic. European ships scoured the coasts and paid in gold, and tons went into English Christmas puddings and Scottish pastries. They were prized in Germany as the *Korinthen* and are part of a German slang term for small, petty, or stingy.[24] Gastouni also exported beef and wheat to the Ionian Islands. Kalamata exported silk. Muslim estate owners in the plains exported wheat to Mediterranean markets and Constantinople.[25]

The ports were key: for an Ottoman official or local notable a port meant gold and tariff revenue, pure and easy cash. The right to collect taxes and tariffs was a marketable and exchangeable commodity, more fungible than land. It was this—the management of revenues—that brought together the notables and merchants of the disparate regions, and they met annually to apportion tax farms and set rates for each region and each notable.[26]

The Morea had been taken by Venice in its last major war with the Ottoman Empire, and retaken by the Ottomans in 1715. Much of the local Christian population welcomed the return of the Ottomans because of their greater religious tolerance and protection for Orthodoxy. The Venetians were Catholic and arrived with priests. The Ottomans taxed in more moderate ways or at least integrated the local elites into the business; the Venetians had pushed them aside. Venetian merchants challenged the Orthodox merchants whereas the Ottomans gave them privileges.[27] When the Ottomans returned they tried and failed to introduce land tenure conditional on military service. Instead the Morea was governed by a system of tax farming: the purchase of the right to collect taxes in a region, in exchange for a flat fee given to the higher authority. The regions became the quasi-hereditary domains of notable families who lived off the local peasants.

Central Ottoman authority was intermittent and irregular. The pasha and his retinue were outsiders who were sent from anywhere in the empire to enrich themselves and secure some revenues for the Sublime Porte—the higher administration in Constantinople—before leaving for another assignment. Below them were the local agas who were usually natives of the Morea. In effect they were permanent office-holders, and the office gave them control of land and revenues. In this manner Muslim notables were the titular owners of perhaps two-thirds of the land and the attendant revenues. The Arnaoutoglou and the Chotoman, for example, controlled the flatlands in a hereditary way.[28] Formally Christian notables owned marginal lands, under a third of the total, where they grew grapes, nuts, and olives on terraced mountainsides and grazed sheep. The key here was control of the springs and streams, which made a small parcel lucrative so long as labor was cheap.

But in the Morea the population was overwhelmingly Orthodox, and Christians outnumbered Muslims by perhaps seven to one, in a total population on the eve of the Revolution of 450,000.[29] All numbers are notional but by any count the small Muslim presence was unusual and remarkable. There was a scattered presence of Jews and Catholics in some towns, and Gypsies who could be of a number of languages and religions. Together these communities may have numbered about 20,000, many of them merchants and craftsmen. The Muslims did not control much military force for lack of a sizable Muslim population and a system of mobilizing them; the center could not provide one except in some strategic ports. This gave the Christian notables an outsized role in governance compared with other parts of the empire. They were deeply involved in gathering taxes, rents, and debts on their own lands and on any other land they managed on behalf of Muslim owners.[30]

These Christian notables were the *kotsabases* (from the Ottoman *kocabaşı*). They were indispensable. Indeed, while the notables sometimes spoke and wrote Ottoman Turkish to maneuver in the Ottoman system, just about all the local Muslims of any status used Greek to maneuver in the Morea. Many of the Muslims were Albanians who did not speak Turkish, and looked at the Ottoman officials as imperious and unwelcome foreigners. Turkish-speaking Ottoman officials were contemptuous of the Albanian-speaking Muslims. The Christian notables meanwhile were likely to speak some Albanian.[31]

In a real sense, Muslim and Christian notables were in partnership. While the pasha and the agas had nominal control over lands and revenues, they formed alliances with the Christian notables and assigned to them the task of collecting. Even the hated tax on Christians was collected by the Christian notables. Working with moneylenders they might extend credits to their Muslim partners to form intricate webs of mutual dependence—the agas dominating the higher offices, the notables controlling the flow of money and credit.[32] Only about a tenth of revenues reached Constantinople. Religious endowments (*vakoufia* in Greek, *vakif* in Ottoman, from the Arabic *waqf*) owned by the imperial family and mosques were also managed by notables. The endowment of Patras sent revenues to the mosque of Ayasofya (Aghia Sophia) in Constantinople, and Pyrgos sent funds to Mecca. Christian notables created their own endowments at monasteries, and with the right conditions they could benefit from the lands tax-free.[33]

The bonds among notables of the two religions were social as well, though after the Revolution the history books have focused on the enmity to the point where good relations are treated as oddities. But good or functional relations were regular. Town marketplaces and trade brought together all the languages and religions, of all the classes. Among notables regular meetings to decide matters of local government and revenues were occasions to share in a coffee, a tea, a pipe, and wine. (Muslims imbibed, contrary to popular belief.) These could be the meetings in, say, Lala overlooking the western coast or Gastouni in the valley below, where agas and notables came together to hire physicians for the community. Or they might be the periodic meetings in each region to agree on plans to rebuild fortifications and roads. Dividing the revenues were the basic and constant occasion for meeting, regionally and in the capital Tripolitsa.[34]

And since the work was about power and money, it spilled easily into marriage arrangements where wealth and kinship were always at stake. In the villages and towns around Monemvasia on the east coast the rates of intermarriage were very high; in 1821 Christian families intervened to save their Muslim kin when the revolutionaries began to kill them. In Mourtatochoria in the west, Muslim husbands had Christian wives.

FIGURE 1.2: "Bazar of Athens," in Edward Dodwell, *Views in Greece, From Drawings by Edward Dodwell, Esq. F.S.A. & c.* (London: Rodwell and Martin, 1821). Collection of the National Historical Museum, Athens. *Markets were a regular meeting place for the various religions and languages of the Ottoman Empire.*

During shared festivals the roasting pans had a section for pork and a section for lamb. Muslim men acted as godparents to the babies of their Christian neighbors, with the blessings of the priests.[35] Muslims honored their Christian neighbors on the latter's name-days with visits and wine.

Lest the point be lost: they worshipped the same saints at the same shrines, organized their rituals around some of the same days, spoke the same languages, sat in each other's homes, and sometimes shared bedrooms and children. Charity also crossed confessional lines. In towns like

FIGURE 1.3. Edward Dodwell, "Festival at Athens before the Temple of The-
seus," 1805. *Festivals were often a shared occasion for the confessions of the Ottoman
Empire. Some Christian saints were considered holy figures by Muslims. Christians
were known to revere Muslims.*

Pylos and Methoni, a few hundred Muslim families were impoverished
and dependent on the Christian notable or merchant for handouts.[36]
The goods and money passing from hand to hand, be they notables sharing in revenues or farmers and craftsmen selling to everyone—all these
were the constant social exchange that were also a bond.

The notables, then, shared in the Ottoman hierarchy of power. They were ambitious and status-seeking. The notables referred to themselves as archons—lords—and to their children as little archons.[37] They vied with each other to gather more tax farms and rents, and they carved out their own estates. Whole villages were in effect their property, the peasants their dependents. They dominated the export trade in the port cities where they worked with Christian and foreign merchants. In lifestyle they shared in an Ottoman culture, be it their robes and furs or the cushioned living rooms and audience halls. Visitors from Europe seeking beds in Christian households were offered divans.[38] Some like the Notaras were educated in Italy, most often as doctors, and their services gave them entry into the households of agas. A line of the Sisinis family of Gastouni were physicians to the agas of Lala. They might command (in addition to Romaic Greek) Albanian, Turkish, and Italian, some also French. They formed marriage alliances with each other so that just about any family was related to any other. On occasion they shored up their overseas trade relations by marrying into foreign families: the Sisinis were partly French for this reason.[39]

In theory the notables were elected by the householders of a given territory. These elections were in fact ritualized acclamations and confirmations of the notable's wealth, status, power, and dominance. These notables in turn elected, selected, or chose who would represent them at the pasha's councils. The notables also had the rare privilege of sending an emissary (*vekil*) directly to the sultan in Constantinople—not even the agas had this representation—and the notables vied among themselves to put one of their own in the post. A notable who managed endowments on behalf of members of the imperial family could mobilize support within the sultan's household and defy the pasha. This gave unusual protection and influence to the Deliyannis clan, for example, which administered the estate of Beyhan sultana, the sister of Selim III.[40] All in all, the notables working with the agas could exercise an open or covert influence on matters including the appointment and recall of Ottoman officials and even the Morean pasha.[41]

And yet Morean politics were dangerous to all concerned. Sultans and pashas intermittently mounted campaigns of executions that aimed at the seizure of lands and revenues. As in Roumeli, one can peruse the catalogues of Christian notables who over the decades fell afoul of a pasha or an aga and were beheaded: a Krevattas and a Notaras in 1764, a Kanakaris in 1770, a Palamidis in 1796, a Deliyannis in 1764, 1770, and 1816, a Zaimis in 1764 and 1787, a Dikeos in 1802. This does not count the extrajudicial murders, such as the poisoning of Papatsonis in 1811. In some Greek histories they are listed as martyrs who died at Turkish hands as a consequence of their purported revolutionary activity. In fact the notables were victims of other notables in alliance with agas and pashas. Deliyannis, the head of the eponymous clan, conspired in the execution of Lontos in 1813 by appealing to the pasha. When the new pasha arrived the Lontos clan arranged the execution of Deliyannis, in 1816. Agreements signed under oath to refrain from having each other murdered were ineffective and thus regular, all the way to the autumn of 1820.[42]

The agas fared little better. A separate catalog could list the many agas who fell victim to an opposing alliance of agas and notables. In 1762 five Muslim notables were executed at the behest of five Christian notables; the latter were executed in 1764 along with the metropolitan Ananias when a new pasha arrived in Tripolitsa. The pasha had two more murdered in secret. The Deliyannis clan arranged the murder of a Muslim assassin and the execution of the aga who hired him. Lontos arranged the murder of Osman aga Marmara. In the years before 1813 the pasha beheaded four more agas along with the dragoman (Christian interpreter, really an advisor) of the Morean pasha. Around Pyrgos and Gastouni in 1815 and 1816, a new pasha took away tax farms from Seit aga and Mustafa aga and provoked open warfare, ending in the execution of both agas and their sons.[43]

The shared enterprise of all notables, Muslim and Christian, was a pitiless exploitation of the Christian peasantry, to a degree that Ottoman visitors found shocking. To the taxation the Christian notables added credit operations. Peasants generally did not hold much in cash, and yet the Ottoman authorities increasingly demanded tax payments in coin not kind. The notables and their moneylenders fronted the tax payments on behalf of households and villages, sums that the villagers could never repay. Instead they sold their liberties and became tenants and bondsmen. Working with merchants and moneylenders, the notable could make a profit of up to 40 percent on a single tax-and-credit operation and claim most of any future harvest. The famous moneylender Tabakopoulos, later a financier of the Greek Revolution, was a creditor to agas, notables, and peasants. In 1819 he can be seen with armed thugs gathering taxes and debts to the tune of 63,000 kuruş (an Ottoman coin, called *grosia* in Greek), about the equivalent of two thousand monthly wages in the region. In total he lent 1.8 million kuruş to Muslims and Christians in the years 1816–20.[44] Through their direct control of lands and villages the notables monopolized peasant labor. Muslim estate owners around Gastouni had to import slave labor from sub-Saharan Africa. Laborers from Venetian Zakynthos came for the harvest.[45]

The situation for farmers worsened as the fiscal crisis of the empire deepened. The Porte imposed new and larger lump-sum levies in a classic system of apportionment and redistribution. Tax bills were lumped onto the regions, the regions lumped them onto the localities, the localities onto the villages, the villages onto the households. In practice this meant that a bloated hierarchy of intermediaries (imperial emissaries, Christian and Muslim notables, merchants, and moneylenders) lived off the peasantry. Tax collection was accomplished with beatings, torture, and imprisonment, and notables hired armed men to protect themselves from each other and also force peasants to pay.[46]

Horrified Ottoman officials enumerated the prisons where delinquent peasants were hung by chains for a day, reeds inserted under their finger-nails, weights placed on the chest, and heads submerged in wet lime. Peasants living in reed-and-mud shacks gathered their belongings and left for less exacting masters. The notables received reports of villages that had simply disappeared.[47] Ottoman officials lamented that in the Balkans generally they had lost half a million subjects (the numbers are notional) to immigration abroad, victims of indiscriminate violence and hopeless indebtedness.[48]

Endemic poverty produced endemic banditry. There are nuanced distinctions that cast bandits as the legitimate formations hired by one or another regional power (*armatoli*) or the untethered thieves who attacked populations and the wealthy (*klephtes*). Later they led the armies of the Greek Revolution. But the shared source of these armed gangs was desperation. Some of these men were Christian and Muslim Albanians who descended from Roumeli before the eighteenth century. Whole regions of the Morea were Albanian-speaking well into the nineteenth century, and some villages and neighborhoods into the twentieth. Albanian marauders were recorded in 1755 in Lala when they robbed and took slaves from the agas. Migrants from the nearby islands of Zakynthos and Cephalonia also appeared as brigands.[49]

The most famous bandits were home-grown, and as Kolokotronis tells it in his memoirs it was a precarious existence. Life expectancy was low, and he lost a father, brothers, and thirty of his thirty-eight first cousins.[50] The bandits in turn made life precarious for everyone else. The sources are littered with cases of ransoming, robbing, arson, and murder. The Napoleonic Wars in the Ionian region offered opportunity to armed men who joined the imperial armies in the tens of thousands (chapters 4–5). During the economic downturn after 1815, when the warring European empires stopped buying supplies and hiring mercenaries from the Morea and Roumeli, unemployment soared. This pool of poor peasants and fighters was the key to the success of the mass uprising of 1821.

3+

It was not obvious that the notables, the necessary and privileged parts of the Ottoman administration, should engage in revolution, and until 1821 they did not. It is likely that the notables from the turn of the century were increasing their command of lands and revenues at the expense of the agas, capitalizing on their command of money, credit, commerce, and peasant labor.[51] Their positions and wealth became hereditary. Individual heads of family might perish but the clans persisted from generation to generation, with only some turnover.[52]

Their expectations were rising and yet dashed with every new wave of violence and economic slump. Tocqueville writing about France in 1789 thought that rising expectations and elite crisis were preconditions for revolution. But revolutions also presuppose that a different future is even imaginable, and this ingredient was provided, in the first instance, by Russia.

Chapter 2

Russia Changes the Balkans

Prologue

IT IS SUMMER 2021 *and I walk along the docks of the town of Naousa, on the Aegean island of Paros. I have frequented the island since I was about ten years old when there was not a tourist to be seen. I then witnessed the successive waves of Scandinavians, British, French, sundry other Europeans, and Athenians who turned the little island into a sea of concrete. Russians came from the 1990s. Taverns and booze cruises abound. I take my children there regularly, and they repeat my mistakes at the bars and discos.*

Only recently have I realized that part of the port was built by Russians to host the Russian fleet during a war against the Ottomans, this one in 1770. They stayed a few years, diverted Ottoman forces from the main front around the Black Sea, and then left the island to its usual combination of farming, viniculture, trade, and piracy.

Few pay much attention to this past, not even the Russian tourists who flocked here until recently. Locals know the facts but see it as a passing intrusion on a Greek national history. "Yes, there were Russians," a shopkeeper shrugged. I contemplate the larger erasure of Russia from the history of modern Greece, including its role in securing Greek independence in 1830. Since the late nineteenth century Greek histories have been oriented to the west, reinforced by the Cold War when a Russian past was awkward. With Russia's offensive against Ukraine of 2022, Greece took the side of Ukraine and a Russian past is more unpopular than ever. Russian tourists have stopped coming.

And yet, in the Morea and the Aegean from 1770, Russians created a precondition for the Revolution that came fifty years later. They did not do this intentionally, and neither nation nor revolution was part of their vocabulary. Instead Russia destabilized the Ottoman Empire and suggested to the Christians of the Balkans that the sultan was not their only option. There were other empires in the neighborhood.

Russia and Ottoman Politics

In the histories of the Ottoman Empire the Russo-Ottoman War of 1768–74 is a turning point. The Ottoman Empire had already been grappling with problems of mobilization, but with this war it entered into a crisis that seemed existential. Russian victories and annexations stimulated more frantic efforts to mobilize resources, and produced more violent local reactions and competitions. The cycle continued with the wars of 1787–92, 1806–12, and 1828–30.[1]

Russia won the wars regularly and annexed the entire northern coast of the Black Sea, from the Danubian region in the west (around today's Romania, Ukraine, and Moldova) to the Transcaucasus in the east (Georgia, Armenia, and Azerbaijan). Russian musings about dismembering the Ottoman Empire heightened the sense of peril. Catherine the Great assimilated her designs on the Ottoman Empire into the Greek Project: a new empire would arise under Russian protection and her grandson was the ruler in waiting: he learned modern Greek. It is not clear how seriously the Russians took the Greek Project; Catherine had ten grandchildren, counting only the legitimate ones, and quite a few projects in play from Poland to China. Her general and advisor Potemkin had a Caucasian Project. Unlike the Greek Project, this plan was carried out.[2]

Russo-Ottoman wars exacerbated the ongoing problem of Ottoman governance—how to control a given territory, how to mobilize men against a foe that was clearly superior on the battlefield, and how to pay for it all. Russia had a standing army and the Ottomans had nothing of the sort, only legions of mercenaries who gathered for a given campaign and then went back to their household economies or to banditry. The

Janissary caste of warriors ceased to be an effective force. Russia worsened the Ottoman crisis and then capitalized on it in careful appeals to
the populations it courted and conquered. The tsarina or tsar could offer
that security of person and property that the sultan could not deliver,
to Muslims as well as Christians.

The problem for the Ottomans was not only the loss of territory. The
Treaty of Küçük-Kaynarca of 1774 as well as subsequent treaties gave
Russia multiple pretexts for intervention in Ottoman affairs. The Danubian Principalities remained Ottoman but with a Russian say in their
governments. Russia (its diplomats held) acquired the right to protect
the Christians under Ottoman rule and this served as a *causus belli* all
the way to the Crimean War in the 1850s. The border was porous and
unstable because it allowed populations to migrate back and forth with
ease. It was never clear if the populations of the Ottoman border regions
would be fighting for tsar or sultan, and they tended to do both. Muslim
and Christian notables alike took advantage of their northern neighbor
to seek refuge when their luck in Ottoman politics ran out or when new
opportunities beckoned. Russia received them all, many of them notables who were integrated into the Russian multiconfessional nobility.
We know more about the flight of the Ypsilanti (Ypsilantis in modern
Greek) and the Mavrogordato (Mavrokordatos in modern Greek) families because of their later role in the Greek Revolution, but Russia gave
haven to the likes of the magnate Tayyar of Trabzond as well.[3] Lesser
Ottoman subjects flocked to Russia in search of commissions in the
Russian army.[4]

This and subsequent treaties created a liminal population of Orthodox Christians who might seem Ottoman in one context and Russian
in another. Thousands of Rum made their way to southern Russia, and
they dominated the export of wheat to European markets as far as Spain
and Britain. "Russian shipping" numbering a thousand ships in the
Black and Mediterranean seas before 1821 was this wave of Ottoman
Orthodox subjects; but so was "Ottoman shipping." By one estimate
80 percent of ships in the Mediterranean in the years 1780–1810 was
owned by Ottoman Christians. Ships traveled with a collection of flags
and chose the appropriate one according to circumstances. In the

eighteenth century Ottoman Greeks sailed under the flags of anything that might resemble a sovereign state: Britain, France, Malta, Minorca, Ragusa, Naples, Jerusalem, Venice, Tuscany, Austria, and the Ottoman Empire. They could fly the special Greco-Ottoman flag, reserved for Christian Ottoman subjects. Loyalties were also multiple and fluid. In the small Orthodox merchant community in Amsterdam families declared loyalty to the Dutch, the Russians, and the Ottomans, all ways to circulate freely and receive protection as they carried out their trades. They kept their options open in 1821 when they both financed the Greek Revolution and denounced it.[5]

Shipowners added the Russian flag which became popular because of the protection it offered, and ship captains flocked to the new Russian city of Odesa to buy the right to use them. They could return to their homelands in the Ottoman Empire and still enjoy immunities and tax exemptions.[6] Merchants in Ottoman lands could also buy a patent (*berat*) from any other power. These were deeds of protection which exempted the holder from certain Ottoman laws and taxes, even if that person was an Ottoman subject living in Ottoman territory. The same people might behave at one moment as Ottoman subjects—the Rum— at other moments as Russian agents—the greki of Russia—or for that matter as the protected agents of a European state as far away as Sweden. European consuls sold these patents liberally because they were a source of income. Such protegés numbered in the hundreds of thousands in the early nineteenth century.[7]

Russia also took an interest in the Aegean region, or what at the time was called the Archipelago or White Sea. (In some Persian and Ottoman cartographic symbolisms, white meant west, and black meant north, hence the Black Sea.) Shipping carrying Russian goods left the Black Sea and necessarily passed through the Aegean Sea and its several hundred islands. The loyalties of such islanders, almost exclusively Christians, were uncertain. In the Russo-Ottoman War of 1787–92 armed ships from Hydra, Kasos, and Mykonos enlisted on the Ottoman side; others from the same islands joined the Russians. As pirates and corsairs they might fall victim to other pirates and corsairs. In 1798 ships from Spetses, Hydra, and Psara were captured by north African corsairs (they too were nominal Ottoman vassals) and nine hundred sailors were sent to the slave markets. The sultan tried to have them released.[8]

The region was directly implicated in the war of 1768–74.[9] The main front was around the Black Sea and as a diversion Russia sent a naval expedition from the Baltic to the eastern Mediterranean that seized some Aegean Islands and based itself on Paros. A detachment was sent to the Morea to stir up an uprising. It was commanded by Fedor Orlov. What to Russia was a diversion was to the locals an upheaval and a catastrophe. The Russian expedition intimated that the Morea might fall under Russian protection. The Russians let it be understood that they held a special place for the locals because of their Classical heritage. Warrior bands and pirates from the southeastern Morea were addressed as Spartans—in 1770 there was no such place—and soon locals were calling themselves Spartans as well. When addressing the Christians the Russians also made much of their shared Orthodox religion, and they referred to the "Russo-Greek Church" though there was no such thing. Then again, the Russians could be many things to many people: they briefly occupied Beirut and flattered these notables as well. Ali bey al-Kabir, the leader of the Mamluk caste of warriors who had ruled Egypt for centuries, took the opportunity to rebel and met with Orlov on Paros.[10] Russian appeals were directed at all elites. The Russians were careful to promise "just" monarchy in contrast to the arbitrariness of the sultan, and to guard the "property, life, and honor" of all notables. Later historians would consider the moment a Greek national awakening; at the time locals saw the Russians more narrowly, as a solution to problems of insecurity and a new opportunity.[11]

The small Russian detachments landed in the Morea in 1770. Some of the notables were openly with the Russians and secretly with the Ottomans; others were openly with the Ottomans and secretly with the Russians. Impoverished peasants fought on both sides. In some initial victories the Russians and their allies took towns and were given their traditional three days of looting, often accompanied by slaughter. Navarino was taken and sacked by a force commanded by I. A. Gannibal, the part-African great-uncle of Alexander Pushkin. Ionian Islanders and

Roumeliots joined in the looting. Christian and Muslim notables fled together to the coastal forts seeking passage or protection. Soon the fighting did not go well for the Russians but nor was this important: it was a diversion. They withdrew and left the rebels to their own devices.[12]

In the aftermath the sultan visited on the Morea an unusual devastation, only some of it intentional. Since the Ottomans did not have a ready fighting force, the sultan delegated the task of punishment to the regional pashas. They in turn hired bands of Albanian mercenaries from Roumeli. Up to ten thousand armed men descended on the Morea to punish and force submission (their mission) and to loot (their main form of compensation). Slave markets from Tunis to Thessaloniki were flooded with Morean slaves, perhaps twenty thousand in total. Tripolitsa was looted and two thousand were killed. Patras was relieved of the rebel siege and then looted by the liberators. Corinth was sacked. In Gastouni the troops erected a pyramid of enemy heads.[13]

Soon the mercenaries were controlled by no one and they attacked populations indiscriminately so long as they had some wealth. Notable families who supported Russia were attacked and expelled, so that the Benakis of Kalamata were one of the few families to lose their Morean position permanently. They subsequently served Russia as merchants, diplomats, and soldiers.[14] But the irregulars attacked wealthy families— Muslim and Orthodox—who had not joined the rebellion. The Jewish quarter of Mystras was left a ruin. Again the peasants paid the price in burned homes and fields, murdered relatives, and enslaved women and children.[15]

And then the irregulars would not leave. For a decade after the rebellion was suppressed, the Albanian warlords remained to loot and rob, making towns, highways, and mountain passes dangerous and lethal. Some of the irregulars formalized their rule and seized titles, lands, and taxes from the agas, and still mounted regular raids to loot. Like any budding notable, they turned their banditry into a protection racket which they called government.[16]

Still the sultan did not have an army to dislodge the Albanians, so he turned to the Aegean fleet. Gazi Hasan pasha was the admiral, and he was also appointed pasha of the Morea. He brought in more troops (often Albanians) and sailors (also Albanians) and hired many more locally. He offered amnesty to anyone who would join him against the first wave of Albanians and offered to buy back their enslaved relatives in north Africa. Muslim and Christian notables hired local warlords and bandits, and together they campaigned across the peninsula to hunt down the marauding Albanians. The Kolokotronis clan appears at this time, as hired warriors for Hasan pasha. The Christian advisor of the fleet Nikolaos Mavrogenis enjoined "elders, notables, honest captains, and other small and big people" to "attack and kill the Albanian warrior bands" and send their heads to the fleet admiral "so that you may be honored," i.e., paid. And so they did: the campaign culminated in 1779 around Tripolitsa and the extermination of the main Albanian force. Their severed heads were stacked into a triumphal pyramid. Many heads were sent onward to Constantinople as trophies.[17] Christian leaders of the revolt pledged loyalty to the sultan, which began with the act of buying a "paper of submission" (*proskynocharti* or *bougiournti*) and continued with new arrangements over tax farms and local order. Some Albanian bands settled down and ruled over territories as agas, for example in Lala in the mountains above Gastouni and Pyrgos.

When the latest wave of hired mercenaries began to maraud, Hasan and Mavrogenis turned on them as well. Among the newest victims were the Kolokotronis family: Thodorakis's father and much of his family were killed following tortures and dismemberment, the children sold into slavery. The survivors escaped into the mountains. In the following decades the surviving clansmen worked for local notables and as pirates and warlords.[18]

In the aftermath Süleymān Penah efendi authored what became a famous diagnosis of the Morean catastrophe and the wider Ottoman crisis.[19] He was an Ottoman statesman and a Morean from the town of Gastouni. He was sent back to his birthplace to fight the rebels and to understand a basic paradox: why a region that enjoyed the protection of its different religions rebelled and joined with a foreign enemy; and why the notables, privileged parts of Ottoman governance, turned on their own regime. His answer was that the region, like so many others,

FIGURE 2.1. "An Albanian of Greece," in Edward Daniel Clarke, *Travels in Various Countries of Europe Asia and Africa. Part the Second Greece Egypt and the Holy Land* (London: R. Watts for T. Cadell and W. Davies, 1813). Greek Library, Alexandros Onassis Public Benefit Foundation. *Albanians, whether Christian or Muslim, were a major demographic group of Roumeli and the Morea, and the major language group of the Aegean Islands. This image was drawn in the Morea (Peloponnese) before the Revolution.*

had become a hierarchy of corruption and arbitrariness that was no longer controlled by the Porte. In each district the agas, the Christian notables, and the administration constituted "a sort of republic, they give and take territories as if they were inherited from their fathers." They were dynasts and tyrants (*tyragni*), as were the notables in Bulgaria, Thessaloniki, Trikkala, Yanena, and Nafpaktos. "What can the poor, ill-fated, and hopeless peasants do" as their land was parceled, bought, and sold with them on it? They became brigands and mercenaries or they left. The higher Ottoman officials who were supposed to be enforcers of moderation and justice joined in the feeding. The authority of the sultan was compromised and his revenues were held back. "The world has slipped out of our hands and it is gone."[20]

Hence the attractiveness of Russia among Balkan notables, a power that might at least provide order. Roads and passages might be guarded by a real army, wealth might be shared with higher officials in predictable and routine ways, property and person might be secure. The Ottoman servitor Mavrokordatos, from a family that had been living off the Danubian peasantry, feared for his safety and joined the Russians. He saw a more stable world under Russian hegemony in the midst of one more Russo-Ottoman war. "All the world is talking of peace!" he exuded in his letter to Catherine the Great. Europe, the Balkans, and even the Ottoman Empire itself might now know order "under the auspices of such a Powerful Sovereign."[21]

The year was 1789 and he could not have been more wrong. Russo-Ottoman wars would remain a fixture on the Eurasian calendar for almost another century. The French Revolution had just begun. The Napoleonic Wars would soon spill into the Balkans and place regime change on the local agenda. And the Ottoman Empire proved no more able than before to rein in local powerful people and impose order. What had changed was that notables now had choices, beginning with Russia in the 1770s, and later also France and Britain. From the end of the century these three powers entered the Ionian region off the Balkan coast and became players in Ottoman politics.

Imperial Reform and Local Experience

Lament and reform became the words of the day, though men like Penah were at a loss to recommend changes. He like many others pined for an idyllic past, what one historian calls "the dogma of the static society." The aim was to freeze the regime into stability by denying change.[22] And yet the real challenge was to manage change. Penah held that the regime was disturbed by individual venality, and the most he could offer was more subordination and punishment—hardly a solution to a problem that was systemic. It added to rather than ended the arbitrariness.

And this was the central paradox of this time in Ottoman history: centripetal tendencies relied on centrifugal forces; attempts to impose order increased the local disorder; any effort to limit the power of the ayans depended on other ayans. Selim III established a new-style standing army and a fisc (a proper treasury) to pay for it. But he depended on the cooperation of regional notables, if only to quash the power of other notables, which meant granting more privileges and concessions to his allies and executing many others. Ayans and notables resisted when it meant rolling back their privileges or allotting them to someone else.[23] Selim was deposed, and the cycle began anew under Mahmud II. Mahmud's decree of February 1816 banned the ayans from buying tax farms and reserved the privilege for the sultan's governors and sub-governors. Locally this unleashed another wave of violence that was fairly termed a civil war,[24] and the notables continued to buy the tax farms.

The prime example of the paradox is Ali pasha of Yanena who from the 1780s to the early 1820s acquired ever more territories and revenues, stabilized the regions he conquered though destroying much in the process, and secured the east–west trade routes. Here was a model of order that was not strictly speaking a centralization of power since it afforded Ali discretion, but his was part of the general quest for stability. He was a supporter of good Ottoman government and supported the reforms of Selim III; he was also enormously powerful in his region and could ignore the commands of the Ottoman capital. When commanded Ali did send armies to fend off Russian attacks and quash agas who showed too much independence or separatist tendencies, but he added their domains to his own and increased his power and territory.

In the process Ali showed alarming tendencies of his own. He carried out his own diplomatic negotiations with Russia, he invited French, British, and Russian consuls to his court, and he monitored his own trade routes that redirected grain meant for Constantinople to his own towns and overseas markets, and he collected his own tariffs. He was defeated and killed in 1822 on orders of the sultan, by a combination of Anatolian mercenaries and Albanian irregulars hired by his regional rivals. "Submit to your destiny," an opposing pasha reputedly told him, "make your ablutions, pray to God and the Prophet, your head is demanded."[25]

Or consider the case of Bayraktar (or Alemdar) Mustafa pasha of Ruse (today in Bulgaria) who dutifully fought the Russians on the Danubian front but demanded new taxable territories to pay for the campaign. In 1808 he marched on Constantinople and installed Mahmud II as sultan, a reformer who would depend on the regional notables and magnates in order to reform. Open warfare erupted. Mahmud's two predecessors (Selim III and Mustafa IV) were murdered along with five current and former grand viziers (chief advisors to the sultan) who were dismembered or poisoned, and along with thousands of ministers, notables, and commoners who were assassinated or killed in the civil strife. Bayraktar died as well.[26] Mahmud continued efforts to rein in the regional powers but faced the same problem: he depended on regional power brokers, for example to fight Persia and Ali pasha. He presided over the loss of Greece in 1830, mainly because he could not mobilize men and resources.

Notables and ayans were dimly aware of the long-term stakes of a strategy that was supposed to make their lives more predictable and secure. To them reform seemed like the tumult they were used to, but worse. In the Morea local notables simply saw a danger to their privileges and a higher body count. They explained their plight in local and personal terms (this pasha and that vizier) and as the continuation of clan politics (the Chotoman against the Arnaoutoglou, the Deliyannis against the Lontos). Whatever Selim's and Mahmud's intentions, locals could only see them as arbitrary, or as they put it in the 1820s, as tyrants. Mahmud may have seen a stable future but the locals saw the violence he brought down on them. In the Morea it meant clan warfare, in Roumeli it was a grab for estates, in Crete it was vendettas.[27] Indeed part of the catalyst for the uprising of the Morea in 1821 was the fact that the notables were expecting that the new pasha, Hurşid, was about to carry out another wave of executions.

Each Muslim and Christian clan hired its armed bands—the Deliyannis hired the Kolokotronis at some point—in order to fight other bands and clans. The bands went out of control. A turning point came in 1805 when one of the Kolokotronis bands attacked a priest carrying tax receipts for the Patriachate, tortured him, and murdered his companions. This was an attack on the Orthodox church and therefore the Ottoman order. The bands were hunted down and exterminated in 1805 and 1806 by an alliance of the pasha, agas, notables, the Christian bey of the Mani, the Orthodox clergy who excommunicated them, and the monks and villagers who denounced them to the authorities.[28] Much of the Kolokotronis family was killed, Deliyannis and the local Ottoman commanders seized their wealth, and the survivors led by Thodorakis burned and looted more villages as they fled to Zakynthos.[29] Chateaubriand, the future French foreign minister, was traveling in the region in 1806 and the aga of Koroni assured him that the road to the hinterland would be safe: "they had just cut off the heads of 300 or 400 thieves."[30]

It was a rare moment of regional consensus, a determination to end the chaos, but any clear direction from Constantinople ended as the sultan was deposed and his officials massacred. In the Morea the notables were left to their own devices, and this meant more local warfare as a new pasha set faction against faction, each hiring more local bandits and still more Albanian irregulars. Scarcely had Kolokotronis been chased to the Ionian Islands than an aga of Lala invited him back to defend him against the new Morean pasha (see chapter 6).[31]

Quo Vadis

If the Ottoman space was not a place of mass religious persecution and oppression, as later nationalist historians would claim across the Balkans, what was it? It was an old regime, with local inflections. As with any old regime facing crisis, the problem was not that repression was systematic. On the contrary the problem was a lack of predictable system, a degeneration of government into arbitrariness and insecurity that

FIGURE 2.2. "Dinner at Crisso, in the House of the Bishop of Salona," in Edward Dodwell, *Views in Greece, From Drawings by Edward Dodwell, Esq. F.S.A. & c.* (London: Rodwell and Martin, 1821). Collection of the National Historical Museum, Athens. *The submission of the supplicant before the bishop is a reminder that the Orthodox clergy were Ottoman figures of power and authority. This scene is around today's Amfissa in southern Roumeli, Greece.*

was felt at all levels of the hierarchy. It afflicted the sultans who were deposed and murdered or could not put their decrees into practice, the notables and ayans who were beheaded and dispossessed, the merchants who were robbed and extorted, and the peasants who were taxed, attacked, and exploited in ever new ways.

Religious tolerance was not the issue because the Christians already had it. Notables and church hierarchs were privileged and integrated into Ottoman governance as tax collectors and forces of order. Church hierarchs defended the Ottoman order because it was their order as well. They handed out excommunications (anathematizations) of rebels liberally—just as in 1821 they would excommunicate the Greek revolutionaries.

Some local populations joined in rebellions but most did not, and rebellions never translated into revolutions—until 1821. Powerful Christians labored to make the system better. Nikolaos Mavrogenis, the Christian dragoman of the Ottoman fleet and later a Danubian prince, sought to make the regime effective, not end it. Raising Christian and Muslim armies, he battled Christian Morean rebels and Albanian marauders in the 1770s, Austrian invaders in the 1780s, Russia in 1790–91, and rebels under Osman Pazvantoğlu. Having seen off the Russians from his native Paros he showered the island with privileges and public works: his marble drinking fountains still adorn the streets of the main town.[32]

The shared complaint among notables of all regions and confessions was about the failure of the regime to provide the order it promised.[33] Ottoman loyalists after 1789 were convinced that arbitrariness was the cause of the French Revolution and warned that a similar fate awaited the Ottoman Empire.[34] Mavrogenis, who had performed impressive services for the regime, was executed during more palace intrigue, his head sent to the sultan. Patriarch Gregory, who excommunicated the rebels in 1821, was himself executed.

3-

That things might be different was a possibility introduced by Russia in the 1770s: it was a model of a centralized state with a standing army that marched by command rather than by negotiation, with a sovereign who might in practice deliver on promises of security. The tsar was an autocrat but perhaps not a tyrant. He would not tamper with the social hierarchy except to make it regular.

FIGURE 2.3. Fountain in Paros, Greece: "Nikolaos Mavrogenis, 1777." Photograph by Yanni Kotsonis, January 2024. *Mavrogenis was a native of the island of Paros and dragoman (Christian advisor) of the Ottoman fleet in the 1770s. After the departure of the Russian forces from the Aegean Islands, Mavrogenis undertook public works projects. This drinking fountain is one of three, made of Parian marble, gifted to an island that was largely arid.*

The next change came to the shores of the Balkans when a new power in the region destroyed Venice in 1797 and seized the Ionian Islands which hugged the west coast of Roumeli and the Morea. For the benefit of the locals their commander styled himself a Greek in origin and encouraged the use of his name in translation. He was Kalomeros, meaning Good Place, which in Corsican was Bonaparte: Kalomeros ton Frantzezon (Bonaparte of the French). Unlike Russia, France did intend to tamper with the social order, and it offered a first experience with mass mobilization.

Chapter 3

Imperial Crossroads

The Napoleonic Wars in the Ionian Islands

Prologue

INDEPENDENCE HALL IN *Tel Aviv, the place where Ben-Gurion declared a new state, is now a museum. The guided tour offers a standard nationalist foundational narrative, its broad outlines familiar from so many others, the Greek included. I fall in with a group of Australians and follow our guide. To illustrate the Jewish diaspora, our guide mentions that she is from Corfu, one of the Ionian Islands that passed between the empires in the eighteenth and nineteenth centuries. It is off the western coast of mainland Greece. Since the 1860s it has been part of Greece.*

I wonder if she considers herself part of the Greek diaspora as well. I approach her after the tour. In fluent Greek, she tells me of her childhood in the main town of Corfu as part of an affluent family of merchants and professionals. During the German occupation, Corfiot Christians saved them from deportation and murder. They made their way to Palestine.

"So you grew up speaking Greek?" I ask.

"Are you joking?" she laughs. "We were educated, we spoke Italian. I learned Greek later."

I am deflated and educated. The Ionian Islands always differed from the Ottoman mainland. They take pride in their politeness. They may look askance at the Greeks of the mainland who seem to them uncouth. To this day well-educated families boast noble lineages, some of them historical, some of them purchased in late Venetian times or granted by one or another empire, and some of them invented. They will readily and proudly recall that they had been subjects of Venice—hence the Italian—and then of France, Russia, and Britain. The towns have a Venetian aspect with ochre and light-blue townhouses and arches. Locals will point to a French commercial arcade here, a British barracks there, a Russian-funded church and school down an alley.

Ionian Islanders are more candid than most modern Greeks that they are the children of empires. It is easy for them because all the empires in question were Christian. The islands had never been part of the Ottoman Empire. Mainlanders, on the other hand, have been busy for two centuries scrubbing away the imperial traces from place names and destroying architectural monuments because their empire was Ottoman. The monuments were mosques and bathhouses, and the place names sounded Turkish and Alba-nian. Slavic also lacks cachet, and those names are mostly gone as well. In the schoolbooks and archeological institutions, the Ottoman era that lasted over three hundred years is called "post-Byzantine."

Ionian Islanders became nationals with an awareness of their multiple histories. Yet I am impressed by the manner in which they skirt over the bloody events that made them who they are.

Empires: The Ionian Islands to 1815

The story of the Ionian Islands from 1797 to 1815 is part of the Napole-onic Wars and also Greek national history. In the Greek histories the era is considered a series of occupations by foreign powers, before the is-lands we handed over to independent Greece in the 1860s. The European story erases the local and makes the history abstract; the local story may be parochial to a foreign visitor. In fact the Ionian region was trans-formed by the European wars and it contributed to those wars. The local became global and the global was translated into the local. Very briefly stated, the events unfolded as follows.

In 1797 the armies of the French Republic commanded by Napoleon Bonaparte destroyed the Venetian Republic. By the Treaty of Campo Formio France annexed Venice's Ionian Islands, off the Ottoman coast.

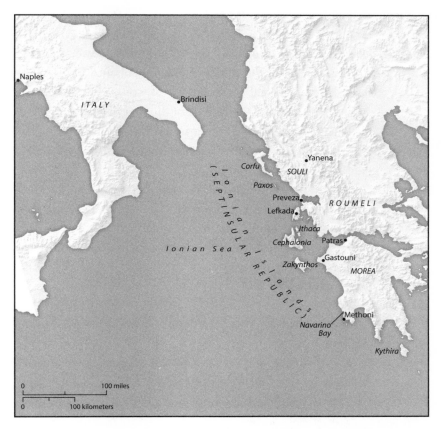

FIGURE 3.1. The Ionian Islands and Ionian Sea around 1800. Credit to Rob McCalebb. *The islands from Corfu in the north to Kythira in the south belonged to Venice until 1797, along with mainland enclaves like Preveza.*

Collectively the Ionian Islands are called the Seven Islands (Eptanisa): Corfu, Paxos and Antipaxos, Ithaca, Santa Maura (Lefkada), Cephalonia, Zakynthos, and Cerigo (Kythira). France also took four Venetian enclaves on the Balkan mainland. In Europe Campo Formio ended the War of the First Coalition. Locally it is known as the time of the Republican French. Bonaparte saw the islands as a way to monitor the eastern Mediterranean and support his invasion of Egypt. More ambitiously the islands were a stepping stone in a conquest that might include the Ottoman Balkans, India, and lands in between.

Simultaneous French invasions of Malta and Egypt implied that the eastern Mediterranean might become a French pond, and galvanized Britain, Russia, and the Ottoman Empire into coordinated action.[1] Britain and the Ottomans attacked the French in Egypt, and Britain took Malta. Russia, supported by the Ottoman fleet, conquered the Ionian Islands in 1798–9. In Europe this was part of the War of the Second Coalition. Locally it is the time of the Seven Islands Republic (also Septinsular Republic), so named after the regime that the Russians installed and protected.

In 1807 Russia, defeated in battle once again, returned the islands to France (now an empire) by the terms of the Treaty of Tilsit, and they came under the rule of Napoleon I. In Europe this was the end of the War of the Fourth Coalition. Locally it was the time of the Imperial French. Finally, Britain took the islands from France in a campaign that ended in 1814. This was the end of the War of the Sixth Coalition. Locally it was the start of the United States of the Seven Ionian Islands, a British dominion that would last to the 1860s when it was gifted to the Kingdom of Greece.

In the course of seventeen years the Ionian Islands experienced a French republic, an aristocratic republic under a Russian autocrat, a French empire, and a British mercantile regime. The changes were accompanied by much blood-letting and what amounted to civil wars. And yet the empires left a shared legacy: they offered the region a first experience of the modern state and the new regime in Europe. Islanders experienced the era as imperial waves, but with some innovations: mass mobilization and centralized state power which they both embraced and resisted. It was not yet a national mobilization, though. It was conducted under the aegis of the empires.

The French Revolution and the Ionian Islands

In 1797 France sent its army and it also sent its revolution, which broke up the old order on the islands.[2] The Ionian Islands under Venice had been a classic old regime divided into legal estates where one's birth determined one's station. The First Class of a few hundred families comprised noblemen with landed wealth. They dominated the administration of the islands. They spoke Venetian Italian (or the Ionian dialect of Venetian Italian), the language of learning, administration, and high status. They could be Catholic or Orthodox. Everyone else was grouped into the Second Class. They were merchants, professionals, and artisans in the towns, and they were the large peasant majority in the countryside. Their language was usually Greek, or its Ionian dialect, and their religion was Orthodoxy.

There was not much sadness over the end of Venice. The worst one could say was that Venice was predatory: emissaries arrived to collect taxes which they kept largely for themselves and then left. The best one could say about Venice was that it was absent: it left local matters to the local nobility. On paper the Venetian merchant houses had a monopoly on the foreign trade of the islands. In practice Cephalonia and Zakynthos boasted merchant fleets engaged in trade, bootlegging, and piracy.

Overnight two hundred thousand people (depending on how one counts) became French citizens, organized into three *départements* of France and governed by the French Constitution of 1795. Declaring these people citizens was a revolutionary act. All islanders had equal legal rights and protections, caste distinctions were abolished, and all men had the right to participate in government in one way or another. Time was reset. The year 1797 became Year Six of the French Revolution and Year One of Ionian Liberty. On local councils the noblemen were joined by Greek commoners, as well as one Coen from the small Jewish community of Corfu. Greek as the language of the masses was to join Italian as an official language. *Liberté-Égalité* were printed prominently on official documents as *Eleutheria-Isotes* and *Libertà-Equivalenza*. The Marseillaise was translated into a song of Ionian liberty. Zakynthians known for their love ballads now sang of "rivers of enemy blood flowing before our feet."[3]

This was the region's first taste of a new regime, and with it came that hallmark of the new regime, the centralized state. That dimension of French power was received with mixed feelings by a population accustomed to a government that was happily ineffective. New taxes were more fair because they were universal, but they were new taxes and they were universal. Worse yet, this government intended to collect them and added to the bill obligatory state bonds. Trade was to be regulated and aligned with French foreign policy. Zakynthians who sold Corinthian grapes to British merchants were cut off from their markets. Bootlegging was to be ended and pirates hunted down. Health codes were strictly enforced and trash and slop could no longer be dumped in the alleys. Quarantine to guard against diseases became stringent and returning sailors were locked away; officials catalogued and killed their dogs. Citizens were required to light the streets in front of their homes, a transparency that was meant to limit criminality and disease but also exposed every street to the scrutiny of the troops who now patrolled regularly. The honorific "*Citoyen!*" sounded less than liberating when it was the prelude to an arrest or a fine, and these were frequent and many. The troops billeted in the homes of the citizens and they were not often welcome and they did not always behave. Looting was a problem throughout this first French period. Appointed officials refused to carry out their duties because they were many and they were directed against their neighbors.

The anticlerical French administrators had it in for the local Catholic church. Locally this meant more sympathy for the Orthodox church as the religion of the majority, but the Orthodox clergy felt threatened as well. Church property was inventoried with a view to taxation or perhaps confiscation. New schools were to be created without the leadership of priests. French officials discussed a vague spirit instead of the Holy Trinity. The troops harassed the bearded and robed Orthodox priests, they carried on business on Sundays, and they urinated on churches before looting them. The new revolutionary calendar had no saints' days and yet saints' days were integral to the way the Orthodox measured time and honored their families and friends. It was easy for an islander to conclude that the French were not simply lay republicans but barbaric atheists.

France had introduced mass politics, and the proof was in the mass movements that rose up to resist the French. The islanders were emboldened by more changes in the geopolitics of the eastern Mediterranean. The Ottoman Empire faced a powerful state on its western Balkan coast and in Egypt. Russian ships sailing out of the Black Sea had to pass through seas monitored by France and harassed by corsairs. Britain's rising power in the Mediterranean and its trade were challenged. All feared France not only as an expansionist state but as an exporter of revolution.[4] Britain joined the Ottomans to attack the French in Egypt and defeated them in 1799. On the Ionian Islands, Russia struck a very rare alliance with the Ottoman Empire to dislodge the French. In 1798 their combined fleet invaded Kythira in the south and moved north, taking the islands one by one.[5]

As the Russians and Ottomans advanced they invited the islanders to support them. Whole villages and towns joined in a mass rising against what was, in substance, a more intrusive and uncompromising form of government and a realignment of foreign trade. The rebels were joined by noblemen who had lost so much of their power; tsar and sultan might restore the old regime. The rebels attacked and robbed the French and their sympathizers, and more generally attacked towns where laws were made and taxes gathered. The French and their local supporters retreated while looting and burning. Regional animosities, clan warfare, and vendettas were translated into imperial allegiances. Many towns and villages raised the Russian Cross of St. Andrew. Some raised the Ottoman crescent. Zakynthos hoisted the Union Jack.[6]

Russia and the Septinsular Republic

The last island, Corfu, was captured in early 1799 and the Russians and Ottomans assumed that their task was complete. They had ended the threat of revolution and curtailed French power. The Ottomans claimed only nominal suzerainty and a vaguely defined role. Russia was to be the protecting power but the fleet was ordered to leave for Italy to continue the campaign against France. Before leaving the Russian admiral, F. F. Ushakov, did try to create a new system of government. Ushakov was something of a liberal for his day. He assumed that the changes wrought by the French Revolution could not be fully reversed. He installed local administrations composed of the old nobility, but he added wealthy merchants and some well-educated professionals who

in Russian fashion became the "personal nobility" (i.e., not hereditary). The latter had to prove that their families had not engaged in
manual labor for two generations.[7] And then, in the spring and summer of 1799, the Russians left.

The Russians left behind mass movements that turned into a civil
war. It was the Russians who had helped create them when they appealed to all classes to attack the French, and the French who were the
original mass mobilizers. Noblemen launched a full-scale reaction and
demanded a monopoly on local power, like the good old days. With the
Russians unsympathetic and then gone, conservative noblemen appealed to the Porte, sent emissaries to Constantinople, and requested
exclusive power. Even the sultan was a better alternative to a government by commoners. The sultan saw them as bulwarks against revolution and agreed to a reactionary constitution.

When word got out that they might be placed under noble rule with
Ottoman sponsorship, townsfolk and peasants took up arms. Republican France looked good again and out came the French tricolors. The
town of Corfu was besieged by a peasant army. Peasant armies marched
across Cephalonia in support of one or another clan or town, under one
or another imperial flag. Soon peasants were marching against the gentry and they set up their own administrations which would abolish
rents. Zakynthos was taken over by a peasant army. Ithaca had no government at all, so far as Russian observers could tell: "they live like Hot-
tentots." Kythira experienced a full-scale peasant jacquerie (*bunt* in
Russian) in which noblemen were killed, their properties reduced to
rubble, and tax and rental records burned. Armed noblemen and their
supporters strung up peasants. "Cerigo" (Kythira) became a word of
caution, on the dangers of democracy or the folly of reaction.[8]

The crisis was resolved because of changes that were occurring in
St. Petersburg. The emperor Paul who had ordered the capture of the
islands was focused on Italy and Malta and ignored the events on the
tiny Ionian Islands. At home he was seen as fickle and dangerous and
there were suspicions that he would no longer prosecute the war against
France. In 1801 he was overthrown and murdered by the supporters of
his son, and his son became Alexander I. He and his advisors appreci-

ated better that Ionian stability was strategically important if the islands were to act as a Russian base.

But the young Alexander was also intensely interested in forms of government and many contemporaries thought he might be a liberal.[9] The Ionian Islands were his first try at constitutionalism. He gathered around himself a Secret Committee of aristocratic luminaries such as Adam Czartoryski, Viktor Kochubei, and Pavel Stroganov. The meetings were part European geostrategy and part political philosophy. They discussed how Europe and Russia itself might benefit from rationalized government. They were stimulated by aspects of the French Revolution which might be correctives to the old regimes. They discussed wider consultation in government and the protection of persons and property. There was talk of constitutions. To some this meant the rule of law, but in Russia this meant orderly and rational autocracy. It was this model that they applied to the Ionian Islands.

In summer 1802, while governing a vast Eurasian empire and waging a European war, Alexander and his advisors considered what would be a suitable form of government for the tiny Ionian Islands. Their aim was moderation and they condemned the reactionary gentry along with the peasant masses. A new constitution was drafted largely in St. Peterburg in 1802 and 1803 by Alexander, Czartoryski, and foreign minister A.R. Vorontsov.[10] A Senate would be elected by the nobility, but this nobility would now include a stratum of men defined by income and education rather than birth. The Russian foreign minister supervised from St. Petersburg to make sure that new men of money and culture entered government. On Corfu the nobility grew from 180 families in 1803 to 475 in 1804—not what we might call a democracy, nor a meaningless gesture. Peasants would be left out and made to submit. Wrote the Ionian senator Teotoki, "their exclusion is founded on a real fact, their poverty."

At the same time Alexander assumed that all islanders were naturally unruly and internecine in their warfare and would require a strong central authority. To enforce his will Alexander sent Giorgio Mocenigo, a diplomat in Russian service whose family came from Zakynthos. He gave him detailed instructions, broad leave to intervene in local affairs, and a Russian army of 1,600 men. Mocenigo promised "liberal government" (*governo libero*) and "civil society" (*civili società*), always backed by an armed force that should be visible and irresistible.[11] The noble assemblies on the different islands were instructed to approve the new regime unanimously. In Corfu Mocenigo and Russian officers observed from the Senate gallery as the representatives of the islands accepted the new constitution. Those who objected were encouraged to change their minds. Aristocrats who appealed to the Porte were frozen out of power. Giovanni Capo d'Istria, Russia's trusted Ionian nobleman, went to Cephalonia and Ithaca to put down violent rebellions and end clan warfare. Holdouts were invited to go into exile. Seeing armed peasants mobilized by all the clans, Capo d'Istria warned of a "Robespierrian terror." The peasant armies were defeated and disbanded.[12]

With a semblance of peace restored, state-building efforts resumed and accelerated. There was more public lighting, sanitation and swamp drainage, support for poor children in new asylums, a postal service, and a new system of public education.[13] Napoleon was intrigued and he asked foreign minister Talleyrand to look into the Ionian experiment. Talleyrand was impressed: it was a "government of enlightenment and experience," introduced by a dictator. If only it had been carried out by France.[14]

Historically and popularly it is usual to see the Septinsular Republic in terms of two legacies. In the first instance it is as a coming together of the Greeks and Russians as co-religionists, a manifestation of the spiritual bond of Orthodoxy. This bond has been overstated. The islanders showed a capacity to work with any number of powers, from Catholics and deists to Muslims and Protestants. As for the Russians, religion was not something to get the fleet to sail and the army to march. The Russians came to evict the French, not save the Orthodox. To be sure, Russia arrived with ecclesiastical proclamations in Greek and Russian. Ushakov extolled the "Russo-Greek Church" though there was no such institution. He denounced French atheism and the antichrist idolater Napoleon. Money was spread to maintain churches. But Ushakov was partial to any organized religion, not only Orthodoxy, and as a Russian he was experienced with Muslims who held positions of authority in the Russian hierarchy. He also extolled Islam which, like Orthodoxy, was a force for hierarchy and stability. The sultan may not have been Christian but at least he had religion.[15]

Anyway, not all Orthodoxies are the same and not all the Orthodox necessarily get along—any more than Lutheran Danes were fond of Lutheran Prussians or Catholic Italians had a weakness for Catholic Austrians. The Russians had little faith in the Ionian Orthodox clergy. Their patriarch in Constantinople was hardly a Russophile. He was an Ottoman appointee and steadfastly supported the Porte in all of its wars against Russia.[16]

Russia came to reform the Ionian church, not preserve it. Russian attitudes toward the church were colored by Russian historical experience. Since the time of Peter the Great, Russian statesmen were suspicious of an independent church and Peter mocked its parochial obscurantism. Peter abolished the Russian patriarchate and enveloped all recognized religions in the bureaucratic procedures of the Holy Synod, headed by a lay official. Over the next decades monastic lands were expropriated. Parallel efforts by Peter and Catherine to join religious with secular education culminated in 1802 when Alexander created the Ministry of Public Enlightenment. Progress in Russia was understood as a state affair. Russian policies were decidedly of the Enlightenment variety.

A century of Russian policy was distilled into reforms in the Septinsular Republic. The Septinsular administration curtailed the church and expanded secular learning, to a degree that the Republican French had only imagined. Mocenigo promised a republic of Enlightenment "founded upon scientific knowledge," a regime that would produce competent men of government, war, and commerce. In this the clergy was not necessarily a help: Mocenigo observed that Ionian priests were often illiterate and could not read the Bible.[17]

To pay for the new schools the republic imposed taxes on the monasteries and closed down several of them—to the chagrin of the church hierarchs from around the Mediterranean who in one or another way drew on the resources of Ionian monasteries.[18] The monastery of Tenedos became a school. Among its teachers was Christoforos Perraivos, the anticlerical, republican, and revolutionary who had joined a conspiracy in the Balkans led by Righas Velestinlis (see chapter 6). His salary was paid with church funds and the curriculum focused on language, classics, and mathematics.[19] Students were drawn from the nobility and the merchantry and they paid a low fee; poor children were to attend for free but it seems none attended at all. The whole affair was delegated to Giovanni Capo d'Istria.

The second legacy of the Septinsular Republic, as any local will say, is that it was the first modern Greek state. In some ways this is true because the republic adopted Greek as its official language, but this was proclaimed in Italian. Too few noblemen in the Senate could speak it, and Italian continued to be the language of official business.[20] Mocenigo observed that noblemen dismissed the Greek spoken on the islands as "vulgar and corrupt" compared with the ancient language they admired. Of the many islanders who spoke Greek very few could write it: when Mocenigo induced the Senate to sign the Constitution in 1803, he noticed that Greek-speaking senators could not write their names. Russia introduced a postal service to carry written words that were usually Italian. If the Septinsular Republic was Greek, it was not yet clear what Greek might mean. Mocenigo mused: "People of quality have for centuries confused themselves with the nation of Italians."[21] The Septinsular Republic was still an imperial product.

Then again, it was not clear what a nation of Italians might look like, either. The Italian Legion that was formed by the Russians on the islands in 1801 had divisions commanded by Charalambos Grigorakis and one Giovanni Coletti—better known as Ioannis Kolettis, a future leader of the Greek Revolution and a statesman of independent Greece (see chapter 14).[22] It was too soon to speak of nations anywhere, let alone decide what nation a person belonged in. Class and empire mattered more than nation. Civil strife erupted along the class and imperial axes, and so did the solution, a republic of the well-to-do, speaking mainly Italian, protected by the Russian Empire.

This did change in the 1820s, with the failed Italian revolutions to the west of the islands and the Greek one to the east. Even then it was not clear what the nation might mean, and who belonged in what nation. Consider the case of a poet. On Zakynthos in 1806, among the pupils in the Russian-sponsored schools was Dionyssio Salamon, later known as Dionysios Solomos and the Greek national poet. Like most students he was instructed in Italian. Modern Greek (*Graiki dialektos*) and Classical Greek (*Elleniki dialektos*) were taught as foreign languages.[23] Only in 1822 or so would a visiting mainlander teach him to use written Greek. Salamon or Solomon chose to become the Greek Solomos and wrote his poetry in Italian and then translated it into Greek. The only poem he wrote directly in Greek was the Greek national anthem, which is still in use today, and is emotive and not entirely grammatical. His Greekness, like any national sentiment at the time, was evolving. It was broadly confessional but not yet married to one language. Meanwhile the poet Ugo Foscolo, another son of Zakynthos, chose to be Italian though in the 1820s asked to join the Greek revolutionaries. The Greeks turned him away.[24]

The Russian moment mattered in a different way. It was a showcase of imperial power that allowed for some peaceful local development, and it probably seemed an improvement on a stagnant Venice and combative France. The empires were still the gold standard of state organization, and local movements demanded the protection of one or another empire, not independence. The republic had a state-of-the-art constitution that was drafted by Russian officials. In this manner an empire had shown how a combination of expanded political participation, a centralized authority, and a disciplined army could bring disorder to an end. The nobleman Zoulatis lauded it as "a power that is firm, vigilant" and offered "security of person and of ownership of property"—what the French had promised but could not deliver.

Whatever else Russia had done, it had secured the peace. It is for this reason that the locals remained calm when Russia changed the constitution in 1806. Russia was preparing for another war with France and wanted a free hand to use the Ionian Islands as a base. Civil rights were repealed, Montecigo was made dictator, and Capo d'Istria facilitated the transition.[25]

Imperial French

The same emphasis on order was the hallmark of the next occupier, France again but this time under Napoleon as emperor. After the massive defeats at Austerlitz and Friedland, Russia suspended its war against France and entered into the Treaty of Tilsit of 1807. The islands were ceded back to France, though the islanders only learned of it when the French fleet arrived.[26] France was no longer the revolutionary force of mass liberation. It embraced some change such as social mobility but controlled changes with hierarchical statuses and a uniform legal code. Power passed to the French army commander, François-Xavier Donzelot, who in effect replaced Mocenigo. Public sanitation and quarantine measures continued apace, and with it the surveillance that these measures implied. Indeed France introduced the hallmark of the modern state, a political police force that monitored the loyalties of the population and invited denunciations. Ionian factions and clans denounced their adversaries with gusto. The population now carried army-issued identification cards. The masses would no longer be mobilized but brought to a "docile tranquility."[27] Napoleon gave new recognition to the churches as guardians of order and the local clergy was put on the state payroll. He showered the Ionian nobility with new titles and inducted many into the new Legion of Honor. Noblemen travelled to Paris for audiences where Napoleon indulged them with tales of their Classical greatness. He was always convinced that the Greeks were vain and open to flattery, and he claimed that as a Corsican he had Greek origins. The Empress Eugenie looked on in Corfiot costume.[28]

Within two years French rule was under threat again. After Egypt and Trafalgar, Britain was the preeminent naval power of the Mediterranean.[29] Britain blockaded the islands using its fleet and corsairs, and cut them off from their supplies from Italy and the Ottoman mainland.[30] The monthly army payroll of 250,000 francs that sailed from Brindisi was regularly hijacked. The islands depended on grain and meat from Epirus and the Morea, but the pashas sent their exports to the British fleet and as far as Gibraltar. The British paid well and the cargos were protected.[31] French diplomats from Constantinople and Alexandria to Naples raced to secure shipments of grain before the British could swoop in with better offers. Donzelot spent more time trying to secure food for his troops and the population than on any other task. He broke open abandoned Russian stores of biscuit, which were rotten but better than nothing. By 1810 he was reporting famine in the town of Corfu and among his troops. He was expecting "the next revolt."[32]

The next revolt came on Paxos in summer 1810. About five hundred hungry locals demanded a British invasion and attacked and killed French sympathizers. Napoleon demanded executions, a total response to stamp out what he saw as treason. Donzelot complied with shootings but reminded Napoleon that the islanders were starving.[33] Customary trade routes between the islands and the mainland, often based on friendships and family relations, were cut off by new and firmer borders between the different powers.

On Paxos the supply crisis had been unfolding since the time of the Russian occupation. Ali pasha on the mainland cut off supplies to the islands when he fell out with one or another occupying power, and Russia banned the locals from consorting with the enemy. A hapless Paxiot named Anemoyannis (Windy John) whose family "traded with the enemy" on the Ottoman mainland was put on public trial for treason. The proceedings were in Italian, and the accused defended himself in Greek as best he could. He pointed out that the "enemy" were his relatives. His incriminating correspondence was addressed to "Dear Cousin" (*Igapimene xadelfe*). The treasonous contraband was olive oil and cheap wine that he exchanged for flour. (The court sampled the wine and agreed that it too awful for bootlegging.) The empires cut across his networks of family and exchange.[34]

All along the Paxiots traded with British merchants whose ships visited under the noses of the French who lacked a fleet to stop them. The entire Ionian Sea basin was flooded with British gold and British calico, rayon, and threads.[35] The French were outraged and helpless but the islanders were conducting business as usual, using family networks and following old trade routes. The idea of total belonging and therefore total enemies was still new.

When the British launched their invasion of the islands, beginning with Kythira, they faced emaciated troops who surrendered and retreated. Locals welcomed the British ships and the restoration of trade, and the British promised to reduce taxes. Out came the Union Jack in town after town.[36] Corfu surrendered in 1814. The islands became the

United States of the Ionian Islands under British protection. British rule would earn a reputation for brutality toward dissent and petty crime, punctuated by demonstrative hangings and public trials. Bootleggers and pirates (mainstays of the local economy) were hunted down. It was also Pax Britannica, remarkably stable, the prosperity of the Ionian ship-owners fed by the trade of the British Empire and protected by the British fleet. Increasingly local affairs were left to a Senate elected by an ever-widening franchise, wider than in Britain itself.[37] It was another imperial experience and a profitable one.

States and Revolutions before the Nation

What, then, was mass politics before the nation, and what was the modern state before the nation-state? Taken together the islands had experienced four regimes that shared a common legacy: they showcased the modern state. The empires shared an emphasis on law and order and promised a return to "tranquility" as the British put it, *spokoistvo* as the Russians put it, *tranquillité* as the French put it from 1807, and *tranquillità* as the islanders put it. Respect for private property for those who had it was a central plank of all the occupiers. The republican French promised it but failed to deliver because they had the impossible mission of introducing order through a revolution.[38] When the Russians arrived they were horrified by the killing and looting between Francophiles and Russophiles. Ushakov promised "personal security and also security of property." He then issued a general amnesty: "All persons, regardless of their religious and national belonging, all inhabitants of the Island and their property, cannot be persecuted, repressed, or insulted for their political opinions." The Russians then delivered peace and stability at the point of a bayonet.[39] Britain imposed an imperious "xenocracy," as a historian usefully put it, founded on law and order as the British understood it.[40] Looking from the Ottoman mainland, this was a model: a centralized state guaranteeing security of person and property, in effect freezing into place existing inequalities. It looked very much like early liberalism.

The invasions of the Ionian Islands opened the region not to nation-alism, not yet, but to a new world of global empires. European warfare exploded into the region and people from the islands and the Ottoman mainland spilled into new imperial mobilities in search of careers and better pay. A person recruited in Ithaca or the Ottoman mainland was serially linked to empires stretching from Vladivostok and India to Mar-tinique and North America. It was a new world and locals lived it as imperial creatures.

Chapter 4

The Magic Lantern of Empire

Greeks on the March for France since 1797

Prologue

IT IS 1980 *and I am in a dimly lit bar in downtown Athens. I am recently out of high school. The man next to me speaks to me in native working-class Greek. As my eyes adjust I realize that he is from sub-Saharan Africa, or so I think. I ask him where he's from and he says Piraeus, the port town of Athens. And before that? Piraeus, he repeats. My surprise owes to the fact that there are not many African-origin Greeks and he is the first I meet. I find it exotic but the man is Greek, because he speaks Greek. I do find it odd when overseas Greeks returning from the United States, South Africa, and Australia organize their worlds into races rather than nations, erasing geographies, cultures, languages, and histories. My classmates and I flinch at their racialized lexicons. They find our mystification mystifying. I am not yet trained in race, but I soon will be as I leave for university and travel the old imperial spaces in Europe and Canada. Later, arriving in the USA as a European, I learn that I am White.*

In the following decades Greece would absorb more migrants from Africa. Their experiences are as varied as any other group of economic migrants. They know hardship, poverty, unofficial bigotry, and sometimes hope when they put down roots and have children. Those children are Greeks and they march with their schools in the annual parades of 25 March to mark the outbreak of the Greek Revolution. Some are chosen by their schools to lead the parade and carry the Greek flag. This is a high honor and meant to make the point, very publicly and at least aspirationally, that they are Greeks. In the 2010s the hero for Greek children is the captain of the national basketball team, a boy born in Athens to Nigerian parents and baptized Yannis.

I wonder why that family adjusted better than, say, the Bangladeshis, who remain transients, cramped into slums and selling flowers and plastic toys in the squares, or placed in barracks and tents and harvesting the fruits and vegetables in the scorching heat. It dawns on me that the Nigerians are Christians and the Bangladeshis Muslims, and I wonder at the significance. Race was never an official category in Greece. But religion is a category that has been meaningful since Ottoman times, through the Revolution, and into the founding of the first Greek state when confession determined the lines of inclusion and exclusion. To this day the Constitution of Greece is written in the name of the Holy Trinity and invokes Our Lord Jesus Christ.

Modern binaries are totalizing but not all binaries are the same. A Muslim might convert to Christianity and vice versa, but how does a Black covert to Whiteness and vice versa?

Then again, why should anyone have to convert from anything?

Georges Ciolly, Ionian Man of Color[1]

The man called Georges Ciolly on his personnel file in the French military archives was baptized Giorgio in Zakynthos in 1771, and he served in the Venetian garrison. One can imagine some sleepy duties: gathering drunks, breaking up brawls at the brothels, inspecting ships in the port on the lookout for bootlegging and disease. When France took over the island in 1797, he became a French citizen and a French soldier. He was promoted to captain. He began to learn French. Within a year he was defending Zakynthos against the combined Russian–Ottoman fleet. When the island fell Ciolly was captured by the Ottomans rather than the Russians. This was unlucky because the Ottomans did not use the category of prisoner of war, governed by protections and the expectation of future release. Captives were war booty, and Ciolly was a slave who would be kept for ransom.[2] Officers were usually high-born and someone would pay a price to have them released.

On the other hand Ciolly was lucky because the Ottomans did not always take prisoners at all. The decline of the rowed galleys had led to a fall in the demand for male slaves. More useful to the Ottoman soldier was the head, the ears, or the tongue. The soldier presenting a body part to his commander could expect a reward, and the company treasurer paid fixed rates out of a special fund. There were more rewards as the trophies were passed up a hierarchy of commanders until they reached the sultan in Constantinople, with the body parts thrown ceremoniously into the yard of the Palace of Topkapi.[3] Ears and tongues traveled well when salted, but heads were more complicated. In fact the victorious soldier carried the dried skin of the head packed in salt, a service performed by the company cook or a local butcher. This was rehydrated and stuffed with hay or sawdust before being presented.[4]

Ciolly and the other survivors were paraded across the Morea and Roumeli and they carried the heads of their dead comrades. In Constantinople the heads were presented to the sultan along with scores of French survivors from other battles in the Ionian and Egyptian campaigns. They were then sent to the dungeons of the fortress of Yedikule (Seven Towers) in Constantinople.[5] Ciolly joined a few hundred French prisoners from around the Mediterranean. The diplomat, spy, and scholar François Pouqueville was among them. Well-off diplomats and officers were imprisoned with their servants and staff and could buy supplies from their captors.[6] The others suffered from hunger and the elements, though over the months they were able to pay the ransoms and they trickled back to France. But not Ciolly: he was from a modest family and was an officer because of French practices that promoted the low-born. In the end Ciolly was released under the terms of the Treaty of Amiens (1802), which made him a prisoner of war rather than a slave. His Ionian homeland was now a Russian protectorate, and he was shipped to Marseille. It was his first time in metropolitan France.

By the time Ciolly arrived in Marseille, the bulk of the released prisoners had already been given hardship pensions and new commissions in the French army.[7] Ciolly encountered army clerks who did not know of the case of the Ottoman prisoners and probably did not know much about the Ionian Islands. The army bureaucrats were baffled. Ciolly insisted that he was a French citizen, but by then the islands were the Septinsular Republic under Russian protection. He was Christian, still a marker of a Frenchman and a European, but he was Orthodox rather than Catholic. He spoke and wrote French but not well, and his native languages were Venetian Italian and Ionian Greek. One commander offered him the status of "Egyptian" and a place in one of the camps for the refugees from France's failed campaign. After all, he was swarthy and from somewhere southeast of France, broadly speaking the Orient or the Levant. Ciolly refused because he was not Egyptian and not a refugee. He was a Frenchman.

Ciolly gathered his paperwork to satisfy an exacting French army bureaucracy. He secured attestations from his French comrades who had defended the citadel of Zakynthos in 1799. A dozen swore that he had fought like any other French officer and was imprisoned with the other French. His commander described "the cruelty, the horrors, and the misery to which we were given by the barbarity of the Turks." That they suffered privations there can be no doubt, but it was a classic Orientalist captivity narrative replete with homoerotic and sadomasochistic intimations, and it did the trick. On 19 Messidor of Year 11 of the Revolution Ciolly's petition reached First Consul Napoleon Bonaparte, who affirmed that Ciolly was a veteran of the French army and reinstated him with the rank of lieutenant.

That settled it for the army clerks: Ciolly was a Frenchman. But what were they to do with him? They still wondered if he was really French and how he could be useful, so they passed his file to recruiters for France's various foreign army formations. France had been organizing all sorts of legions, regiments, and battalions for national and regional groups. There were formations of Irish, Swiss, Italians, Illyrians, Croats, Poles, Albanians, Greeks (in Egypt), and Egyptians (Copts).[8] These were formed partly to satisfy a hunger for more soldiers to carry on France's seemingly endless wars. But they were also an affirmation of the principle of nationality. European armies had always hired foreigners to fight the wars of a monarch; both Britain and France sent German mercenaries to fight in the American War of Independence.[9] Now foreigners were organized as national units, to affirm that such a nation existed and that France was its liberator. Ciolly did not call himself a Greek, and anyway the Greek formation had been disbanded after Egypt. The options were open.

Among these foreign formations, France formed a battalion for people who were Black (*noirs*) and People of Color (*hommes de couleur*), official racial terms tracing to the slave colonies of the Caribbean. Slavery had been abolished by the republic but the racial terms were very much alive and practiced. The battalion was named the Pionniers Noirs: the Black Sappers or Scouts. In contrast to the national and geographic formations, this one was racial. It could draw troops from any geographic location speaking any language, so long as they seemed dark and so long as they were Christians. Recruiters were struggling to meet their quota, and the clerks were struggling to make sense of Ciolly. A clerk had an idea: "We propose him for the Black Battalion."

Ciolly was categorized as a Man of Color, meaning a person who was mixed race and not a slave. Blacks on the other hand had most often been slaves. Ciolly was made a lieutenant (later captain) in the Pionniers Noirs. There he joined hundreds of People of Color and Blacks from across French, formerly French, and adjacent non-French territories. He reported to the storied Joseph-Damingue Hercule (or Hercule Domingue, or simply Hercule). Hercule was an African-Cuban slave raised in Bordeaux, the capital of the French slave trade in the eighteenth century. Hercule was emancipated and fought for the republic that had freed him.

This was in effect a racially segregated formation and it was illegal. France had disallowed such units in 1798. Many of the Pionniers were French and in theory it did not matter that they were Black.[10] To allow for the racial principle, the battalion was sent to Naples, a de facto French dependency but technically not France. There the battalion became known as the *Royal Africain* or *Real Africano*, though the vast majority were not from Africa but the Caribbean. In Italian they were called the *Mori* (Moors or Blacks). It was used to patrol the coasts down to Calabria where it hunted rebels and bandits working with the British. Our last record of Ciolly is from 1809, when he asked to be assigned to the Ionian Islands, his birthplace and once again part of France. We do not

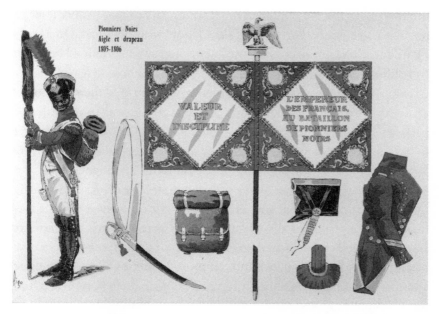

FIGURE 4.1. "Pionniers Noirs. Aigle et drapeau, 1805–1806" (The Black Sappers. Eagle and Banner), nineteenth century. Plate 109 of "Le Plumet," vol. 4, d'Albert Rigondaud dit Rigo, Paris, Musée de l'Armée. © RMN-Grand Palais / Art Resource, NY. *The Black Sappers were formed originally of Haitian refugees and prisoners held in Ajaccio, Corsica. They served in Italy and the Russian campaign, 1812–14.*

know whether he was transferred. We do know that the Pionniers were at the invasion of Russia in 1812, and they surrendered in Danzig (Gdańsk in Poland) in 1814.

How did Ciolly become a Man of Color? The answer lies in Saint-Domingue, today's Haiti, which on the eve of the French Revolution was a slave colony. France's conduct in the Caribbean (as a kingdom, a republic, an empire, and a kingdom again) is a shameful chapter in that country's history.[11] On Saint-Domingue the French Revolution was embraced by free People of Color. They were joined by Blacks who were emancipated in the region in 1793 and on all French territories in 1794. For some French republicans this was a moral necessity for the homeland of the Rights of Man. For others who wondered whether Blacks were human it was an expedience: the freed slaves could be used to fight the vestiges of the old regime in the Caribbean. For many more it was a mistake since France still needed slave labor to supply sugar. On Martinique and Guadeloupe, slavery was reimposed and maintained until the Revolution of 1848.

Saint-Domingue was different. Former slaves formed their own army under the former slave Toussaint Louverture. He was more or less a partisan of France until Napoleon sent an army to subjugate the island in 1802 and reimpose slavery. Toussaint and his army were now fighting for their personal liberty, which came to mean independence. Over the next two years the French force was decimated by disease and battle losses in a campaign that was as amoral in conception as it was a humanitarian disaster for the islanders. Even as thousands of islanders were butchered and drowned, the lines of color were never clear. France recruited hundreds of Blacks and People of Color on Saint-Domingue and brought others from nearby territories. With the reconquest in tatters, shiploads of these veterans of the French forces were evacuated to France. Prisoners taken from the army of Louverture were sent over as well.[12] Both groups, the pro-French and the pro-Louverture, landed in camps in Ajaccio, Corsica where they were placed in labor brigades.

The refugees and prisoners in Ajaccio became the core of the Black Pioneers, which was formed in 1803.[13] In their practical quest for more troops, the recruiters used race to make use of manpower and to erase the political differences among the recruits. When some officers queried about the fact that some had fought for the independence of Saint-Domingue and others for France—surely some were more trustworthy and deserving of reward—the recruiters insisted that there was no difference between those who fought on the side of Louverture and those who fought against him. Their race overrode their differences. So while the names on the rosters were clearly marked "for Louverture" or "for France," the recruiters told officials to ignore the distinction.

The army recruiters in Paris searched for more Black people and they sent queries to the police in cities and port towns. The police responded with a veritable census of Blacks in France. Some were French, born and bred. Many more had arrived in France in the 1790s, from colonies like Martinique and Guadeloupe.[14] Others were from Granada, Louisiana,

St.-Lucie (today's Saint Lucia), the west coast of Africa, and Egypt. The police lists named tailors, launderers, cooks, domestics, prostitutes, professional soldiers, farmers, and fishermen. The racial categories were at best inconsistent. For all their claims to genealogical or legal accuracy, these were political terms and open to change, and in this context the terms were gradually merged into a single category. Terms like *noir*, *nègre*, *mulattre*, *quarteron*, and *homme de couleur* were used pretty much interchangeably, always with the same outcome in mind: eligibility for the Black Pioneers. The officers and NCOs were mixed: some were White, some were Black, and some were Men of Color. In that last group fell the officer Ciolly.

The problem for us is not that Ciolly was placed in the wrong category; it's that the categories were contingent and specific to French colonial politics. There is nothing universal about the meaning of skin color. Ciolly ended up a Man of Color because a clerk wrote in the margins of his file, "C'est probablement un homme du couleur" (This is probably a man of color). Another notation in the margin doubted the entire story as too improbable: "Cela est il bien vrai?" (Is this really true?)

One can well understand both reactions to Ciolly's file, and they remind us that the categories Greek and European were also in play. The region whence Ciolly came was Greek by French cultural tradition, and European on some maps. To a French colonial mind trained in race, Greeks were necessarily White insofar as they were Europeans and Christians; Blackness had to do with the western colonies and Africa. Viewed this way, the clerk who designated Ciolly a Man of Color would have been acting out of ignorance of Classical learning. A well-educated Frenchman—officers learned strategy and history beginning with the ancient Greeks and Romans—would have known that Greeks and the cradle of European civilization could not be Black or Men of Color.

But the well-educated officer would be wrong, precisely because of his Classical education. An experienced Frenchman would have known that people from sub-Saharan Africa reached Europe not only though the western hemisphere and the European empires, but more easily through Egypt, Arabia, and north Africa. Perhaps sixteen thousand slaves from sub-Saharan Africa were imported to the Ottoman Empire in any given year.[15] Koroni and Methoni in the southern Morea were entry points for slaves shipped through Arabia and the Barbary who were put to work on Muslim estates. But in the Ottoman Empire slaves were not taken on the basis of skin color. Nor was this the Atlantic, and Blackness did not mean a life sentence stripped of humanity.

Rather, Ottoman slavery adhered to laws about confession. Plenty of African-origin people lived in Ottoman Europe, many of them Muslims who served as soldiers, servants, laborers, and officials. A slave could advance: many of the sultan's highest administrators were slaves. Moreover slavery was not a Black phenomenon. Any Christian caught in battle might be sold into slavery, and most of these Christians were White by the standards of the day.[16] Whereas some symbolic geographies made the region Europe and White, other geographies made the Ionian basin the Levant, Turkey, or the Orient. Ergo: someone from the Ionian region need not be White.

Ciolly himself was unclear about his color; he only stated that he was Zakynthian, French, and Christian. He did not use the terms Greek, White, or Man of Color. It is not clear that he cared. When he asked to be transferred, he may well have mentioned that he was in the wrong race; NCOs from France who asked to be repatriated did make that argument. He only stated that he wanted to go home. But it would be wrong to posit that anyone had a natural place based on skin color, that the NCOs belonged in France, or that Ciolly was miscategorized. They were all imperial creations, one way or another, as was their color: Hercule the African-Cuban from Bordeaux, Ciolly the French Man of Color from Zakynthos, the Haitian veterans of all political persuasions, the officers, cooks, prostitutes, and tailors dotting French towns and ports, and the White NCOs who became White because of the imperial context. French recruiters made the racial dichotomy real in their search for soldiers. Ultimately the dichotomy traced to a French liking for sugar.

Ciolly was operating by different categories: service to be sure, but also confession. So were the French who formed national battalions, but of Christians only. The Haitians, the other Caribbeans, the French Whites and Blacks and People of Color, Louisiana Blacks, the Egyptians Copts, the Ionian Islanders (Catholic and Orthodox) were all Christians. Europe had plenty of Muslims, and the French made a brief effort to recruit defecting and captured Janissaries. Nothing came of the undertaking and their archival files are empty, save a list of names written in Ottoman.

Confession was the point where Ciolly and his employers understood each other. The axis of religion was quiet under the French Republic, meaningful but muted by its anticlericalism. At the very least, Christianity was a marker of civilization. The contrast to Islam (usually painted as barbaric and used interchangeably with Turk) was persistent. The Christian element was pronounced under the French Empire which, among other things, reinvented a sense of church-infused hierarchy and gave new prominence to the established religions.

Only some of the imperial categories made sense locally. Race would not take hold. Bishop Ignatii, an Ottoman Christian who defected to Russia and advocated for the Greek Revolution, placed the Greeks alongside the Haitians as people fighting for freedom. He was scathing in his criticism of the French who did not recognize the humanity of a Black person. The Blacks now lived in liberty, "like other enlightened nations."[17] The Haitians were Christians, and Christianity meant Enlightenment. It was the Muslims who were—in the common terminology of the time—"inhuman" (*apanthropi*).

Religion was already a meaningful signifier in the Ottoman Empire. It was a way to organize its populations using clerics, powers of tax collection, and spiritual rewards and punishments. The new empires in the region were also infused with religious meaning but brought something different: Christian supremacy and even Christian exclusivity. This did take hold and the Greek Revolution was a war waged by Christians only, in pursuit of a Christians-only state. In the massacres and battles of the 1820s there was no evidence of people dying as races on any side; in the mass enslavements there was no talk of skin color. But tens of thousands died and were enslaved as religions.

To the Europeans the violence of the 1820s was all very Oriental, barbaric, and messy; to the Ottomans it was all very European, simple, and pitiless.

❧

An afterword to this story of race was to be seen in the ruins of the Morea at the end of the 1820s, when French troops arrived to evacuate the last of the Muslims from the emerging Greek state (see Epilogue). The nation that was being founded was based on Christianity, and the new Greeks took this seriously to include some and exclude others. As the French soldiers went from village to village to sort out the Muslims from the Christians, they encountered an odd third category: sub-Saharan slaves on the estates who had survived the war. There were about 150 such people near Patras, 200 near Gastouni. Near the slave market of Koroni were the villages of Arapochori (Village of the Blacks) and Sklavochori (Village of the Slaves). The French probably wondered if Blacks belonged in the newest European state. The new Greek state listed them as *arapades*, meaning people who had arrived through Arabia or the Arab world. (Today the term is derisive.) But they were Christians and therefore Greeks.[18] They stayed, and their descendants are still there.

The Magic Lantern

What should one call the traveling soldiers of France like Ciolly? After Greek independence French archivists classified them as grecs and gave them their own file box, but they were originally mixed with all other French soldiers. If one opens their files they reveal themselves as French always, Greek sometimes. But these labels are secondary. The supreme label throughout is soldier, the category that got them a place in the archive. France was a career that opened to them a new imperial world.

Stamati Bulgari (or Stamatis Voulgaris) is well known in Greece. He was a low-born Corfiot who joined the French Republican forces as they withdrew in 1799. He was trained as an army engineer in Paris. From 1807 he was back on French-held Corfu as an officer and sent to reconnoiter the Ottoman mainland in anticipation of an invasion. After the fall of Corfu in 1814 he was evacuated to France and fought during the One Hundred Days alongside his commander on the islands, Donzelot. Thereafter he served the Bourbon king and he inspected the French Caribbean where again he met with Donzelot who was the governor of the slave colony of Martinique.

In 1823 Bulgari joined the One Hundred Thousand Sons of St. Louis in a French "crusade" to put down the liberal revolution in Spain, as another revolution was unfolding in Greece. Liberal revolutions were not to his liking, or at least not to the liking of the Bourbon monarchy, but by 1826 France had warmed to Greek independence as a Christian rather than a liberal cause (see chapters 7 and 16). With the Ottomans and Egyptians defeated, France sent an expedition to stabilize the Morea and evacuate the surviving Muslims, in anticipation of a Christian Greek state. Bulgari, now Voulgaris, was sent to the Morea to plan the reconstruction of Greek towns that had been razed during the revolutionary war. By 1831, now a battalion commander, he retired to Corfu on a French pension. The army, he wrote, was a "magic lantern," a device that projected images and transported viewers to faraway lands. The French army transported him to places of which he had never heard, wielding power he never could have imagined as a boy in Corfu. His name at his death was again Bulgari.[19]

France was a calling and an opportunity. One of Bulgari's patrons all along was Count Nicolas de Loverdo of Cephalonia. He served the French Republic in Paris where he had been a student in the 1790s and was a member of the Committee of Public Safety. He then served Napoleon across Europe, then Louis XVIII during the One Hundred Days, then Charles X. It's safe to say that he was a committed army man and flexible in his ideologies. He commanded forces that put down the Spanish Revolution in 1823, and for this he was decorated by Ferdinand of Spain and the Russian tsar. He helped plan the Morean Expedition at the end of the Greek Revolution. He helped plan the storming of Algiers in 1830. His name is on the Arc de Triomphe.

Another Cephalonian family, the Bourbaki (or Vourvachi) remained fiercely French and divided along French political lines. These were a family of Ottoman Cretan Christians who had migrated to Venetian Cephalonia and received noble titles, and from 1797 embraced Republican France. Constantin joined the French as a captain and aided Ali pasha in his planned attack on Lefkada, i.e., against the Septinsular Republic.[20] Denis (Dionysio) fought during the One Hundred Days and refused to submit to Louis XVIII. Denied a commission after the Restoration, he joined the ranks of unemployed European officers until opportunity beckoned in Greece. He was killed at the Battle of Kamatero near Athens in 1827. His head was sent to Sultan Mahmud II. Joseph stayed on the Ionian Islands, pledged allegiance to "the most just hegemon of the earth—Napoleon the Great." He fought against the British and Kolokotronis. He stayed after the French defeat and committed suicide, lamenting his persecution as a Frenchman under British rule, and as a Bonapartist in a French community of royalists.[21]

Denis's son Charles made his name in the storming of Algiers. By 1870 he was a general in command of an army in the Franco-Prussian War. In defeat Charles took his army to Switzerland where it was disarmed and sent back. He attempted suicide with a pistol but succeeded only in denting his forehead. The Bourbaki spawned a school of mathematics but they did not know it. Decades later a group of French mathematicians saw the name on street sign and found it amusing. They created Nicolas Bourbaki, a fictional mathematician, and under his name they published that series of theses that became the New Math. Their group was and is the Bourbaki Society.[22]

The Zakynthian Psimaris who had been enslaved in 1799 along with Ciolly made his way to Egypt only to find that the French had lost and left. He went to France and continued to study and serve. His last record was to ask permission from the Ministry of War to marry the daughter of the grocer Maribaud at 330, rue St-Honoré, in Paris.[23] Constantin Philippis, born in Constantinople and a migrant to Corfu in the 1790s, became a veteran of at least three armies—once for the French Republic, once for Russia, and once for the French Empire. He was evacuated to France after the fall of Corfu in 1814. Termed Greek in his papers, he received an army pension and declared, "I have no other *patrie* but France."

One may wonder whether countries and empires were opportunities as much as sentiments, careers and callings as much as loyalty, and whether they saw the distinction.

The "Greco-French" Nation

With the Greeks and would-be Greeks following imperial trajectories, it is little wonder that the Paris-based intellectual Adamantios Korais— another francophile transplant—could not quite picture an independent Greek state. The issue was which empire the Greeks should join. He opposed revolutionary movements of the Greeks until one had already broken out, in 1821.

Korais is a dominant figure in modern Greek philology. He was born an Ottoman subject and spoke Romaic Greek and Turkish. After a career in trade, he studied at Montpellier and landed in Paris as a scholar. He was mainly an editor and publisher of Classical texts. He had a role in the standardization of the modern Greek language which integrated ancient words and idioms and expunged foreign borrowings. After his death in 1833 this artificial language became an official language of government and education. It was called "purified" Greek (*katharevousa*). In effect it rendered generations of Greeks illiterate and insecure as they struggled through official documents, supplicated before bureaucrats, and wrote their school assignments. It held that place until the 1970s.

In 1800 Korais looked forward to the emergence of a coherent Greek people following a long period of education and enlightenment. In the meantime, Korais saw the future of the Greeks under the umbrella of France. In 1800 he published his "Warrior Hymn," a battle march of the modern Greeks, which called for Greeks to fight for France in Egypt. Writing in Greek, he concluded: "They are not Greeks [Graiki] or French [Galli], but a nation of Greco-French [Graikogalli]." As for the mass of Greek-speaking peoples in Ottoman lands, his recommendation was that they pick up books, or at least listen to those who wrote them. When the Greek Revolution did break out in 1821, he thought it was premature by decades.[24] He sent to the revolutionaries his collected editions of ancient Greek texts.

Before 1821 powerful empires were irresistible and independent nations were the fantasies of the few. Much the same was true of Ottoman subjects, the would-be and future Greeks across the Ionian Sea who were drawn to the model of the centralized and stable state. For some this led to service for the empires. For others it sparked ideas about how the Ottoman mainland could be reformed or the regime overthrown. And for still others it inspired a reaction against the dangerous influences of the Enlightenment, revolution, and Europe itself.

Chapter 5

Enchanted

Ottoman Christians, Imperial Service,
and National Myth

Prologue

IT IS 2018 *but I am stuck in 1807. I spent time in the military archives in Vincennes where I read the records of Greeks who served in the armies of France.
I followed the career of Nicole Papas-Oglou, a colonel in the French army. In
1807 he was seconded to Ali pasha of Yanena to help organize an invasion of
the Ionian island of Lefkada, which was under enemy Russian rule. In the
history books he is portrayed as one of the "Greeks of Napoleon."*

*Now, in the archives of Corfu, in the town's coastal fortress, I learn about
the same campaign, but from the other side. I read about the people who
gathered under the leadership of Count Giovanni Capo d'Istria to defend
Lefkada from Ali pasha and Papas-Oglou. In the books the defense of
Lefkada is treated as a gathering of the Greeks.*

*The two stories—the planned attack on Lefkada and the planned defense
of Lefkada—are not told as part of the same campaign. The books skirt the
fact that Greeks were on opposite sides. The problem is the label. In the 1940s
well-meaning French archivists added "Greek" to records of men who had
Greek-sounding names or places of origin, and this is how Papas-Oglou acquired the primary marker of "Greek." Inside the file he is a French soldier.
As for Capo d'Istria, he did not call himself Greek until much later in his life.
He was a Corfiot and an aristocrat, and to many he was a Russian because*

he was in Russian state service. He calls the mercenaries he hired from the mainland "greci," because they were Christians, though they tended to speak Albanian as well as Greek.

I begin calling the archival game "Find the Greek," whereby any source is combed for traces of the nation. We do much the same with celebrities as we remark on "the Greek-descended actress Aniston" or "the Greek-descended actress Rita Wilson," and now "the Greek actor Tom Hanks." We refer to "the Greek-descended Senator Tsongas" and "the Greek-descended Governor Dukakis", and pass quietly over an American vice-president who landed in jail for corruption and a director of the CIA who justified the US attack on Iraq in 2003. There is the Greek-born George Papanicolaou, inventor of the Pap smear. There are even the crazy rich like Jamie Dimon of Citigroup, and on-line debates about whether Bezos is a Greek name. (It is not.)

But there's a difference when it comes to the archives. Today one can speak of a diaspora because the creation of independent Greece provides a point of origin and return. But people who lived before 1821 are categorized as Greek before there was a Greece or a shared understanding of Greekness. My work is cut out for me: to put these people back in their places and better under-stand what Greek might mean before Greece. I need to put them back in the empires.

The Meanings of Greekness

Like many nations, the idea of a coherent Greek people began as a for-eign import. Travelers from Europe and the United States arrived in the Ottoman Balkans convinced that there was such a thing as Greece, popu-lated by Greeks. It matters that they were singularly interested in Greeks as opposed to the many other populations that inhabited the region. Such visitors were on Classical tours of the ancient sites. Increasingly from 1797 they were officers, diplomats, and spies seeking allies and inva-sion routes. Such travelers termed all Orthodox Christians Greeks in English, grecs in French, and greki in Russian, and applied to them names that locally had not been current for centuries. They sought Spartans in lands called Vardounia, Mani, and Mystras. They sought Thebans in a vil-lage called Istefe, Olympia in a place called Fanari, and Piraeus in a port

called Porto Draco, Porto Leone, and Aslan Liman. Into the 1820s foreigners arrived with maps with Classical names and employed the locals
to tell them what these places were called now.[1] Some of the answers are
still tentative. It is still not clear that the Ithaca of Homer is the island
called Ithaca today.[2]

As for the wider territory and region, Catherine the Great implied
that it was liminal when she queried: "Is the Mediterranean European
or not? And the [Aegean] Archipelago? The first is between Africa and
Europe, the second between Asia and Europe." Her officers who arrived
in the Morea sought out Spartans and Sparta. (There was no such place
in 1770, but there had been and there would be.) Warriors, pirates, and
notables from the Mani Peninsula soon came forward to claim the title.
Like so many admirers of ancient Greece, the Russians carried off "marble things" and placed them in museums, in this case the Hermitage.
And like later visitors, the Russians were disappointed when they met
the would-be Greeks. Wrote Orlov: "The peoples here are liars who
swindle, they are fickle, reckless, and cowardly." Like later visitors he
explained the Greeks' distance from their Classical heritage not in the
obvious way, the passage of over two thousand years and conversion to
monotheisms, but "the legacy left by the Turks."[3]

The people they amalgamated into the Greeks called themselves different things: Romios (Ottoman Orthodox), Graikos (Orthodox from
lands west of the Balkans, sometimes Russia), Albanian, and a host of
names derived from their regions, towns, and villages of origin. For the
visiting Europeans the one overarching term that encompassed all of
them was not national at all: Christian. To trace a line from the ancient
Greeks to the Christians they called Greek was not at all an obvious
thing to do because the populations had undergone some big changes,
like wholesale baptism. And since no one in the region still sacrificed to
the twelve Olympian gods, one could well ask why the Christians had
to be the ones they called Greeks, rather than, say, Muslims or Jews.
Muslims in Athens were proud of the Acropolis they had inherited and
invested it with biblical meaning. The Morean pasha sponsored the first
organized digs at ancient Olympia. Other pashas were avid collectors
of antiquities, and very many of them spoke and read Greek.[4] The

conclusion of the Europeans that the Greeks could only be the Christians owes to the fact that the visitors were claiming the Classical past as their own past. Seeking their own origins as Christian Europeans, they insisted that the cradle of civilization should be Christian, too.

The term "Greek" lost much of its usefulness when applied in practice. Very often the travelers were disappointed by the human material they found—in substance, peoples in slippers rather than Hellenes in sandals. Some were not interested in the people at all. The diplomat, classicist, and spy William Martin Leake described Ottoman Greece as "the thinly populated province of a semi-barbarous empire," made interesting "almost entirely by connexion with ancient history." Leake lamented that he could not understand Romaic Greek in all its varieties and it had traveled too far from the Classical Greek he knew. Much Greek pronunciation had been "infected" with Slavic sounds, and the Greeks sprinkled their words with sounds that Xenophon never used, like "sh" and "ch."[5] What should be pronounced "Tripolitsa" was spoken as "Tripolicha" (or the even more Slavic "Drobolicha"), and "Katsonis" was pronounced "Kachonis." His French counterpart and rival Pouqueville alternated between disgust with people who "more foreign to Europe than to Africa," romanticization of those he decided were Greek, and real confusion about who the Greeks were. He might call the same people Greek or Albanian because they were very often bilingual or multilingual. As a rule, though, the Greeks were Christians; the Muslims were Turks.

As the European armies and navies entered the Balkan region from 1797, "Greek" became a practical matter, its fluidity a matter of military concern. Soldiers and spies sought out allies who might join them, and assumed that local Christians were likely to support a European power against the Ottomans. But they learned that language, religion, and ethnicity did not predict loyalties. Such was the case with the French spy "Guillaume" who was sent to Epirus in 1810 to reconnoiter for an invasion and seek out allies. "Guillaume" was Frederic François Guillaume de Vaudoncourt, an army officer. He set off armed with texts about ancient Greek and Roman wars. He traced ancient routes that might be used by French sailors and soldiers, and he spent a good deal of time guessing the ancient names of current locations. He expected to encounter Greeks with whom he could collaborate.

He returned in despair: there was no way to predict alliances. Rather than coherent peoples—Ottoman, Greek, Albanian, Turk, Christian, or Muslim—"One could view them as an aggregation of provinces that have particular and different interests."[6] No single category held its members together, and people whom he expected to be on the same side were likely to fight among themselves. Locals could pick, choose, and change their employers and patrons in ways that seemed to outsiders devious or treasonous, Levantine or Oriental. Locals serving a given empire fought against other locals serving a different empire in a way that seemed fratricidal.

There was a bigotry that allowed such visitors to condemn what they saw as barbarous, and forget that they practiced barbarities of their own. They condemned local notables like Ali pasha for fickleness and Oriental deviousness because he switched alliances, but European powers changed alliances with abandon and attacked each other without warning, but with the proper diplomatic language. Their killings were systematized in modern armies. On the other hand, Europeans were observing (and naming Oriental) something that was real: the absence of a coherent state that could mobilize people and resources into a single policy. It was as if Marseille opted out of the Napoleonic Wars or Cornwall looted Exeter. The issue was a lack of solidarities that might predict preferences and the absence of a supreme authority—a state— to hold people together. Orders from even the most supreme Ottoman authority—or especially from a distant sultan—were the start of a negotiation or could be ignored altogether.

The arrival of the new empires from 1797 gave the region more empires from which to choose. The pay was good, the punishment for failure was something other than slavery and beheading. One might better understand how an Ottoman subject acted in the new imperial intersections and remember that their actions were imperial, not national. At least not yet. In 1821, the Christians sought help in their existential struggle with the Porte. The locals represented themselves as Greeks, and gave the Europeans what they had been looking for all along: the living proof of their own origins.[7]

The Adventures of Nicole, the Greek Roman Mamluk Ptolemean Frenchman of Çeşme

When Korais published his "Warrior Hymn" in 1800 and identified "a nation of Francogreeks," he was referring to the Greeks fighting for France in Egypt. Hundreds and perhaps thousands of Ottoman Christians flocked to the side of France and converged on the Nile. It is possible that Korais was referring to Colonel Nicole Papas-Oglou, the name that is used on the man's French military record. He was a storied adventurer also known as Nikolis, Hadji Nikolas, Papasoglou, and Papadopoulos. (Papasoglou is Turco-Greek for Papadopoulos, "son of the priest." Hadji meant that he or his forebears had gone on a pilgrimage to the Holy Lands.) He signed his name Nicole.[8]

Papas-Oglou was made famous, though not by name, in 1819 by the banker-turned-novelist Thomas Hope who may have acquired Papas-Oglou's memoirs and published them as his own fiction. *Anastasius, or, Memoirs of a Greek*, was a huge commercial and literary success across Europe, published just in time for the Philhellene Grecomania of the 1820s. Hope did not initially claim authorship and readers guessed about who may have written the book. British literati found the knowledge of the Levant so authentically Oriental that it must have been written by Byron. Byron thought it must have been written by a Jew.[9] The French Bonapartist historian Boppe, who reintroduced Papas-Oglou (by name) in 1900 as a Bonapartist hero, thought that the detail of *Anastasius* was so exact that it must have been Papas-Oglou's own memoirs, published by Hope just as soon as Papas-Oglou died.[10] The Greek historian Rados introduced Papas-Oglou to a Greek readership in 1916 as a proto-national of a future Greece: he insisted that he must have joined the Greek revolutionaries before he died in 1819, though this is wholesale invention. He agreed with Boppe that details of *Anastasius* matched the archival (French and Egyptian) record of Papas-Oglou's exploits.[11] Be that as it may, our primary sources written in French and Arabic are plentiful enough to put together a plausible picture of an imperial creature, before a time when changing sides was considered treason. Like so many honorable warriors of his day, he was a mercenary in search of a good employer, and France was the closest he came to a cause.

Papas-Oglou was born a Christian in Çeşme near Izmir on the Aegean coast, in 1758. Hence his original surnames in Greek, Ottoman, and Arabic are variations on Çeşmeli. He was from a family of landowners and merchants, and trade often spilled into soldiering. His first military experience was as a boy in the Ottoman navy under Hasan pasha and the Christian dragoman Mavrogenis. He arrived with the fleet in the Morea to put down the marauding Albanians in the aftermath of the Morean rebellion of 1770 (see chapter 2). He reached Tripolitsa in the central Morea in 1779 where the Albanians met their end. At some point, in 1785 according to Arabic sources, he was hired by Mamluk commanders in the Aegean Sea who were opposing their nominal sovereign, the sultan. He brought them to Egypt with a large reward in his pocket and a price on his own head. He lost his land in Çeşme and his family was sold into slavery. In Egypt opportunity beckoned, and he became an admiral in the Mamluk fleet commanding three hundred other Ottoman Christians.

When the French arrived in Egypt and defeated his fleet in 1798, he became an officer for France, for an initial payment of 1,000 thalers. (These were Dutch or Austrian currencies, in English "dollars.") He was valued because he knew the region, he could navigate the waters, and he spoke Turkish, Arabic, Maltese, Romaic Greek, and now French. The French put him into a new Greek Legion in Egypt. With the French defeat on the Nile he was evacuated to Marseille. There he joined groups of other veterans from Egypt (Orthodox and Copt), the Ionian Islands, the Ottoman Balkans, and sub-Saharan Africa (Ottoman soldier-slaves who went over to the French). "Syrians" were probably Assyrian Christians.[12] The French termed them all "Orientals," the catch-all for swarthy people hailing from the east and southeast of France. They were formed into the Bataillon des Chasseurs d'Orient (the Oriental Scouts or Oriental Light Infantry).

So the Rum-turned-Mamluk became Oriental and French. He was a colonel co-commanding the Chasseurs with a Coptic officer by the name of Gabriel Sidarious. In 1806 he was given leave to locate his family (or one of his families; he may have had a few) who had been taken as slaves, and recover some of his estates around Çeşme. He spent time in Constantinople. Using his new clout as a Frenchman he was able to return with his wife and a promise of restitution.

After a spell fighting in the Adriatic, his commanders sent him on a secret mission to Ali pasha in Yanena. It was 1807. At that moment France, Ali, and the Porte faced a common enemy on the Ionian Islands: Russia. The Ottomans had been allies of Russia for a brief moment in 1798–9 when they evicted the French from the Ionian Islands, but the Ottomans and Russians returned to their usual enmity in a war that lasted to 1812. France sided with the Porte and Yanena. In Yanena Papas-Oglou sought recruits for his battalion. Papas-Oglou had rich experiences and Ali pasha befriended him and picked his brains. Papas-Oglou told Ali of Palestinian rebels, Mamluks, the great palaces of Cairo, and the French and British.[13]

At that moment Ali held much of the Balkan coast across from the Ionian Islands, and he was planning to take the island of Lefkada from Russia and the Septinsular Republic. Papas-Oglou took charge of Ali's Greek and Albanian soldiers and organized the siege of Lefkada using knowledge acquired as an Ottoman sailor and a Mamluk: naval operations and amphibious landings. On the opposite shore were the forces of the Septinsular Republic including Russians, islanders under Giovanni Capo d'Istria, and more Christian mercenaries speaking Albanian and Romaic Greek.[14]

What to call these people? The islanders called themselves Septinsulars and named their specific islands of residence. What they thought of the enemy assembling on the opposite shore was more complicated. As a sample we have the correspondence of one Anna Giourga Setini of Lefkada who could see and hear the enemy across the narrow channel. In her letters to her sister who was away on Corfu, she wrote that she could hear "the Turks" across the straits speak Greek and French. "Turk" to her meant anyone working for the Ottoman Empire; it was not at all ethnic or in this case even confessional. She singled out one with a loud and commanding voice: "the French colonel named Haji Nikolaos Ptolemean the Greek."[15] Ptolemean meant he was Egyptian, but not of the Arab and Muslim variety. She meant the descendants of one of the generals of Alexander the Great who ruled Egypt, of whom the last in the dynasty was Cleopatra. To Setini Papas-Oglou was a Ptolemean and also a Greek and a Frenchman in a collective of Turks. One should marvel at the combination of labels, and then ask if we can do any better.

The invasion was called off when France reoccupied the Ionian Islands. From 1807 Papas-Oglou served around the Ionian and Adriatic seas and by 1813 he was the commander of the mainland outpost of Parga, with a garrison of French, Italian, and Epirot fighters. They awaited an attack by the British. The end came when the Christian Pargans, starving and cut off from their usual trade routes, hoisted the British flag, killed off part of the French garrison, and opened the town to the enemy.[16]

Papas-Oglou and the Chasseurs returned to France, and they were disbanded in Lyon after the first defeat of Napoleon in 1814. Their future in the restored Catholic kingdom did not look bright, and during the One Hundred Days they rallied to Napoleon. In May 1815 they paraded on the Champ de Mars, and there were reports of a colorful procession, a "strange mix of officers, Mamelouks, and negroes." Following Waterloo the survivors were sent to Marseille to a refugee camp for Orientals. Rumor had it that most were massacred during the White Terror as Bonapartists, possibly also as Blacks, People of Color, Orientals, foreigners, and non-Catholics. We know that Papas-Oglou survived and died with his pension of 1,800 francs, in 1819, a Frenchman.

Papas-Oglou was, successively, an Ottoman subject, a Mamluk admiral, and an Oriental French officer. For a time in Egypt he was a Greek commanding a Greek Legion. He called himself grec but this did not prevent him from fighting other grecs. He also called himself French. His career was always imperial, and there was no nation to join or betray.

Regional, Imperial, and National: The Souliots[17]

The new empires in the region hired tens of thousands of Ottoman subjects at any given moment, and these soldiers served all sides of any conflict. Whole communities were in motion as the soldiers moved with their families and livestock from one ally or employer to another. Most of the future military leaders of the Greek Revolution were veterans of these armies, among them the Moreans Kolokotronis, Anagnostaras, Mavromichalis, Vilaetis, Petimezas, Fotakos, and Nikitaras. Today one need only mention the names and their Greekness is not in doubt. But during the Napoleonic Wars they were likely to be fighting each other because they were serving opposing empires, and they switched empires as circumstances changed.

The most storied of these regional warriors were the Souliots.[18] We know a bit more about the Souliots because their descendants became prominent generals and statesmen in independent Greece and cultivated the image of their Greek origins and cause. The clans and their names are synonymous with revolutionary heroism. Names like Botsaris and Tzavellas are as recognizable and evocative in Greece today as Garibaldi in Italy. Markos Botsaris was killed during the Revolution and became something of a cult among Europeans who recreated his death in chinaware, statues, and paintings. Before becoming Greek—in 1822, specifically, with the defeat of their most recent employer Ali pasha of Yanena—the Souliots were many other things, and they fought for and against every conceivable power in the region, for and against Muslims and Christians, and often among themselves. They were a source of intrigue since the end of the 1790s when the Europeans encountered them, and the intrigue evolved around the central question of who they were.

Souliots were a collection of herding, trading, marauding, and mercenary clans on the western Balkan coast, across from the northern part of the Ionian Islands. They spoke both Greek and Albanian and some Italian and Turkish. They were Christians but they spent as much time fighting Christians as any Muslim enemy. They regularly fought among themselves. The most known enmity was between the Tzavellas (Xhavella in

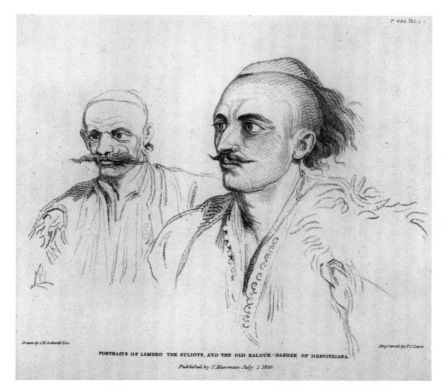

FIGURE 5.1. "Portraits of Lambro the Suliote, and the old Balouk-Bashee of Dervitzina," in Thomas Smart Hughes, *Travels in Sicily Greece and Albania . . . Illustrated with Engravings of Maps Scenery Plans &c. In two volumes,* vol. 1 (London: J. Mawman, 1820). Greek Library, Alexandros Onassis Public Benefit Foundation. *The scene is a reminder that Souliots and Ottomans often served on the same side. A* bölükbaşı *was an Ottoman captain in command of a* bölük, *smaller than a regiment.*

Albanian, at the time also known as Giovelli and Tziavella) and the Botsaris (Boçari, also Bozzari and Bozziari). In the 1790s they had alliances with pashas and beys on the Ottoman mainland, and with Venetians on the Ionian Islands, and these alliances changed frequently.

The arrival of France in 1797 expanded their possibilities. At that moment the Porte was fighting alongside Russia against France, and in 1798 Tzavellas sold his services to France in the area of Preveza. Preveza was a mainland outpost of the Ionian Islands. Tzavellas was to defend the

FIGURE 5.2. "View of Albanian Palikars in Pursuit of an Enemy," in Thomas
Smart Hughes, *Travels in Sicily Greece and Albania . . . Illustrated with Engravings
of Maps Scenery Plans &c. In two volumes,* vol. 1 (London: for J. Mawman, 1820).
Greek Library, Alexandros Onassis Public Benefit Foundation. *The Albanians in
question are Souliots, irregulars who could fight on unusual terrain. A palikar
(palikari in Greek) was and is a Balkan term for a warrior or a strapping man.*

town from an imminent attack by Ali pasha. Giorgos Botsaris was paid
to join them, but some of his clan also received payment to let Ali's
troops through.[19] This they did, and the massacre that followed at Preveza and Nicopolis was infamous back in France for its beheadings, the
taking of body parts as trophies, and the arrival of 150 French survivors
at the prison of Yedikule in Constantinople. They joined the other
French prisoners from the campaigns on the Ionian Islands like Ciolly,
and in Egypt like Pouqueville.[20]

    With the French defeated the Souliots entered into new agreements
with Ali. But in 1800–04 Ali turned on them as part of his campaign to
stamp out banditry and local power centers. He began by hiring the
Botsaris to attack the Tzavellas. Ali then turned on the Botsaris and
pursued them to the coasts. The survivors made it to the Ionian Islands,

now under Russian rule. Starving and unemployed, the refugees turned to stealing livestock, grain, and wood fuel from the populations of Corfu and Paxos. The men refused to work as anything but mercenaries. They spent their days cleaning their guns and singing Albanian songs while the women managed the households.[21]

The Souliots were a problem for the Russians because they looted and might work for an enemy. So the Russians hired them. Some were sent to campaign in Italy, in a group of Ottoman Christians numbering fifteen thousand. Some were formed into the Legion of Light Irregular Riflemen, also called the Corps of Epiro-Souliots and the Legion of Greek Light Infantry Scouts. The names of the formation suggest the vagueness over who they were. The Russians printed a military manual for them in which they cited their national hero Skederbeg, who was by most reckonings an Albanian.[22] In 1807 some were deployed to defend Lefkada against Ali pasha and Papas-Oglou.

Then came the Treaty of Tilsit of 1807 that handed the islands back to France. The Russian emissary Mocenigo commended the Souliots to the French as a gesture of humanity. To expel them would send them into the hands of any number of enemies on the mainland, including each other. So in that year the arriving French organized the Souliots and other mainland Christians into a new formation and called it the Albanian Regiment because the Souliots did speak Albanian. It was placed under the overall command of Christakis Kalogeros. It mutinied. Its complaint was that Christakis was not a clan leader and he was not a Souliot. He was not even a Romaic Greek. He was a Graikos (Orthodox Christian but not Ottoman) from Preveza.

The French commander was baffled. "Albanians!" he wrote. France did not need or want them but France had given its word to the departing Russians. Now "you refuse to recognize the chief of your nation," by which he meant the Graikos Christakis. In fact the Souliots were not thinking of nations, they were thinking of clans and regions. To calm them the French sent a commander who had served in Martinique and had experience with colonials. He was succeeded by Colonel Jean-Louis-Toussaint Minot, chosen because he had fought in Egypt, which was broadly speaking the Levant.

When the British attacked the Ionian islands of Zakynthos, Cephalonia, and Ithaca, about half of the Souliots employed by France switched sides. On Lefkada they split in two, and French Souliots fought British Souliots who were bolstered by Moreans like Kolokotronis and Nikitaras. The Souliots who remained in French service were concentrated on Corfu with their families and declared themselves Napoleon's "most loyal subjects."[23] The Souliots who joined the British were reconstituted as the Duke of York's Greek Light Infantry, while Kolokotronis pledged allegiance to "my King," George III.[24]

Corfu surrendered in 1814. The Greek Light Infantry was disbanded and they joined the tens of thousands of European soldiers who were unemployed. The lot of the Souliots after 1814 was mixed. Some starved, begged, and stole. Some joined other mainlanders and went with their British commanders to Naples to reconstitute the army of the Kingdom of Two Sicilies. Others made their way to Egypt to serve Mehmed Ali.[25] Ali pasha of Yanena was still an option and the leaders of the Botsaris and Tzavellas clans were given new estates.[26]

In 1821 the Souliots were not part of the Christian uprising that became the Greek Revolution. They were embroiled in the conflict between Ali pasha and the sultan. They began by serving the sultan against Ali, then threw in their lot with Ali, just in time for his defeat in early 1822. The Souliots were once again refugees and now they had fewer options. In the past they had taken refuge on the Ionian Islands but these were now British. The British were interested in stability, and while they accepted them as refugees, they did not employ them and they were not welcome. As the Christian uprising against the sultan took hold and endured, it was a good time to think Greek: it was a new option and perhaps their last one.[27] Lord Byron, who was beginning to dabble in the Greek Revolution, hired some of them using his own funds. Some made their way to the Morea where they were hired by one or another faction of the Greek revolutionary movement.

That they were Greek they were now sure but they meant it in a limited way. Having been told for so long that they were the heirs of the ancient Greeks, they decided that only the Souliots were Greek. In the cafes of Missolonghi in western Roumeli, a Greek revolutionary base on the Ionian coast, they ordered around the other Christians as reayas because the Souliots "alone enjoyed the privilege of being Hellenes."[28] Still they hedged their bets. A Souliot commander warned his employers to pay them well and pay them soon. Otherwise "we will go Turk" (*tha tourkepsoume*).[29]

Who, at long last, were the Souliots, men who we know spoke Greek but swore and sang in Albanian? One option was to consider them Greek because of their later role in the Greek Revolution, but a French army report of December 1807 was not confident. "They have a certain pride, the unique heritage of their ancestors, of which they have but a very confused idea."[30] Visitors debated hotly whether they had origins in Classical Greece, or had arrived in the region a few decades before 1800 from parts and cultures unknown, an offshoot of one of the many Albanian tribes. The Greek revolutionary Perraivos who campaigned alongside some of them on Lefkada in 1807 noted that the Souliots had no knowledge of ancient history at all.[31] That they spoke Albanian is one of the awkward truths of the Greek Revolution, but in this the Souliots were not exceptional. Most of the Greek revolutionaries from Roumeli spoke Albanian, as did most of the Greek sea captains from the Aegean Islands.

When the French diplomat and future Philhellene François Pouqueville encountered the Souliots on the Ionian Islands, he was sure they were Greek and not at all Turkish (meaning Muslims, whom he detested). But their dialect of Romaic was mixed with their dialect of Albanian in ways only they understood. Pouqueville was determined to separate their speech into two standardized languages so as to make them Greek–Albanian. In his presence and at his behest two generations of Botsaris dictated an Albanian–Greek wordbook to the third, Markos. The manuscript is in the Bibliothèque Nationale in Paris.[32] Pouqueville was not alone in his confusion. Capo d'Istria called them greci in 1807 but in 1818 and 1820 he referred to them interchangeably as Souliots, Greeks, Albanians, and Macedonians.[33]

It is doubtful that the Souliots were confused about who they were. Part of their lore relates to the fact that they were freer than a straightforward citizen of a nation or the subordinates of any one state. Their changing loyalties were a form of liberty. The Souliots were Albanian, Rum, later Greek too. They were soldiers of Venice, Ali pasha, the Ottoman Empire, France, Britain, and Russia, and sometimes of more than one power at a time. It is arguable that they settled on being Greek in the 1820s because they had finally run out of options.

Enchanted: The Nationalization of an Imperial Story

Consider the rich mix of peoples who were brought together around the Ionian Islands thanks to the Napoleonic Wars, and focus on the campaign around Lefkada in 1807. In one way or another, the campaign involved Papas-Oglou and several persons associated with the Greek Revolution of the 1820s, among them Capo d'Istria, Kolokotronis, Perraivos, Anagnostaras, Petimezas, and some of the Souliots. It was portrayed in later decades as a meeting of the national leadership-in-waiting. The problem is that they were fighting on different sides and against each other; and they themselves did not refer to themselves collectively as Greeks. It is a case study in the way pre-national events have been reshaped to fit a later national narrative.

In 1807 Russia was the formal protector of the Ionian Islands but distracted. Russian battalions and flotillas came and then went off to other Mediterranean campaigns. Ali pasha of Yanena saw an opportunity to seize the island of Lefkada. Lefkada is separated from Epirus by a narrow channel that could be crossed easily by barge or ship. Today it is spanned by a short bridge. With Russia's commitment uncertain, and with the Porte and Russia once again at war, it seemed to be easy pickings. So Ali assembled his usual mix of armed Christian and Muslim Albanians. His advisor for the assault was Papas-Oglou, on loan from France and experienced in amphibious landings.

Perhaps to Ali's surprise, the Russians and the Senate of the Septinsular Republic mobilized. Russia sent ships and soldiers to provide the core of the defense Lefkada. The Senate appointed Count Giovanni Capo d'Istria Extraordinary Commissar and the Russian emissary Mocenigo made him de facto commander. Local men aged sixteen to sixty were drafted to build defenses out of stone and earth—a testament to the kind of mobilization of which the Russians were capable. But getting the locals to fight was a different matter, so the Russians hired, as was often the case, Ottoman Christians from the mainland. Joining them was Perraivos, the Roumeliot revolutionary-turned-teacher at the former monastery of Tenedos, who came to enlist. Anna Setini of Lefkada—the person who termed Papas-Oglou "Ptolemean the Greek"—wrote to her sister on Corfu that Perraivos was a Romios, but more importantly he was billeting in her sister's home. "Major Perivos and his evil smell are almost unbearable."[34]

Once the fortifications had been completed, Capo d'Istria invited the Russian and Ottoman warriors to a banquet, to celebrate a job well done. This was the banquet at the cove of Magemeno (Enchanted), a storied meeting that is part of the lore of prerevolutionary Greece. His- torians looked back on Magemeno as the foreshadow of the Revolu- tion. Over the following decades historians added new details. More and more future revolutionaries were placed there. Capo d'Istria wept as he hugged his fellow-Greeks. The attendees raised their swords and swore to fight for Greek independence. The enemy was not the Alba- nian Ali and his Muslim, Catholic, Orthodox, and French soldiers but the Turks.[35]

Our only source from the time—in fact, the source for the entire story—is Capo d'Istria, who wrote two reports on the affair, in Italian. He tells us something different. In his private report to Mocenigo (his superior in the Russian hierarchy) he was matter of fact and noted that the warriors drank quite a lot. In his report to the Ionian Senate, more literary and elaborate, he described it as an affair of the Septinsular Re- public, employing foreign (i.e., mainland) mercenaries. He was not sure what to call them. His scribe wrote down that they were "our brave men," and the Count scratched it out and replaced it with "greci." He did not call himself or the Ionian Islanders greci. In his native Italian he invited the warriors to return when needed: "they left persuaded that the Republic will always be their patria."[36]

His patria was the Ionian Islands. He could not recall most of the leaders' names because they were too exotic. (Whether a name like Goat-John—Katsikoyannis—is easy or hard to remember is debatable.)

He did remember "the wise and brave Bozzari," a leader of the Souliots, but it is not clear that his clan, or which members of his clan, were part of the operation. According to Perraivos, Kizzo (Kitsos) Botsaris had bought land and sheep on the islands and wandered over to the banquet to greet his old comrades from Souli. The Ionian Senate, meanwhile, was not at all fond of Botsaris and the Souliots because they were bandits and tended to steal. Capo d'Istria's friend and co-commander at Lefkada, the Bishop Ignazio, looked forward to the day when the Souliots would be destroyed. "It is high time, friend, that the bad behavior and arsons of the Souliots on the islands and in our tsifliks [estates on the mainland] bring us to war against them."[37]

Among the names added to the banquet and the campaign by later historians is Kolokotronis. Indeed Capo d'Istria later recalled that he met Kolokotronis at this time. One historian depicted Kolokotronis sailing the coast, protecting the banqueteers, and saluting them from his ship. It is true that Kolokotronis was in the harbor of Lefkada, but he was in the brig of a Russian ship on the orders of Count Capo d'Istria himself. Kolokotronis had recently been chased out of the Morea as part of the campaign against banditry (see chapter 2), and he was in exile on the islands and unemployed. He had bought shares in a ship and had been hired by the Russian commanders to harass Ali's forces. As was typical in these cases, the crew of shareholders (*interesadi* in Greco-Italian) had agreed that the booty would be shared in proportion to the shares they held in the ship. Kolokotronis, his cousin Yannakis, and their comrade Petimezas would receive 5 units each, and the captain Anagnostis Papageorgiou would receive 12.5. The latter is better known as Anagnostaras, later a hero of the Greek Revolution.[38]

Now they were corsairs flying the Russian flag, though they were not particularly good at following orders. Kolokotronis was a Morean, and it was consistently true that he avoided campaigning outside of his Morean homeland; those were not his wars. He insisted that he be allowed to raid the Morean coasts, where he knew the terrain and the players. The Russians refused because the Morea was still supplying food to the islands, even as the Russians were once again at war with Yanena and the Ottoman Empire.[39] Nevertheless the crew raided towns in the

Morea near Patras. They burned villages, gathered loot, and took slaves for ransom whom they brought to Zakynthos. In response the Morean Ottoman authorities seized Ionian Island ships or prevented them from landing in the Morea. The islands were threatened with food shortages. The authorities on Zakynthos and the Septinsular Senate demanded that Kolokotronis be stopped and punished. Mocenigo ordered Capo d'Istria to arrest Kolokotronis. And so he did.

On 20 July 1807, sitting in the brig of a Russian ship, Kolokotronis dictated his supplication to Capo d'Istria, using Romaic Greek interspersed with the Italian terminology of the islands. He pleaded with "his most excellent count Ioannis Kapodistrias Extraordinary Commissar" to release him from jail and from service since he was not worthy to serve a power such as Russia. And could the commissar please pay him his back wages of 1,500 kuruş? Kolokotronis was released and sailed away on a fleet of ships raiding in the Aegean, or what he called the Levante. It was perhaps the only time he campaigned outside the Ionian basin and the Morea.

But what to make of the campaign, Magemeno, and the converging hyphenated Greeks? Labels were varied and to today's reader confusing. Ottoman Greek Moreans under the Russian flag fighting for a Septinsular Republic and raiding their own homeland, speaking a mix of Romaic Greek and Italian. Romaic Anatolian Greeks from Egypt under the French flag fighting for the pasha of Yanena joining with Christian and Muslim speakers of Albanian, Greek, and French. A Corfiot aristocrat receiving orders from both a regional Senate and a Russian emissary, hosting Orthodox Greco-Albanians and addressing them in Italian. The labels were all regional; the powers imperial.

The interesting story is how the space between empire and region was filled with a nation, and how they all became, or were rewritten as, Greeks. That is a story that began in 1821.

Chapter 6

Ottoman Echoes

The New Empires and Balkan Politics

Prologue

A DRIVE TO *the village of Monastiraki high in the Peloponnesian mountains, facing the Ionian Sea to the west. I am in search of the stronghold of the fabled Ali Farmaki who fought alongside Kolokotronis against the Morean pasha. Impressed by the view, I drive onto a curb and burst a tire. A farmer and his Albanian worker pull over. They learn that I am a historian and ask me to tell the story of their village and Ali Farmaki. My story told, they nod their approval and fix my flat tire.*

I'm not sure which part they were nodding to. I like to think that there are lessons to be learned from the story of Ali and his friend Thodorakis. I told them of a time when Muslims and Christians conspired together to challenge the pasha, a time when the Morean peninsula was multiconfessional, a time when notables of all religions and languages could work together to defy authority and fleece the local peasantry.

I spoke of those events as local folklore and Greek history, as my audience expected. In fact, local history had gone global. Across the Ionian Sea from where we stood, the Ionian Islands were conquered successively by France, Russia, France again, and Britain. On the Ionian Islands they each imposed a version of the modern state. Gazing from the Ottoman Morea, men like Ali and Little Theodore could imagine an alternative to the Ottoman order for the first time. Others could imagine revolutions, and they inspired in still others the idea of counterrevolution.

Righas and Ottoman Revolution

The most famous and early echo of the French Revolution in the Ottoman Balkans was Righas Velestinlis (or Righas Fereos). Less than a
decade after the outbreak of the French Revolution he wrote about a
revolution in the Ottoman Empire. Righas was the product of a merchant family in Roumeli, a Vlach who spoke the Greek lingua franca.
He did well. He traveled the trade routes up and down the Balkans,
straddling the Russian and Ottoman spheres that intersected in the
Danubian Principalities, and making forays into Austria. He was multilingual, literate, and erudite. He was captivated by the French Revolution's vision of republican citizenship. He was rare among Christian
Balkan activists because he did not anticipate a simple change in rulers,
and he did not direct his appeals to princes, kings, and emperors. He
called for an indigenous mass uprising ending in a mass state of rights,
equality, and protection. He dabbled in Classical texts but disparaged
the pretentious scholarly obsession with the ancient Greek language.
He dismissed this as "Hellenism," confined to the overeducated few. He
wrote in the vernacular about the Greek present, and had in mind
masses of people. Greece was a social question, not a scholastic one.
Ancient Greece mattered for what it taught the contemporary Greeks
about civic virtue and liberty.[1]

French agents in the Balkans in 1790s thought that merchants and
clerks were the Ottoman sans culottes who might lead indigenous
movements,[2] and Righas is a case in point. Against the Ottoman reality
of autocracy tempered by anarchy, Righas proposed a new Greece modeled on the French constitution of 1793. Like that model, he promised
legal equality and a broad franchise for men regardless of religion. He
anticipated security of person and property, rights for employees, and
the cancellation of debts. All men would serve in the army, and women
would march with javelins in order to avoid close combat. His understanding of his projected republic was broad, expressed in a famous
map: it would include all the Balkan peninsula and all its peoples as they
were understood at the time. He termed this future federation Hellas, a
Classical reference, but also termed it Graikia, its modern sequel.

The inhabitants of this federation would be Greek in the sense of speaking Greek as a lingua franca, which many of them already did. They would be the Romios, the Montenegrin, the Vlach, the Serb, the Bulgarian, the Jew, and the Albanian. Muslims were equally deserving of liberation from their tyrant the sultan, the agas, and the Christian dragomans. He had relations with Pazvantoğlu, the sometime Muslim rebel in the area of Vidin. All were victims of the Ottoman insecurity. What seems today to be problematic—the assimilation of non-Greeks into a new Greece—was to him not a problem at all because neither he, nor his contemporaries, thought in terms of ethnic nations. He was a humanist, and human divisions were historical and artificial. He dreamed of human liberty and it was incidental that it would be achieved in a Greek lingua franca.[3]

His group was exposed by a Christian merchant. He and his comrades were arrested in Austria in 1798 and handed over to the Ottomans. The dragoman of the Porte at that time was Constantine Ypsilantis (father of Alexander, the Greek revolutionary of 1821) who did not quite defend Righas but recommended a moderate punishment because Righas and his ideas were clearly nonsensical and Righas obviously unwell.[4] Nevertheless Righas and some of his comrades were executed. To the Ottomans he was "the one called Riga the mapmaker" whose maps threatened Ottoman territories. Apparently the Ottomans hastened to execute him because they thought Pazvantoğlu was planning to rescue him.

Very few Orthodox Christians came forward to defend him, many more denounced him, and the church excommunicated him and his followers. Patriarch Gregory V called for his "deceitful" and "corrupt" writings to be seized and burned, and so they were. His legacy was preserved largely by his comrade Perraivos, the officer who later taught on Corfu and joined the defense of Lefkada in 1807 (see chapters 3 and 5). The Bishop of Yanena demanded that Perraivos be executed as well.[5] Korais followed the drama from Paris and lamented the executions, but he did not endorse the program of radical revolution.

Righas was partially a precedent for the Greek Revolution that broke out in 1821: it was the mass movement he had called for. It was a break from intellectuals like Korais who had called for education, gradualism, and elite tutelage, and a departure from the many who saw the future of the Greeks in one or another empire. But the Revolution of 1821 added something that Righas had not anticipated: a liberation not of people, but of nationals, into a state reserved only for the Christians.

The Church, Counterrevolution, and Counterenlightenment

Righas did not have a place for the clergy in his imagined Greece. This is understandable. The Orthodox Church was an institution of Ottoman governance and decisively aligned with the sultan against foreign enemies and subversive ideas.[6] As the Porte began to focus on the twin threats of French revolution and European conquest, it turned to the patriarchate and the Orthodox hierarchy to shepherd the Rum away from sedition. The clergy responded dutifully. An earlier curiosity about Enlightenment and matters French was replaced by a coordinated campaign of anti-revolutionary publications and repressions. Tracts denounced either the Enlightenment as a whole, or its secularizing and republican outcomes in France. Church pamphleteers recommended submission to the parallel hierarchies of Orthodox church and sultanic monarchy. The "Paternal Instruction" of 1798, written by Patriarch Anthimos of Jerusalem, was only the most famous and it was relatively mild in tone. A pamphlet of 1802 denounced "the zeal of those philosophers who return from Europe." Other leading lights of the church published refutations of heliocentric astronomy. Theologians from the Ionian Islands like Voulgaris and Theotokis who had tried to reconcile church with Enlightenment turned to categorical condemnations of Voltaire.[7]

The patriarchate issued elaborate adulations of Mahmud II:

His sacred majesty, following upon the unrivaled, farsighted, and wisest providence with which, to the admiring amazement of all political observers, wonderfully governs His God-guarded realm, persecuting all sorts of vice . . . royally awards to the various peoples which find

FIGURE 6.1. "Un Prêtre Grec et un Turc" (A Greek Priest and a Turk), 1819, in Louis Dupré, *Voyage à Athènes et à Constantinople* (Paris: Dondey-Dupré, 1825). *The scene is in Athens. The man on the right is likely Mehmet aga Salam, the emissary of the grand vizier in Athens. It is a reminder that the Orthodox clergy were part of the Ottoman administration.*

succor under his mighty wings, the liberty to establish and cultivate all those projects which contribute to their moral order, the improvement of each people and the advancement of human learning.[8]

This was not the stuff of national revolution. Church hierarchs were tax collectors who gathered revenues from all the Orthodox and they were invested in the Ottoman regime. In the two decades before the Greek Revolution the sultan strengthened their powers. Patriarchs readily and frequently condemned and anathematized rebels and urged submission to the sultan. Righas and his co-conspirators were condemned by the patriarch. The Souliots were anathematized when they were fighting against the Ottomans. Kolokotronis was anathematized twice that we know of, in 1805 and 1821. Leaders of the Danubian Uprising of

1821 like Ypsilantis were all anathematized. All the Morean rebels in 1821 were anathematized by at least one of the Orthodox patriarchs of Constantinople, Antioch, and Jerusalem, some by a few.[9]

One can well appreciate why the church would take second place to the national cause when the Revolution broke out in 1821. In 1820 and early 1821 the church was busily dismissing headmasters in Greek schools that taught the Enlightenment, science, and Greek national sentiment. When the Revolution did break out in 1821, the patriarchate roundly condemned it. Quite a few Morean clergy joined the uprising in order to protect their region, but they did this in defiance of their superiors and out of solidarity with their Morean friends and relatives.

Epirus and the Morea: "Bonaparte Wants to Screw Our Mother."

Ali pasha of Yanena was the ruler most directly affected by the new empires in the Balkans. The empires arrived in the Ionian basin, and his territory faced the Ionian Sea. His power had been on the rise since the 1780s. When France, Russia, and Britain competed in the region after 1797, he played the powers against each other. His leverage was his control of food exports to the Ionian Islands and the imperial armies, and the passage of trade to and from Constantinople.[10] He joined Russia in its attack on the French on the islands in 1798 and took the mainland enclaves for himself. He then joined France against Russia and threatened Lefkada. He invited the powers to send consuls to his capital and watched as they competed and intrigued. By 1810 or so he tacitly aligned himself with Britain which paid well for local output. European diplomats and soldiers found him untrustworthy and Oriental, but Ali was practicing something that should have been familiar to any European diplomat: making and then breaking agreements when it suited his interests.[11]

The arrival of the new empires was also a threat, and it spurred Ali to consolidate his rule. He stamped out local power centers in a series of campaigns that extended his territory north and south along the Ionian coast. He used notables to fight notables and warlords to fight warlords. He assimilated the survivors into his administration. At one point or another, he had hired virtually all the future military leaders of the Greek Revolution who hailed from Roumeli, including all the Souliot clans, and including the future statesman Kolettis. Warlords who became famous Greeks in the 1820s, like Androutsos and Karaiskakis, had worked for Ali at one or another point. Kolokotronis refused because he considered himself a Morean and Roumeli a foreign land.[12]

Ali gained a reputation for extreme violence and this was well deserved, but his goal was good government.[13] He was a state builder. He imposed an order that allowed for smoother trade and tax collection, the building of roads and bridges, and the funding of centers of learning. He endowed mosques, churches, and synagogues. The regional language of learning was Greek and Ali was fluent—it was the language he used to correspond with his sons—and Greek flourished in schools, in monasteries, and in his court.

The Porte was suspicious of Ali's power, to be sure, and there were rumors that he intended to create an independent state or even convert to Christianity.[14] Later Ali and the sultan would go to war, and in early 1822 Ali was killed and Yanena sacked. But for the time being his policies aligned with those of the Porte: he had stabilized the region. The French complained that he was defying the Porte's support of France in 1810 and 1811 by expanding trade with Britain and starving the Ionian Islands, but Ottoman policy was tending in the same direction no matter what the official declarations.[15] British naval and mercantile power was irresistible and anyway Britain was the only power not likely to dismember the Ottoman Empire. Better a weak Porte that was open for trade and monitored from the sea.[16]

The Porte asked Ali to achieve the same stability in the Morea, to Ali's south. In the Morea too the new empires were a source of concern. Napoleon contemplated an invasion of the Ottoman Balkans ever since he took the Ionian Islands in 1797 and his officers openly boasted that the Morea was next. Corsican spies of Greek origin, the Stafanopoli, were sent over to reconnoiter. In the following years locals expected an invasion by either Russia or France.[17]

Ali agreed and in 1807 sent his son Veli to become the Morean pasha. Veli pasha proceeded to stamp out banditry, sent irregulars to quash local power centers, executed more agas and the Morean dragoman, and centralized trade policy and revenues. He gave privileges to churches and allowed Christian schools to open. He gave approval to excavations of ancient Olympia and received reports on their progress. Some thought he had a bias in favor of the Christians and the notables, even at the expense of the ayans. In fact, as was usual for the region, Veli was siding with one alliance of notables against others. And if he was fluent in Greek and preferred it in his correspondence, this was not unusual for a Muslim in the region. Greek was the common language, Albanian was not yet a written language, and few here wrote Ottoman.[18]

In the Morea the empires were the cause of an economic boom and Veli weighed his options. France, Russia, and Britain competed in the Morea for supplies for their armies, navies, and Mediterranean possessions. Prices rose. Exports of oil, grain, and meat did well. So did timber exports from the west coast. Carpentry and metal-working supported shipbuilding, and gunpowder mills in the mountain towns of Dimitsana and Divri boomed. Like his father, Veli directed more exports to the British. In 1810 alone he contracted to deliver 30,000 kilograms of wheat to British-held Malta, and more was destined for Sicily, Spain, and Gibraltar. British ships docked freely in the Morea and bought up the supplies needed by the French Ionian Islanders. The British trade in Corinthian grapes continued unimpeded. The French were not pleased.[19]

Also displeased were Morean notables who were on the wrong side of Veli's imperial realignment. Veli took away the tax farms of some families and gave them to their adversaries. Taxes went up—good news for the notables—but only his favored families benefited. And Veli planned to take a larger share for himself.[20] Among those losing out were the kotsabase of Gastouni, Giorgos Sisinis, and his allies, the agas of nearby Lala. They were on the west coast and their exports had been sent almost entirely to Zakynthos and Cephalonia, a few hours away by boat. These islands were now part of the French Empire and under British blockade.[21] Veli's deals with Britain cut them off from their main markets.

The resistance of the local agas became open and in 1808 Veli mobilized a force of 1,200 Albanians. They marched on Lala and the agas fled. One of them was Ali Farmaki—Ali Poison, so named because of his jaundiced appearance. He retreated further up the mountains to the stronghold of Monastiraki and closed himself in the tower with a few men. Desperate, Ali sent word to his friend Kolokotronis who was in exile on the island of Zakynthos. Their fathers had been allies and adoptive brothers. Kolokotronis recruited a band of warriors and about sixty made their way to Monastiraki. Veli tried to tunnel the tower to blow it up, failed, and then negotiated. Kolokotronis was allowed to go to Zakynthos. Ali was supposed to go to Tripolitsa to submit, but instead he escaped with Kolokotronis. He died soon after. Kolokotronis, respectful of his friend and his religion, arranged for Farmaki to return to the Morea to die and be buried at home.

Also in contact with the French commanders was Yakoub aga, Ali's brother, and he joined forces with Kolokotronis. In secret he was also working with Sisinis. Together they played the imperial card: while Veli was turning to Britain, the conspirators turned to France and met with French agents. Later they met with Donzelot, the commander on Corfu, and asked to be introduced to Napoleon. In a series of exchanges they and their secretaries told the French a story of Morean woe. The region as a whole was in disarray and squalor, they said. Veli was raising taxes on everyone and seizing the tariffs. The notables had generously offered him the equivalent of 300,000 French francs, Veli's share of the Morean revenues; Veli greedily demanded 3.5 million. The notables were impoverished. Veli was having Christians and Muslims killed. He was selling Muslim and Christian boys and girls into prostitution.[22]

They told the French that the entire Morea was ready for a change in rulers, and that notables from across the region were with them. Many of them were related by blood and marriage, and Yakoub named relatives and allies as far away as Monemvasia. If France were to invade and expel Veli pasha, Muslim and Christian notables would pledge allegiance to Napoleon. Ottoman rule in the Morea would end. The notables would maintain an army of 4,000 but France would pay for it and France would not interfere in local affairs. Indeed France would receive

FIGURE 6.2. "A Mosque at Gastouni," John Spencer Stanhope, *Olympia; or, Topography Illustrative of the Actual State of the Plain of Olympia, and of the Ruins of the City of Elis* (London, Dodwell and Martin, 1824 / Athens 2010). Greek Library, Alexandros Onassis Public Benefit Foundation. *Mosques were a common sight in the Morea before 1821. Very few have survived, none as working mosques.*

nothing at all, other than the thanks of the notables. The notables— impoverished by Veli, they lamented—would have to keep all taxes and tariffs for themselves.

They then proposed a constitution for the Morea. The Morea would be ruled by a council of notables that was half Christian and half Muslim, without French interference but protected by France. Local councils would be weighted according to local demographic conditions, in some places with a majority of Muslim notables, in others a majority of kotsabases. Both religions were to be protected and tolerated. There were special provisions for Muslims who would find themselves a small minority, outside the Ottoman structure, protected by a Christian emperor: they would have separate religious courts and would be allowed to bear arms.

The proposal was remarkable, not the least for its gall. The French were to invade to secure a republic of kotsabases and ayans who would now share their revenues with no one else—not the pasha, not the Porte, not the French. Their exploitation of the peasants would be unimpeded. It was a novel constitutional document with detailed provisions for religious tolerance, equality among notables, and the disposition of armed force and revenues. At the heart of the matter, observed a French agent traveling the region, was not religion or systematic repression; it was the chronic insecurity of the notables who were wealthy and privileged but could be killed and expropriated at any moment. They complained of general disorder and asked for protection against the Christian armed men as well as Veli. They also feared the mass of poor peasants: if the notables and ayans were to act alone against established authority, the peasantry might turn on them.

Sisinis and Yakoub devised a plan that was still recognizably Ottoman: the rule of the notables over a hapless peasantry and religious pluralism. It was also new and French: there would be security of (notable) persons, (notable) properties, and (notable) revenues. The plan would freeze the vast inequalities of the region into a permanent arrangement, in effect a version of European liberalism where certain property rights were absolute. Arguably this is what the notables saw in France and why they saw the French Empire as an improvement on the Ottoman order. No longer a carrier of revolution, France under Napoleon represented hierarchy, stability, and the protection of their persons and properties. Indeed, according to a French agent on the ground, Yakoub and Sisinis thought that Napoleon as emperor would prevent any revolutionary movement from unfolding and there would be no threat to the privileges of the notables.[23] Protected from arbitrariness from above and mass movements from below, it was a solution to the Ottoman disarray.

Veli knew what was happening because he was intercepting their correspondence and he took the threat of a French invasion seriously. His network of Christian spies in the Morea and on the islands, probably his privileged slaves, pursued Yakoub and promised the arrest of the "apostates." Their regular and elaborate reports ("I slavishly kiss the traces of your bright feet") kept him informed of Yakoub's movements and schemes with the French. Anyway, the uncles of Yakoub and Ali Farmaki had already denounced them to Veli.[24]

Veli's response was remarkable because he too proceeded from a sense of Morean notable solidarity that was multiconfessional. He had no Ottoman force to draw on so he mobilized the notables with whom he was allied and with whom he did business. They should provide men and pay for Veli's Albanians. Among his Christian allies was the bey of the Mani ("I slavishly submit, I kiss your hand") who offered his support and asked by-the-by whether Veli planned to buy up his crops of acorns and oil. Others offered to support him if he were to appoint their clan or faction to rule locally.[25] They came to him to supplicate and negotiate in the town of Kranidi on the eastern coast of the Morea.

Veli sounded the alarm. In perfect Greek Veli warned the notables: "Bonaparte wants to screw our mother!" (*O Vonapartis theli na mas gamisi ti mana!*)[26] It was a marvelously colloquial expression of geopolitical alarm, as effective as any ministerial report. One should admire Veli's command of Greek idiom. The term was and is a way to say that someone will inflict extreme damage. And Veli implied that Muslims and Christians shared the same mother because they were all Moreans. He appealed to their sense of self-preservation and their liking of privilege and wealth. Veli was still the sultan's partner and nominally his vassal, but the sultan was far away. Lacking a force of his own, the sultan expected Veli to settle matters using local notables and irregulars. Both sides could only speak in terms of the region and there was no mention of a common Ottoman home, only a Morean one. That the conspirators could now appeal to France shows why the problem was becoming a matter of survival. It was a regional conflict of notables, conducted in the space of an imperial rivalry.

It all came to nothing because the British were conquering the Ionian Islands and France was on the retreat.[27] Always the optimist, Kolokotronis abandoned the French plan and donned the helmet of a British dragoon. Yakoub continued to make his case to France in 1810 and 1811, and then made his way to Constantinople to find supporters, all along pursued by Veli's spies. He returned to the Morea and organized mutinies of the coastal garrisons in 1812. That was probably the last straw for the Porte because Veli could no longer maintain order. In that year the sultan took the pashalik away from Veli. Veli would later be hunted down and killed, not long after the fall of his father in 1822. Yakoub fared better under the new pasha and it seems that his French plot was forgiven.[28] Sisinis was never exposed. He continued to work in the Ottoman administration. He thrived as an exporter, landowner, and tax farmer.[29] With Veli gone, the notables of both religions returned to their factional alliances and continued to have each other killed.

Around 1810, then, all sides spoke of regions and empires with no mention of a nation in between. And yet in 1821 these same Christians spoke of the nation. This brings us to the key question surrounding the Greek Revolution. Why was the Greek Revolution Greek, a national movement of Christians only, directed against all Muslims? How did Sisinis, who worked so closely with the agas of Lala, set about killing them in order to enter the pantheon of revolutionary leaders? In January 1815 Sisinis signed his name and affixed his seal alongside ten agas of Lala and Gastouni, to an agreement to jointly pay for medical services in the region. In 1818 and 1819 he was contributing to the rebuilding of forts to defend the Ottoman coasts, with Muslim agas paying one-third of the cost and Christians two-thirds. In 1820 he gathered taxes and rents and shared them with his Muslim partners. In summer 1821 Sisinis attacked the Muslims of Lala with armed men and canon, and killed and evicted the very men with whom he had collaborated in the preceding months.[30]

Or consider the notable Sotiris Charalambis in Kalavryta, who was married to Sisinis's sister Viktoria. As late as December 1820, or three months before the outbreak of the Greek Revolution, he was busily corresponding with his agents in Constantinople, in secret code. The subject was not revolutionary conspiracies, but the deadly matter of tax farms and tax collection, wondering how he would survive the latest political intrigues involving Muslim and Christian notables, the Morean pasha, and the Porte. A few months later he was a leader of the Greek Revolution.[31]

FIGURE 6.3. Karl Krazeisen, *Georgio Sissini*, 1829. © National Gallery, Alexandros Soutsos Museum, photograph by Stavros Psiroukis. *Giorgos Sisinis was the kotsabase of Gastouni and a part of the tax-farming Ottoman elite. His family remained prominent tax farmers and civil servants after independence.*

The question applies not only to Sisinis and his kin but to the entire stratum of Christian notables who were implicated in Ottoman administration and quite suddenly abandoned the regime in favor of a nation. Something similar may be asked about the warlords who served every possible power in the region before setting off a nationalist uprising. And the same may be asked about the merchants of the Aegean Islands who enjoyed autonomy, privileges, and wealth as they moved the trade in the eastern Mediterranean and the Black seas.

The answer has a lot to do with Russia. It was Russia that led Europe into a new era of Christian assertiveness at the Congress of Vienna and in the Holy Alliance. And Russia was the home of tens of thousands of

Balkan Christians who came north for wealth, careers, and opportunity. For all their differences of region, language, and dialect, in Russia they were all greki and they were all privileged. The plot to create an independent Greece was hatched in Odesa and grew out of a novel Greek assertiveness, entitlement, and coherence, all incubating in Russia.

And yet no one was more surprised by the Greek Revolution than the Russians themselves.

Chapter 7

Capo d'Istria, Kapodistriia, Kapodistrias

A Short History of Europe, 1776–1831

Prologue

MY ACQUAINTANCE IS *well educated and aware of it. He outlines his lineage as the descendant of Ionian Island gentry. Like many people from the region, he is fiercely proud that the first governor of Greece was a fellow-islander and aristocrat, Giovanni Capo d'Istria. We agree that the Count enjoyed a remarkable career. He helped govern the Ionian Islands under Russian occupation, and he became the foreign minister of Tsar Alexander I at Vienna in 1815. I wonder aloud how the Count felt when he disembarked in the Morea, for the first time in his life. He saw a war-torn region, armed and impoverished peasants, entitled tax farmers who had recently been Ottoman notables, and warlords who had fought for just about anyone until they threw in their lot with the nation. The nation notwithstanding, the Greeks were still fighting each other when he arrived.*

I remark, "He must have thought that he had come to a land of savages."

My companion rejoins: "I think so too." Our grammar leaves room to think that he means that the Count looked down on the mainland Greeks, or that he himself does.

Certainly the Count changed in profound ways, and he embodied the movement of Europe as a whole from regions under empires to nations with regions. People of the revolutionary era had to arrive at the nation—it was not preexisting—and allow national feeling to supersede station and locality. The Count's personal journey embodied the journey of a country, a continent, and ultimately the world.

Yet the man in his many incarnations and languages was always one thing: count, conte, graf, comte, *and* komis. *He was an aristocrat and he had a view of rule and authority that was superordinate, and he had learned it in his upbringing and in Russia while serving an autocrat. He was that kind of liberal. The people needed guidance, education, and authority. He had little time for rapacious notables and warlords whom he treated with contempt. This worldview got him killed in 1831 at the hands of Morean notables.*

The view of government as lofty, conducted for the good of the people without asking the people, remains one of the models of rule in independent Greece. Power is superordinate. It might be carried by dictators or by finance ministers. It implies that Greeks cannot govern themselves, and quite a few Greeks agree to this day.

From Venetian Nobleman to Russian Statesman

The man baptized Giovanni Capo d'Istria was a child of the revolutionary age—he was born in 1776 and died in the wake of the 1830 revolutions in Belgium, France, and Poland—but he was not a revolutionary. A liberal and an aristocrat from the island of Corfu, he chose gradualism. He witnessed revolutions in Italy as a student, and saw the arrival of the republican French on Corfu in 1797. He was put off by the revolutionary violence and supported the Russo-Ottoman invasion. He ran the Ottoman naval hospital on Corfu and reported to the Ottoman admiral. When the Russians imposed a new order of expanded participation by the nobility and the affluent merchantry, he sided with Russia and did its bidding. For a man of his station, this was a little radical. His father Antonio-Maria had been petitioning the sultan to reinstate the aristocratic monopoly on power, but Giovanni thought that the old regimes needed guided reforms.

In 1804, still on Corfu, he was appointed Collegiate Councilor in the Russian civil service. This was a reasonable choice for a moderate liberal. Alexander I was widely seen as a liberal himself, and the two men shared an interest in constitutional experiments and aristocratic republics. He put down both pro-French republican insurgencies and reactionary plots intending to reinstall an oligarchy of titled landowners. Change was needed, he held, but it was to be managed by an educated, affluent elite that was backed by firm power. The power in this case was the Russian army. He became an admirer of Montesquieu, for whom constitutions and order came before popular sovereignty.[1]

When the French returned to the Ionian Islands in 1807, the Russians invited him to St. Petersburg. He entered into the Russian service rolls as Ivan (or Ioann) Antonovich Kapodistriia. He was at home in the prenational, cosmopolitan European aristocracy of the capital. The Russians in turn valued him for his fluent French (the language of diplomacy and nobility) and Italian (the language of diplomacy in the Ionian and Adriatic basins). He had pedigree and he knew the region. That he was an Orthodox Christian, like his new master, made the relationship more comfortable. Then again, Russia was cold. "It's all crystals," he remarked to supplicating Moreans searching for appointments, and he advised them to head south.[2]

In 1811 he was at the Russian embassy in Vienna, a specialist on the eastern Mediterranean and reporting to the ambassador on Ottoman Balkan affairs. In his reports he organized the world by confession, territory, and the sovereignty of monarchs and aristocracies. In the current war with the Porte, he opined, Russia might appeal to the Orthodox Christian Slavs of the region, the Bulgarians and Serbs, and it might mobilize the Greek-speaking Orthodox. If Russia were to peel territory away from the sultan, then the region could fall under the protection of the Orthodox tsar. Russia might sponsor new principalities, and Ali pasha of Yanena might become the king of an independent Epirus or a larger multiethnic and multiconfessional Greece. It would be easier if Ali were to convert to Orthodoxy: he would be brought into the world of European diplomacy and become part of Russia's Christian umbrella.[3]

By 1815 Russia was triumphant and the preeminent power of Europe. The Count sat beside Alexander at the Congress of Vienna. By year's end he was the tsar's foreign minister and he shared that role with Karl Nesselrode. In diplomacy he became known as Jean Capodistrias. He knew his place. The tsar was an autocrat who set his own foreign policy and conducted diplomacy personally. Alexander surrounded himself with advisors who tended to be intelligent, cultivated, worked within the parameters he had set, and in the last analysis obeyed his orders. The Count fit these criteria and he implemented Alexander's orders all the way to 1821, when the Greek Revolution produced a rift.

The Congress of Vienna decided the boundaries and regimes of the new Europe, and inaugurated the Congress System that managed European affairs until 1826. The monarchs and diplomats would fight off challenges to borders, they would put down liberal movements in the different Italian and German states, and they would quash mass movements anywhere. The Count was responsible for Ottoman policy. He periodically and privately thought it was time for another Ottoman war over the northern Balkans, but the tsar was categorical: the peace must be maintained at all costs. Instability in that region would draw the European powers into a vacuum and they would fight each other for the spoils. The Count understood. All the way to late 1820 he warned Ottoman Christians that Russia would not come to their aid if they rebelled. Russia might lobby on their behalf but the Christians would have to reconcile with their sultan.[4]

Within this Europe, the assembled statesmen decreed the size and character of states. In theory the nature of each regime would depend on how the assembled statesmen assessed the civilization of each country.[5] In Sweden the Bonapartist general Bernadotte could remain as constitutional monarch. In Naples the Bourbon king could return to rule in an unlimited way over a reanimated Kingdom of Two Sicilies. Switzerland could be a confederation and remain without a monarch: the Count went there in 1813–1814 to mediate among the cantons and draft its constitution. Poland would be a kingdom with a constitution. It had once been an independent commonwealth with a large nobility accustomed to ruling. But as a check on Polish unruliness its king would be the Russian autocrat and constitutionalism would have its limits. Alexander dutifully addressed the Polish Diet, but he warned that its prerogatives were conditional. In the face of any disorder "the strong arm of authority will make itself felt."[6] This pretty well captured the nature of his liberalism. France under the restored Bourbons would have a charter that gave the vote to a tiny aristocracy as a way to put a check on an unreliable king. Alexander and Europe's diplomats were not out-and-out reactionaries, though they could be and became so in 1820 in the face of the Mediterranean revolutions.

If this patchwork of European regimes seems arbitrary, that is because it was. In the last analysis there was no way to scientifically determine what regime a given territory deserved. The powers declared that they ruled by a benevolent Christianity, but the maps they produced and the regimes they decreed depended on the jockeying of the powers, which in practice meant Russia in the lead, Britain, Prussia, Austria, and, increasingly, a restored Bourbon France. The rights of religious minorities entered the lexicon but in no consistent way—for Jews but only if they were in Germany, for Catholics if they were in the Netherlands, and for Muslims not at all.[7]

It takes the discernment of Glenda Sluga to point to what should have been obvious: policy swings and about-faces were contained within a newly assertive Christianity. Policy could move from liberal to reactionary, and from constitutionalist to absolutist, but all of these outcomes assumed and presumed that Europe was more Christian than ever before. For Alexander and the Count, liberalism and constitutionalism played out in a world of Christian civilization, not vice versa. References to God, Christ, the Trinity, and Providence suffused any political or diplomatic pronouncement.[8]

The new spirit was expressed in the Treaty of the Holy Alliance that was signed by Russia, Prussia, and Austria. The three would actively ensure that borders and regimes did not change without their approval. The continent may be divided between states, but they were all part of a single entity, "one great Christian nation" in which the strongest states dominated. They would base their actions not on the self-interest of each monarch, but on a notion of a collective European good animated by "the eternal religion of God our Savior." One might pass over such language as nonsense, as did Britain's Castlereagh, but Alexander

I meant it and he believed in this Europe. The role of the monarch was to wage war against "Satanic power," whatever foreign or domestic form it might take.[9] British statesmen who found the rhetoric far-fetched nevertheless agreed that Christianity and geography combined to give definition to the continent, and they also employed the religious idiom.

The Ottoman Empire was excluded from the deliberations because it would be too dangerous to tamper with it, but there is more. The sultan was not invited to Vienna because his territories were outside Christian Europe and the sultan was a Muslim sovereign.[10] The southeastern boundary of Europe that was drawn at Vienna was geographic, ending in the Ionian Sea. But the boundary was also religious and demographic in that the European continent, its states, and its peoples were Christian. Talk among some powers to include the Balkans in the Vienna settlements ended when the sultan declared he would not participate in "any System of European politics." European diplomats were happy to leave it at that.[11]

This was the Europe the powers decreed but it did not always make sense. If Europe was decidedly Christian, what was the status of the Christians of the Ottoman Empire? Europeans were Christians, but were all Christians Europeans? The problem lay in a tension in the Treaty of the Holy Alliance. It defined Europe and its populations as Christian, but invested political importance in the sovereigns or the aristocracies. In one of his edits to the treaty the Count and his deputy proposed that Christian values be the defining feature of Christian peoples and therefore of Europe. In the Balkans it could give significance to the Christianity of the sultan's subjects, despite the Islam of their ruler, and make the Balkans the business of Europe. Austria's Metternich objected: it suggested that subjects had a say in who they were and might feel entitled. Rather, the monarch lent identity to his subjects. Metternich prevailed but the tension never went away. In 1820 the Count pointedly stated that Napoleon had been defeated in 1812–14 by the mass mobilization of soldiers fighting for their fatherlands. He was no revolutionary but also not a believer in unreformed old regimes. Somehow millions of subjects had to be accounted for.[12]

For the Count and his deputy, Alexandre Stourdza, the sultan was more than non-European, he was the enemy of Christendom and Europe. Stourdza in particular was a true Orthodox believer and a fanatic by many measures, and he detested Islam and "the Turks." He came from a family of Ottoman Orthodox servitors in the Danubian region who fled to Russia and received estates populated by peasants. His two uncles remained as Ottoman diplomats and were executed when the sultan was dissatisfied by the Treaty of Bucharest of 1812. His animus against the sultan was matched by his piousness in Europe. Stourdza was the brains behind the Carlsbad Decrees of 1819, when the murder of a prominent writer prompted the monarchies to place limits on German university autonomies, secret societies, and the press, and gave the universities more religious content. At moments like these their liberalism had clear limits, though Stourdza had none to begin with.[13]

All the way to 1821 a Greek state or territory was not on any agenda. Even the private musings of the Count and Stourdza tended to be about Ottoman Christians who were subjects of past treaties—Wallachians, Moldovans, and Serbs—and about places that actually existed in diplomacy, from Alaska to the Ionian Islands. The Greeks were not a subject of any treaty, and Greece did not exist on the official maps. The two men agreed that the Greek people, whoever they were, would find accommodation in and among the empires, and for the time being most of them were subjects of the sultan. At Vienna diplomats set aside sessions for the abolition of the slave trade and for Jewish emancipation in Germany, but not for Greece and the Greeks. Quite a few people later associated with the Greek Revolution were present, but in 1815 they served one or another empire and said little to nothing about a Greece.[14]

Greek in Russia

To be sure, the Count was sympathetic to the Greek cause, but his homeland was Corfu. He regularly used his position to advocate for the Ionian Islands before the emperor and the other European powers.[15] Unlike Greece, the Ionian Islands existed as a place in European diplomacy, and they were ruled by Britain which had conquered them in 1814 and did not intend to leave. The Congress of Vienna confirmed this and also made the islands a European affair. At the time the Count and Alexander had agreed that British rule could be felicitous to trade, education, and civil rights for the affluent.[16]

The Count worried that the agreements of 1815 were being dishonored by the British governor Thomas Maitland, who overrode local prerogatives in exchange for peace and trade. The islanders should be happy, Maitland told them in 1819, that they enjoyed "the most perfect internal tranquility," that their shipping was booming, and that the value of Corinthian grape in which they traded was high. The European Congresses of "wise, moderate, and most fortunate" monarchs promised the "permanent tranquility of the World." In 1821, with revolutions breaking out in the northern Mediterranean, he told them they should feel lucky that they were not part of the "catastrophe" and that they were not infected by the "Political diseases." The quarantine he imposed was as much a way to screen for subversives as diseases.[17]

The Count's visit to the Ionian Islands in 1819 was in a private capacity, to arrange family affairs. He met with the mercenaries he had employed at Lefkada in 1807 (as well as Kolokotronis whom he had imprisoned), with new waves of Christian refugees from Ali pasha's lands, and with islanders outraged by British conduct. His message was consistent: Russia, and he as Russia's servant, could not be involved in subversion, and they would have to find accommodation with the British.[18] On the other hand, Russia did have the right to inquire because the Ionian Islands were formally part of Europe and therefore the Congress System. Arriving in London soon after, the Count brought letters from the tsar that raised questions about the Ionian Islands, though not protests. Alexander I took an interest as a favor to his loyal servitor. The tsar wrote to Wellington as a fellow Christian "of our Holy Religion." The Count too wrote to Wellington and Bathurst (the colonial secretary) in the name of his Ionian "co-citizens," and raised the matter of representation and high taxation. The British were clear that this was the affair of no other country.[19]

When an uprising broke out on Lefkada and Zakynthos not long after the Count's visit, Maitland was convinced it was the work of the Count and the "Russian Party" on the islands.[20] Maitland intercepted and avidly read the Count's correspondence with his brother, and his brother's correspondence with anyone, in search of the incriminating evidence which he never found. Still he concluded that the unrest was the result of "the intrigues of Capo d'Istria himself." When rebellion broke out on the Ottoman mainland in 1821, Maitland again blamed the Count and Russia.[21] No matter how much he protested that he was a Corfiot and servant of Russia, British officials insisted he was a Greek.

And it is true that around this time the Count began numbering himself among the Greeks, at least in some connections, and his sense of his Greekness was a product of his years in Russia. He was part of a recent wave of Orthodox arrivals. Soldiers, clergy, and nobility had been migrating to Russia in search of careers since the fall of Byzantium. The Byzantine princess Sophia Paleologina had married Grand Prince Ivan III as Byzantium was falling and Muscovy rising. The Russian double-headed eagle was copied from a church in Mystras. The new and large wave of migration began with the Ottoman wars of the 1760s onward. People who were unlikely to mix in their previous lives came together in Russia: Ionian theologians, Ottoman bishops, Danubian princes, and Ottoman administrators and diplomats.[22] There were tens of thousands of merchants, sailors, farmers, and soldiers who flocked to Russia around the Black Sea (see chapter 8). The Count did receive the petitions of his new compatriots but station and status still mattered more. Their interactions were those of lord and supplicant. The Count responded with a mix of *noblesse oblige* and romantic admiration for the rough men he admitted to his offices. They inhabited different social and cultural worlds and he was capable of dismissing them as low-born clerks and upstarts who should remember their place.

The Count's world was that of aristocrats, officers, church hierarchs, and state servitors. He arrived in St. Petersburg in 1808 young, alone, on a modest stipend, and very cold. He lived with two churchmen, one of them his comrade from the defense of Lefkada in 1807. Ignatios had been a bishop in the lands of Ali pasha of Yanena and defected to the Russians on the Ionian Islands to become Ignazio and Ignatii. The churchmen urged the Count to learn proper written Greek though he never did.

He was a prolific correspondent but the first known letter he wrote in Greek was from 1808, to his Greek tutor. He wrote to his father regularly and dutifully, but only once in Greek. He entered into pacts with circles of Greek-origin Russians and expatriates to speak and write in Greek only. In practice it was too easy for them to fall back into Italian, French, and Russian, but the shame he expressed of being a quasi-Greek who spoke Greek haltingly and wrote it rarely tells us that his Greekness was now mattering more.

His growing consciousness of being Greek owed in part to his reception in salon culture as the Greek they expected him to be. He fell in with aristocrats who became advocates of Greek causes. Chief among them were the Stourdza siblings, Roxandra and Alexandre, the Count's deputy. To give them national labels would not make sense, though many have since tried. They most often wrote their names in French (Stourdza). With a boyar father from Moldavia they might be thought of as Romanians or Moldovans (Sturdza). With a Christian mother from Constantinople they might be seen as Greeks, or as Alexandre put it, Greek by descent (Stourtzas). By upbringing and service they may seem Russian (Sturdza). Deeply religious Alexandre supported causes that were Christian and not necessarily national. Roxandra was at the center of this circle and perhaps the Count's love interest, though she was by now married to a German prince. She was among that cohort of impressive women who facilitated diplomacy at Vienna; we have since mistaken the dances and dalliances for frivolity.[23] All in all, the Stourdza siblings were what later would be called Philhellenes, friends of the Greeks but not necessarily Greek themselves. They were aristocrats.

Meanwhile, beyond the general statement that the Greeks were Orthodox and ancient, the Count, like Stourdza, thought that the Greeks were not ready for independence or even autonomy. The national marker was something increasingly real in their minds, but still subordinated to the religious marker and in diplomacy irrelevant. Whoever the Greeks were, they existed in the supranational empires. One can well understand this perspective. Most of the people who might be called Greeks were mere commoners. They were merchants, sailors, farmers, herders, and mercenaries, hardly the material of a state leadership. The Morean and Roumeliot notables were not a nobility as they understood it, entitled and cultivated in the European way and organized into corporate protections and autonomies. They were insecure tax farmers. The more education they had, the more likely they were to be implicated in the Ottoman hierarchy. The example was the Phanariots, well-educated and wealthy families of Constantinople, who congregated around the patriarchate in the Phanari district. A few defected to Russia and quite a few were executed, but the vast majority stayed in the Ottoman Empire as advisors, translators, diplomats, and tax farmers.

According to the Count, the Greeks needed a good education, one person at a time, as part of civilizing process that would last indefinitely. Around 1814 the Count, Bishop Ignatii, and the Stourdza siblings directed their attention to the Society of the Friends of the Muses (Philomousos Etereia). It was nominally centered in Athens, but the society gathered its funds from the aristocracies and courts of Europe whom the Stourdza circle lobbied in Vienna in 1814 and 1815. Its funds were held in Bavaria. The tsar and tsarina contributed along with other monarchs, princes, princesses, and bankers. Soon the society reached into the Greek merchantry based in Russia who may have lacked status but did have a lot of money. The caviar merchant Varvakis was the largest donor. The society used its funds to finance the education of Greek youth in Germany and Italy. Who the Greeks were was still vague, but as a rule they were not Muslims, who were excluded. Slowly, very slowly, the Christians would become the core of an enlightened and responsible people, perhaps circulating in the empires, perhaps taking the leadership of one or another autonomous region that might sprout up during some future realignment of imperial forces.[24]

But a national revolution, of Greeks or anyone else, was anathema. Revolutions broke out in Spain, Piedmont, and Naples in 1819 and 1820, and the revolutionaries demanded constitutions and forced their kings to agree. It was at this moment that the Congress System acquired its reputation for out-and-out reaction. Never mind that these movements also claimed to be thoroughly Christian, and specifically Catholic. Their crime was to demand constitutions, including political participation by wide or narrow swaths of the population, and to do so without the agreement of the powers.

Alexander requested a meeting of the powers and they met at Troppau (Opava, Czech Republic) in 1820 and Laibach (Ljubljana, Slovenia) in 1821. They delegated Austria to send troops to quash the revolutions in Italy and in effect convert the Two Sicilies and Piedmont into Austrian protectorates. The Spanish Revolution dragged on until the Congress of Verona in 1822 delegated France to send an army to put it down. The French army marched in 1823 as the One Hundred Thousand Sons of St. Louis, a Christian crusade.[25] In that army, by the by, were the Ionian Islanders who had entered French service, Bulgari of the "magic lantern" and his patron, Loverdo.

The Count and the Revolution

Another uprising was brewing in the Balkans, in the name of the Greeks, but none of these statemen knew of it until it broke out in early 1821. But we do know what the Count thought of the idea of a Greek conspiracy against the sultan. Whatever his sympathies for Greeks under Ottoman rule, a plot against the sultan was subversive, a disruption to the peace, and dangerous for the Ottoman Christians. On four occasions from 1817 to 1820 men representing a secret organization (the Friendly Society) aimed at overthrowing the sultan asked if the Count would lead or support it, and four times he refused.[26] The Count was scandalized and called one of them insane to his face before having him put under surveillance and thrown out of Russia. He dismissed the leaders as "pitiful merchant clerks," people with "no particular occupation or status," "bankrupted by their own conduct," seeking support for a patria because they themselves were rootless. Over the years he urged other Greeks to have nothing to do with them. His objection was not simply that his hands were tied by the emperor; he thought it was a very bad idea. An uprising by a few upstart fanatics would invite reprisals against all the sultan's Orthodox subjects who would pay a real price.[27]

The conspirators offered the leadership to another Greek aristocratic transplant, Alexander Ypsilantis, and in April 1820 he accepted. Ypsilantis was from a family of Phanariots. His grandfather Athanasios had busily put down rebellions against the Porte in the 1760s and 1770s but fell out of favor and was executed by torture. Alexander's father Constantine had been a dragoman at the Porte, Prince of Moldavia, and finally Prince of Wallachia. He defected to Russia in 1806 and was based in Kyiv. The Ypsilantis sons were educated in officer schools at Russian expense. Alexander Ypsilantis served as the tsar's aide-de-camp and lost his arm in battle against France in 1813. In St. Petersburg Ypsilantis was a regular among the Greeks of the salons, he was a cousin of the Stourdzas, and he was acquainted with the Count. The tsar took an interest in helping the family reclaim their lost Ottoman properties and Russian emissaries were making the case before Ottoman officials as late as February 1821.[28]

Imagine the tsar's surprise when he learned that Ypsilantis had led a small army into the Danubian Principalities in February 1821. It was a personal betrayal and it cast suspicions on Russia. Ypsilantis the *Russian* general had crossed into the Danubian Principalities from *Russian* territory at the head of a revolutionary army including *Russian* volunteers. The conduct of Russian officials also gave the appearance of Russian complicity. Russian commanders along the border in the south had given Ypsilantis and his volunteers passage into the Danubian Principalities because they could not imagine he was acting against the tsar's wishes. Russian emissaries were accustomed to lending support to Ottoman Christians during small conflicts but did not understand that this was a nationalist movement and not Ottoman politics as usual. Ypsilantis had spoken of a rebirth of ancient Greece but the Russian commanders thought it fanciful. Russian–Greek diplomats in the Ottoman Empire had joined the society or tacitly supported it but it is not clear that they understood what they were joining. The Ottomans and the European courts assumed that the Greek uprising was Russia's doing.[29]

Only the Russians knew that the Greek Revolution was not a Russian conspiracy. The Count was given the task of renouncing Ypsilantis. He did so publicly, and even in his private correspondence he expressed the same refrain: "we are making, and will make, all pronouncements, telling the truth: that we knew nothing about this and we do not want to know anything." The Foreign Ministry told its emissaries abroad that Russia expected the sultan to "snuff out the revolt at its very beginning," and the tsar agreed to let Ottoman forces enter the Danubian Principalities to suppress the rebels. When the uprising spread to the Morea and Roumeli, the powers were no more sympathetic, and envoys from revolutionary Greece were turned away from the Congress of Verona in 1822. There Alexander told the French Foreign Minister Chateaubriand that nothing would please him more than a "religious war against the Turks," but never at the expense of the European consensus. With Russia in the lead, all the European powers condemned the Greek uprising categorically as an illegitimate conspiracy against a legitimate ruler, Sultan Mahmud II.[30]

Perhaps the more profound truth that hardly anyone appreciated was that autocratic, anti-nationalist, and legitimist Russia had incubated a nationalist, revolutionary, and conspiratorial movement in its own borders. The cluelessness of Russian officials, the Count included, had something to do with the fact that the conspiracy was of lower-class Greek merchants with whom aristocrats like the count had few contacts. It turned out that the upstart clerks had set off a mass movement.

The Count and the Argument for Greece

It was from around this time that the Count entered the final stage of his evolution and became decidedly Greek. He adopted the idiom of the nation, and he crafted the argument for Greek independence. That argument was ignored by Europe for the moment, but it was available when European courts changed course in 1826.

The change in the Count was partly a matter of conviction and choice. He had dismissed the idea of a Greek uprising, but now that it had happened he would salvage what he could. He advocated for the Greek cause in the Foreign Ministry, and later to anyone who would listen. For a few months he was able to persuade the tsar to make a stand for the Christians who were being arrested, executed, and attacked by Muslim crowds around the Ottoman lands as reprisal for the uprising (see chapter 10). Moreover the sultan closed the Bosporus and Dardanelles Straits to European shipping and threatened the person of the Russian ambassador.

It was a splendid moment for another Ottoman war; it had been almost ten years since the last. But none of the other powers were willing to go along and Russia would not act alone. It would deal a fatal blow the Congress System of European consensus. Alexander was probably the last monarch to believe in the Congress System and the Holy Alliance as a principle and as a practice. Metternich sent troops to Italy and acquired protectorates. France sent troops to Spain to reacquire great power status. Russia maintained the consensus by doing nothing in its own interests. The Count told Alexander as much, quite bluntly, and he was largely right.[31]

Behind the official scenes the Count worked closely with Stourdza and Greeks in Russian service to make a novel case, an argument in favor of the Greeks. It was true, they wrote, that the Mediterranean revolutions were liberal and subverted Christian monarchs. They were rightly being suppressed. But Stourdza wrote that "the cause of the Greeks must never be confused with that of revolutionaries in France, Italy, and Spain." The Count wrote that the Greeks had nothing to do with the "Jacobins" of Europe. The Greeks were different because they were fighting a foreign, Muslim conqueror. Christian kings were legitimate, but Muslims ruling over Christians were not. For over three hundred years the Greeks had never acceded to their conquest, they held. Not only that, but the sultan was a barbarian, served by a barbarian Muslim people. This was not a revolution at all, but a war to reclaim liberty. It was not an insurrection but a war "of a people against a people, between the Muslims and the Greeks." The Turks aimed to "exterminate" the Christians. The Greeks were merely defending their land and lives against a foreign invader.[32]

The idea that the Ottoman Christians were conquered tributaries was not entirely new: the Russian Foreign Ministry had offered up the argument in 1815, in the event that the tsar chose to intervene on behalf of the Serbs.[33] Over the decades populations of Serbs had served the Ottomans against the Austrians, the Austrians against the Ottomans, and most recently the Russians against the Ottomans. Russia had enlisted Serb warrior communities in its last war against the Ottoman Empire (1806–12) and had secured privileges for the region in one more imperial re-alignment. Like the Greeks in the same period, the Serbs chose among empires and depended on the empires to settle matters in their favor. The Serbian uprising was quashed in 1813 but Russia continued to advocate for the Serbs and secured Serbian autonomy in 1830.[34]

All of this was a familiar state of affairs whereby the empires reached agreement and the local warlords accommodated as best they could. What was new in the arguments of the Count, and what was new about the Greek uprising, was profound: it was a not an imperial conflict, and it was not one more uprising led by warlords and notables. It was a war of peoples. The Christians were Greeks and the Muslims were Turks. The 1815 memorandum had referred to Christians first and foremost, some of whom were in Serbia; in 1821 the Count and his collaborators referred to Greeks, juxtaposed to Turks. They were *nations*, totally co-herent, totally opposed to each other, and mutually exclusive. In their writings every Christian in the rebelling regions, regardless of language or even allegiance, was a Greek; every Muslim, no matter what he or she spoke, was a Turk. They had never mixed. The Greeks had never been integral imperial subjects, but tributaries to an alien sovereign. The church had ensured the continuity of the nation and it was the guardian of the Greek nation. That nation had existed through centuries of Turk-ish rule.[35]

The Count's argument about the Greeks was disingenuous. What made a Christian king any less a conqueror, his taxpayers any less his tributaries? Since when had European peoples agreed to be ruled by their absolute monarchs? The argument was also inaccurate. For three hun-dred years the Christians mixed with the Muslims in the administration at all levels and indeed made the Ottoman system work. The moneys of the Ottoman state were moved by Christians, as was the commerce. Ottoman taxes were collected by Christians. Christians and Muslims lived in the same towns and villages, they traded, they intermarried, they converted, they spoke the same languages, and they worshiped some of the same saints at the same shrines. As for the church, the hi-erarchs were creatures of the sultan who appointed them to govern the polyglot Orthodox flock, and they were also tax collectors. The patriarch hastened to excommunicate rebels, and in 1821 he did the same. The patriarch always sided with the sultan in wars against Russia, the shared Orthodox faith notwithstanding.

And the argument was brilliant. The Count pushed against the faultlines of the entire post–Vienna settlement that was founded on the legitimacy of the monarch, but also the Christianity of Europe and its peoples; that excluded the sultan from Europe and ignored the fact that his subjects were very often Christians; and that drew a boundary of Christianity along the Ionian Sea, ignoring the fact that just across that boundary the population was majority Christian. This was the time to declare that the Roumeli and the Morea were European and Christian, a region in which Muslims did not belong. It smacked of eschatology, as two forces entered into a combat to the death, in a place where only one of them could remain. It was God's revelation. Stourdza mused about the end of time.[36]

The Greeks in Russian service created a loop. The Greek and pro-Greek diplomats in St. Petersburg circulated their ideas to Russian–Greek diplomats abroad, and the latter sent the ideas back to St. Petersburg to be assimilated into the language of Russian diplomacy. Russia's consul in Turin was, of all people, Giorgio Mocenigo, the man with Zakynthian origins who had been the Count's superior during the Russian rule of the Ionian Islands. He explained to his Austrian counterpart what the Count had been writing, that the Greek war was "completely distinct from" the Italian revolutions. He then reported the exchange back to Nesselrode, Russia's co-foreign minister.[37] At the Congress of Verona in 1822 the Greek–Russian diplomats present began to refer to "Greece" in their official documents, and to a war of independence rather than a revolution.

The language was deployed most famously in Russia's ultimatum to the Ottoman government in July 1821. It was delivered by Ambassador Stroganov in Constantinople and came to naught, but it did implant a thinking that would matter later. Stroganov admitted that the sultan had the right to put down a rebellion, but the response of the Porte was violence against all Greeks and all Ottoman Christians anywhere in the empire. They were being punished as a collective. (In this there was a lot of truth: see chapter 10.) Stroganov protested that the Porte was operating on an entirely new axis: "never in Turkey has a general proscription enveloped a nation [*une nation*] in its entirety, nor delivered the Christian religion over to the most bloody outrages." And never had the sultan armed "the totality of its Muslim subjects" to attack all Christians. The sultan had created a simple binary of Greeks and Turks. As a consequence, and since Europe was Christian, the Greeks had become "a European cause." Over the months other new terms popped up in official Russian documents. The Greeks were fighting to defend their "fatherland" (*otechestvo*)—a early and rare statement that a specific land was theirs.[38] Whatever the Greeks were before 1821, the Ottoman Empire and Russia were making them into a nation—the one by victimization, the other by martyrology.

The Russian–Greek luminaries also tutored Greek revolutionaries in the languages that would elicit European sympathy. The early Greek proclamations cited liberalism and this would have to end. At that moment the powers were quashing liberal movements in the name of Christian legitimism, and the Greeks were alienating conservative opinion. Russian statesmen had written to the Count privately, saying that they would have supported the Greeks if only they had claimed to be Christians rather than liberals, martyrs rather than revolutionaries. So the Greeks of the Foreign Ministry used the network of Russo–Greek clergy like Ignatii to send urgent warnings to the rebels: under no circumstances should they style their movement a liberal one, directed against a monarch. The Friendly Society that planned the uprising should be shunned.

The Greeks should claim no fraternity with the other Mediterranean revolutions, and exiled veterans of the other Mediterranean revolutions should not be allowed to fight for Greece. (For this reason Santarosa of Piedmont served the Greeks under a pseudonym, as a private.) It should be a religious war. A Christian king ruling absolutely was benevolent; a Muslim monarch was a tyrant because he was not Christian. The rebels got the message, and what had been announced as a liberal revolution in 1821 was rechristened a religious one in 1822.[39] And soon the Revolution became the War of Independence.

Greek in Greece

People of all walks of life seized opportunities, saw others foreclosed, and made choices. We have seen this in the profiles of low- and high-born soldiers and notables, and in this regard the Count was no different. He made his way from imperial cosmopolitanism to national belonging in part because he had few remaining options.

By December 1821 the Count was no longer invited to meetings on the Ottoman crisis. He asked why and one can understand the reason. The Count led a war party in the Foreign Ministry but the tsar was not deciding on war, only on more protests. Alexander cooled on his minister and delegated the conduct of foreign policy to others who were compliant and not Greek, led by Nesselrode. Alexander came to rely on the advice of Austria's Metternich who was vehemently hostile to the Greek cause. Moreover the Count's moderate liberalism was no longer useful to an autocrat who was drifting toward religious obscurantism, Bible societies, and political reaction.[40]

The Count was still a Russian servitor but put on a leave of absence. He left Russia in spring 1822 and went to Geneva. He was well received because of his work to restore the peace and draft the Swiss constitution in 1813–14. He was not wealthy, and by the standards of an aristocrat he thought himself poor.[41] In Geneva he was sponsored by the banker Jean-Gabriel Eynard, a financier of governments who had represented Geneva at the Congress of Vienna. Eynard was a liberal of sorts who was sympathetic to the revolutions of the Mediterranean, but by 1823 these had been defeated and only Greece was still in insurrection. From that year he dedicated his talents and some of his own wealth to the Greek cause in Switzerland and France, and sent thousands of appeals to wealthy and powerful Europeans. By then Eynard was at the head of a new movement, Philhellenism (see chapter 16).

Together the Count and Eynard were careful in defining the Greek cause, since they were appealing to people from antagonistic camps in European politics. Some Philhellenes were liberals, others conservatives; some were constitutional monarchists and some were in favor of absolute monarchy; some were republicans and some were Bonapartists. But all of them were situated in a sense of Christian civilization, be it secular or religious. They found common cause in the Greek War.[42] This was a struggle of a Christian people against Muslim barbarity. It was Greek against Turk, and complexity be damned.

It was not mere tactics to dissociate the Greeks from the Italians and Spaniards; it reflected a real difference that made the similarities between the different revolutions superficial. To be sure, in Spain and Italy the revolutionaries issued constitutions and proclamations that gave rights and citizenship to the Catholics, just as the Greeks favored the Christian Orthodox. But Italy and Spain were already overwhelmingly Catholic, and to declare the Catholics sovereign and free was to give rights to almost everyone. In Roumeli and the Morea, proclaiming a land of Christians was to overthrow the demographic status quo because so many inhabitants were Muslims, some also Jews.[43] Such a Greece would not confirm the demographic reality; it had to be created by removing the Muslims, one way or the other.

This implication was contained in a map produced in Geneva by the Count and his aide Moustoxidis. Mapmaking could be dangerous, as "Riga the mapmaker" demonstrated with his execution (see chapter 6). But Righas's map had included all the peoples of the Ottoman Balkans. The Count and Moustoxidis produced a map that showed only Greeks (Christians), the majority, and Turks (Muslims). The map showed Greece as geometric regions, which made the underlying argument neat and rational. Captions showed the populations of each region and the total: 886,000 Turks and 2,910,000 Greeks. One can take the numbers lightly, and set aside the fact that very many of those counted spoke neither Greek nor Turkish. It is perhaps the first example of a map that represented the Balkans as demographic nations. All Muslims were a Turkish people, all Christians a Greek people. With its geometric and symmetrical form and simple arithmetic, it was a masterful exercise in simplification, representing conclusions as obvious. It was a binary conflict in which the Greeks had the greater claim to the land because they outnumbered the Turks.[44] Today this approach is a geopolitical commonplace, though no less contentious. At the time it was revolutionary. The Count described it as "geographical observations." It was wholesale demographic reordering.

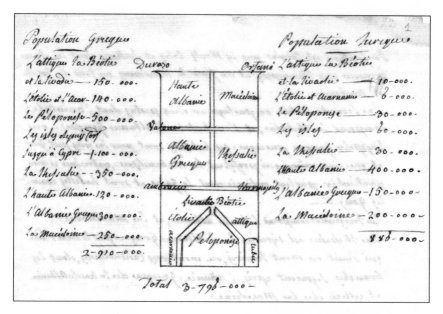

FIGURE 7.1. Map of the Morea, Roumeli, and Islands from "Observations géographiques" (Geographic Observations), a collaboration of Ioannis Kapodistrias and Andreas Moustoxidis, 1824. Benaki Museum, Historical Archive, Kapodistrias Collection, box 41, doc. 23, p. 23. *This is the first known map of the southern Balkans to organize territory by nations, Greeks and Turks. Note the rational, geometric formation of regions which implied self-evident simplicity.*

The Count had more freedom and fewer options. He could not go home to Corfu. There the British rulers saw him as a subversive, part of an imagined Russian party bent on undermining British rule. British authorities believed that he was somehow behind the 1821 uprisings.[45] Tsar Alexander I, who was still nominally his master, wished he would stay away from Corfu, lest his presence in the region cause alarm among the powers. The next tsar, Nicholas, wished him to stay away from Russia as well, lest his presence be seen as a support for a war party. All the other powers continued to assume that he was a Russian agent.

The Count hoped he would be reappointed to his old post, but his situation of being neither in active service, nor released from his obligation to the tsar, was untenable; he was neither fully Greek nor fully Russian. In December 1826 he traveled to St. Petersburg for the last time and delivered to the new tsar his report—in effect an account of his life—in the hope of being reinstated. Nothing came of it so he asked to be released from Russian service. In June 1827 Nicholas I agreed.[46]

Just then the Count had an entirely new option. While visiting St. Petersburg he learned that he was being offered the governorship of Greece by one of the Greek national assemblies. He was to be a governor (*kyvernitis*), almost a president, but not quite, since it was not clear if his office was meant to be the transition to a monarchy. The leaders of the Greek revolutionaries were warring among themselves again and they landed on his name as a compromise: he was a Greek who was an outsider to Greek politics, who in fact had never stepped foot on the Ottoman mainland. He was not aligned with any of the Greek factions. The Greeks valued his social station: he had an aristocratic title and he had some clout in Europe, and perhaps (the myth never went away) he represented Russia. Eynard promoted his candidacy across Europe precisely because he was not a Greek but a "foreigner" and could be better trusted.[47]

The Count would only accept the governorship if he had the support of the European powers, and by then the European powers had warmed to the Greek cause and soured on the sultan (see chapter 16). Suffice it to say here that change was initiated by the new tsar Nicholas I, who had enough of being held back by the European consensus, and drew France and Britain into an alliance in support of the Greeks. It marked the end of the Holy Alliance and the Congress System. Austria with its vehement opposition to any national movement was left isolated. Greek independence was sealed by one more Russo-Ottoman War. The Treaty of Adrianople of 1829 mainly concerned the Danubian Principalities, the Caucasus, and Black Sea navigation, but it also required the sultan to accept his loss of Greece. In 1830 the London Protocol finalized the matter: Greece would be an independent state.[48]

The Count's arguments about the exceptionalism of the Greeks gave them cover. The Greeks were waging war, not revolution. They also accepted the Count as governor, though with reservations: he was an aristocrat and a statesman with whom they could communicate (culturally and in French), but the British and the French still suspected that he was a Russian agent.[49] Ever since the French had been evicted from the

Ionian Islands in 1798–9, French officials were certain he was a Franco-phobe. Talleyrand had called him "the most malicious of men, distin-guished by hatred against France."[50] Indeed the Russian foreign minister, Nesselrode, looked forward to ongoing *"intimate"* (his emphasis) rela-tions, and expected him to do Russia's bidding.[51] But the Count by now saw himself as a Greek. Russia was one of the foreign powers. He ac-cepted support wherever he found it.

Eynard arranged his passage from Italy.[52] Arriving in what was becom-ing Greece, he traveled on French, British, and Russian warships. His new country's dependence on Europe was clear. This was not something that was forced upon him: he was an aristocrat and he believed that the future of the Greeks lay with the European courts, and that only the courts could decree a new state. Certainly the Greeks could not go it alone. When he arrived in Nafplio, which was the provisional capital in early 1828, two warlords were bombarding each other. The government, such as it was, had been evacuated. There was no revenue to speak of and he depended on subsidies and loans. Russia gave him small handouts to cover his expenses and some impressive grants—2 million francs here, 200,000 rubles in gifts from the empress, and then a monthly stipend of 300,000 francs. More came from the other powers and Eynard.[53]

The Count, now Ioannis Kapodistrias, was experienced with Europe but not with Greece. In Greece he spent much of his time doing what was expected: scribbling notes to the foreign powers, still in French and Italian, and advocating for his new fatherland despite his compatriots. Real power still formed around the warring clans which he bypassed as unbecoming of a state. To the notables and warlords he used Greek, a simple and colloquial one that added crudeness to the contempt he expressed: they were "dogs," useful to "wipe up the filth," "the ruin of Greece," and poorly dressed.[54] If he was popular among the villagers whom he genuinely wished to help with land grants, he had no direct links with them and was not one to mobilize them. He was still the aristocrat, in a land without an aristocracy.

He lasted as president for almost four years before he was murdered. The reason had to do with his understanding of government and rule. The qualities he brought to the Morea included a liberal, aristocratic, and Russian penchant for supreme and centralized rule that treated the masses benevolently but did not ask their opinion. He distrusted the intermediary strata of notables and merchants who interfered with his mission and were the antithesis of good and systematic government. Like the Russian nobility, they were meant to be conduits, not obstacles. He surrounded himself with outsiders, many from the Ionian Islands and Russia. He proposed land redistributions which would make citizen–farmers of the peasantry but also circumvented the regional notables who had their eyes on the same lands.[55]

With independence at hand, this violent agglomeration of peasants, warlords, and notables were still fighting over the charred remains of the Morea. They needed a firm hand. He had operated this way on the Ionian Islands under Russian occupation, but in the Morea he did not have a Russian army and he did not have an aristocracy to lean on. He would have been the greatest of leaders, quipped a visiting European, if only he had an army, but since he did not he was a tyrant.[56] Aegean Islanders were in open rebellion against his government and forming a separate administration. Members of the Maniot Mavromichalis clan killed the Count in Nafplio in October 1831. It was Sunday and the Count was on his way to the Church of St. Spyridon, the patron saint of Corfu. Some of his compatriots expressed sympathy. Korais thought that he deserved it.

The final evolution of the Count tells us how the Greek Revolution was accepted internationally, sincerely by multitudes of Philhellenes, and as cover for geopolitics by statesmen. Diplomatically, it came down to one proposition that until then had not been obvious: Christians were Greeks, Greece was European; the Turks were neither Christian, nor European. This settled at long last the old question: Who are the Greeks? Soon there would be a border and a map, which for the time being would settle the other old question: Where is Greece?

A New Paradigm

Greece was meant to be an exception, a unique solution to a regional crisis. The powers cited universal principles of humanitarian intervention, the rights of religions, and the campaign against slavery, but applied them in such a way as to pertain to Greece only.[57] The Count had insisted that it was the exception, but then again all nationalists think that their nations are exceptional. The sponsoring powers also insisted that the peculiar combination of Muslim rule over Christian peoples made the case for the Greeks exceptional. But the Belgians were also exceptional when the powers in that same year, 1830, bowed to revolutionaries to create a Catholic Belgium out of provinces of the majority-Protestant Netherlands. France was exceptional when Charles X was overthrown just days after agreeing to full independence for Greece, and the powers acceded to the July Revolution to allow France to become a more expansive constitutional monarchy under a new dynasty.

The Greek king would be king of Greece, not the Greeks, a way to insist that he did not rest on the Greeks for legitimacy. But the powers had used the principle of popular mobilization to decide the borders of the Greek state: it would be the territories that had risen up against the sultan in a sustained way. For all their insistence that the Greek state was a decision of the powers, and that sovereignty rested with a monarch, their decisions kept returning to some sort of recognition of popular sovereignty and the nation under arms. The united front against popular sovereignty cracked when Louis Philippe became king of the French, and Leopold became the king of the Belgians. Later the powers would yield to allow a king of the Greeks as well.

In the Balkans the exceptions multiplied because the whole region had Christian majorities under Ottoman rule, and the exceptions became a pattern. Over the next century of war and mass uprisings, the Balkans were simplified into countries of absolute belonging, of unities that created outsiders and absolute enemies. The new lines of unity and exclusion continued to be confessional. The Balkans became less Islamic by the decade.

Greece, it turned out, was the rule.

Chapter 8

The Greek Merchant Conquers, and Becomes Greek

The Russian Origins of the Greek Revolution

Prologue

I MEET MY colleague in his living room in an affluent part of Athens in 2017, the so-called Northern Suburbs that are a market for Lacoste, Ray Ban, and BMW. They give the country many of its governments. These neighborhoods tend toward a quiet, confident patriotism.

We are picking each other's brains. He is deep into research about his ancestors and plans to write a book about them, as people of a certain age will do. They migrated to Odesa, where they helped build the new city on the Black Sea. We speak of men like his ancestors who carried wheat from Russia to the cities, ports, navies, and armies of the Mediterranean. The Napoleonic Wars had created a boom, but the wars ended in 1815. We then jump to 1821 and the outbreak of the Greek Revolution, a plot hatched in that same city of Odesa.

"I wonder what happened from 1815 to 1821," I muse. "The Revolution seems to have come from nowhere." These were prosperous subjects of the empires, and in Russia they were privileged. Quite suddenly they took up arms and demanded a nation.

My host looks at me with annoyance tempered by pity. "We were waiting for '21."

In Greece 1821 is a thing, like 1776 in the USA and 1789 in France. We are lending a year a predictability, as if someone in 1815 knew what would happen in 1821. One could wait for it to arrive, like a train arriving on time—except that the schedule was drafted after the train had pulled into the station. I notice the collective "we," as if we are on a temporal continuum and we were also there in '21. I have heard it so many times before. "We took Monemvasia in '21." "We fought the Turks at Lala."

On one matter my host and I agree: the answer lies in Russia.

The Greek Merchant Conquers[1]

The history of Greek nationalism is the history of trade. Prosperous merchants across the Mediterranean financed a boom in Greek learning. Networks of merchants were also networks of nationalists carrying books, pamphlets, and ideas. Some of them carried a revolution. If one were to put a date to the blossoming of Greek nationalism, it would be 1800–21, when Greek merchants combined wealth, ideas, and conspiracy that took form in Russia. The new national creed was loaded onto ships and exported to the Balkans. Such nationalists placed themselves on a timeline that stretched to Classical times and Byzantium, and yet the idea of a Greek nation was quite new. It all happened quite suddenly.

In the Balkans in the eighteenth century Greek dominance of overland trade was a fact, but the coherence of the Greeks as an ethnic group was new and evolving. In large part "Greek" designated a profession. From the Danubian region to Egypt, Romios and Rum in any language could mean "merchant," as did Gòrög in Magyar. By "Greek," contemporaries meant the Orthodox Christian who spoke Romaic Greek in commerce; it was not what today would be called a nationality. People who spoke Vlach, Albanian, and Roma at home spoke Greek in their businesses, and they were all Orthodox.[2] Muslims spoke it as well. In Yanena it was the main language of public life, administration, and learning. Ali pasha used Greek to correspond with his children, his servitors, and his slaves.

On the sea, people called Greeks had sailed the Mediterranean for millennia, and in early modern times had followed the path of Spanish conquest to reach the new world. Through Spain groups of Greeks joined Pizzaro in the conquest of Peru and promptly mutinied. Others settled towns in Florida.[3] The Spanish called any foreigner on a ship a griego, mutated into the slang for anyone speaking gibberish, and finally any foreigner at all: a gringo, a variation on "all Greek to me."[4] Greeks accustomed to calling foreigners barbarians—the speakers of bar-bar—got their comeuppance.

The outright dominance of Mediterranean trade by Greeks was a phe-nomenon that began around the mid-eighteenth century and was ac-complished by around 1800.[5] It was the product of two geopolitical shifts: the decline of maritime France and the rise of Russia in the Black Sea. The Seven Years' War ended in 1763 in a resounding French defeat and it occasioned a larger decline in French naval and merchant power. Until then French agents and ships were to be found in even small Medi-terranean ports. By way of example, French merchant houses had agents in the Morea's ports of Nafplio, Koroni, and Methoni. In Kalamata they exported silk. French merchants married into Morean notable families such as the Sisinis and the Notaras. From 1763 France was on the retreat and in the 1790s the shipping of revolutionary France was chased out of the eastern Mediterranean after defeats in Egypt, the Ionian Islands, and Malta. Venice, another maritime power, collapsed in 1797.[6]

The merchants who dominated the Balkans spilled into the sea in the wake of the retreating French. They were helped along by Russia which entered the Mediterranean just as France was leaving. In 1768, a mere five years after the end of the Seven Years' War, Russia went to war with the Ottoman Porte. The Treaty of Küçük-Kaynarca of 1774, as well as subse-quent wars, clarifications, and treaties, gave Russia the right to navigate the Black Sea and pass through the Bosphorus and Dardanelles Straits into the Mediterranean. In those same wars Russia conquered the north-ern coasts of the Black Sea from the Ottoman Empire. Russia annexed territories from Bessarabia and Moldova to the Trans-Caucasus.

The Russian conquest of the Black Sea coast set the scene for a boom in the export of wheat. In the beginning Danubian wheat was carried to Russia's new ports to the east, of which Odesa (now in Ukraine) was the most important. By 1800 the wheat came from the Russian hinterlands, by land and by river, from existing grain-producing regions and from the vast expanses that were now named New Russia. From the new ports the merchants shipped the wheat to European regions that were not producing enough of their own: Britain chronically, France regularly, and Italy intermittently. Soon Russia was supplying the Ottoman capital Constantinople with wheat grown on lands that had recently been Ottoman, sent from coasts that had also been Ottoman, and carried by merchants who had been or still were Ottoman subjects.

Russia had little experience in Mediterranean trade, and the wheat was carried mainly by ships owned by Ottoman Christians. Along with wheat the ships carried animal fats that lubricated English machinery, oil that lit up English streets, tallow soap for English workers, and wool for English weavers.[7] One merchant invented the process for transporting caviar as we know it, though this was a side-business. Yannis Varvakis was a merchant from the Aegean island of Psara who served Russia in the war of 1768–74 and settled in Astrakhan as Ivan Andreevich Varvatsi. He invented a technique for transporting Astrakhan sturgeons' eggs in order to satisfy the Orthodox Balkan demand for crushed fish roe (*tarama*) during the religious fasts. Later he fed the aristocratic hunger for clumps of whole fish eggs on bread.

This upward trend in trade contained spikes and booms. During the Napoleonic Wars the warring powers sought grain for their armies and navies and for the territories they controlled, and Russia had surpluses to sell. Blockades and counterblockades cut off supplies in a given region and the new supplies were from Russia.[8] A volcano in Asia in 1815 affected the European climate into 1820 and depressed northern and western European production, though no one at the time made the connection.[9] The threat of famine was met with more supplies from Russia.

There were busts, too. The peace of 1815 ended wartime demand and a localized crisis reverberated through the sectors that had supplied the armies and navies. Protectionism in Britain (the Corn Laws) and France from 1815 disrupted demand. But wheat exports continued and Russia set a new record in 1816 and 1817.[10] The upward secular trend—the long-term trajectory rather than the year-on-year change—was unmistakable and it would continue into mid-century. New port cities boomed.

FIGURE 8.1. The World of Greek Trade and Mobility around 1800. Credit to Rob McCalebb.

Odesa was founded in 1792 and by 1813 had a population of 35,000. About a thousand carts laden with wheat arrived per day. In 1796 the port welcomed sixty ships, and in 1805 over a thousand.[11]

The ships that carried these goods were owned and manned by Ottoman Christians, and these Christians settled the new towns which became their bases of operations. The first wave of settlement started after the war of 1768–74. These were veterans who had served Russia, and by treaty they were allowed to return to the Ottoman Empire or resettle in Russia. The shrewd ones did both and became merchants in both empires. Veterans were settled in new towns as military colonists with tax privileges, with the requirement to serve in times of war. Kherson was built in 1778 under the command of I. A. Gannibal, Pushkin's great-uncle who had commanded Moreans during Russia's expedition in 1770; he brought Morean veterans as settlers. Thousands followed in the 1790s as they sought opportunity, fled regional wars, and escaped harvest failures.[12]

Merchants came from islands like Spetses, Hydra, and Psara. These islands were strategically situated on the routes that brought Russian wheat out of the Black Sea and into the Mediterranean. Even when they were based on their home islands, they could fly the Russian flag and carry goods in and out of the Black Sea. The merchant Benaki made his money selling the patents to fly the Russian flag to newcomers in Odesa. Ottoman Christian ships were known to fly flags from a good dozen European states and statelets, but most often they alternated between the Russian and the Ottoman flags. If Russia enforced its right to navigate the Straits linking the Black and Mediterranean seas, the sailors might choose the Russian flag and benefit from Russian protection. If another war led the sultan to close the Straits, they might fly the Ottoman flag as subjects of the sultan and freely navigate Ottoman waters.[13]

Ionian Islanders entered the trade as well, under a succession of flags representing the powers that ruled them: Venetian, French, Septinsular (under Russian protection), Russian, and British. And as always they were also bootleggers who supplied all sides of the Napoleonic Wars. The British Corn Laws of 1815 banned grain imports from outside the empire, so Black Sea grain was carried to Zakynthos. Officially Zakynthos was importing more wheat per capita than a Zakynthian could possibly consume and live to tell of it. But Zakynthos was now a British protectorate and the wheat was sent onward to British territories as far as London under the British flag.

Ottoman shipping, Russian shipping, and British shipping were very often Orthodox shipping, or in the shorthand that most Europeans used, it was Greek shipping. And as Greeks these diverse merchants formed transimperial networks that began in Russia's new Black Sea ports and spread wheat, money, kin, and clerks across the Mediterranean and beyond. From Russia, Greek agents set up offices in ports from Alexandria to Marseille to Gibraltar, and the Greek community in Austrian Trieste expanded. Large and wealthy Greek communities were formed in strategic markets such as London and in entrepots and banking centers such as Livorno. The merchants added to the already large Greek communities of Izmir and Constantinople.[14]

The ships also carried books and ideas from colony to colony. The Boubas brothers of Russia traded in red cotton thread from Marseille, clothing, Russian fish, and Greek books. The start of the nineteenth century was a boom in Greek printing of books, pamphlets, and journals, some driven by a market of affluent readers and some financed by wealthy merchants around the Mediterranean.[15] Indeed this new learning was mainly a phenomenon of the settlements outside the Balkan peninsula. People leaving their homelands can be more patriotic than those who stay behind. The journals in Greek that flourished in the period 1800–20 had readers who lived overwhelmingly in these colonies; only seven in a hundred subscribers lived in what would become Greece. The Greek texts were almost entirely funded by the overseas Greeks and printed in one or another merchant colony in Europe.[16]

The merchants democratized an educational tradition that had been limited to the literate few. For some time Orthodox clergy and literati had been gathering and printing texts in Greek and translating contemporary works from other European languages. This phenomenon has since been termed a Neohellenic Enlightenment, an exploration of theology and religion as they applied to the secular world. Some of this had a Russian dimension, what has been called an Orthodox Enlightenment, under Russian auspices, which linked theology with contemporary problems of government, sovereignty, and science. Often such literature asked what it meant to be an Orthodox subject in a world of empires that lacked any place called Greece. Their answers very often led them to the tsar, their patron and protector. The Ionian clerics Voulgaris and Theotokis who went to Russia, and later men like Bishop Ignatii and Stourdza, are examples.[17]

These same tendencies were harnessed to the needs and interests of the rising merchantry, increasingly literate and functioning largely in Greek, and catering to a growing lay readership. They were part of the movement from esoteric philosophical texts printed in ancient or ecclesiastical Greek that few could understand, to publications using the vernaculars of the time.[18] Many of the wealthy merchants who financed these works were, again, people originating in the Balkans who spoke Albanian, Vlach, Serbian, and Bulgarian but were Greeks in public speech and education. The new schools taught bookkeeping and also Greek culture.[19]

And soon, certainly by the turn of the century, they showed an interest in the *genos*. The term had been around for some time but now spread to ever growing strata of merchants speaking and writing in Greek along the trade routes they traveled, which is to say all the Mediterranean. Genos may be mistranslated as race. More accurately it implied a shared heritage, expandable and open to newcomers who shared in the faith and acquired the language. It implied a community of the Orthodox Greeks anywhere, speaking Greek in commerce, at church, and perhaps at home, and claiming a continuous heritage stretching back to Classical times and Byzantium.[20]

Perraivos, the comrade of Righas Velestinlis whom we saw on Lefkada in 1807, was an example of this movement of people, goods, and ideas and their merger in to a new understanding of Greekness, this one also armed. He was a Roumeliot and a radical nationalist and republican. He had good relations with Muslim and Christian dignitaries in the Danubian region and did well as a merchant. In the Balkans in the 1790s, Perraivos awaited merchants who brought him the latest books and pamphlets. He fell in with the revolutionary Righas whose main activity, and the crime that got him executed, was publishing pamphlets and maps. He fled to Corfu under French republican occupation and managed the printing press that issued revolutionary proclamations. When the Russians came, he taught at the new schools opened under Russian patronage and overseen by Count Capo d'Istria, and merchants brought him the books. In 1817 we find him in St. Petersburg petitioning on behalf of his comrades to emigrate to south Russia, and he himself relocated to Odesa. It was where the money was. He brought with him his books and joined in the conspiracy that would launch the Greek Revolution, the Friendly Society. In 1821 he was in Epirus and the Morea to prepare for the uprising. His biography combined arms, trade, and learning into a composite picture of a Greek nationalist.[21]

Women too, by now well educated, many of them in Italy, engaged in the translation of literary works into Greek, and contributed to the larger library of modern Greek. They helped build a transimperial community of—the terms still varied—Romans, Graiki, or whatever the equivalent in the local language. With a Classical heritage revived, they also adopted the ancient term Ellinas (Hellene) to describe the modern Greeks. Such writers showed sympathy for the Greeks under Ottoman rule and drew on the Enlightenment to argue for their liberation. As a rule, liberty did not mean independence, but delivery from a tyrant into the hands of a Christian enlightened absolutist. Monarchy and empire were still the obvious forms of polity.[22] In some cases the European cultural scene of letters and enlightenment did translate into revolution: the wealthy and aristocratic Manto Mavrogenous of Trieste outfitted and commanded quite a few soldiers and warships in the 1820s, in support of the Greek Revolution.

Greekness consolidated in these places. In their homelands they spoke a variety of languages and dialects. They might look askance at the Romios or Graikos who lived nearby. The Moreans looked across at Zakynthos and saw a foreign place dominated by the Franks (Catholics or broadly western Europeans). Wrote Kolokotronis, "They thought of Zakynthos as we think of the farthest place in the world . . . America seems to us as they saw Zakynthos, they said it was in Frankia." The Zakynthians returned the favor: seasonal workers brought to pick the grapes got off the sloops in the Morea and spat on the ground: "Cursed exile!" (*Katarameni xenitia*).[23] Kolokotronis, meanwhile, referred to the Aegean Archipelago as the *Levante*.[24]

For Kolokotronis something changed when he settled down in Zakynthos, now as a trader and shopkeeper. He probably learned to read here. He was reading new kinds of texts addressing the world around him, not long-dead ancients and not the afterlife. In the Morea priests only knew and spoke of the scriptures, and they used a language that was incomprehensible to laymen. "It was not until I went to Zakynthos that I found the History of Greece in simple Greek." He was reading the books being financed and circulated by that wave of up-and-coming and affluent merchants.

He continued: "The French Revolution and Napoleon, in my opinion, opened people's eyes. Before there was no knowledge of nations, they thought kings were gods on earth, and they thought that anything they did was good." Kolokotronis had discovered popular sovereignty, and this would give direction to a man of violence whose understanding of politics had gone little beyond clan, region, and empires. His violence in future would be national. It did not make him a republican or a democrat per se—he was neither—and sovereignty need not lead to elections and constitutions. But it did lead him to consider a new kind of warfare, mass mobilization, or what the French called the *levée en masse*. The nation would exist insofar as it was on the march.[25]

Something similar was at work in the wider extent of the Mediterranean, in the countless merchant settlements that stretched from the Russian coast of the Black Sea to Italy and Egypt and as far away as London. In the merchant outposts both the Zakynthian and the Morean were Greeks living in a Greek quarter, attending the same church, and sending their children to the same schools to learn the same dialect and history from the same books. They learned of religion but now also of the genos. This was a new way to be Greek that went beyond trade and prayer.

The six brothers Zosimas are emblematic of these Greeks in a number of ways. They came from Yanena in the Ottoman Balkans where their father had already been a merchant in the mid-eighteenth century. Two brothers set up shop in Nizhyn (today in Ukraine) a year after the Black Sea trade routes were opened by the Treaty of Küçük-Kaynarca in 1774. Two other brothers established themselves in Livorno. Their exceptional wealth owed to Russian wheat, and Russian wheat financed a Greek cultural boom. They financed schools, libraries, and orphanages for Greeks in the Ottoman Empire and Russia. Theaters performing in Greek and promoting the idea of a modern Greekness popped up in Odesa. And they financed books, among them the multi-volume series Hellenic Library edited by Adamantios Korais, beginning in 1806. The books were distributed to shops in Livorno, Venice, Trieste, and Vienna.[26] Quite a few figures associated with Greek nationalism or revolution of one sort or another were the product of these merchant

circles. Korais himself was a merchant from Chios and Izmir who settled in Paris, and Righas was a Roumelian merchant and commercial
facilitator.

The coherence of the Greeks was reinforced by the fact that in most
places, from Italy westward, they were a small minority of outsiders. The
confessional markers still mattered and the Greeks were eastern Christians surrounded by majorities of Franks—Catholics and Protestants.
The markers Greek, grec, greco, and grek placed them lower on the social
hierarchies, or in separate categories living in their own quarters. That
they were merchants placed them below the nobility. They were on a
level with the Jews and Armenians with whom they competed. They did
well if one measures success in silver and gold, but these were regimes
where status could count for more. Greek aristocrats in the empires, and
not the Greek merchants, had the exalted status. Then again, the merchants had something that aristocrats did not: while men like Capo
d'Istria contemplated their Greekness in French, Italian, and Russian, the
merchants actually spoke and read the Greek vernacular.

Greek in Russia[27]

Being a grek in Russia was different, and cities like Odesa, Kherson, and
Taganrog were not just more colonies among others. Here they were
the exceptionally privileged Orthodox subjects of an Orthodox monarch. They were not questionable Christians as they were in the west,
but members of the dominant and predominant religion of the Russian
Empire. They were not quasi-Orientals as they remained in much of
Europe, with the stigma of the Levant and the Great Schism. In the
north they were the original Orthodox Christians. Very many were well
off and some were fabulously wealthy.

The Greeks in Russia were part of a wave of colonizers recruited to
populate Russia's Black Sea coast. Most of the new territories were
dubbed New Russia, and they had a thin population made thinner by
the flight of many Ottoman subjects. To Catherine the Great and her
advisors, this land needed people. Land would be made valuable by
settlers who engaged in what Catherine and her advisors considered

to be productive labor, and at first they did not mean merchants. They meant farmers, shepherds, and artisans. In the 1760s Catherine's governors drew up plans to attract settlers from abroad and provide them with subsidies, land grants, and tax privileges. The Russians were not particular. Recruiters were sent out with pamphlets in German, Italian, Serbian, Romaic Greek, and Romanian, to places from Sweden to Persia.[28]

The region acquired a multiconfessional and polyglot population. The majority of the new settlers were Ukrainian and Russian peasants, but their numbers and occupations were depressed by limits on peasant mobility. Half of the peasantry in European Russia were serfs tied to their masters, the other half state peasants tied to the land. Abroad Russia sought anyone who could settle the land and introduce new techniques in husbandry, farming, and small manufacturing, and anyone who might pick up a gun or sword in times of war or at least stay neutral. Early waves came from what are today Romania, Moldova, Serbia, Montenegro, Bulgaria, and Greece. Later waves included Mennonites, Prussians, Swedes, Swiss, Neapolitans, Corsicans, Britons, Polish Catholics, and Polish Jews. They all were given privileges unknown to Russian peasants: large farms, freedom from taxes, freedom of movement, and stipends.[29]

For some the land was a source of income and speculation. An allotment of at least 30 hectares was more than a Russian peasant could ever expect and it was a lot for Balkan settlers who had farmed small parcels and marginal lands, in places known to produce only "people and rocks." (The specific reference is to Hydra.) The parcels could be a few hundred hectares if the settler recruited other settlers. Of course there was corruption. Captain Gorakopulo came to Kherson with colonists but not enough of them, so he invented many more in order to increase his land grant and status. The scheme was the inspiration for Nikolai Gogol's *Dead Souls*, about a merchant who trafficked in people who do not exist. Gogol's merchant smacked of unscrupulousness and he in turn was modeled on the merchant Bernadaki, a Greek born in Taganrog in 1799 who became wealthy in the vodka business. He later funded the Greek community of St. Petersburg around Greek Avenue, Greek Gardens, and Greek Square, all centered on the Church of St. Dimitrios (now the October Concert Hall). Later he funded the University of Athens, and insisted it maintain the name of the most illustrious Russian Greek. Hence its formal name, National and Capodistrian University.[30]

As wheat exports boomed, settlers moved into trade and more merchants arrived from the Aegean and Ionian regions. They were given their own administrations and a few towns were founded by Greeks exclusively. The model of Greek self-government was Nizhyn. Ottoman Orthodox merchants had been granted privileges under the Hetmanate of Bohdan Khmel'nyts'kiy in the seventeenth century, and under Russia in the eighteenth these privileges were renewed.[31] Nizhyn was strategic because it was on the frontier with Poland and the Ottoman Empire. Russia used these merchants to do what the Russians did not do themselves: carry goods on a north–south axis, through territories that the Russians knew less, using languages that the Russians did not know at all.

The town merchant guild, the Rum Brotherhood, doubled as a town administration. They were granted land, subsidies, tax exemption, exemption from military service, and their own church and schools. From Nizhyn they could move about the empire unmolested and often duty-free.[32] Today Nizhyn is adorned with monuments to its luminaries, such as the Zosimas brothers. And to cucumbers: from the eighteenth century Greek merchants perfected and exported a famous variety of pickle, and it is a major export of Nizhyn today.

As the frontier moved southward to the Black Sea, Nizhyn became a hinterland but maintained its privileges. Newcomers from the Ottoman Empire paid to join the Rum Brotherhood of Nizhyn with privileges and trade permissions which they carried anywhere in the empire. From Nizhyn Greek merchants took up residence in places like Moscow (again Zosimas), St. Petersburg (Bernadaki), and, from the 1790s, the new cities of Odesa, Taganrog, Ekaterinoslav, Kerch', Enikal, and Kherson, as well as Mediterranean ports like Livorno (Zosimas once again). The Melas family used its base in Nizhyn to send scores of family members to St. Petersburg, Odesa, Taganrog, and Constantinople. Emmanouil Xanthos, who was one of the founders of the

FIGURE 8.2. Monument to the Nizhyn Cucumber. Photograph by Valerii Ded. Wikimedia Commons / Panoramio / CC-BY-3.0 DEED. *Greek merchants in the eighteenth century exported the pickles around the Mediterranean and eastern Europe, in barrels. Pickles continue to be a major export of the city. This monument is in front of the pickling plant of Nizhyn.*

Friendly Society that launched the Greek Revolution, was a merchant registered in Nizhyn.[33]

In Taganrog too, town government was Greek government, and the town had a Greek church and a Greek commercial school. In Mariupol' all men who were Greek could vote in elections for the town magistrate. Russia expected the town and its twenty-two surrounding villages to develop agriculture and husbandry and they did: in 1824 a census counted 31,000 horses, 116,000 cattle, 268,000 sheep, and 27,000 Greeks. Others were brought to the region to grow crops and soon wheat predominated. Settlers from the Balkans brought the main export variety, Arnautka

FIGURE 8.3. Tomb in Nizhyn Cemetery: "Nikolai Pavlovich Zosima, Greek Nobleman and Cavalier of the Commanding Order of the Savior." Photograph by Natalia Dmitrenko of the Nezhyn Spaskiy Regional Museum, 2023. *Nikolai Pavlovich was one of six brothers who purchased their merchant statuses in Nizhyn through the Greek Brotherhood that administered the city. From there they established agencies across Russia and the Mediterranean, including the banking center of Livorno. Their fabulous wealth financed Greek institutions and publishing, most famously Korais's Hellenic Library series.*

(from the Turkish word for Albanian). Viniculture in the Crimea took off with the import of the Corinthian grape, here called Kokur (from Korkiry, meaning Kerkyra: the Greek name for Corfu).[34]

Numerically speaking the Greeks were a small minority in most towns, and claims that the wave of Greek migrants numbered 250,000 are vastly exaggerated, no matter how expansive one's definition of

Greek. In Rostov or Nikolaev where they were the first arrivals and then overwhelmed by many others. Still they were given their own quarters and their own sub-administrations, and in Odesa and Elizavetgrad (Yelysavethrad) they modeled their communities on the Nizhyn Brotherhood.[35] Surely this heightened their sense of coherence but such privileges were given to other communities as well.

That the Greeks were convinced of their own exceptionalism has to do with their domination of trade and the unusual wealth that some of them accumulated.[36] In Odesa the Greeks comprised as little as 5 percent of the total population in 1817, depending on who was counting and how; other estimates seemingly included all Ottoman Christians and estimated that they comprised a third. Be that as it may, their numbers mattered more if they are viewed as merchants and guild members (34 percent of the total in Odesa), and even more if one counts the value of the capital they declared as members of the merchant guilds (62 percent of the total capital).

Most telling of all was their hold on imports and exports. In Taganrog in 1783, Greeks carried 64 percent of all trade; in Odesa in 1810, they carried 90 percent. In Odesa some Greeks did spectacularly well and they moved into finance: they were among the founders of insurance companies and quite a few banks across the Russian Empire.[37] If one considers that ships and merchants labeled Russian were very often Greek (Ottoman Christian and Ionian); that the same was true of most of the merchants designated Ottoman; that the same was true of British shipping which was often Cephalonian and Zakynthian; and that Greeks entered the ports under a dozen or so flags, then one appreciates that the shipping of the region was, in ethnic terms, Greek.

The Greeks Become Greek in Russia

Russian wheat made the Greeks rich, and it also made the Greeks Greek.

The ethnic label was being employed more readily in Russian practice, and adopted by the Orthodox merchants themselves. In the early days of settlement, around the time of the war of 1768–74, not many of the settlers were labeled Greek. Rather than ethnicities, the Russian authorities counted religions, and all the Ottoman Christian settlers fell under the category of "foreign co-religionists" and people of "the Greek faith." The merchant guild of Nizhyn was named the Rum Brotherhood, i.e., Ottoman Orthodox. The Russians sometimes named them for their territories of origin. By that measure the largest groups were Montenegrins, Bulgarians, Vlachs, and Moldovans who had fought for Russia in the many regional wars and arrived in Russia over land. Serbs who had changed their allegiances from the Porte to Austria now offered their services to the tsar. They founded New Serbia on the frontier with Poland. What they spoke is anyone's guess, since again the term referred to their geographic origins. By one count most of the Serbs spoke Moldovan, many Wallachians spoke Serbian, and many Greeks spoke Albanian and Bulgarian.[38]

Different Balkan Orthodox settlers came by sea and they were sometimes called Greeks, sometimes Albanians, and sometimes Vlachs, Serbs, and Bulgarians. These were the merchant warriors from the Aegean Sea and Roumeli who had fought on the Russian side in the various Ottoman wars. They were often given the blanket name "Albanian" because they did speak Albanian and called themselves Albanian or *Arnaut* (the Turkish word for Albanian). Some were formed into the Albanian Force (*Arnautskoe voisko*) and used to guard the new frontier.

As more Balkan Christians arrived, they brought with them the commonplace of their region, which is that any Christian engaged in commerce used Greek and was referred to as Greek. The very people the Russians had called Albanians so recently were now called Greeks. The Albanian Force morphed into the Greek Infantry Division. Vlachs came from the Balkan mainland as Rum and in Russia became Greeks. Shipowners from the Ionian Islands who had been classified as Venetian and later British were increasingly merged into the Greeks as well. Aegean Islanders who spoke Albanian more readily than Greek joined the Greeks. By the nineteenth century there was scarcely a mention of Albanians and Arnauts.[39] In Odesa Greeks were organized into the Greek Magistracy and it included people who spoke Bulgarian and Serbian.[40]

Nizhyn was again a precedent for this merger into Greek. Ukrainians and Russians had long considered Nizhyn to be the definitive Greek city, but fundamentally it was a legal term for a merchant registered in the merchant Brotherhood. It was also confessional, which is why it was first named the Rum (Ottoman Orthodox) Brotherhood. By the end of the eighteenth century the legal term had demographic and ethnic meaning and it assimilated people who were not native speakers of Greek. A plurality of Nizhyn merchants came from Yanena, and among them was a large contingent of Slavs who in the Balkan tradition spoke Greek in business; and also in the Balkan tradition, they were assimilated into the dominant category of Greek and were part of what made Nizhyn Greek. The Bulgarian Palauzov was registered as a Nizhyn Greek in 1821. The very wealthy Vasil Aprilov, also of Nizhyn, was registered as a Greek. He attended the Greek gymnasium in Moscow as a Greek, for a time funded the Greek Revolution, and later became a Bulgarian. Under the Hetmanate in the seventeenth century the Greek administration had been called the Brotherhood of the Rum, a reference to their Ottoman Orthodox origins and trade routes; later, under Russia, the town administration was named the Magistrate of the Graiki.[41]

Mariupol' is another example of the merger. The Orthodox Christians who lived in the Crimea under the Ottomans had been evicted by Russia during one of the wars, lest they side with the Porte. They crossed to mainland Russia and founded Mariupol' as a majority Greek town in 1779. The Russians termed them Greek because they were Orthodox Ottomans, but with doubts. They dressed like Tatars and spoke Tatar, and their liturgical texts were in Tatar using a Greek alphabet. When they spoke Greek they used a dialect that no other Greek could understand (*Roumeika*). But the label grek held, and these Greeks learned the Romaic dialect, employed it in public, and educated their children in a shared Greekness, even as they used Tatar at home.[42]

The ethnic label could erase the status distinctions as well. Unusually for Russia where everyone was placed in a distinct legal estate (*soslovie*), the Greeks were organized into a single group. Whatever their differences in origins, and even when they were given titles (the Zosimas,

Varvakis, and many others), they were given land and privileges "regardless of status" (*zvanie*) and they could vote so long as they were Greek as the term was by now understood. Peasants, warriors, sailors, merchants, artisans, and clergy—all fell under the label. In St. Petersburg the Greeks were granted a secondary school to train officers, the Corps of Foreign Co-Religionists, and it was the only officer school that was open to students of any social class, so long as they were Greek and Orthodox. Later heroes of the Greek Revolution were its graduates.[43] Schools were set up for the "Greek merchant estate" exclusively, while the "Helleno-Greek school" (*Ellino-grecheskoe uchilishche*) was open to all estates, so long as the students were Greek.[44]

They were getting the status they thought they had deserved all along, though they were still learning what it could mean to be Greek. They were not dominant numerically but like any budding nationalist they were certain that they were unique. Who else spoke a language that had been in use for two or three millennia, in more or less the same places? (The Armenians and Italians, probably.) Who else could claim to be the fount of organized Christianity? (The Ethiopians and the Armenians had cases to make.) Who else could claim to be the cradle of European culture itself? (Here the Greeks were given a monopoly.)

The Russian Greeks carried their self-awareness back to the Ottoman Empire. For the most part these Greeks still had homes, relatives, and trade in the Ottoman Balkans and the Aegean Islands. G. Varvoglis made his money in Russia and came to Tripolitsa, the capital of the Morea, and his Russian wealth financed his entry into the Morean elite when he became a notable and moneylender. Others returned to finance schools and libraries as the Zosimas brothers did in Yanena, but the examples are myriad. Russia's Greeks were constantly circulating and appeared across the Ottoman Mediterranean.

The contrast to their status in Russia was stark. Being a reaya would no longer do. They may have made money but in the Ottoman lands this affluence could be fleeting as they were swept up in one more regional war, where they confronted pirates, bandits, and irregulars who lived by looting or enslaving them. Officials took their wealth as taxes and booty but in no regular way. In Russia the corruption was regularized and predictable. The Sekeris brothers of Tripolitsa went to Russia when their father, a successful merchant, was murdered. In Russia by contrast a strong state gave them a safe haven, guaranteed their lives and properties, rewarded them mightily, did not enslave them or murder them, and often did not tax them at all.

The Russian Greeks also carried home a specific understanding of "Turk": a foreign and absolute enemy. In Russia "Turk" did not refer to Muslim and Turkic peoples in general. Russia's own Muslims were integrated into the Russian systems of estate and confession as Tatars and Bashkirs.[45] In Russian "Turk" meant the Ottomans, the enemy whom generations of Russian soldiers and officers had been trained to fight. Russian documents and literature could be vehemently Turkophobic, but again they were referring to a foreign enemy. Greeks in Russia carried this inflection back to their Ottoman homelands where it no longer referred to a foreign enemy but to the people in the next house, village, or town. When the Russian–Greek general Ypsilantis, another officer trained to fight the Turks, crossed into the Ottoman Empire in 1821 to begin the Greek Revolution, he brought with him a notion of Turks as a total enemy that was not familiar to many of the Ottoman Christians. He was asking that the Christians turn on their neighbors, sometimes their relatives.

We can now better appreciate why the conspiracy that launched the Greek Revolution began in Odesa, why Odesa was not just another city, and why so much of the material support for the Revolution came from Greeks of Russia. The triumphant Russo-Greek merchant armed with gold, cannon, and the gospel of the nation met with Greeks across the Mediterranean. The dignities and securities they had acquired under the tsar might be transferred to their compatriots in the Ottoman Empire. In substance, the Russian merchants proposed that the Ottoman Rum of the many localisms, languages, and dialects were all Greeks, in lands that should be ruled by Christians. By their reckoning, Ottoman insecurity owed not to the general crisis of Ottoman governance, but to the

fact that the Christians lived under the rule of Muslims. The disorder of
the Ottoman lands was ordered into a confrontation of Turks and
Greeks.

The fateful meeting was in 1820, between Russia-based merchants
and Morean notables at a time when the latter were especially vulnerable. Since 1815 the grand vizier had been replacing governors as part of
a new effort to concentrate or at least regularize power. More Morean
notables were being executed. In late 1820 they were convinced that the
new pasha was about to unleash more violence. Perhaps a cause supported by Russia (so they were told) was their way out, and in 1820 they
began to join a secret society founded in Odesa. Within a year the
Morea was in revolution.[46]

It all happened quite suddenly. It started in 1814 and exploded into
the world in 1821.

Chapter 9

Greece-on-Danube

A New Conspiracy and a New Uprising, 1814–21

Prologue

IT IS 2021, *the bicentennial of the Greek Revolution. My friend is Pontic Greek, meaning a Greek of the Black Sea region. He lives in Moscow. He regularly sends me pictures of his travels with his family. This batch is of a monument to Prince Constantine Ypsilantis, in a church in Chişinău, Moldova. Constantine was a Phanariot, a privileged Christian from Constantinople. He served the sultan as grand dragoman and ruler of Wallachia and Moldavia. He defected to Russia. Constantine's son Alexander became a general in the Russian army and aide-de-camp to Tsar Alexander I during the final campaign against France. He became famous when he commanded the first Greek uprising of 1821, against the wishes of his master the tsar. The uprising was secretly organized in Russia (today's Ukraine and Moldova), and carried out in what is today Romania.*

It failed.

My friend is proud that the Greek Revolution was launched from what used to be the Russian Empire, and I have questions. The monument in Chişinău bears the epigram "For Faith and Patria" in three languages— Greek, Romanian, and Russian—so it is fair to ask which patria is at issue. His son Alexander, the Greek revolutionary, never visited the lands that would become Greece, though his heart arrived after his death and it was preserved in a church in central Athens. The rest of him came in 1964. Where was his Greece, I wondered? Why was Alexander originally buried in Vienna and kept there (most of him) for so long? Why is Constantine still at rest in Kyiv?

Why not? my friend replies, and I realize I am asking the wrong questions. People who might be termed Greek were spread out across the Mediterranean and Black seas, and they might be called Greek as well as many other things. There was no clear understanding of where Greece should be located or who comprised the Greeks. The Greek Revolution of 1821 was started in what is today Romania by a Russian general of Ottoman and Danubian ancestry who had recently decided he was Greek, leading bands of armed men who might be called Greek but just as readily Albanian, Bulgarian, Serb, and Romanian. Had this initial uprising succeeded, I may have grown up in Athens as a diasporic Greek, gazing longingly at a Danubian homeland with Bucharest as its capital, perhaps taking out Pontic citizenship and learning Pontic Greek. As it happened Ypsilantis failed and a different uprising to the south, in the Morea, succeeded. So it is my friend who is diasporic, my Greek became standard Greek and he learned it, and he took out Greek citizenship.

It all seems clear today as we straighten the line to Greek independence, but at the time there were many lines and they were crooked.

The Friendly Society

The year 1814 is a landmark in Greek history. In Odesa affluent merchants founded the System of Greek Insurers (*Systima ton Graikon Asfaliston*), renamed in 1816 the Company of the United Greek Insurers (*Eteria ton Enomenon Graikon Asfaliston*). It announced the arrival of the Greeks as men of finance as well as trade. The insurers dedicated part of their revenues to a school for the children of Greeks who would be taught bookkeeping along with language, history, and religion, in effect training their own heirs and clerks.[1] In Vienna in that same year Greek-Russian aristocrats launched a fund-raising operation in favor of the Society of the Friends of the Muses. Capo d'Istria and Roxandra Stourdza tapped into their links to raise money for the education of Ottoman Christians in Italy and Germany. It was the gradualist approach to the Greek cause. Finally, in Nizhyn in that year, the Greek school moved into a new and better building.

More obscure at the time was the Friendly Society (*Filiki Eteria*), also founded in Odesa in that same year 1814.[2] The society was obscure by design. It was a secret, conspiratorial organization aimed at overthrowing the rule of the sultan over the Christians. Secret societies were common in Europe. They were most often after-hours gatherings of writers, professionals, and students who discussed literature and philosophy. Secret rituals gave them a sense of mystery and exclusivity, and the Friendly Society adopted its rituals from the church and the Masons.[3] Some of the societies discussed politics. European conservatives thought they all led to radicalism. The Carlsbad Decrees inspired by Stourdza closed secret clubs in Germany in 1819.

The Friendly Society was obscure in another sense. It was founded not by aristocrats who hardly knew of its existence until later and largely disavowed it; and not by the higher merchantry that was funding books, churches, and schools. It was founded by three clerks, less-than-successful merchants named Nikolaos Skoufas, Athanasios Tsakalof, and Emmanouil Xanthos. They were all Ottoman Christians who had made their way to Russia and traveled the trade routes of the Mediterranean. That they were not aristocrats or even well-off, not well versed in the world of European diplomacy, and mystified by the strategic subtleties that kept the Ottoman Empire intact, allowed them to think differently and radically. The founders believed in a Greek nation in a way that few others did, and dreamed of its violent liberation by the work of Greeks like themselves—Christians at the very least, Greek speakers in their public life. And they were serious, going as far as to murder members who in one way or the other threatened their plans— Nikolaos Galatis who spoke openly and recklessly of secret plans, and Kyriakos Kamarinos who threatened to reveal that the society was based on the fiction of the tsar's support.[4]

Looking back it should have been perfectly clear that they had chosen the perfectly wrong time to plot a revolution, using a secret society of the sort that the European governments were stamping out. Still they told themselves and new inductees that the tsar secretly supported them. Better-informed men like Capo d'Istria refused to lead them and told them they were unwell. The Count dismissed them as "clerks," and the governor of Russia's southern provinces later lamented that they were "of the most base extraction." Others found their ignorance remarkable.[5] When the European powers sent armies to quash the revolutions in Italy in 1820, the Greek conspirators might have realized at long last that "no" meant "no." Instead the conspirators made their plans concrete and put them into action in 1821. It seemed exactly the wrong thing to do.

It also helped that they were not intellectuals, and what they proposed was outside of the mainstream of Greek intellectual life. To be sure, Greek uniqueness was being promoted in all its forms by poets, playwrights, storytellers, and Classicists. One can forgive the Friendly Society for thinking this translated into a demand for a separate status and a revolution. In fact, even the most elaborate versions of a Greek people, some combination of a continuous language and the Orthodox faith, were qualified by the reality of empire and doubts about whether the Greeks were prepared for government. Intellectuals tended to agree that the future of the Greeks lay in one or another imperial orbit, usually France (Korais) or Russia (Capo d'Istria and church exiles like Ignatii). The rule everywhere was cautious patriotism, made all the more moderate by the reality of the imperial worlds in which they were all implicated and vagueness about who the Greeks were, who they should be, by what measure, and where exactly. Even the Friendly Society left open the question of what freedom might mean, and there was no clear and consistent call for an independent country. It simply called for freedom from Muslim rulers and probably assumed that the Greeks would be freed into the Christian empires.

And yet one can understand why they had reason to hope: they were reading from the script of the Holy Alliance. The European powers in 1814 and over the next several years were announcing their Christian piety and returning to their Christian foundations, with Europe defined as Christianity in contrast to Islam. With Tsar Alexander I invoking Jesus, God, and the Trinity in almost anything he wrote, and periodically waging war against the Porte, one can understand why they expected his backing. Soon after the Greek rebellion broke out, some of its leaders wrote to Alexander "the very powerful and the very pious Emperor," insisting that they were acting in the spirit of the Holy Alliance and asking to join it, in favor of legitimate monarchy and against "nomadic barbaric hordes."[6]

At the very least, one can understand why they, not part of the higher authority structure of Russia and unfamiliar with the distinctions between piety and legitimacy, could misunderstand Alexander and his ministers when they said they stood for the established order and had no intention of destabilizing the Ottoman Empire. Legitimacy to the conspirators could mean throwing off a Muslim tyrant, justice the restoration of Greece to one or another Christian ruler. "Base extraction" let the conspirators imagine what the well-educated and the savvy could not. In the 1810s and into 1821 such merchants were able to misunderstand some basic realities: that the Count and the tsar would, despite what they said, support them; that the Mediterranean revolutions would pave the way for their own; and that Europe would rush to support them.

If their timing was wrong for the courts and intellectuals of Europe, it was right for many Greeks, especially merchants. The Friendly Society rode on the merchant networks to induct members (and conduct business) across the eastern Mediterranean. The three founders collectively traveled routes linking Patmos, Yanena, Arta, Izmir, Trieste, Constantinople, Moscow, and of course Odesa where they all met.[7] In the first few years the society was limited to the Greek merchantry of Russia. In 1817 they had only forty-two members.[8] Soon they had members from around the eastern Mediterranean, Livorno, and Pisa. In 1820 they approached notables in the Christian-majority Morea who had money and authority, and also mercenaries from the wider Ionian region who knew warfare.

By 1821 membership was around one thousand. Most were still merchants. At that moment many of the members were suffering from poverty due to the economic downturn that began in 1815, and they equated their misery with the Turks, the nation with their salvation. Skoufas of Arta in Epirus was a hat-maker and small-time merchant who was bankrupt in 1814. Better-off merchants stood mostly aloof until 1821, though the Sekeris family did provide some funds, and it is significant that they were wealthy but insecure. They hailed from Tripolitsa in the Morea where their father had been murdered. They left and did very well as merchants in Odesa, Moscow, and Constantinople.[9] Be they bankrupts or millionaires, they shared in a sense of heightened expectations, of unjust insecurity. They shared the belief that there was a different way to live and that way was national.[10]

The Prince and the Plot

But the conspiracy lacked social status, and the leaders thought they needed pedigree to lead them. They turned to the Count Capo d'Istria, who turned them down four times (see chapter 7). They then turned to Prince Alexander Ypsilantis. Ypsilantis came from a family of Phanariots, those privileged and wealthy inhabitants of the Phanari or Lighthouse district of Constantinople, who served the Porte as administrators and interpreters. Their service to the Ottoman regime could be lucrative. When the stars aligned at the Porte, they were sent to rule the Danubian Principalities as princes and dragomans, and they exploited the region with impressive fervor and thoroughness. To the Orthodox Romanian peasantry and merchantry the Phanariots were the cruel face of the Porte in the region. Some of the native boyar landowners detested them because they themselves had been displaced to make room for the Phanariots, beginning in the early eighteenth century.[11]

With Russia regularly on the scene from the 1760s, some Phanariots fled to Russia. Branches of the Ypsilantis and Mavrokordatos families are examples. The Russians received them but had no illusions about their conduct in the Balkans. Constantine Ypsilantis asked to be given control of the Ionian Islands when Russia seized them in 1799, and to rule them as a prince. Tsar Paul I feared he would do for the islands what he had done for the Danubians: it would mean "the poverty and ruination of the Christians."[12] In the Danubian region Russia intervened on behalf of the "indigenous people" and against the Phanariots who were, after all, Ottoman instruments.[13] Proposals that the Phanariots be sent to other Balkan regions—like Serbia in 1805—were rejected by the Russians for the same reason.[14] Some Phanariots were open to changing masters but the vast majority did well by serving the sultan, even as some of their members were executed in the course of political intrigues and realignments. But they were not people to join or lead a subversive movement, not to mention a national revolution.

Alexander Ypsilantis was from a Phanariot family but he was different. He was raised in Russia and very privileged, and he circulated among people who were newly aware of their Greekness. Unlike the other Phanariots who were a part of Ottoman governance, Ypsilantis was imbued with a deep antipathy for "Turks" (meaning Ottoman Muslims). He was a Russian general, and part of the esprit de corps of a Russian officer was to fight in the routine wars against the Ottoman Empire. Ypsilantis accepted the leadership of the Friendly Society in April 1820, his sense of Greekness outweighing his oath to the tsar. The deal was sealed amid embraces and cries of "Long live Hellas, long live liberty, long live the aristocracy."[15]

The conspiracy now had a more diverse membership. By 1821 merchants still dominated; wealthier merchants joined in larger numbers once Ypsilantis assumed the leadership.[16] In addition to merchants, it had professionals and notables (each about a tenth of the membership). The core members remained Greek Russians and Greeks in the Danubian region, and together they amounted to about 40 percent of the membership in 1821. It had some clergy though not many: priests in the Ottoman Empire were unlikely to support a movement against the regime in which they were invested. It did not have many mercenaries (seventy-eight persons) but the ones they had would prove decisive when the rebellion became a war. And it was led by a prince.

The notion that the society represented all social groups is only narrowly true: it had six peasant members out of a thousand, at a time when the Ottoman Christians were overwhelmingly peasants. The near absence of peasants was consistent with political thought at the time, whereby anyone but a peasant or a slave had political importance. Their absence is nevertheless surprising given what would follow in the Morea: a mass movement of peasants. It was certainly a surprise to the members of the society who unleashed something they had not intended. But this is exactly what would make the Revolution revolutionary and unprecedented.

In terms of who the Greeks were, the Friendly Society was clear: the vast differences of dialect, language, region, and social station would be overcome by the very simple label "Greeks." They were also exclusive, in a break from Ottoman, Russian, or any imperial tradition: their initiation ritual included the pledge to "not accept any hetero-national" (*alloethne*) as his brother. They were the Greek-speaking Orthodox of the Balkans and the islands, supported by the Greek-speaking Orthodox anywhere. They were arrayed against the Turks (the Muslims). They were vague about the many Orthodox who did not embrace the new Hellenic creed, and they said little about the majority of the Balkan peninsula who did not speak Greek at all. The society's vision of a reanimated Byzantium implied that they would be incorporated as subjects with one or another status, so long as they were Christian. In practice only a few self-declared non-Greeks joined, among them the Serb warlord Karađorđe (also Karadjordje) who was then out of favor with the Ottomans. His rival Obrenović was on the sultan's good side and he rebuffed them, and arranged for Karađorđe to be killed. His head was sent to the sultan.

Ethnic belonging was still an evolving concept and people still had choices, and many people in the region could fairly represent themselves as more than one nationality, depending on the context. Balkan Slavs like Aprilov declared themselves Greeks and joined, though later changed their minds and became Bulgarians. Some people who joined the Friendly Society and started the rebellion appear in the Greek sources with their names spelled in the Greek manner (Giorgios Olympios, Ioannis Pharmakis, and Savvas Fokianos), with the assumption that they were Greeks. In the Romanian sources they appear with their names written in the Romanian manner (Iordache Olimpiotul, Ioan Farmache, and Sava Fochianos). They may also appear in Serbian (Kapetan Jorgać). The Prince of Moldavia was supportive of the society and expected that he would become prince of the whole region once

Russia (he thought) intervened, and as Michail Soutzos he appears as a Greek. Elsewhere he appears as Mihail Suțu, a Romanian or Moldovan.[17] No Muslims were inducted, and on this at least the members could agree: the enemy was all Muslims, whom they called Turks.

Led by Ypsilantis they now had a plan. In Izmail in October 1820 the conspirators agreed that the uprising would take place in March 1821. The prince would land an army of volunteers and mercenaries in the Morea. Someone would alert the members in the Morea. Here the Christians were in the majority, and from here his forces would fight their way northward to the Danubian Principalities.

Ypsilantis then decided unilaterally to begin the Revolution in the Danubian Principalities rather than the Morea. It is likely that he wanted to claim his ancestral home and made this his priority. Greece would begin as some sort of formation around the western Black Sea: an Orthodox crescent from Constantinople to Bucharest, in a relationship with Odesa, Russia, and Russia's Greeks. The tsar might back him despite what the tsar said about revolutions and secret societies, in which case fighting on a territory adjacent to Russia would make it easier. Certainly Ypsilantis and the society had been spreading the word that the tsar secretly supported them, though based on no specific evidence; the claim was somewhere between wishful thinking and outright deception. But the claim was one of the main reasons why so many joined the conspiracy and the rebellion.[18]

By choosing the Danubian Principalities Ypsilantis could also draw on Greek resources and volunteers from the Russian side who would cross the border easily. Anywhere from three to seven thousand Russian Greeks from the Black Sea basin and Greek boys from the universities did join him. The bulk of the funds, guns, and ammunition for his campaign came from the Greeks of southern Russia.[19] He may also have hoped that his invasion would link up with the uprising, just then underway, of Romanians under the warrior Tudor Vladimirescu. Vladimirescu had indeed cooperated with the Friendly Society, though he cooperated with other groups as well. He was sometimes referred to the leader of a Serbian movement. He had followers who spoke Serbian and

Albanian, as did Ypsilantis. Nationality was still a new concept.[20] Vladimirescu started his attack around 18–22 January, Ypsilantis on 22 February (both Old Style).[21]

In practice the decision to start the uprising in the Danubian region made little sense at all. Russia would in no way back him. It was a place with few people who might call themselves Greeks, and a shared religion was not enough to overcome social antipathies. His would-be ally Vladimirescu equated the Greeks with the Ottomans, and just about anyone in the region saw the Phanariots as exploiters. This meant that it would not be a mass uprising but more an invasion from Russia and an insurrection of leaders and mercenaries. Anyway, it is not clear that Ypsilantis the aristocrat and general wanted a mass uprising. While he spoke in general of an uprising of Greeks, he meant the usual cast of warlords and notables, but only the Christian ones. He feared the uncontrolled violence of the mob (in Russian, the *bunt*). Peasants had no place in politics. His outlook was aristocratic, and his campaign was military rather than social.[22]

The uprising began in February 1821 as something familiar—a mobilization of diverse warlords and mercenaries—but aimed at something new: a purely Christian movement. Ypsilantis led about a thousand mercenaries across the Prut River and into Jassy (Iaşi, today in Romania) and dispersed the small Ottoman force. In Galaţi his mercenaries slaughtered Muslim families in their homes along with captive Ottoman soldiers, and pillaged towns and villages in between. He advanced to Bucharest and proclaimed the Greek Revolution in letters to the tsar: "Save us, Sovereign" and "Liberate us, Sovereign." More ominously, he asked the tsar to evict the Turks and "cleanse Europe of these bloody monsters." To the Greeks (meaning Orthodox) who did not join his movement, he promised anathema and called them "bastards and Asiatic germs."[23]

The rest went poorly.[24] Vladimirescu's uprising was directed against the Phanariot princes and in public he appealed to the sultan for support. The Russians found Vladimirescu's appeals familiar from the politics of the region, asking the sultan to support him against the privileged who exploited his people. The outcome might have been a new interimperial accommodation that left him with a better deal. Ypsilantis by contrast was calling for a "war of religion" that "comprises all his nation" and planned to "die or exterminate."[25] Here was something new.

Ypsilantis led an ever-shrinking band of followers. He had Vladimirescu murdered as a traitor to the Greek cause, though again Vladimirescu did not fancy himself a Greek. Ypsilantis appealed to the patriarchs of Constantinople and Jerusalem who duly excommunicated him. Prince Soutzos was sympathetic when the plot seemed to be a Russian operation, but he fled when he realized it was not. The patriarch excommunicated him anyway.[26] The European monarchs and diplomats who were assembled at the Congress of Laibach denounced Ypsilantis. Russia could have claimed the right to intervene based on past treaties, or it could have objected to Ottoman troops entering the region, but Alexander held back to let the Ottomans do their work.[27]

Already in April, Ypsilantis's Balkan mercenaries were asking Alexander I to extract them. Some commanders sought the forgiveness of the sultan and at least one converted to Islam.[28] In June his last remaining followers were the Sacred Band of officers and students, most in their late teens and most from Russia, and they were slaughtered at the Battle of Dragatsani (today in Romania, Drăgășani). The prince was not at the battle and he escaped into Austrian territory. His exit was not dignified. He denounced his surviving followers as unworthy traitors and a "cowardly herd of people." He cursed his commanders and renounced a founder of the Friendly Society as "unscrupulous and depraved." The Austrians kept Ypsilantis in prison at the tsar's request. He stayed there until the year of his death, in 1828. About forty thousand civilians spilled into Russia in 1821 to escape Ottoman reprisals.[29]

That could well have been the end of the affair. Europe was mobilizing against revolutions of any sort and allowing the sultan to do the same in the Balkans. The Friendly Society had planned a next insurgency in the Morea, and it was terrible time to contemplate more insurgencies. But the Moreans knew of the beginning of the outbreak in the Danubian region, not its end. In March they rose up, in part because they believed that Ypsilantis was victorious or soon would be, the tsar was on his way or soon would be, and Christian Europe had blessed them or soon would. In fact they were alone, joined only by some of the Aegean Islanders and Roumeliots. The only independent country to support the Greek Revolution was Haiti. So did the Knights of Malta, but the knights no longer had Malta and they were no longer knights.

Much to everyone's surprise, their own included, the Moreans overthrew the Ottoman order in the peninsula.

Chapter 10

Outbreak, 1821

The Elite Rupture in the Morea

Prologue

THE PORT ON *the southeastern Peloponnesian coast, what used to be called the Morea, is used by small fishing boats and pleasure crafts. The town attracts vacationers from inland areas of the Peloponnese and the occasional foreigner. I am with my children who want to swim off the piers.*

A northern wind is blowing in the Aegean. "A lot of Beaufort," a café owner says, referring to the pre-metric measurement of wind. Sailing boats have come to harbor to wait out the storm. Among them is a boat with an American flag, its two Turkish owners, and their Turkish crewman. As my children scream and jump off a lighthouse and splash into the clear water, I approach the men offering a cigarette, and they offer me coffee. They explain that they will not leave the boat because of the public health rules that require them to quarantine. We are in the midst of the coronavirus pandemic. The rules are laxly enforced, we all know, but they worry that the rules might be strictly enforced if Turks are the ones bending them.

It's a pity, I tell one of the owners, who speaks good English. There's a lot to see here, each village and town with its own history. Not far away there are villages that were once Muslim, side-by-side with others that were and are Christian. Christians and Muslims were once neighbors, and this was once a shared Ottoman space. We are both its descendants. We use some of the same vocabulary, we eat some of the same foods, we practice similar rules of hospitality. We still both know that tobacco breaks the ice. The coffee we are drinking is a legacy too: it is that sweet black kind with silt on the bottom.

It all ended in 1821, I add, referring to the outbreak of the Greek Revolution. I wonder if he recognizes the date.

He does: "It was the first genocide."

There it is: the G word. The man is expressing matter-of-factly what is a commonplace where he comes from. In Greece the term is avoided. I do have reservations. Today the term has legal definition and weight, but the world did not have a name for what happened here in the 1820s other than war, revolution, and massacre. We might use a current term and project it backward, but was Genghis Khan guilty of genocide? The Crusaders who slaughtered Muslims in the cities they sacked? It is too often a rhetorical bomb that ends any attempt to understand, and I want to be understood sooner than cause shock.

Moreover, in early 1821 it was not clear if the Greek Revolution was to be a war of religions and nations. The Muslims of the Morea were on the losing side of what was, in part, a class war against privilege. The combatants of 1821 did align themselves along a Greek–Turk axis and the class dimension was marginalized, but this dichotomy was new and served the interests of privileged Christians who feared they were next. The categories had to be created before they could be acted upon, and they were being created from the year 1821, in the course of the killing. Still, it is worth talking about it, and I have my first explicit exchange on the matter with a Turkish boat owner on the Peloponnesian coast two hundred years after the fact.

Anyway, I ask him, what are we to make of 1923? Was it also a genocide? Again, he recognizes the year: the founding of the Turkish Republic, when the Muslims of Anatolia became Turks and overthrew the remains of the Ottoman Empire, all in the midst of a war against Greece. It ended with mass murder and the eviction of some 1.5 million Christians from the new republic. Greece in 1821 was only the beginning.

The man nods acknowledgment without agreeing, but he puts aside his caution. I drive him, his crewman, and my children in their laps to a nearby bay where an ancient city is submerged, and we snorkel above ruins that we agree are neither Greek nor Turkish. They are Roman. "We have them too," he smiles.

On the Eve: Fear and Circumstance in 1820 and 1821[1]

Knowing what we know about Ottoman Morea, a revolution was not an obvious development. Most of the people who became revolutionaries in March 1821 had not planned a revolution even a month previously. It takes quite a lot of circumstance to convince most people that their routines of survival, however precarious, and the terms of their labor, no matter how meager the rewards, should be shattered. Surviving and perhaps thriving from day to day, year to year, and generation to generation was its own form of inertia that made change seem untoward. The Morean Christian notables who later claimed to lead the Revolution had been part and parcel of the Ottoman order. An uprising meant disrupting their lifelong accommodation with the Ottoman system that had netted them wealth and status. Even when some of them perished in the seemingly endless power struggles, their heirs were allowed to replace them. The lineage continued. In this there was an immortality.

Ending the complacency involved some confusion, some misunderstanding, and some circumstance. It also took the madness of some people whose fanciful and dangerous dreams of 1820 became normal as the world aligned with them in 1821. The nation made sense of what they had done.

In 1820 and early 1821 the Christian notables had reason to worry. It was time to buy the tax farms, which was always a delicate process. A new governor was arriving, and that was cause for more worry. Hurşid pasha meant to force the notables to send more revenues to the regional and imperial capitals. His arrival in 1820 could have heralded another wave of violence.[2] This was unsettling but also familar. In November 1820 the notables and the church hierarchs gathered in Tripolitsa to submit.

The usual worry was heightened when the Christian notables were told to accept a quicker pace of payments for the tax farms they were buying. In Gastouni, Sisinis and lesser notables were surprised and did not give a response, perhaps waiting to be offered better terms. Their

Muslim counterparts wondered why the Christians were delaying. The agas sent word to the Christian notables that there could be consequences and the notables rushed to agree to the terms, but the agas remained suspicious. The Muslims were also put on alert by warnings they had received from their Christian notable friends, to the effect that some sort of conspiracy was underway. They wondered if these were all connected.[3]

In February the Christians were thrown into trepidation because Hurşid pasha invited the notables back to Tripolitsa. This could mean another periodic consultation, but it could mean a general rearrangement of power and more bloodshed. Some notables and priests heeded the call and came to Tripolitsa. To this day it is not clear if they were hostages or guests. They were probably a bit of both. At least one feared for his life and converted to Islam, and later he oversaw the torture of others until they did the same.[4] Others ignored the summons and fled the Morea. Others temporized, feigned illness, and went into hiding. Their Muslim counterparts in these localities, by now alarmed, demanded that they return, as reassurance; the Christians took the demand as a threat.[5]

At that very moment, from February 1821, the Morea was touched by wider imperial crisis that turned worry into alarm. This was the fighting in the Danubian Principalities, organized by the Friendly Society and headed by Ypsilantis. In the first instance this was not a Morean affair.[6] To be sure, many of the Morean notables had joined the Friendly Society in very recent times, mostly in 1820, some only a month before the uprising of March 1821.[7] How much the Morean notables understood the national message of the Friendly Society is not clear. Some of them joined but thought the society odd and upstart, populated by uncouth merchants from Russia. They may have pledged to become Greeks, but they were more importantly notables in charge of regions and revenues, at the head of their respective clans. It was tax season.

Younger notables and the sons of notables were more receptive. They had been better educated in matters Greek and national, at local schools and with local tutors, or in foreign travel and study, exposed all along to the new kinds of books that carried messages of national belonging. But their fathers were wary. They were curious about the plans of the society and made inquiries, but they refused its requests for funds. Kanellos Deliyannis who lost his father to the executioner in 1816 was more taken.[8]

The Moreans became embroiled in the conspiracy because the society had decided that there would be an uprising in the Morea, though the Moreans did not know it. This was decided at a gathering of the society's leadership in the town of Izmail in October 1820. The meeting set the date: 25 March 1821. Only one Morean was present.[9] He was Grigorios Flessas-Dikeos, a monk from a family of notables around Kalamata. He later became an archimandrite, a monastic hierarch one rank below a bishop, and he was popularly known as Papaflessas—Flessas the Priest. He was an outlier known for radicalism and confrontation, perhaps a touch of madness. He had alienated the Morean bishops and notables who treated him as maladjusted. He was "vein, unpredictable, and dangerous." They transferred him from one school and monastery to another but he kept getting into trouble. He threatened Ottoman authorities with violence. He fled the Morea with a price on his head, first to British Zakynthos and then to Constantinople where he was inducted into the Friendly Society. Its radical aim gave him a simple template to understand himself, his otherwise erratic conduct, his isolation in his own class, and his purpose. He was a Greek opposing Turks in a historic and epic battle of religions and now nations.

Papaflessas was not candid with anyone. When he met with the leaders of the Friendly Society in Izmail in October 1820 he announced that the Moreans were willing and ready to start the uprising. This was untrue. Quite the contrary: when he arrived in the Morea at the end of 1820 and told the notables that they were expected to rebel, neither he nor his tidings were well received. In Argos he demanded money, and the Perroukas family of notables refused. An enraged Papaflessas wanted to have them murdered. In Vostitsa a gathering of regional notables and clerics confronted him. His loose talk of an uprising could lead to loss of life and property and threaten the system of which they were a part. In substance Papaflessas proposed that they attack their neighbors, partners, and sovereign rulers and instigate a Morean civil war. Moreover a new movement of all Christians would unleash popular furies that would be directed against the notables: who would control the peasant masses once they were armed and emboldened? The notables agreed among themselves to lock him up in a monastery before he caused real harm. Papaflessas had come with an armed guard and he walked away unmolested.[10]

Papaflessas was in a hurry. He was supposed to await the arrival of Ypsilantis but intended to go ahead without him if necessary. He was supposed to work with the Morean notables but intended to start an uprising with or without their agreement. He told them he was going to start killing Turks. This would implicate all the Christians who would have to arm themselves if they wanted to survive Ottoman ret-ribution. He went south toward Kalamata and gathered fighters along the way. In the south he awaited the arrival of shipments of gunpowder. Here too he encountered something less than nationalist altruism. The notable in charge of the port was Petrobey Mavromichalis, the Otto-man appointee responsible for local order, and Petrobey treated the arrival of the gunpowder as an opportunity. Before unloading the ship he demanded 1,000 Mahmuds (Ottoman gold coins) and a share of the gunpowder.[11]

That the notables listened to Papaflessas at all owes to another un-truth he told, that Russia would support an uprising of the Christians. It was a claim that had been deployed repeatedly by the leaders of the Friendly Society. It was one of the keys to their success and helps ex-plain why many notables had joined. This would make the conspiracy a familiar imperial intrigue, not an upheaval. In the exchanges among notables and representatives of the society in the months before the outbreak, notables thought they were negotiating with Alexander I and his emissaries. Some members thought that the mysterious references to "the Authority" (code for the leadership of the Friendly Society) was code for the tsar. A Russian army would come.[12]

Mavromichalis was intrigued by the prospect of a Russian interven-tion but he wanted to be sure. He was first told of it in early 1820 and he sent his agent to visit Capo d'Istria in St. Petersburg and confirm it. The Count was categorical that this was not a Russian venture and did not have Russian support. He gave the agent a letter to that effect and the agent set out for the Morea. Now the leaders of the society were alarmed. If word got out that Russia was not behind the conspiracy and in no way supported it, the plans of the society would be ruined. The leaders of the society had the emissary murdered on a ship crossing the Danube.[13]

In early 1821 Papaflessas again told the Morean notables that Russia would support them, and this gave them pause. Russia had been thrashing the Ottoman Empire with regularity since the 1760s, so a venture backed by Russia had good chances of success.[14] The plans of the society could produce a change in rulers rather than social orders, a clash of empires rather than a mass uprising. Papaflessas told the notables that they would replace the agas as the rulers of the Morea. If Russian merchants and a Russian general said that the Russian Empire was backing them, and since the Moreans knew no better, then it was plausible that Papaflessas was telling the truth. But they trusted him very little, and they demanded proof that Russia would support them. In the meantime they would wait.[15]

Rupture

And then, in March 1821, the solidarity of Christian and Muslim notables collapsed in a dynamic of mutual suspicion, each convinced that the other was going to attack. Some Ottoman officials knew that some sort of uprising was planned. The British commandant of Zakynthos had warned the Morean pasha, and Christian notables had warned their Muslim friends.[16] Their fears were seemingly confirmed on 14 March (these dates in the Old Style or Julian calendar). Armed men led by a village elder named Solotis (a.k.a. Nikolas Christodoulos) ambushed Ottoman Muslim tax and loan collectors and left three dead. On 16 March the same band killed another eight Muslim tax enforcers in one village, and two more in another village along with their Albanian guard of twenty-eight men.[17] Also on 16 March, the old bandit Chondroyannis (Fat John) attacked and killed the Muslim Seyd Hamoudz Lalioti; only later it transpired that his real target was the Christian moneylender

Tabakopoulos to whom he owed money, and Seyd was merely his body-guard. The attackers in all these cases were not following the orders of the Friendly Society but it could well seem that they were. The local notables had not ordered the attacks but rumor spread that they had. Muslim suspicions were seemingly confirmed when a panicked Christian notable ordered the murder of fifteen Muslims who he wrongly thought were a punitive squad. To the south, the aga Arnaoutoglou had the Christian elders of Kalamata arrested.

To some agas the attacks added to other sources of suspicion, the failure of the Christians to buy the tax farms and their failure to go to Tripolitsa when ordered by the pasha. In some areas the Muslims armed themselves and prepared for battle. When Christians in Patras began to leave to avoid the anticipated violence, the Muslims took this as a prelude to an attack on themselves and began to move on the Christians. The Christians were sure they were being attacked and now this was true. Bishop Germanos called for armed men to defend them. And now, from late March onward, the Christian notables were convinced that the pasha and his supporters intended them harm. The invitation to Tripolitsa seemed like a prelude to another massacre, and the agas were mobilizing against the Christians. The kotsabases hired local fighters and threatened violence if the Muslims approached. In Gastouni Sisinis hired three hundred armed men and warned the Muslims that he had ten thousand. To the Muslims this confirmed their worst fears: the Christians were on the march, and now this was true. Messages from Christian notables and clergy to the Muslims around Lala that they stay put lest they be ambushed may have seemed like sound and friendly advice on most days in a land plagued by banditry; on this day, 26 March, it seemed like a threat, and it probably was.[18] Around Gastouni the agas agreed to kill all the Christian notables.[19]

Christian warlords made the rebellion a fait accompli. Kolokotronis arrived from Zakynthos. He was joined by his comrades from his fighting days on the Ionian Islands. They maneuvered around Kalamata and began campaigning on 22 March.[20] Fighters fanned out across the Morea and looted Mystras before moving on Monemvasia.[21] By attacking Muslims, the fighters dragged the populations of towns and villages to the point of no return. All these Christian populations would be held collectively responsible, and punishment would be brutal.

In place after place Christian fighters told the Christian townsfolk and villagers to arrest the Muslims. The locals complied in a half-hearted way. The Muslims were their neighbors, friends, and relatives, so they asked them to stay in their homes or simply not leave the area. Fighters working with the Deliyannis clan entered the town of Lagadia and saw that the Muslims were still free and mingling with the Christians, and that the Christians were planning to submit to the pasha in Tripolitsa. So Deliyannis's men killed forty Muslim families on the spot and ended any possibility of reconciliation with the pasha.[22] Petrobey Mavromichalis of Mani made the break on 22 March, alongside Kolokotronis: he had offered to protect the Arnaoutoglou family, then decided to take them hostage, and then had them killed or sent to villages as slaves.[23]

The Muslim communities were overwhelmed by the Christian numbers, and there was not much in the way of an organized Ottoman force to protect them. They had always depended to some extent on the Christian notables for their protection. Now the Christians had turned on them. Muslims gathered their valuables, evacuated villages and towns, and headed for the coasts. From there they could wait in the forts for reinforcements or board ships to safer parts of the empire. Others went to the walled town of Tripolitsa, the seat of the pasha, where they thought they would be safe.[24]

The Muslims of Lala organized a frontal attack. Lala was a military community based in the mountains that ruled over the plains of Gastouni and Pyrgos. We saw in chapter 6 that Ali Farmaki and Yakoub aga were based here and had collaborated with Sisinis and Kolokotronis against the Morean pasha, Veli. Now Sisinis was their enemy. They mounted their horses and charged. They were defeated by a combined force of regional notables like Sisinis and his hired fighters, Ionian veterans like Vilaetis, peasant bands from the wider region, and bands of Ionian Island peasants led by the Cephalonian Metaxas. In June the Muslims abandoned Lala and made their way to the coast. Lala was looted and torched. Arriving in Patras, the agas murdered their Christian secretary.[25]

Still it was not clear that this was exclusively a confrontation of religions. Muslim and Christian notables had showed signs of solidarity. When the Morean pasha had invited the kotsabases to Tripolitsa, some of their Muslim counterparts warned them not to go; the pasha was their shared enemy. Christians in some towns warned the Muslims of impending attacks and gave them horses to make it to safety.[26] In the early days of the uprising some agas assumed that they were dealing with the usual banditry and asked Christian notables to provide armed men to suppress them; the agas assumed they were all on the same side.[27] Retreating Muslims around Argos who thought the violence was an attack on privilege invited the Christian notables to join them and save themselves; when they came to rescue the Christian counterparts, the Christians thought it was an attack on themselves, and so they attacked the Muslims.[28] When warlords prepared to massacre the Muslim population of Monemvasia, Christians from surrounding villages tried to stop them: some were their relatives.[29]

In the confusion over who was on what side and indeed what the sides were, Christians killed each other as well as Muslims. Some of the Christian fighters who arrived from the Ionian Islands recalled that they were not quite sure why they were in the Morea; perhaps it was a looting expedition.[30] Certainly a lot of peasants thought it was just robbery. The fighter Nikitaras traveled the Morea to stir up rebellions but the Christian populations refused to give him supplies, which he had to seize, and they denounced him to the Ottoman authorities. Kolokotronis threatened the reluctant villagers with "fire and axe."[31] Zakynthians who had come to fight the Muslims alongside Sisinis in June 1821 began looting the properties of Sisinis in July.[32]

If this was a revolution, as the Greeks quickly termed their actions, what kind of revolution was it?

The Sultan Unifies the Christians

The uprising of March 1821 did become a national war. This owed in part to the sultan's reaction which treated the Christians across the Ottoman Empire as an undifferentiated mass of rebels. Ottoman legal subtleties distinguishing rebel from loyal subject were overwhelmed by a practice on the ground that visited vengeance on the Rum as a whole. The sultan's own sweeping commands for all Muslim men to arm themselves against all the Christians made the violence a confrontation of the believers and the infidels. In the Morea and parts of the Aegean Archipelago, the Christians could resist collectively: they were islands or near-islands with Christian majorities. Elsewhere they experienced looting, enslavement, and massacres.

The sultan read events from Constantinople, and not very well. He was convinced that the Danubian rebellion of Ypsilantis was organized by the Phanariots, and he was wrong. Quite the contrary, some Phanariots converted to Islam to prove their loyalty and save their lives, and many rushed to prove their loyalty by denouncing other Christians. The sultan also suspected that the rebellion was the work of the patriarch who himself came from the Morea, and again he was wrong. The patriarch dutifully anathematized the rebels and gathered names of alleged Christian culprits; the grand vizier had them rounded up and they were imprisoned, exiled, or executed. Nevertheless, on Easter Sunday the patriarch was murdered and strung up at the door of the patriarchate, in the last analysis for his failure to control his flock.

Most importantly, the sultan was confident that the uprising was Russia's doing, and once again he was wrong.[33] If anything blinded the Porte to the reality on the ground—an indigenous mass uprising—it was this belief that Russia planned or backed the Greek rebellion. It was true that Ypsilantis was a Russian general and his forces including Russian volunteers crossed from Russia. But Russia raced to disavow the general and denounce the rebellion, and gave the sultan permission to send troops into the Danubian region.

The sultan then went further and unwittingly changed the axis of confrontation. He called on all Muslims to arm themselves and put the Rum—all the Rum—in their place. The Porte invoked an imagined past in which the believers would set aside their differences and become united by religious fervor. It was the "duty of all believers of all classes" to unite under one banner.[34] This was a search for a social foundation in the long term, and an effective fighting force in the short term. Every

Muslim in all parts of the empire should mobilize. And since the sultan could not pay them, their reward would be loot. This was the significance of declaring the Christians rebels as collaborators of a foreign power, meaning Russia. Collaboration was cause to strip populations of their protected status and declare them *harbi*—warring enemy non-Muslims. This allowed Muslim fighters to loot Christian properties and take Christian slaves.

How many Christians were killed in Constantinople, Anatolia, the Aegean Islands, and Roumeli is unknown, but it is certain that passive innocents were killed in much greater numbers than actual rebels.[35] The refrain of the Porte to local commanders was regular and numbing: "kill the infidels, take their property, and enslave their families."[36] The ensuing violence was random as local Ottoman officials tried to understand their unusual orders, to turn on populations that had not rebelled and whom they had been mandated to protect. In some towns the Christians were left alone and given protection. In others the sultan's call produced mob violence and looting, with young men shooting at Christian passers-by. Lists compiled by the patriarch were used to round up Christian boys and men for forced labor in mines and foundries. Clergy were rounded up and hanged in the squares around Constantinople. In far-off Syria, Christians who scarcely knew of the rebellions were punished. In Haifa the governor destroyed churches and monasteries. The commander of Iraklio, in Crete, was ordered to execute the local bishop.[37]

The Ottoman fleet was purged of Orthodox Christian sailors; this measure sent unemployment soaring and sent unemployed sailors into the rebel fleet. Ottoman merchant vessels as far away as London dismissed their Christian crews and abandoned them on shore. Others were arrested. In the Mediterranean, Ottoman ship captains were ordered to "massacre all the rebellious enemies of our religion . . . enslave their offspring, confiscate their property as booty . . . destroy their bases." On the Aegean Islands commanders had similar instructions: "They are to be executed, their offspring are to be enslaved, their properties are to be seized and distributed among Muslim warriors as bounty."

The slightest suggestion of rebellion was justification for soldiers to kill the men, "enslave their women and children, pillage their properties and goods, and burn their dwellings to the ground." In some of the instructions killing, enslaving, and pillaging was not only allowed but required, and the commanders were reprimanded for showing leniency.[38]

The Porte was explicit: "the Rum infidels" were guilty *as a whole*, including "low born and high born alike," who were united in "martyring any Muslim they can lay their hands on." Regular instructions in 1821 declared regions rebellious "in their entirety" and the Christian population guilty of "collective treason." In 1822 the Porte issued more statements to governors and commanders that the sedition of the Rum was "universal," and commanders were ordered to launch wholesale attacks on towns and islands.[39] The ultimate goal of the Porte was the submission of the Christians, and even in 1821 the grand vizier outlined the terms under which the Rum could be readmitted to the "circle of obedience." But massacres continued throughout the decade, and while some places like Aghios Efstathios were shown mercy, others like Ayvalik and Samothrace were destroyed.[40] It looked to the Christians that they were being collectively targeted, and in many cases they were. It was hard to behave as a distinct notable, peasant, cobbler, sailor, or merchant when they were all being attacked as an undifferentiated population of Christians. They were all the same, whether they liked it or not.

Not many regions of Christians were able to resist or flee when Ottoman retribution was organized or sudden. The surprise of the locals was all the greater because most had not rebelled at all and expected to submit to the arriving Ottoman forces. In Samothrace 200 were killed, 1,400 were enslaved, and 400 were left at liberty. Forty live men were sent as trophies to the sultan and were forced to carry a revolutionary flag. At the palace of Topkapi their leader shouted in vain that it was not his flag but was forced by his captors to carry it. The town of Ayvalik on the Anatolian coast was burned to the ground, the men killed, the women and children sold into slavery. Naousa near Thessaloniki was destroyed in March 1822 and the sultan expressed pleasure at the severed heads he received. On Kasos in 1824, five hundred men were killed outright and two thousand women and children were enslaved. Also in 1824, Psara was depopulated by massacre, enslavement, and flight. Smaller massacres and enslavements occurred along the routes followed by the Muslim fighters around Roumeli. From the island of Evia came reports of sixty priests (most likely monks) impaled in the town of Mantoudi.[41]

The most notorious massacre of Christians was in Chios in 1822. It was the largest murder of any population, Muslim or Christian, of the entire decade. Chios was a prosperous island of farmers and merchants, known as the source of the valuable gum mastic that only grew here and was a monopoly of the sultan. The population had stayed aloof of the uprising, and in 1821 the sultan ordered local commanders to protect the island's Christians. This changed when Christian outsiders arrived to force them into rebellion—the tactic that had forced many regions into rebellion since the outbreak of March 1821. Now all Christians on Chios were rebels, with the exception of the villages where the gum mastic was produced. The grand vizier presented the fleet's attack on the island as a military operation and the massacres of civilians as "battles," and he encouraged the attack as "courageous" and a "religious obligation."[42]

The Ottoman fleet arrived in Chios in April and let lose a campaign of murder and pillaging, and the regional slave markets were flooded with Christians. The commander wrote of "booty and slaves in quantities never before seen or heard." Notables and clergymen who offered to submit were cut down.[43] The sultan received more loads of severed ears and heads. When the admiral of the Ottoman fleet was killed by a Greek fireship, the soldiers extended the terror to the remaining protected villages where mastic was produced; this was the part to which the Porte objected.[44] Estimates of the victims vary widely. According to one common estimate, probably on the high end, of a population of 120,000 Christians perhaps 23,000 were killed, 47,000 were enslaved, and 10,000 more died of hunger and epidemic. Observers in Europe were rightly horrified, and Delacroix launched his career as a painter of oil on canvas with his famous work, *Scenes from the Massacre of Scio*.

It was one of the events, and one of the paintings, that would turn European educated society in favor of the Greeks.[45]

The Christians Become Greeks

Christians in most regions were defenseless, but the Morea was different. It was almost an island, its coasts could be defended by the Aegean fleets that had joined them, and its population was overwhelmingly Christian. This demography and this geography allowed the rebellion to take root and organize into a mass mobilization. The question is how a rebellion, even a mass rebellion, became a national revolution.

The answer is that the immediate events of spring 1821, like all events, were the concentration of decades of change. The Revolution was in an immediate sense a conspiracy of merchants, notables, and warlords, but over the decades various trends had converged to create the idea of a modern Greek, an absolute category that was juxtaposed to another absolute category, Turk. The arrival of new empires suggested there were alternatives to the Ottoman order. Cycles of boom and bust heightened and dashed expectations, leaving more people of all walks of life with the conviction that things could and should be better. European influences valorized the Christians above all others and depicted the sultan as illegitimate and Muslims as foreigners. All these tendencies were distilled by a very recent wave of ideologues bearing the gospel of the nation who proposed that the nation was the new solution to the old problems. The confusion of March 1821 released the otherwise familiar violence into a new binary of Greek and Turk, and consolidated all these changes into a new praxis, the nation under arms.

The change was expressed in the very idiom that the rebels used to describe themselves. What foreigners in Europe called Greeks had been a mix of peoples who went by a variety of names, all related to the imperial spaces in which they traveled. In the Ottoman Empire they were the Rum, from the Ionian Islands westward they were the Graiki, in Russia they were the greki, elsewhere they were Greeks, greci, and grecs. "Genos" had implied an affiliation of the Orthodox anywhere and was also trans-imperial; that the patriarchate used the term is a good indication that it was not subversive or even national.

But the revolutionaries were using new labels. In contrast to the imperial and confessional terms for themselves, the revolutionaries adopted a term that was very old but new to them: Ellinas, usually transliterated as Hellene. Literati and scholars had used it to refer to a Classical past but rarely to the populations of the present. In 1821 it referred to the rebelling Christians. According to the notable Kanellos Deliyannis, "a handful of Peloponnesian men put forward that name 'Hellene.'" It caught on instantly because it explained, to themselves and to others, that they were members of a nation rather than subordinates of a monarch. It referred to the current, living Orthodox Christians as a free-standing people who existed independently of the empires. The idea that they were the heirs of ancient Greece and Byzantium also spread. The Greeks were a historic people, and they were a modern, coherent people who existed in Vostitsa and Mystras, Hydra and Athens.[46] As Kolokotronis put it, "Men's communities were small, it was only our revolution that associated all the Greeks."[47] Local labels were still common and meaningful—they still are—but in the course of 1821 "Hellene" joined them. It is still what the modern Greeks call themselves in their own language, and the formal name of the country is the Hellenic Republic.

For a moment, in 1821 and 1822, the idea of a Hellene could also overcome class animosities. It allowed the Christian notable to insist that the enemy was the Muslim notable but not himself; and it legitimized the Christian peasant who took up arms against privilege, beginning with Muslim privilege but perhaps not ending there. Indeed the hostility of notable and "the people" (laos) was enduring and mutual. Over and over the Christian commanders in the Morea had to hold back the armed peasants who begged permission to kill the kotsabases. In Roumeli in 1821 and 1822 warlords fighting in the name of the Revolution attacked Muslims and also killed quite a few Christian notables.[48] Over the next few years Athens and its Christian notables suffered more violence at the hands of Christian fighters than they did from the Ottomans.

The notables for their part never stopped being resentful that they had been forced into a revolution. The bishop Germanos of Patras, who ultimately blessed the Revolution, remained uneasy that he was riding a wave of peasants ("the poor reaya"). Notables blamed the Friendly Society for embroiling them and riling up the young notables with false promises of Russian support. Whatever the Friendly Society had intended, it became associated with the rising up of the poor against the privileged. "A curse on Dikeos [Papaflessas] who came here," one of them wrote.[49]

On the Aegean Islands the notables had been forced into revolution by unemployed sailors. Their ranks swelled as the Ottoman fleet dismissed them in 1821 and unwittingly created a rebel fleet. On Hydra the sailors were led by the captain Antonis Oikonomou and the notables never forgave him. In December 1821 the notables had Oikonomou hunted down and murdered.[50]

In August 1821 the Hydriot notable Ioannis Orlandos wrote to his father-in-law of the "labyrinth of misfortune into which the unscrupulous have submerged us." Men like Orlandos were ambiguous about the Revolution, at times regretful. In 1822 Orlandos crossed from Hydra to Nafplio in the Morea to negotiate the surrender of the town's remaining Muslims. Under a flag of truce he was the guest of Mir Yusuf el-Morani. Orlandos lamented that it had ever come to this. He blamed the "ridiculous mob" which, if not handled properly, would turn on the Christian notables next. In a subtle rebuke to his host Orlandos said that the rebellion was succeeding because of the disarray of the Ottomans and their inability to mobilize an army. The dismissal of the Christian sailors from the Ottoman fleet was a double damage: it made the Ottoman fleet ineffective and left the island notables with a mass of the unemployed. The old regime could not protect itself and justify its existence. Here there was no talk of nations and liberty, only of saving what could be saved. His complaint about the old regime was that it bred "insecurity" (*anasfalia*), not a lack of freedom. And the best Orlandos could hope for was a new order that might offer security and predictability, preserve his status and wealth, and preserve his life.[51]

The notables had not asked for a mass movement, and now they would try to define it as national rather than social. Anyway, by the end of 1821 the notables needed the mass movement. Ypsilantis had failed and the Russians were not coming. Any hope that the other Mediterranean revolutions might let Greece ride a wave of success were dashed as the continental powers coordinated their suppression.[52] The Moreans, some Aegean Islanders, and some Roumeliotes would be facing the Ottomans alone, and they would need more than a few mercenaries.

Chapter 11

The Nation, Unbound

Prologue

"WHERE IS DERVENAKIA?" *I ask out the window of my car, to a woman waiting on the side of the road next to an abandoned railway station. It is April 2018 and I have left the highway in the northeastern Peloponnese, around the site of ancient Mycenae.*

"I don't know, probably that way." She motions beyond the abandoned railway line.

I am in search of the site of the battle of 1822 when a massive Ottoman army arriving from the north was defeated by the Greeks. Just about any Greek has heard of the Battle of Dervenakia but not many know how to get there. Shrugs, sweeps of the arms, and a general beckoning toward a mountain do not help, and a lone road sign is pointing the wrong way.

At last I am answered accurately by a bright boy of about twelve attending a gas station, in the village of Aghios Vasilios (St. Basil). "Aghios Vasilios, of Corinthia," he says knowledgeably, distinguishing his village from the many others of the same name. "And you? Where are you from?" "I live in New York, of America." He grins broadly.

During my quest I stop to inquire near a beaten-up pickup truck parked on the side of a country road. A woman and her child are standing next to it. Behind the truck I see a man on a prayer rug, and I am embarrassed when I realize what I am interrupting. I also appreciate the historical irony. They are Syrian refugees who have managed to find work in Greece. And yet it was here, almost two hundred years ago, in the passes surrounding this valley, that the multiconfessional empire died at the hands of the nation under arms. The region had not welcomed Muslims in almost two centuries. Times are changing, I hope.

I found the site. It is marked, inevitably, by a statue of Kolokotronis. He was one of the thousands of men and women who were there in 1822, commemorated by no monument at all.

What Made the Revolution Revolutionary?

By the autumn of 1821 most of the Morea had been cleared of Muslims. In town after town, village after village, at the molecular level of neighborhoods, alleys, and households, Muslims had been killed or they had fled. Violence had been common enough in the region, and in 1821 armed men and women sought out loot as they always had and they took slaves as they always had. But the new, additional object of the violence was people as such: the destruction of an entire category of the population. History books do mention the massacres and lament them as unintended excesses, but this will not do. The massacres were not the unfortunate and regrettable side-effects of warfare, but the very point of the war. They were part of an attack on privilege, and Muslims were privileged. And it was a way to ensure that the Ottoman order and the Muslims with whom the old order was identified would never return.

Such a thorough and sudden demographic change—the disappearance of perhaps forty thousand people—took more than some bandits, mercenaries, and warlords. The books and the statues commemorate individual commanders, but campaigns around Tripolitsa and Dervenakia involved tens of thousands of people. They were armed peasants. The men who chased the Muslims out of the towns and villages, the women who carried supplies and also fought, and the people who surrounded their new enemies in the forts and walled towns were the laos—the people, the masses. The Morea had been experiencing an economic slump since 1815 and this produced legions of unemployed youth for whom fighting was a reasonable option. In the past this may have meant banditry; now it was a national movement. The ranks of unemployed sailors from islands like Hydra swelled when they were dismissed from the Ottoman fleet. In the past this was a cause of piracy; now it was a national cause.

Others had their parts to play, to be sure. The Morean notables provided logistical support, and only they knew how to move wheat, meat, and ammunition in the quantities needed. The Ottoman system they managed became the Greek system in 1821. Moneylenders who had financed the Ottoman order now lent their money (with interest) to the revolutionary cause. Warlords, many of them the veterans of the various Napoleonic campaigns, added a strategic and tactical leadership. It was they who taught peasants the basic rules of warfare, that victory meant loot and slaves, and body parts meant rewards. The notables oversaw production, moved goods, and collected taxes. But none of this would have amounted to a revolution had it not been for the mass mobilization they fed, financed, and led. It was this that made the likes of Kolokotronis a revolutionary rather than a rebel, the leaders not of bandits or mercenaries but of a whole nation. It accounts for the success of the Greeks from 1821: the promised Russian support did not materialize, and the Greeks won their battles because they capitalized on their one advantage, their numbers. Finally, it was specifically a national revolution because, for a moment in 1821 and 1822, the different classes were fighting on the same side.

It was mass mobilization more than anything else that made the Greek Revolution revolutionary. And it was this top-to-bottom confluence of all the Christians that made the Greek nation and spelled the end of Islam in the region. There had been no movement like it in this place but there would be many more elsewhere. It was the start of the Balkan Century of national mass mobilizations, of the demographic reordering of religions and languages into new nations. In the Balkans it meant the near-end of Islam. In Anatolia in 1923, it meant the near-end of Christianity.

3+

From spring 1821 the shared goal of the Greeks was to defend the island-like Morea from Ottoman reconquest. Everyone expected an onslaught.

The warlords approached village elders to point out men who would fight. The elders threw in their lot with the warlords and directed poor peasants to the military camps and the sieges.[1] Soon the notables, themselves facing Ottoman retribution, gave their blessings and began directing money, food, and ammunition to the newly formed armies. They may not have supported an uprising before it occurred, but now the issue was their own survival.

The villagers came to defend themselves, and some received pay.[2] Most came because they were promised loot, the lifeblood of any military campaign in the Balkans. Every attack on a Muslim household or armed force was also a looting expedition. The retreating and besieged Muslims left with their most valuable possessions, and pursuing and defeating them meant acquiring a small fortune in coin, fine embroidered clothing, ornamented weapons, copper pots and pans, and a dowry of linens for the daughters. If the violence became unusually wanton, it was because the newly armed men were also driven by a sense of social justice and revenge against their superiors whom they blamed for their immiseration. In 1821 the parting of ways of Muslim and Christian notables legitimized them: their violence was justified and well rewarded if it was directed at Muslims. The matter of the Christian kotsabases who had also ruled over them, and intended to do the same after 1821, was postponed. In the meantime the kotsabases, the warlords, and the villagers, each carrying their own motivations, blended into what became the nation.

These were the people who drove the Muslim populations out of each village and town. They drove them into coastal towns. Some of the refugees boarded ships, but others were trapped and closed themselves in the forts and awaited the relief that never came. As the besieged Muslims ran out of food and water, they surrendered with terms arranged with the Christian commanders who promised them their lives in return for their wealth. The peasant-soldiers would have none of it. They wanted loot and they wanted justice. In case after case the surrendering Muslims—men, women, and children—were attacked, stripped of their valuables, enslaved, and often murdered. In the Morea alone, massacres were recorded in Arkadia (today's Kiparissia), Navarino (Pylos), Kala-

vryta, Kalamata, Gastouni, Pyrgos, Acrocorinth, Nafplio, and Monemvasia. The bishop of Methoni who was at the surrender of Neokastro
(the newer fort of Navarino, today Pylos) added abject cruelty: tired of
the shooting and stabbing, he abandoned sixty surviving families or
four hundred people on a small desert island where they died of exposure and thirst.[3]

The People under Arms: The Massacre of Tripolitsa

The largest single mobilization of 1821 took place in the autumn around
Tripolitsa. It is a study on the kind of mass warfare that was being unleashed and the new ideology that made this violence legitimate and
total. Tripolitsa was on the central plateau of the Morea and it was the
Ottoman regional capital. It had a population of perhaps ten thousand
before 1821, including Orthodox, Muslims, Catholics, and Jews. In 1821
its population and wealth increased as perhaps eight to ten thousand
Muslim refugees streamed in with their valuables. Christians were there
as well, some of them local residents, some of them notables who were
ordered there by Hurşid pasha earlier in the year, and some refugees
who had fled the armed peasants. Armed local Muslims and their hired
Albanian cavalry patrolled the region and skirmished with Christian
bands from around the Morea. In August, following a series of defeats
on the open plains, they were trapped in the city walls. The Christians
besieged the town.

The siege of Tripolitsa was nominally commanded by Kolokotronis
along with notables and fighters from across the Morea. The siege was
in part a strategic operation that would remove a threat from the heart
of the Morea, but such a task required more men. Warlords and notables hired some but they were not many and they were expensive.
To attract more men the commanders promised loot, which was the
reward for any victorious fighter. So the commanders used the Ottoman administrative hierarchy of notables and village elders to spread
the word that Tripolitsa held enemies, and the enemies held wealth.
A soldier could expect a small fortune, if only he defeated the people
within the walls.

Thousands responded. In the course of September about twenty to twenty-five thousand men were camped around the town, organized by region. Most were Morean peasants. Sailors arrived from the coast under the command of the formidable Laskarina Bouboulina, the Albanian-speaking widow of a merchant from Spetses. (She was also the in-law of Kolokotronis.[4]) The army outside outnumbered the population inside. If we take the figures seriously (they are always notional), it means that about 5 percent of the Morean population, 10 percent of all men, and a higher percentage of adult men were armed and surrounding the city. Kolokotronis intended to negotiate a surrender which would have entailed the distribution of some of the loot to the soldiers, to himself, and to the other commanders.

It slowly dawned on the Muslims inside the walls that help was not coming. The Muslim dignitaries began to negotiate with the Christian commanders. In their despair the besieged families delivered valuables to Kolokotronis as a guarantee of a peaceful exit when the time came. Some of the Albanian guard agreed to leave with terms and Kolokotronis promised them safe passage. Some of them made it to the coast and boarded ships. Others were attacked along the way, killed, and stripped of their valuables. Kolokotronis was ashamed; he had given his word.[5]

And then the commanders lost control. Soldiers and their lower-level leaders saw the negotiations and saw the wealth being brought out, and thought they were being cut out of the deal. Enraged, they went around the other side of the city, away from the main camp, found a gate unguarded, and breached it. They hoisted their flag over the mosque of Nakip effendi, and the army streamed in. The eyewitness Anagnostopoulos kept a diary. "After the voices of the soldiers there were the screams of the women and children," he wrote. "The evils that began today are indescribable; a person with any feeling should weep." It was the start of a butchery in which perhaps fifteen thousand men, women, and children were killed, most of them in the first few hours of Friday, 23 September. Families opened their doors and begged for mercy in vain. The last holdouts were burned alive in their homes on Saturday, 24 September. Those who escaped the town were hunted down in the fields. Bodies lay in streets, doorways, homes, and the surrounding hills and villages. Kolokotronis remembered the events in his deadpan style and offered his own numbers: the Greek force "was cutting and killing from Friday to Sunday, women, children, and men, 32,000 . . . That's how it ended."[6]

The commanders came in after the soldiers, guiding their horses over the bodies piled in the narrow streets. They and their scribes rushed to buy the loot off the soldiers at bargain prices, and later left with cart-loads of treasure. Kolokotronis was said to have left a rich man with fifty-two loads of booty. They then went to the administrative building in search of hostages who could be ransomed or exchanged. Hurşid pasha was away, but the commanders captured his harem and the Otto-man administrators, who would have a high value. The captives were distributed among the commanders. Ottoman sources hold that only ninety-seven Muslims survived the massacre.[7]

It will not do to refer blandly to the "fall" or "battle" of Tripolitsa. It was a massacre, mostly of unarmed civilians. It was the largest massacre of 1821 but it was not exceptional in character. It followed countless others that had taken place in the towns, forts, and villages of the Morea, and they all aimed to destroy an entire category of people. The slaughter was almost complete and we should ask why. It was partly because the soldiers were inexperienced and the commanders power-less to stop them. But the soldiers did not simply take loot, they went into a rage that exterminated the population. It was an expression of deep resentment that was untethered and legitimized as the "nation" of "the Greeks"—terms that were just then become widespread. The violence was total because it was waged by and on totalizing categories, these ones ethnic and national. The vanquished did not have the right to exist, and this applied to the collective of a total enemy—men, women, and children.

But the violence was not only sectarian; it was also class-based. Trip-olitsa was the capital, the place where taxes were gathered and whence the reaya were ruled, and this made the rage a generalized attack on any moneyed privilege they found—ayans, kotsabases, and merchants and shopkeepers of all the religions. If the army gathered outside was Christian and Greek, the population inside was mixed and imperial.

Once inside, the peasant-soldiers sought out anyone with wealth, including Orthodox clerics and Christian notables.[8] Torture and vengeful cruelty was visited on a Christian notable whose family watched as he was dismembered so that he would reveal any hidden treasure. The histories list quite a few Christian notables who died in Tripolitsa and intimate that they were killed by Muslims. Given that the Muslims were planning to surrender, this is unlikely, and it is probable that they were killed by the frenzied Christian soldiers. The notables Yannis Perroukas and Sotiris Kougias perished. Stavrakis Iovikis survived and escaped to Constantinople. The Jewish population was decimated—we know of one man named Kanon who was taken for ransom—because they had valuables.[9]

Tripolitsa put an end to Islam in the Morea, but it also put an end to imperial pluralism and cohabitation.

The End of Empire: The Battle of Dervenakia

The battle of Dervenakia of summer 1822 was another campaign of mass mobilization but of a different kind. There was no longer an indigenous Muslim population to speak of, so it was a clear-cut confrontation of two armed forces, an army coming from outside the Morea and another one mobilized to defend it. It was an empire against a nation.

By the end of 1821 the Morean peninsula was in Greek hands, save some coastal forts and towns, and any threat would come from without. But the Porte only had so many forces, other fronts were more important, and the Porte had to choose which war to fight. A war with Persia lasted to 1823. Fears of a war with Russia persisted and troops were sent north to the Russian border. And a serious rebellion was underway in Epirus where Ali pasha had finally broken with the sultan. Roumeliot pashas aligned with the Porte gathered up mercenaries, most of them Albanians and some Anatolians, and together they surrounded Yanena. They took it in January 1822 and sacked it. In the next months they mopped up holdouts like the Souliots. These delays and distractions, and more profoundly the inability of the Ottoman Empire to mobilize adequate armed force and then supply it, is what allowed the Morean uprising to take hold in its first year and a half.[10]

With Yanena taken and the Souliots defeated, the same Ottoman army marched on the Morea. Anatolian mercenaries and Albanian irregulars were joined by irregulars recruited along the way, including Christians. The army numbered between twenty and thirty thousand, which was quite large for that time, and in summer 1822 it was camped around Corinth in the northern Morea. Their commander, Mahmout Ali pasha of Drama, or Dramalis to the Greeks, was to lead them to Nafplio, the principal town of the eastern Morea, stopping for supplies in Argos. Ultimately the army was to take Tripolitsa on the central plateau and from there fan out to crush the Christian rebellion in the whole Morea.

It was well understood that slaughter and enslavement awaited the locals before their formal submission was accepted and politics rearranged, as they always had been.[11] In the meantime, upon entering the Morea they killed Christian men and took their heads as trophies, took female slaves, and looted property in just about any town they occupied. With drums beating and colorful banners unfurled, songs sung in all the Balkan languages, supplies and loot carried on camels, donkeys, and mules, and slaves bound in columns, it was to be a reconquest and the performance of an irresistible Ottoman power, fueled by the promise of more loot and slaves.

But Dramalis was an outsider who did not know the terrain. He commanded his forces to routes without water, to towns burned and depopulated by both Christians and Muslims, past crops burned by the Greeks, all during the hottest month of unusually hot year. Reaching Argos they found cinders, poisoned wells, and none of the food they thought was there. The mercenary Deli Mustafa, on horseback since Anatolia and Yanena, recalled that he was afraid of Kulli Kutran (Kolokotronis, "the principal bey of the infidels") of whom he had heard gruesome stories. He was also afraid of thirst because he could not find water. In late July the army was demoralized and starting to die, beating a hasty retreat to the wells and supplies of Corinth through tall mountains and narrow passes.[12]

The passes are what gave the ensuing battle its name. A *derbent* in Persian-Ottoman is a pass. Dervenakia in Turko-Greek means "the Little Passes." Kolokotronis intended to start the attack at these passes, where the Ottoman army could be trapped, but he needed more people. He had gathered some of his fighters and paid others to come, but they were not many and some were fleeing. Men like Petrobey Mavromichalis of the Mani wavered and proposed negotiations with the Ottomans, perhaps a new submission under terms that would leave them alive. Dramalis offered money. Kolokotronis would have nothing of it and he replied to Petrobey and other kotsabases in a letter dripping with sarcasm. "Glorious bey and all-noble archons," he began. "It is not worth our while to trade our big interests for the little ones, as we did so often in the past. We do not want that money or to sell our patria itself." Kolokotronis really did think strategically and he really was exceptional. This was an opportunity to gain a country, not a tax farm.[13]

One might understand Petrobey sooner than Kolokotronis because the Ottoman army was massive. But Kolokotronis had in mind a different kind of warfare, a mass mobilization. He sent out word to the town and village elders that this army needed to be stopped before it could fan out and attack towns and villages. And he explained that this Ottoman army was special. Having come from the sacking of Yanena, it carried precious ornaments and metals from the court and palaces of Ali pasha. It had sacks of coins loaded on valuable horses, mules, and camels. It had beautifully ornamented rifles, powder horns, swords, cannon, powder and shot, chests, and embroidered vests and cloaks. It had a lot of coffee, brass coffee-mills, and copper coffee-pots. Kolokotronis exhorted the villagers with a combination of local patriotism, warnings that they would be killed or enslaved, and the promise of the riches of Yanena.[14]

The histories emphasize the commanders who launched the initial attack that broke the Ottoman formation. But that was only the beginning. The campaign lasted months, and it was conducted as an ongoing mass mobilization of peasants. It stretched from Nafplio in the east toward Patras in the west, and it involved the pursuit of thousands of Ottomans in the regions in between.[15]

Kolokotronis's aide Fotakos remembers it as protracted a *levée en masse*. Peasants arrived from all over the Morea, organized village by village, with their womenfolk carrying supplies. Men who had never killed were told that this killing was just and it would be rewarded. In one episode, Kolokotronis came across a young shepherd who seemed oblivious to the meaning of the campaign. Kolokotronis indoctrinated the shepherd and told him that killing these men was justified, glorious, and profitable. The shepherd went into battle with his staff. At the end of the day he reappeared proud and elated, with weapons taken from the men he had killed. It was a better living than herding sheep and it was the right thing to do.

The rebels gathered on the heights and fired at the army below, moved in with their swords, gathered the loot, and moved on to start anew. Women threw boulders over the cliffs and scurried down to gather the booty from the dead and fleeing. The Ottomans dropped their treasures to slow the Christian pursuit. The Ottomans were pinned down and blocked by the enemy, by each other, and by the dead men and horses that began to roll down the hills and pile up in heaps. Their cavalry and artillery were useless.

It was a rout. Two to five thousand Ottomans died on the spot that first day, which was a lot for this kind of warfare. The remaining Ottomans dispersed into the scorched plains of Corinth, Nemea, and Argos, and found water if they were lucky. More often they died of thirst, starvation, and armed attacks. Over the next days and weeks more armed men and women arrived from more villages, "rabid with grief" that they had missed out on the loot, only to be told that the surviving Ottomans still had a lot of valuables to yield. They would have to be hunted down and stripped of their wealth. In this manner the campaign continued into the fall.

The peasant mobilization was well organized, directed by women and elders. Fotakos looked on fondly as peasants formed human chains and "worked like ants" to carry the booty to their carts and villages. Women led columns of new horses, mules, and camels laden with new treasure. They kept some of it for themselves and contributed some of it to the village reserves. It was also time to harvest the Corinthian grapes and there were always British merchants waiting for them off the coasts. Battles were interrupted and others initiated over the grapes. A band of sixty men under the mercenary Anagnostis Petimezas attacked an Ottoman force as it harvested. The Greeks in turn were wiped out by another Ottoman force that wanted the same grapes.[16]

The estimates of Ottoman dead vary. Fotakos estimated that of an army of 30,000, about 6,000 made it back to Corinth that fall. Kolokotronis thought that 4,000 made it out of the Morea alive, of an army of 32,000. Deli Mustafa thought that 30,000 died out of an army of 55,000.[17] Locals recounted stepping over human bones for years. Kolokotronis in his memoirs offered a brief, deadpan account of what was indeed a brilliant plan, the killing of 28,000 men and the capture of 20,000 riding horses, 30,000 mules, 500 camels, cannon and cannon balls, "treasures and beautiful weapons," and a lot of coffee.[18] Mustafa lamented not the violence, but that he was on the losing side.

Years later Fotakos was still haunted by what he saw. With the battle of the first day decided and as dusk fell, he witnessed the slaughter of the Ottoman sick left behind in mobile hospitals. They covered their eyes so as not to witness their own deaths. As he left the battle site, his horse stepped on the stacked bodies that had rolled down hills into the path. A mass of wounded shouted out from the darkened ravines. Their voices mingled with those of the slaves who had been collected from the surrounding villages and abandoned, still bound, during the rout. In the ravine were the speakers of Albanian of the various groups (Gegët, Shkodër), Greek, Bulgarian, and Turkish, the Orthodox, Catholics, and Muslims, the slaves and their owners.

Fotakos heard the empire die in the Little Passes, vanquished by a nation under arms:

> Each cried out his pain to his friends, some in Turkish, some in Albanian, some in Romaic Greek, and we could only hear their voices far away and deep in the ravine. Oh Hasan, Oh Dervisi, Oh Ahmet. Oh Thanasi, Oh Konstanti, giam Geka, giam Skondra, giam Christian, I'm a woman, I'm a Christian, I'm a slave. . . . Our souls were between our teeth, from fear and from sadness and from hunger.[19]

And then the army of villagers melted away with their new wealth. Cajoling and threats could not change their minds. There was no more loot to fuel their patriotism and the immediate threat was over. Kolokotronis shamed them but to no avail. The warlord Plapoutas wrote to the elders across the Morea to send the men back or face his wrath. To "old man Boukouras" in the town of Magouliana in central Morea he demanded that the men return "if you do not want your homes to be burned, the people to be beaten."[20] It had been the same at Tripolitsa: "Ten days [after the storming] all the Greeks left with their loot and went back to their provinces with their enslaved men and women."[21] It would be possible to mobilize men for particular campaigns, such as the siege of Patras in 1822. Here notables and warlords offered food and pay and promised loot. But there was no standing army, save gatherings of a few hundred Greek students from Europe and European officers seeking fortunes. These formations rarely saw combat, and when they did they were decimated.

Then again, all the way to 1825, the Greeks did not need a standing army because they faced no invader. The sultan had run out of armies. The Ottoman fleet avoided engagements, and more coastal towns were abandoned to the Greeks for lack of supplies and reinforcements. Well into 1825, the rivalrous pashas of Roumeli sabotaged each other's efforts to mobilize armies. The Albanian clans competed among themselves and decided whether and for how long they would commit to a given campaign. Some refused to fight if the warfare was dangerous.[22]

The Greeks had a breathing space of about three years to deliberate over the nature of their new nation, and promptly turned on each other.

Chapter 12

The Nation, Limited

Prologue

IT IS A *typically hot summer evening in Laconia as the villagers awake from their naps. It is a village of low stone and plaster houses and terracotta roofs, of tall church domes and bell towers, all looking down on a fertile valley on one side and up at a tall mountain on the other. The deafening sounds of the cicadas are joined by the occasional goat or dog. Soon there are sounds of spoons in coffee cups and women yelling greetings and news to their neighbors.*

This is my grandfather's village, where we maintain the family house. I am standing with my neighbor who knows quite a lot about local history, though he always apologizes for being "a foreigner"; he's originally from the next village. We gaze at the mountainside above, at a group of abandoned houses that are on no map and appear like dots in the pink evening light. I have known that settlement since I was a child, and I know that the last family moved away in the 1970s when the state failed to provide the village with electricity. My children know it as the Ghost Village and visit it at dusk with flashlights and gleeful terror. The locals call the settlement Saint Theodore.

I have always had questions about the village and only vague answers. Why are the homes there different, larger, older, and even palatial? Why is there no church? I have gathered some information in the archives in Athens, and my neighbor brings it together in a rapid-fire narration. Turks lived there. They controlled the supply of water to the valley, they owned the water-powered mills, and they were rich. The biggest house with the arched cellars and large ovens was the bey's. The Turks left in 1821. The Greeks took over their homes. Do we know anything about the people who left? No, nothing, they were Turks (sweep of the hand), they went home to Turkey.

The archival record corresponds with most of what my neighbor told me, though it turns out the bey was an aga and the Turks were Muslims of unknown mother tongue. When the Christian uprising broke out in 1821 some were killed on the spot and the others fled to the coastal fortress of Monemvasia. Many were killed in a final massacre in July. The survivors who boarded ships for the Ottoman Empire (there was no Turkey) were not going home; they were leaving their homes and they were refugees.

I fall into my usual pondering of what people can do to people, of the violent place that this was, so at odds with the friendly place that it is today.

"But there was a boy," my neighbor adds, and my head perks up. This is not in the documents. It is part of the oral history of the village, the knowledge handed down from generation to generation for two centuries. The fleeing Muslims left behind a child. According to the practice of the time, he was too young to be killed and so was raised Christian and fed by the whole village. He was given the nickname that means "of the street." And the Boy of the Street thrived. Today the surname is sprinkled around the villages and towns of the valley, in households and businesses. Branches of the family immigrated, and the name can be found from Florida to Quebec. In the 1950s the immigrants sent back funds to build a church, some 100 meters down the hill from Saint Theodore.

Nations can do many things. Nations empower. Nations destroy. Nations redeem.

Body Parts and Slaves

The human body has always been a marker of status and it has always been a commodity. In the regional warfare of the Balkans this meant the body parts that were collected after a battle as trophies and the whole body of the captive who might be ransomed, killed, or enslaved according to status, gender, and value. These were the practices of the Ottoman Balkans, and the Greeks of 1821, lest we forget, were Balkan Ottomans in 1820. As rebels the Greeks followed the same practices but turned the status hierarchy upside down. At first glance this was mimicry, but the new conditions of nationalism gave violence and slavery a different meaning. It had a new finality.

Ottoman fighters sent from the north and Anatolia to retake Roumeli and the Morea entered the Greek War with practices that were well established. The memoirs of Deli Mustafa, the mercenary who was at the Battle of Dervenakia, was vague about the nature of the campaigns he fought. He was content that he was fighting the infidels. But he was very specific and detailed about the heads, tongues, and ears that he and his comrades took at every opportunity—what he took, where, when, and what reward he received. (See chapter 4 on body parts as trophies.) When Mustafa took his first Christian head, he and his father gave a prayer of thanks and of hope that they would kill many more infidels. The commanders and regional governors gathered these body parts and presented them to higher-ups. In October 1821, a hundred heads from the massacre of Samothrace were on display at the pasha's residence on the mainland across from the island.[1] Loads of heads and ears from Chios reached Constantinople and were ceremoniously thrown on the ground before Topkapi Palace. In 1826 the sultan proudly showed the British ambassador 5,498 ears collected after the fall and massacre of Missolonghi.[2] It was the symbol of awesome power and complete vanquish.

Kolokotronis knew these practices well. As a bandit he and his clan cut off the heads of their own dead in order to deny the enemy a trophy. Small battles broke out to recover the heads of dead comrades and reunite the heads with the bodies.[3] Kolokotronis was also a practitioner. At one point during the Revolution he offered a thaler (about a quarter of a mercenary's monthly pay) for every head that was brought to him.[4] Deli Mustafa recounts that the Greeks collected heads in quantity. In one skirmish he escaped death when his Greek pursuers stopped to gather heads, and in victory the Greeks gathered heads and rolled them to the Ottomans to demoralize them.

Slavery was more nuanced. In Ottoman theory not every captive could be enslaved. Muslim men defeated in battle could be executed and dismembered but not enslaved, and this was a mark of status. Deli Mustafa avidly gathered slaves and did not distinguish between Greek rebel and Christian loyalist; but he was careful to verify that they were not Muslims. On the island of Evia he came across a harem of sub-Saharan African girls and women. Their race was not the issue, but their religion was. He made inquiries to confirm that they were Muslim, as they claimed; they were and he released them, reluctantly because he lost a large payment. Whole regions were declared rebellious and the populations subject to slavery, and this was both retribution and a way to pay the soldiers.[5]

The practice of slavery was also gendered. While the men were often killed and dismembered, the Christian women had value. Slaves flooded the Mediterranean markets whenever a large town fell—tens of thousands in Chios in 1822 and perhaps four thousand in Missolonghi in 1826—but there was a steady flow from ongoing campaigning until the end of the 1820s. Again Deli Mustafa was proud to describe the female slaves he took during his campaigns through Roumeli and Evia, and was especially keen on virgins who were more valuable. He sold them up a hierarchy of commanders who took them to the coasts and sold them to slavers. Greek, Muslim, British, French, and Austrian shipowners carried and traded in Christian slaves around the Ottoman markets and among themselves into the 1830s.[6] Battles were fought over slaves, and battles were abandoned as the soldiers went off to capture women. Deli Mustafa thought that the Battle of Dervenakia was lost because the Ottomans broke ranks to gather slaves and ignored the enemy amassing in the cliffs above.[7]

If adult males were valuable as body parts—they were mature and irredeemable—male children up to the age of twelve could be bought, sold, given, and raised as Muslims in Muslim households. As children they were redeemable. Their fates varied. This was not the Atlantic slave trade, and Ottoman slavery was not the commodified, final destiny of the captive. It was not the erasure of the person. Some were worked to death in mines and queries or sold into sex work, but some became household servants and some had bright futures. Ottoman commanders who waged war against the Greeks were themselves former Christians who had been raised as Muslims. Omer pasha Vrioni was an Albanian child convert from Christianity. Mehmed Rashid pasha (known as

Kioutachi to the Greeks) was the son of a Georgian clergyman who was
sold as a slave in Constantinople. Hurşid pasha had also been a slave
from Georgia.[8] By the same token, one child survivor of the Chios massacre of 1821 became the prime minister of Tunis, and another became
Ibrahim Edhem pasha, grand vizier to the sultan in 1877.

Atlantic slavery was color-coded, "white slavery" was to the Europeans
a special affront, and Europeans and Americans paid ransoms to free
White captives from the Ottomans. The Calvocoressi line of American
military men were descended from a boy from Chios who was brought
by Christian missionaries, raised in the United States, fought in the American Civil War, and became an admiral. His son fought in the Spanish-
American War, and a direct descendant in the Second World War.[9] The
orphaned John Celivergos Zachos from Constantinople was sent to Ke-
nyon College to study medicine and he ended his life as a lecturer at Cooper Union College in Manhattan. In the Morean village of Skourochori,
a Christian boy was captured around 1826 or 1827 and sent to Alexandria
as a slave.[10] He was ransomed by one or another Christian and returned
to his village. His name was "Panagos son of Skouras" (Skouropoulos).
His descendants immigrated to America and invested in nickelodeons.
Spyros Skouras became the chair of Twentieth Century Fox, his brother
the chair of United Artists.

Kolokotronis accepted that enslavement was normal in his letter to
an Ottoman commander. He expected the Ottomans to take Christian
slaves and did not object in principle; his own men were doing the same
to Muslims. He objected when the Ottomans burned the valuable olive,
fig, and mulberry trees belonging to Christians. "That's not military
work because the soulless trees are not against anyone, only people are
against you and are an army, and you enslave them, and that's the right
of war."[11]

The Greeks took slaves as well, and the banning of slavery and the
slave trade by the Second National Assembly in 1823 was widely ignored.[12] We know that the first Muslim slave was taken on 22 March 1821,
the daughter of the Muslim dignitary Mourati who was one of the first
to be killed around Kalamata. She was given to the warlord Anagnostaras in recognition of his seniority.[13] The commanders were most inter-

ested in the high-office and high-status Muslims who could be ransomed. The ransom money mattered because it could be enough to pay for a campaign, feed an army, and enrich the victor. The Greek government, always strapped for cash, was interested in the captives for the same reason. It sent a survey to the localities in 1825 and learned that every region of the Morea had slaves belonging to notables (Palamidis and Mavromichalis had quite a few), clergy (Papaflessas), warlords (Yannakis Kolokotronis), and many simple peasants. The list separated out the high-born who might have value when ransomed. Austrian and French ships arrived to bid on them, with the intent of reselling them to one or another Ottoman authority.[14] Muslim survivors of the massacre of Navarino of 1821 were still living as slaves in the area of Zarnata on the Mani peninsula in 1829.[15] Rumor had it that these slaves were kept into the 1830s despite the many bans.

Slavery was a big business by local standards. During the massacre of Tripolitsa in October 1821 the commanders went straight to the administrative building to save and capture the pasha's retinue and an assortment of military and civil commanders. Over the succeeding months they kept them alive until one or another Ottoman paid a price. The last was sold by Kolokotronis in 1823. Hurşid pasha's harem was especially valuable. This was the pasha's household and family and he would pay handsomely to get it back. The Greeks needed the money quickly: the Ottoman fleet was anchored in Gallipoli and planning to sail into the Aegean, perhaps to attack the Morea. The Hydriot fleet was poised to engage the Ottomans, but it would not sail until it had been paid in cash, in advance.[16] The ransom was finally paid and the harem released on 16 April 1822. Some of the ransom was directed to the fleet and it sailed on 20 April, but it was too late: the massacre of Chios was already underway.[17]

The Greeks generally killed adult Muslim men outright. Those who survived were put to heavy labor, such as digging trenches and hauling artillery. In Tripolitsa after the massacre they were made to bury the dead before disease could break out, though disease broke out anyway. The slaves died of overwork, exposure, disease, hunger, and mob violence. Some men were brought to the home villages of the soldiers where they were put to work, very often to death. Ship captains from Hydra and Psara captured Ottoman ships and threw the low-value passengers and crews overboard in the open sea, and kept the high-born as hostages. They killed them if they seemed a burden or a threat. Perhaps two hundred were massacred on Hydra in June 1825 when they were suspected of sabotage. Prisoners dropped off on Naxos and Kea were murdered by the locals.[18]

Captured Muslim women and children were different, as they were in Ottoman practice. Any boy up to age twelve, and most women, could be baptized and inducted into the household. Orphaned children from Muslim families in the Morea were rescued by Greeks and baptized.[19] Younger Muslim women became concubines to commanders and notables. Papaflessas traveled with his Muslim concubine and their children. The notable Palamidis had a few concubines; he also baptized and married the daughter of an ayan in Tripolitsa, Suleyman Boussos; Palamidis had been his dragoman.[20] Kolettis, the mercenary, physician, and politician from Epirus, had five concubines.[21] For a few decades after the Revolution a Sisinis son cohabited with Aïsha, the daughter of Halil aga Hotoman zade, and they had a son together.[22] Father Sisinis boasted a full harem and displayed it as sign of his new status: he had taken the place of the agas.[23] The Cephalonian revolutionary Konstantinos Metaxas received a whole harem from the warlord Tsongas of Roumeli, as a gift.[24]

Peasant soldiers also took slave girls and brought them home as concubines. One hundred women survived the massacre of Navarino in 1821 and they were taken by the fighters. Soldiers leaving the massacre of Tripolitsa offered up girls at very low prices, and travelers passed homes with Muslim girls on display, for sale. The low price was a sign of oversupply.[25] Soldiers also baptized and married their captives. In the Morea later in the decade, in what is today Laconia, veterans demanded that the village priest baptize their captive children and women. "Old Man Giatrakos" demanded that his enslaved Muslim woman be baptized so he could marry her. If the priest refused the parishioners threatened to go to a different village and pay the fees to a different priest.[26] European officers who had joined the Greeks chose slave girls though they called it a rescue. A conscientious and rules-bound English officer wrote around to ask if it was legal for him to own the Muslim girl he had bought.[27]

Confession, Conversion, and Citizenship

All in all, religion carried clear implications for all sides: members of one religion did not enslave their coreligionists. But the boundaries between the religions were porous since both allowed for conversion. Religion was fixed but the people were not, and this suggests a malleable understanding of the person that was latent in both religions. In the Ottoman period, Christian slaves might convert to Islam in order to gain their freedom, either immediately or upon the death of the master. Whole Christian communities converted after the Ottoman reconquest of the Morea in 1715, including for example families from around twenty villages near Gastouni and the collection of villages to the south called Mourtatochoria.[28] The issue was partly survival, partly the privileges that came with being a Muslim. From 1821 Christians converted to Islam when they were captured; it probably saved them from death or slavery though the Porte trusted them very little.[29]

Likewise, in the 1820s in Roumeli and the Morea Muslim survivors asked to be baptized in order to avoid death and enslavement, and they numbered in the thousands.[30] The practice was controversial and was debated by revolutionary leaders in 1822. There was general agreement that Christians could not be enslaved, even recent converts; the question was whether the converts would revert to Islam when the opportunity arose and give the enemy intelligence and local knowledge. This happened in the Morea and Roumeli as territories changed hands, and for this reason there were calls to kill all captives before they could convert.[31]

After independence in 1830 the matter of conversion had a new practical importance: Muslims were expropriated but converts to Orthodoxy could claim the properties of their dead or departed parents and grandparents. A man marrying a Muslim girl could claim her family's property, which probably explains why Christian leaders like Palamidis married their concubines. As late as the 1860s, Muslim men who had fled returned with baptismal certificates and claimed their lost properties. The Greeks doubted their devotion to the cross, but religious labels did matter and very many converts were given title to the properties.[32]

This painstaking attention to confession relates to the nature of Greek citizenship as it was being defined in the 1820s: Orthodoxy was the only bond that could bring together such diverse peoples into a single community, despite their differences in language, dialect, region, and social status. To question it would be to question the founding principle of Greek nationality. Starting with the local proclamations of spring 1821, the Greeks were defined as those who believe in Jesus Christ and acted in the name of the Holy Trinity. There were provisions for non-Christians, which would have meant Muslims, Jews, and pagan slaves from sub-Saharan Africa.[33] They could petition to stay, but they were the exception and their rights would be incomplete. Some proclamations banned them from participating in politics and owning land.[34]

Anyway, tolerance was not the same as freedom of conscience. The former required a deliberate recognition of a heterodox religion, while the latter implied that one's religion did not matter. In practice and in word, Greece was becoming a polity where religion mattered very much, and Orthodoxy was to be predominant and dominant. The rules were loosened for Catholics, of whom there were quite a few on the Aegean Islands of Naxos, Andros, Tinos, and Syros. Ultimately Catholics were given full rights of citizenship: French warships had been sent in the 1820s, in part to protect the Catholics, and the Greeks were anxious to keep France satisfied.[35]

The emerging country of Greece was recognizably Ottoman in the sense that it used religion to order the population. But the Greeks were doing something new because only the Christians had a right to live on that land; all others had to petition, though there were not many left to take advantage. The Ottoman space was multiconfessional and it was meant to remain so. The collective Ottoman assaults on Christians of the early years of the uprising were extreme and in places unprecedented, but such actions were not intended to end the presence of the Christians in the Ottoman Empire. Even during the horrific massacres the Porte insisted that its ultimate goal was the submission of the reaya, not their eradication. The survivors were meant to be reintegrated. For example, the survivors of the massacre of Ayvalik in 1821 were given assistance to rebuild their town in 1825. The survivors of the massacre of Naousa were invited back in 1825, as were the survivors of the massacre of Missolonghi in 1826.[36] By contrast, Muslims of the new Greece were not meant to be there at all.

Nor was the Greek case comparable to other parts of Europe. Multiconfessional empires like Russia integrated the non-Orthodox into the polity, as did other Eurasian empires. European countries from Italy westward were already overwhelmingly Christian and relatively homogeneous. To declare that the citizenry of Spain or Naples was Catholic was to elevate almost all men to citizenship. By contrast, Greece in the 1820s became homogeneous by eliminating the Muslims altogether. Muslims would have to convert, leave, or die. Offering tolerance was not of much use when there was no one left to tolerate. This made the Greek Revolution unique among revolutions to date: it was a demographic reordering that rendered a multiconfessional space monoconfessional.

The Nation and Total War

In creating and then practicing this new and absolute category, the Greeks were empowering one population; they were effacing another which responded with mystification; and ultimately the new enemy responded with a realization that they were dealing with something entirely new which the Greeks called the nation.

In terms of empowerment—a new sense of rights and entitlement for those who had little of either under the old regime—one might cite the heady atmosphere outside the walls of Tripolitsa in the fall of 1821, when perhaps twenty thousand armed villagers gathered to take loot and take revenge on the people inside. The diarist Anagnostopoulos describes the moment when the lesser commanders and soldiers suspected that the notables and higher commanders planned to take the loot for themselves. They were outraged and they put to work their new national label: "They want proof that they are Greeks [Ellines] and they are no lower than any other." The Revolution had given them not simply the possibility of over-throwing one of their oppressors, but a language to demand more and better, an equality with others on the basis of their new national belonging.[37] Given the mass murder that followed, it was a macabre way to demand rights, but it was a demand for rights nonetheless.

Similar demands appear in other records. The attack on Lala in June 1821 almost failed because the armed villagers from the region refused to follow the notables who were keeping the loot for themselves. Kolokotronis brokered a deal that gave every fighter a share of "all movable and immovable property" that was seized—from evacuated homes and farmland to portable valuables.[38] In a similar vein, soldiers in Roumeli complained bitterly that Kolettis traveled with five slave girls, while the humble soldiers went hungry and had no slaves. So they kidnapped the girls.[39] In a brutal time and place this was entitlement.

The mystification concerns the Muslims who were confronted with a new kind of force that they did not understand: the nation. To be sure, Ottoman administrators knew of revolutions and their liberal roots, but they were bemused when confronted with a people absolutely united and absolutely exclusive.[40] Since 1821 the Porte was outraged that the Rum would attack Muslims as a whole and defile the religion; tellingly they could not explain it. The Rum, wrote the grand vizier in summer 1821, "have united, low-born and high-born alike, without cause, in order to engage in treason and abominable deeds against the Sublime State of Islam and against anyone who calls himself a Muslim." The Rum, he noted in another missive, "were willing to go so far as to sacrifice their malignant lives" for some sort of cause. They occupied and held territories no matter how many armies the Porte threw at them, and sometimes held their ground to the death when the reasonable action would have been to flee. Their "obstinacy" threw Ottoman commanders "into consternation." The rebels ignored the many privileges they had enjoyed before 1821 and they refused offers of generous terms of submission. Tiny boats and fireships defeated the mighty warships of the Ottoman fleet. "This situation astonishes all faithful believers."[41] It was an unfamiliar kind of fanaticism.

The grand vizier was describing nationalism without knowing it. It united all its social strata, it was a cause higher than their individual lives, it drove them to do things that did not make sense, it induced them to fight against the odds, and it destroyed the old order of multi-confessionalism. The vizier could see that something was different but again could not explain it. While he referred to the rebels as the Rum, meaning the Ottoman Orthodox, he noted that they had taken to call-ing themselves Yunan, the Turkish term for an ancient Greek. (It derives from Ionia, the Classical name for the Aegean coast of Anatolia.) The vizier found the label both comical and befuddling.[42]

In that same vein of mystification, we return to Tripolitsa and con-sider an exchange that took place shortly before its storming in Sep-tember 1821. The Greek commanders and the Muslim leaders met for a parley and a possible surrender with terms. The diarist Anagnosto-poulos kept an account of the exchange. The Muslim delegate asked, very simply, who the Greeks were in the imperial scheme of things. He knew of Muslims and Christians who fought for a sultan, and of Chris-tians who fought for European monarchs, but he had not seen Morean Christians—now Greeks—fighting for themselves.

With his imperial mindset, the Muslim wanted to know what impe-rial power was behind the uprising. "Do you have a superior?" If there was to be an agreement of surrender, "Who will sign?" In the first in-stance the Greeks wanted to impress upon the Muslims the hopeless-ness of their position and wove a tale that they probably did not believe themselves. The Russians supported the Greeks, they said, which by then should have been obviously false to all but the Muslims who were cut off from the outside world. Alexander Ypsilantis was the tsar's man and he was sending his brother Dimitris to represent him. All the Chris-tian monarchs were gathered in Vienna to back the Greeks. Replied the Muslim: "Then they made an unjust decision if they so decided; they should not have decided without telling us."

So far the Greeks told a familiar story of imperial rivalry, but the Greeks added something different: they were backed by the powers but they were not fighting for the powers. They were fighting for their "pa-tria" (*patrida*) and the "whole nation" (*ethnos*). In that case, asked the

Muslim, who would sign a surrender agreement "for the whole nation?" "Agas!," Kanellos Deliyannis interrupted, "be careful, God is present." Setting aside Russia and Europe, he said: "The fate of the Greeks [*Griki*] and Turks of the Peloponnese rests with us the representatives"—not the empires. Rejoined the Muslim negotiator, a new reality dawning in him: "It is so, it is so. Oh, humanity, humanity!" (*Etzi ine, etzi. A! anthropotis, anthropotis!*)[43] The questions of the Muslims were answered, their confusion swept away, by the absolute destruction that followed.

A similar exchange took place in Athens where Muslim notables had withdrawn to the citadel of the Acropolis, surrounded by waves of bandits who were deploying the new national idiom. They asked of the besieging rebels the familiar question: Who were they? "We are Greeks" (Ellines) fighting to free the patria. The Muslim, a Greek speaker from the area, responded: "And what are we? Aren't we Greeks?" "But you are Mohammedans." "Then why don't you become [Muslims] too and we will all be free." The Greek retort, of sorts, came in the shape of the pieces of the butchered notables showered down from the walls of the Acropolis on the astonished crowds below.[44]

Another exchange involved the high-status survivors of the massacre of Tripolitsa who were moved about the peninsula before being ransomed off. There was no place to escape in what was now an island of rebels, so the captives had some liberty to move about the villages where they were held. On occasion the captives visited their captors, for example to celebrate the name-day of one of the Christians, and drank a few too many toasts to the celebrants. They had long conversations with Panos, the eldest Kolokotronis son. Tired of being called "Persians" in contrast to the Greeks, a Muslim declared: "We're Greek too because we were born and raised in Greece, so were our fathers and ancestors. You should not call us Persians and kill us, since outside of faith we are brothers." Panos changed the geographic imaginary: "You came from the deserts of Arabia and you conquered our country, you took our farms and our freedom and you tyrannized us."[45] Needless to say the Muslims were neither Persians nor Arabian nomads, and most of them were Moreans, but that was beside the point. The Muslims were prisoners, the Greeks were winning the war, and the Greeks set the terms of the nation. Muslims were foreigners.

In terms of the dawning realization that this was all something new, we have the testimony of the Morean Mir Yusuf who visited Tripolitsa when Ibrahim pasha took the city in 1825 (see chapter 15). He knew that the population had been massacred, but massacres were not uncommon. Instead he was horrified that the Muslim cemetery had been ploughed under and made into arable land. He understood now that the war was meant to erase his kind completely, his past and his ancestry and therefore his future, and his confusion became a deep despair.[46]

Further north, in Roumeli, Muslim Albanian mercenaries also learned that the lines of confrontation, inclusion, and exclusion were new. In November or December 1821 the Muslim Albanian warlord Tahir Abbas (Abazis to the Greeks) came to Arta and Missolonghi to see if he could work with the Christian rebels. To him any unrest was an opportunity to join one or another side, share in the spoils, and participate in any new distribution of privileges. Religion had never been an obstacle when it came to striking new alliances. To wit, at that time Abbas was fighting alongside Christian mercenaries on the side of Ali pasha of Yanena.

Now there was a war in the Morea and opportunity beckoned. Abbas met with the local Christian warlords who were comrades from past campaigns, and he proposed that they offer their services to the Moreans. Together as "Albanians, Roumeliots, and Souliots" they made overtures to the notables and promised to come south to join them. They never followed through. What Abbas found as he traveled the region disgusted and horrified him. The Muslims men had been killed, and the women were kept as sex slaves or they had been baptized. The mosques had been destroyed. The lines of simplification were new, stark, and unmistakable. This was a new world, not like the old one, and as Muslims Abbas and his men were likely to be the next victims. They spent the remainder of the decade offering and withdrawing their services to successive Ottoman commanders. For the Porte this was back to business as usual: the sultan pardoned them for their support of Ali, appointed them to high positions, and planned to have them murdered.[47]

3+

1821 was a revolution, no doubt. It was a demographic revolution that ended Islam in the Morea and reserved the space for Christians. It was a national revolution, a mass mobilization that brought together disparate populations to form the modern Greeks. The Revolution was foundational and the legacy is enduring. Over the next century independent Greece would expand its territory, and the template of 1821 was applied almost everywhere. The homogeneity of the Greek people today, with over 98 percent Greek Orthodox, owes to the events and precedents of 1821.

But the Revolution had not produced a state, only an agglomeration of regions that were themselves loose associations of localities. Standing in the way were the Morean notables who had gained the most from 1821, did not intend to share their good fortune with other regions, and set about reestablishing the hierarchy that placed them on top and the peasants on the bottom. For them the Revolution was over. For others it was incomplete.

Chapter 13

Republics of the Privileged

Greece in 1823

Prologue

25 MARCH 2021, the bicentennial of the Greek Revolution. The public commemorations have been uninteresting, the traditional speeches filled with one-dimensional heroes and massacres recast as great military victories. It is all the more disappointing because I have been following the bicentennial observations of the death of Napoleon, where scholars engage in public debate about his life and legacy.

In my car leaving Athens, I scan the radio and hear more speeches and documentaries narrated with deep voices and soundtracks of cannon and Peloponnesian clarinets. I land on what is obviously a low-budget, obscure station with a small radius of coverage. I can hear the speaker light his cigarette and pause for his drags. He is on a rant about corrupt Greek politicians, a vague Europe of euros and technocrats, and Greek plutocratic bankers. And then he turns to the kotsabases, the Ottoman Christian notables who took over the Revolution and used it to rule over the population as exploiters and despots. He declares that the Greeks are being squeezed today by the latter-day kotsabases, the governments and the wealthy, making the anniversary a reminder that the Revolution is unfinished.

When he moves on to the Freemasons I turn off the radio. But as with any such rant I try to clear my head of the clutter of nonsense and identify the truth it contains.

The Persistence of the Old Regime

The Greeks in 1824 were a nation racked by internal divisions, and the nation lacked a single authority to lend it coherence. Both problems related to the Morean notables who remained in control of their respective localities. They continued to exploit their villagers without having to share the money with the agas, and they were suspicious of any authority that questioned their supremacy in their regions. They stood in the way of any institution that might be national. Greeks from other regions called the kotsabases proud, which was an insult taken from scripture.

When the Revolution broke out in spring 1821, the Morean notables formed authorities that were local and dominated by themselves: the Messinian Senate in Kalamata, the Community of Ilida in Gastouni, the Directory of Achaïa in Patras, the Chancellorship of Corinth, and the Chancellorship of Argos.[1] In May the localities formed the Peloponnesian Senate, using the ancient name for the Morea. This was a gathering of notables who confirmed their own supremacy. The old districts were renamed eparchies. The kotsabases became eparchs. Through the Senate the notables discussed which campaigns to support. Coordination was made easier by the fact that virtually every eparch was related to every other by birth or marriage. But each eparch had his own armed force and each made the final decisions about his own eparchy.[2]

The coordination of the Peloponnese was loose, and its coordination with other regions was looser still. Most of the Aegean Islands stood aloof of the Revolution, but three islands joined the Moreans in 1821: Hydra and Spetses which were just off the eastern coast and dependent on Morean trade, and Psara with its formidable fleet of armed merchant ships. They governed themselves, as they had in Ottoman times. Their small ships were successful against the Ottoman fleet, and their fireships terrorized Ottoman captains who avoided battle. The Ottomans lacked experienced crews: the sultan had dismissed the Christian sailors who now, unemployed, joined the Revolution. The grand vizier exhorted the fleet to engage the enemy and support the land forces but the fleet's encounters with the Greeks had ended poorly. Their ships hugged the coasts and stayed in the bays.[3]

Together Hydra, Spetses, and Psara boasted about two hundred armed vessels but they each set their own goals and they usually campaigned separately. No doubt they were animated by patriotic fervor, but they also expected pay for any support they offered to the Moreans. The Revolution after all had been a solution to the unemployment of the sailors, and the sailors expected rewards. Sometimes they refused to sail until they were paid, which is why, as seen in the previous chapter, Chios was left undefended in 1822.[4] In 1825 Ibrahim pasha of Egypt was able to land in the Morea without interference, and for the same reason (see chapter 15).

In Roumeli two administrations came into being. These were putatively governed by two arriving Phanariots, Alexander Mavrokordatos in the west and Theodoros Negris in the east. The regional notables and warlords accepted them as a compromise—better outsiders than one of their rivals—and because they were polyglots who knew diplomacy and Europe.[5] But the Phanariots were dependent on warlords who were cooperative when they were paid, and unreliable even when they were. To say that either of them governed their regions would be an exaggeration. Mavrokordatos had money to hire armed men but his influence was limited to one town, and even there he was under threat by other armed bands. Negris had no resources and he soon left.

That some form of national authority was needed even the Morean notables accepted. There would be Ottoman attacks from Roumeli and the Moreans would need the Roumeliots to intercept them. There could be attacks by sea and the Moreans and Roumeliots would need the island fleets to guard the coasts. Funds and supplies would have to be gathered and moved about. The revolutionaries wanted international recognition, but there was no one government to recognize. The new Greece might seek loans on the foreign bond markets in the way that Latin American revolutionaries had raised money in London, but which faction of the revolutionaries represented Greece, and what state would owe the money?

In December 1821 the regions came together in the First National Assembly at Piada, later rechristened Epidavros after the nearby archeological site. Most of the attendees were Morean notables supplemented by Aegean Islanders and Roumeliotes. The Phanariots based in Roumeli came to offer their experience. The sparse representation of clergy spoke to the subordination of the church to the national cause—the opposite of the later depiction of the church as the repository of nationhood, and despite the myriad artistic depictions of priests at the center of the Revolution. The uprising of 1821 had also been a revolt against the church as a component part of the Ottoman order. Those clergy who had thrown in their lot with the revolutionaries tended to be locals, with ties to the Morean notable families. From this time Greek politicians began the process of separating the church from the patriarchate which was so deeply implicated in Ottoman governance. In its place would be a national church with some influence and wealth, but subordinated to the national state. The Christianity of the revolutionaries mattered, but they did not need the clergy to prove their Christianity and it did not mean ceding power to priests. The priests were there to bless what the notables decided.[6]

Piada was the assembly that proclaimed the Greek uprising a "Holy War" and formally declared Greek independence.[7] In January 1822 the assembly agreed on a Provisional Administration for all the main regions, but it was federative insofar as it recognized the four distinct regions as "the peoples" (not the people) of Greece. It called each region a *klase* (class or category): the Morea, eastern Roumeli, western Roumeli, and the three islands. These were each accepted as they were, i.e., various forms of oligarchy proclaimed by oligarchs themselves, with one or another degree of support or tolerance from the masses of armed men.[8] The regions themselves were federative, so the Greek polity of 1822 was a federation of federations.

Not that constitutions, liberalism, and the Enlightenment were what made most people take up arms in 1821. Men like Mavrokordatos came to the Piada assembly armed with sample constitutions in a sincere effort to enshrine the principles of nationality and liberal citizenship. They were not naïve and they well understood that their work was not what motivated the fighters; it was an aspiration for the future and a showcase for Europe. This and later national assemblies—there would be four in the 1820s and one more in 1832—approved detailed provisions about the nature of the new regime. Some of these provisions are significant because they confirmed certain realities, like the primacy of Christianity in the new nation, and the idea of a Greek (Ellinas) as the primary marker of the population. Others, such as a franchise and elections, were fictions. They would become significant later, in the 1840s, when they were cited as precedents in new constitutional arrangements.[9]

At issue in the 1820s for the mass of armed peasants was something more profound and direct than the written word: popular sovereignty in the form of mass mobilization and a new sense of entitlement. The victories of 1821 and 1822 would have been unimaginable if peasants had not armed themselves and marched—to kill and pillage, to be sure, and also to overthrow a regime of deep exploitation and attain a better life. It was fair for them to ask what the Revolution was about, whether blood had been spilled to enhance the position of the notables. The notables may have taken on new and exalted titles, but they were the same Ottoman kotsabases who had squeezed them for so long, hand-in-hand with the agas and pashas.

For the Morean notables the issue was direct control over resources and people. Legalistics and institutions were useful if they served that purpose and dispensable if they did not. The peasant mass movement of 1821–2 was necessary to the survival of the notables and they supplied it, but thereafter they expected peasants to resume their place of subordination. Provisions for the popular election of the delegates and eparchs (the notables) were fictions and the notables continued to be self-appointed. Each notable confirmed the status of the other. Each aspiring authority had to begin its overtures by affirming the local rule of the notable in question.[10]

For example, in anticipation of the national assemblies, Sisinis in Gastouni organized proclamations from the villagers and clergy that recognized him as their plenipotentiary. When his primacy was in doubt, as it was in 1823–4, Sisinis's men visited the elders and householders and invited them to affirm that their notable was their "head" and eparch, and to confirm that the eparchy would follow its own "system." In nearby Pyrgos the Avgerinos family of notables organized similar petitions. That "system" amounted to the primacy of the notable in question, and the same notables were proclaimed eparchs and plenipotentiaries to the national assemblies with predictable regularity.[11]

The Provisional Administration was only as powerful as the people who occupied its offices. In 1822 at Piada the Phanariots Mavrokordatos and Negris were given the highest offices of president and vice-president. But they represented the Roumelian regions that were the least coherent, and they lacked power bases of their own. The Moreans called them "foreigners," "outsiders," and "men without a patria."[12] Commands sent by Negris and Mavrokordatos carried little authority and no force. Instructions sent by ministers, Morean notables like Mavromichalis and Notaras, came from men with real power bases, so that any instruction they sent was a negotiation with recipients who had power bases of their own.

A Second National Assembly, at Astros in April 1823, was again dominated by notables. It did abolish the Peloponnesian Senate, so that the rivalries of the notables were transferred to the new national institutions. The Moreans probably thought that the abolition of the Peloponnesian Senate would allow them to take control of an emerging national government. The Roumeliots and Aegean Islanders probably thought that the Moreans would be subordinated to a national authority. More notables from the Aegean Islands joined these institutions and pushed for a real national policy, but they were just more voices in a cacophony of localisms. Soon the Aegean Islanders and Roumeliots formed a rival administration. Indeed intermittently throughout the 1820s the Greeks had more than one set of people calling themselves a government. Whenever a faction fell out with a formal authority, it simply formed another one.

The administration(s) as such did not have much money so it sustained itself by selling the tax farms to the notables. In 1822 this arrangement was formalized, so that each eparch who bought a tax farm was responsible for delivering a flat sum in return. Sisinis, for example, owed 40,000 kuruş in exchange for the right to collect taxes in the eparchy, and he then haggled with government agents over the amounts and timing of payments.[13] (The Greeks still counted in the Ottoman currency.) Notables did channel resources to the government when it suited them, and warlords did allocate a portion of the loot after battles, but in this there was no consistency. Hence the administration scurried to take its cut of ad hoc sources of revenue: the high-status Muslim hostages who were held by the notables and warlords, the Corinthian grape harvest which was technically national property but controlled by the notables, and the loot gathered after the fall of a town or the defeat of an army.

In practice there was no national strategy, only a succession of campaigns, and each notable could decide which campaigns to support. In 1822, Sisinis readily joined with other regional notables in the siege of Patras, which was near his home turf and allowed the Ottomans to strike out at will. Patras also had loot for the taking, and for this reason Sisinis struck a deal with neighboring notables to exclude all others from the campaign and the booty.[14] Here he did show his use, and indeed only the notables had the experience and networks of agents and enforcers to mobilize resources. Sisinis "gave us everything," recalled Kolokotronis, who commanded the siege. He sent to the army's camp four thousand sheep and eighty cows and ensured that whatever the soldiers ate was replaced. He sent bread. He paid the gunpowder mills of Dimitsana, Divri, and Douka (today Neraida) to supply Patras and Missolonghi.[15] He more or less supported the Christians holding Missolonghi across the Gulf of Corinth on the Roumelian mainland because it was a forward defense for his own region.

As for the fleet, Sisinis sent supplies when it guarded his own coasts. In August 1822 he sent livestock and hard tack because he feared that a new Ottoman attack would come from across the Gulf of Corinth and pass through his territory. But four months earlier neither he nor the other notables sent money when the fleet was meant to protect the islands of the eastern Aegean Sea. That was not a Morean affair.[16] The failure of the notables to pay the fleet consistently was a chronic problem in the 1820s, and so was the refusal of the fleet to fight unless paid.

In addition to being given the tax farms, the notables expected repayment for their outlays. For this reason Sisinis's records are very detailed and careful, if not necessarily complete and candid. He calculated his expenses in kind and in money, submitted invoices with 8 percent interest added, and for the moment accepted bonds that gave him priority in buying the revenues of his region. When he was asked to support campaigns he had not approved, or even to deliver the pre-arranged payments from his tax farms, he protested that he was poor, demanded that he be paid himself, and presented a bill for 1.5 million kuruş.[17] His records show that he received small handouts from one or another authority but nothing like the amounts he thought he was due. "Are these the rewards of the patria?" he protested.[18] Again, the government did not have much to give him, so in the meantime the notables were paid with tax farms.[19]

The character and names of the revenues themselves had changed only slightly. Discriminatory taxes on Christians were abolished but the notables collected the other Ottoman taxes, under the same names, and added the sale of bonds which the population was required to buy. They took control of the fisheries, and they controlled the tariffs at the ports.[20] The notables also took control of the lands that had been abandoned by the fleeing Muslims. These were termed national lands: technically they did not belong to anyone and their distribution would be decided in the future. But in the meantime they were managed by the notables. Some were taken by warlords. Kolokotronis and his sons were now owners of estates and revenues across the Morean peninsula.[21]

The same applied to workshops and mills abandoned by the Muslims. These were rented out and the notables collected the rents. Sisinis received regular and detailed reports from his agents. "I rented the mill of Hasan aga in Tragano to Mr Anagnostis Votzou for the year," reads one report. "Alexis rented the bakery of Osman effendi for 50 kuruş," "That of Hadji-Ibrahim to Mr Avgerinos—48," "That of Mullah Hasan to the same," "That of Bekir effendi to Stamatis," and so on. The properties monitored by Sisinis alone ran in the hundreds. He also took responsibility for the harvesting of the Corinthian grapes that were once controlled by Semseti bey.[22]

All in all, the notables saw the Revolution as a confirmation of their wealth and status. Having overthrown the agas, they would replace them. Wrote Deliyannis when queried, "Of course this eparchy belongs to the Deliyannises exclusively."[23] Notables held court in their fortified mansions, with supplicants kneeling or lying prostrate. Supplicants chose to "humbly submit" (*tapinos proskino*). Deliyannis was addressed with new and old honorifics: "Most brave lord" (*geneotate archon*), "Your brilliance" (*eklamprotate*), "Your excellency" (*exochotate*), and, covering all the possibilities, "most brave and all-noble master, my lord, Mister Kanellos" (*geneotate kai panevgenestate afthenta mi archon Kirie Kanelo*). Village women asking Sisinis for compensation for the loss of their sons in battle wrote as "your slave" to their "archon." A later biographer described Sisinis in terms that were meant to be admiring: "And the poor respected him, lying on the earth and submitting, and he cared for them as a brother and father, warden and physician, advisor, etc." George Finlay, the historian who was also there, put it differently: peasants recounted that they were not permitted to address Sisinis unless they fell on their knees. Sisinis demanded his sons be addressed as beys; Mavromichalis had always been one. Notables appeared with their Muslim concubines, some with full harems of Muslim girls.[24]

The popular anger was palpable. Papaflessas denounced the notables as sultanic and arbitrary. Kolokotronis thought that the notables were trying to grab the land for themselves and "wanted to leave the people naked"—though his family was also busily acquiring estates and tax farms of its own. "The people [laos] always meant to kill the archons," he recalled, what he termed "the people's fever."[25]

Exit the Friendly Society

From the point of view of the notables, the Revolution was over as soon as the sultan had been overthrown and the agas eliminated. Hence the ignominious disappearance of the Friendly Society. The notables never forgave the society for the uncontrolled outbreak of spring 1821, and they were contemptuous when it did not deliver the long-promised Russian intervention. Others such as Count Capo d'Istria and Bishop Ignatios likewise disavowed it: it smacked of conspiracy, Jacobinism, and Carbonari, and it would alienate European opinion.[26] The society had provided a national idiom and a mobilizing ideology when these were needed. But the Morean notables stopped acting in its name soon after the uprising had broken out.

The legacy—for some the stigma—of the society was carried by Dimitris Ypsilantis who had arrived in the Morea in summer 1821 to claim overall leadership of the Revolution. He was the younger brother of Alexander and a sergeant in the Russian army. He claimed to be the representative of his brother and therefore the society, and he let it be understood that he was the advance guard of a Russian army. To that extent he carried some authority, but not much. He tried and failed to take overall command of the Christian forces. He tried and often failed to prevent some of the massacres of surrendering Muslims, he tried and mostly failed to claim a share of the loot of Tripolitsa, and he tried and mostly failed to control the ransom money that was received in exchange for high-ranking Muslim captives. His influence evaporated when it became known that brother Alexander had been routed and the Russians were not coming. The Morean notables dismissed him as the "the plenipotentiary of nothing and the representative of a non-existent Authority"—i.e., the Friendly Society. By year's end even Mavrokordatos, himself an outsider and isolated, had denounced Ypsilantis, the Friendly Society, and all talk of more revolution. He delivered to the First National Assembly a long letter from Bishop Ignatios denouncing the same people.[27]

Ypsilantis's only option was to appeal to poor village soldiers or claim to speak on their behalf, and it does seem that villagers saw him as an alternative to the notables. In some proclamations he denounced all those who had participated in the Ottoman system, which meant the kotsabases as well as the agas. He termed the notables "Turk-worshippers and Turco-kotsabases." Papaflessas, who was hostile to the notables, urged Ypsilantis to lead the soldiers against the notables and he refused: he understood that the notables were needed, and he was not one to feed what he thought was the mob. But the exchange did set off a riot. At the village of Vervena near Tripolitsa about five thousand armed peasants surrounded the notable Deliyannis with the intention of killing him, the other archons, and perhaps Kolokotronis as well. Kolokotronis held them back with the argument that it would look bad in

Europe. Some months later soldiers again asked his permission to murder the notables and again he refused. Arguably the reckoning was postponed by the rush to attack and plunder the Muslims and then guard
against Ottoman retribution.[28]

The notables understood that they were vulnerable. At the national
assemblies of Piada and Astros they appeared with small armies to
guard them while other armies of peasant soldiers camped nearby. Peasant soldiers asked when "our afentis" (lord) Alexander Ypsilantis was
arriving to become king, but he was by then in an Austrian prison.
When the First National Assembly met, Dimitris was not invited and
he was given an honorific title. No mention was made of the Friendly
Society, and its emblems were not adopted as the national emblems.[29]

The Greeks Face Each Other

Dimitris Ypsilantis was not the main problem faced by the notables; he
was an annoyance and a disappointment. Their problem was their own
rivalries, complicated by the emergence of the warlords as an additional
force, all of them feeding once again on a disgruntled peasantry. The rivalries broke out into open warfare in 1823, what they called a first civil
war. This was largely a fight among notables and warlords from the Morea.
Putatively they used the government institutions created by the national
assemblies, but different factions split into competing government institutions. They struck and broke agreements with each other, with the notables of the islands, and with politicians from Roumeli. Kolokotronis was
given and then stripped of overall military command, and he in turn
moved against opposing alliances of notables.[30]

Civil war may be too refined a term for what was occurring on the
ground, a mad grab for the money of villagers and a free-for-all of notables, warlords, and bandits organized by clan and region.[31] Sisinis
faced the incursions of nearby notables who sent men to loot villages
in his region. He hired Souliot mercenaries to protect himself. But he
was also facing the wrath of the armed villagers who dared defy him.
Before there was one tyranny, he wrote, that of the sultan. Now there
was a tyranny of the many, a "hell" of "anarchy, murders, kidnappings,

and all the evils." Sisinis lamented that he was promised "Philadelphia," that they would "make Greece into America, but now—banish the thought!"[32]

In the territories of Deliyannis in October 1823, the warlord Dimitris Plapoutas took villages and collected revenues that had been bought by Deliyannis. Deliyannis sent men who killed villagers, looted homes, and tried to dislodge the intruders. In nearby villages still other armed men, these ones lesser Morean bandits, moved in to make their own claims. "I have no beef with the poor," the barely literate Vasilis and Panoris wrote to the villagers, in letters dated "today." But they wanted payments. If the villagers did not come to him to pay up then "my whole band will come and then don't complain . . . I swear, get ready, and whatever happens will be on your necks."

Villagers mobilized against different claimants and Deliyannis's managers warned him to stay away so as not to cause more "dissatisfaction and unrest." His extractions were already too high. Villagers also mobilized against each other. Elders in one village threatened the elders of another to "take your village with muskets." The other elders replied: "we see you're in the mood for a fight because that's how you've been watered" (taught), and prepared for battle. Still they asked how.it was possible that Christians were now fighting Christians and poor villagers were fighting other villagers. "We are tyrannized and victimized, not just us but the whole eparchy," and together they should fight off the armed bands that were robbing the villages. The Provisional Administration asked the same question—how could Christians kill Christians—and offered to mediate, which was ignored.[33]

And there matters rested as the revolution entered its third year in 1824, an ongoing discussion of what were called "Greek things" (*Ellinika prammata*). It was a nation divided horizontally by wealth and status and vertically by competing localisms and regionalisms. Greece was a republic of notables and warlords in the Morea, competing and now fighting over a mass of villagers. The three Aegean Islands were republics of shipowners and notables in an uneasy alliance with sailors, and each island governed itself. In Roumeli the two administrations scarcely existed in 1824. Mavrokordatos pretended to lead in western Roumeli, and mercenaries followed his money. With the warlords fighting among themselves and defecting, Greek-held territory in Roumeli was reduced, ultimately, to the town of Missolonghi, which endured sieges until 1826. In eastern Roumeli the administration of Negris disappeared altogether, sidelined by waves of Christian armed factions who were as likely to kill each other as any Ottoman invader.[34]

The Morea was the core of the Revolution but the Morean notables refused to think nationally. Others did. For some time the Aegean Islanders and Roumeliots had been demanding that the Moreans merge their regional cause into the Greek one and consider the needs of a larger Greece. The Morean notables could remain the "fathers" of the Morea and the Hydriots could become the "fathers" of the nation. The Aegean Islanders and Roumeliots were not entirely altruistic, to be sure. The nation was a way to dilute the power of the Moreans and give themselves a platform through which they could extend their own power. Then again no nation is born only of fervor and ideals, and the unfolding of a Greek national idea was a typical mix of loftiness and self-interest. Nations are also about raw power, and for the time being the carriers of the national idea could not compel the Moreans to become good national citizens.[35]

This changed in 1824 when the idea of a Greek state triumphed. It traced to some British Romantic poets, some savvy Greek politicians, and some rough Roumelian mercenaries. They were brought together by a speculative bubble on the London bond market.

Chapter 14

The Second Revolution, 1824

London Bonds, Roumeli, and the Sack of the Morea

Prologue

MY CAB DRIVER *talks a lot, as do many cab drivers in Athens. He asks me what I do for a living, and I make the mistake of answering candidly that I am a historian. Every Greek is a historian and cab drivers are also lecturers with a captive audience. When I tell him I am writing on the Greek Revolution, I wonder why I am being so frank. I resign myself to hearing a short course on Greek history with ample hand movements, and I pray that he keeps at least one hand on the steering wheel.*

But the driver now speaks less and actually asks my opinion. "Is it true that Androutsos was a traitor?" Androutsos was a warlord from Roumeli who went down in the history books as a national hero, but Greek historians have pointed out that he went over to the Ottomans. He asks about another hero, Karaiskakis, and points toward the port of Piraeus and the soccer stadium named after him. Karaiskakis was put on trial for treason because he struck deals with his old comrades in the Ottoman forces. "And these men made the Revolution," the driver says through clenched teeth.

The man is right to wonder what he was taught in grade school, as was I. I propose to him that there is no harm in stating the facts of the Revolution while still celebrating the Greece that came into being over the next two centuries. It produced citizenship. In 1844 Greece was the most democratic regime in Europe, with universal manhood suffrage. The veterans of the

Revolution made that happen in a coup. Something must have gone right. I do not think he hears me.

As for the warlords, I am not sure that treason is the right word for men who spent their lives hiring themselves out to a rich variety of masters. The nation was too new for them to understand it as an absolute commitment. They could and often did sell their services to Muslim notables and overseas empires, or simply carved out their own fiefdoms where they visited a brutal terror on the inhabitants. These were men I would not want to meet in a dark alley. One can muse about how bad people can produce good results, or about how bad times produce bad behavior, but this would be platitude.

Their most enduring accomplishment sometimes goes unnoticed. They achieved the destruction of the old regime in the Morea, something of a second revolution. In 1824 these pitiless men crushed the Morean notables, and they did it for pay and loot. The politicians who hired them to take the Morea also seemed flawed, as will any person who is looked at too closely, and their motives seem impure: to remove their rivals and seize power. The mercenaries knew what they were doing: making a living. Together they made way for a national space.

There was a liberalism in what they produced, and we might miss it because they were dressed in kilts and spoke Albanian. Like budding liberals anywhere, they created a higher authority that might stop them from killing each other. The Greek factions and regions would share power and negotiate the terms of their participation in the nation and admit, finally, that they owed something to Greece.

For all this to happen the victors of 1824 needed a lot of money. They found it in London.

Philhellenes: Soldiers, Liberals, and Speculators

Europe experienced a wave of sympathy for the Greeks from 1821, and in 1823 the French gave it a name: Philhellenism, a term borrowed most likely from Phillip II of Macedon or the ancient Parthians. The first large wave of support occurred in Russia, which had a tradition of sympathy for the Greeks—as heirs to the ancients, as the fount of Orthodoxy— stretching back to 1770.[1] Public support was carefully aligned with official policy. It took the form of relief for the tens of thousands of refugees who came across the Ottoman border as they fled the war zones as early as March 1821. The support came from the government ministries, regional governors, and the Russian Orthodox church. Aristocrats and merchants channeled funds as well, and some peasants and serfs dropped coins into the collection boxes. State and private funds paid to liberate Christians taken as slaves. But in keeping with policy there would be no Russian military supplies for the Greek fighters because Russia until 1826 would not recognize the Greek cause. They were rebels, deserving of charity and no more.[2]

To be sure, Greek merchants based in Russia could operate from other cities like Livorno, but few in Russia could defy the autocrat and few probably even wanted to. It was well understood that Christian charity was one matter, policy and warfare entirely a matter for the tsar. The poet Pushkin is a good example of this stance. He always treaded a fine line between implied defiance of authority and ultimate conformity. His early enthusiasm for the Greeks yielded to disappointment when he met the Greeks, in this case merchants in Russia's south. His expectations crashed against the reality of people whom he considered overtly materialistic, philistine, and lower on the status hierarchy. He came to see the Greek War as an occasion to expand Russia's imperial power, alongside campaigns in the Caucasus which he joined as an observer. By the time he died his romantic death (defending his wife's honor in a duel), he mentioned the Greeks rarely and with contempt, as an addendum to imperial ambition.[3]

To the west the first wave of Philhellenism took the form of officers and NCOs who had been seeking work since the end of the Napoleonic Wars. It is not clear that these volunteers were believers in the Greek cause or that they are rightly termed "friends of the Greeks." Some were no doubt fighting for liberty, but many were not particular about who paid their wages. Some were in one way or another political, in the sense that their politics made it hard to find work in Europe. Bonapartists were denied commissions in their home countries, and veterans of the defeated Italian and Spanish Revolutions were again without a master. But this did not necessarily mean they would opt to serve the Greeks. To put

FIGURE 14.1. Memorial to Paul Marie Bonaparte at the Church of Aghios Nikolaos, Spetses, 2023. Photograph by Alexandra Manoli. *This Bonaparte was Napoleon's nephew. He volunteered to fight for Greek independence but was not handy
with weaponry and shot himself. The locals preserved his body in a barrel of rum
until a French warship collected the barrel and the Bonaparte in 1832.*

this in perspective: the pool of unemployed soldiers in Europe was vast,
and quite a few enlisted under Ali pasha in Yanena, others under the
sultan. It is likely that many more served in Egypt under Mehmed Ali
than served in Greece, and anyway Mehmed was a better paymaster.

But many did serve the Greeks. In the 1820s hundreds of these veterans made their way across the Adriatic and Ionian seas from France,
Italy, Switzerland, Germany, the Netherlands, Poland, Scandinavia, and
Austria. There were a few Americans like the nephew (he claimed) of
George Washington, William, who like so many of the volunteers was
killed in battle. Napoleon's nephew Paul Marie came as well and died in
1827 when he accidentally shot himself.[4] His Greek hosts, unsure what

to do with the body of a Bonaparte, preserved him in a barrel of rum until someone French could fetch him.

The volunteers searched in vain for the "Greek Army" in order to receive their commissions. But there was no national army as they understood it, only irregulars employed by local warlords and notables and peasants who gathered and dispersed as they saw fit. Instead the volunteers formed into regiments and battalions named after their leaders (Regiment Baleste, Regiment Tarella), their patrons (the Byron Brigade), or the cause (Philhellene Battalion, Sacred Band). They were tiny formations, with perhaps one to two hundred men in each, most of them officers, very often dueling among themselves, and in every case undersupplied, underpaid, and hungry. When they agreed to serve "the Greeks" (one or another faction of Greeks or other patrons who might pay them) they were sent into battle by inexperienced civilians, putatively backed by Greek irregulars who practiced a very different warfare.[5]

One can understand the clash of military cultures. The Greek irregulars found Europe's vaunted "discipline" odd and suicidal as the European officers marched mindlessly into enemy barrages and kept marching as their comrades fell dead around them. By local practice they should have run for cover on a hillside, and this the Greeks did as they abandoned the Europeans alone on the field where they died in large numbers. The pattern began at the Battle of Peta in July 1822 where the Philhellene Battalion was destroyed, with two-thirds killed on the field and the prisoners beheaded and impaled. It ended with the Battle of Kamatero outside Athens in January 1827. It was here that Denis Bourbaki of France was killed and his head sent on to Constantinople (see chapter 4). Many more volunteers succumbed to hunger and epidemics, and survivors begged for passage back home. In substance the Europeans had been trained for the wrong kind of warfare, they never understood Balkan tactics, and they did not belong to the clans and regional networks around which Greek formations cohered. Kolokotronis quipped that the problem lay with the unruly Greeks but also the ignorant newcomers: "Let Wellington give me an army of 40,000 and I can command it. But if they gave *him* 500 Greeks he couldn't command them for an hour."[6]

The Greeks were scoring victories on their own. The military significance of the Philhellenes was negligible. When the European soldiers fought, they lost. The conclusion back in Europe that the volunteers were "martyrs of the Crusade" and "Holy Martyrs of the True Faith" was the most they could salvage from what was basically a disaster. Survivors moved on to other employers, including Mehmed Ali of Egypt who was preparing to invade the Morea. Some converted to Islam.[7] Italian revolutionaries—these ones true believers—who had come to lend their support after the defeat of their movements were marginalized. The Piedmontese Santorre di Santarosa was allowed into the Greek forces as a private, once he agreed to use a pseudonym; his history of liberal revolutionary activity could be embarrassing. He died in battle. The Italian liberal Vincenzo Gallina arrived in 1821 with crates of sample constitutions and co-wrote the Greek one. He found a career as a clerk for a Dutch shipowner in the Black and Aegean seas.[8]

Civilian Philhellenes had a more tangible effect on something less tangible: public opinion in Europe. The European press was filled with fanciful stories of the Greek cause that portrayed the Greeks as heirs of the ancients and martyrs of Christianity. Hundreds of books, pamphlets, and articles came out with dramatic narrations of Greek heroism and death, often written by people who had never been to the region. They are a good source on European imagination and fantasy and no less important for it. Ottoman Muslim barbarity was related in detail while massacres perpetrated by the Christians, though known, got less press. Reports of the massacre of Tripolitsa were overwhelmed by the massacre of Chios which entrenched the trope of Christian martyrdom. It was common to see calls for a "crusade," a battle of the "cross against the crescent," a war to evict the Muslims who were "the common enemy of mankind."[9]

Their effect on their own governments was small. The European courts treated the Greeks as rebels, no better than Carbonari, and threats to the status quo. As a result Philhellenism in its early years was quasi-oppositional and at odds with official policies. Soon the French government clamped down on the fundraising and closed the port of

Marseille to officers trying to reach the Greeks. German states banned the Greek committees and prohibited the movement of funds and men. Austria supported the sultan steadfastly. It blocked efforts to raise loans for the Greeks or use Trieste for the passage of volunteers and supplies.

The London Greek Committee was different because it was generally tolerated by the British government. It was founded in 1823 by men who tended to be liberals, many of them members of parliament, and saw in Greece a cause of liberty. It helped their cause that the British government wavered. Each new cabinet or minister produced a change in policy in one or the other direction. While officially Britain was neutral and thus traded with both sides of the Greek War, some ministers like Wellington were plainly hostile to the Greeks who were destabilizing the eastern Mediterranean. By contrast Foreign Secretary George Canning was sympathetic. He made his views plain when he attended a banquet of the London Greek Committee, though the king reprimanded him.[10]

More profoundly London was different because it was the center of global finance and it was in the midst of an impressive financial bubble. The post–1815 slump had ended and the City was awash with money seeking a good return. British government bonds were safe, so safe that the interest paid fell from 5 percent to 3.5. Instead brokers sponsored bonds for foreign governments that were riskier but offered the bondholders better terms. There were higher rates of interest. There were special provisions that repaid the first few years of interest out of the loan itself (a sinking fund), meaning that a part of the loan never reached the borrowers. And there were discount rates, or gaps between the nominal price and the amount actually paid for the bond. A bondholder who had bought, say, a 100-pound bond might pay only 70 pounds, but would be repaid the full 100.

Publicly held sovereign bonds, as opposed to loans from banking houses to states, were a new business. They were invented to help France pay its indemnities after the Napoleonic Wars. Soon brokers offered bonds on behalf of well-established powers like Russia, Prussia, and Denmark, emerging states like Mexico, and states that had not quite come into existence, like the regimes of Brazil, Peru, Colombia, and Chile. The bonds were lapped up by people who could combine their liberal principles with a hefty profit. The prospectuses that introduced the bonds described lands of plenty, paradisal places of minerals, agriculture, and hard workers and yeomen that awaited the savvy investor who would own a piece of a country before it even existed.[11] In 1821 the enterprising Gregor MacGregor offered bonds for the land of Poyais in Central America, a veritable Eden, and the bonds sold well. But he had invented Poyais from whole cloth: there had never been such a place and there never would be, and both Poyais and MacGregor became bywords for an elaborate scam and investor gullibility.[12]

Greece was another such paradise. In 1823 agents of the Greek government (in fact, from the faction of islanders who would soon be arrayed against the Morean notables) arrived in London and were introduced to liberals of the London Greek Committee and brokers in the City. Before long they were arranging a bond issue in the name of "the Greek government." In this land of opulence and riches equal to that of "the whole South American continent," of philosopher–farmers and pious laborers nearly Calvinist in their ethic, the borrower could invest in a Christian cause and make quite a profit in the process. The London Greek Committee would ensure that the loan reached "the Greek government" so that it could be employed against the Ottomans. Lending to the Greeks was at odds with British government policy of neutrality but it was not illegal. Respect for the markets was an article of faith, as the Russian ambassador in London explained to his perplexed superiors in St. Petersburg who already thought that British diplomats were clerks for the merchant houses (which in fact they were). Now, it seemed, the banking houses were dictating foreign policy.[13]

The bond issue for Greece sold well because of its exceptionally good terms: a good rate of interest at 5 percent, a hefty sinking fund to cover the first two years of repayment, and a discount of 41 percent. For every 59 pounds spent to buy a bond, the lender could expect 100 pounds back, plus interest. The brokers and intermediaries took their commissions. Members of the Greek Committee came away with impressive profits by capitalizing on rumors and news that pushed the bonds up or down. After all the deductions were accounted for, the nominal loan of 800,000 pounds yielded a net amount of 308,000.[14] That latter amount would be sent to Greece.

The terms were terrible but the Greeks were focused on the enormous sum that they could pocket at that moment. There was no Greek state to be held accountable, and no certainty that a country of Greece would come into being. Greek national budgets were imaginary and hardly ever collected and spent.[15] The Greek representatives in London might agree to anything (arguably, they did) because their accountability was notional. There was gold to be had right now. Hence when the Greeks were offered a second loan in Paris but with better conditions in the long term, they opted for another loan in London because the immediate net payout was larger.[16]

And the sum really was spectacular for the Balkans, what the Greeks called "vast" and "massive" (ogodes). By one estimate the 308,000 pounds of 1824 was the equivalent to 10 million day-wages in the Morea. It could pay for thousands of mercenaries and could buy quite a lot of patronage. The sum could turn the politics of revolutionary Greece in favor of the faction that received it, and the Greek factions vied to be recognized as the Greek government.[17] The London Greek Committee seemed only vaguely aware that there were multiple factions claiming to be the Greek government, and that the men before them in London were Aegean Islanders, at odds with Moreans.

The decision—who represented Greece and who would receive the money—rested with the commissioners of the London Greek Committee in the Ionian region. One of them was the poet Lord Byron.

The Prince and the Poets

Alexander Mavrokordatos was a Phanariot prince. He was a member of one of the families that ruled over the peasantry of the Danubian Principalities on behalf of the sultan. Like many of his kin he was well educated, wealthy, worldly, and destined for a career in Ottoman diplomacy. He fell out of favor at the Porte and he fled to Austria, then Russia, then Pisa. No doubt he was in search of a purpose and a career, and what he found was a calling: liberalism. It addressed his immediate circumstances—what is the proper, regulated relationship between the person and power—and it gave him a goal: some form of rights and legal equality before the law or at least a higher authority. He ordered dozens of volumes from booksellers and immersed himself in the liberal classics. His newfound liberalism merged with his newfound nationalism, expressed in a memo. In it he wrote that the internal crisis of Ottoman governance led to violence and insecurity (the liberal critique), and the retrograde character of Islam versus the civilization of Christianity led to barbarities (the nationalist case). In the Balkans the predominance of Christians should lead to the overthrow of the old order.[18]

In Pisa he fell in with Percy Bysshe Shelley, the Romantic poet who was part Classical traveler, part exile, because he had eloped with Mary Godwin, soon to be Mary Shelley. As a Greek and a prince, he had cachet and pedigree, and the couple received Mavrokordatos regularly. Mavrokordatos shed his Ottoman robes and donned a frock coat. He found Mary impressive in her talent and intelligence, and he sat for days on end with Mary who taught him English. His languages now numbered seven, by other counts eleven. He taught Mary Greek, and the Shelleys told the prince of the southern Balkans which the prince had never visited.

Together the Shelleys and Mavrokordatos learned of the Greek uprising in the Danubian region and the Morea. There was still some confusion about who the Greeks were, and they mixed up their rebellions when they termed it a rising of "the Servians, the Epirotes, and the Souliots."[19] But they did know that it was a Christian movement and they termed it "the war of the Cross against the Crescent." Soon Mavrokordatos was on a ship from Marseille to revolutionary Greece and he expected to become its leader. In a narrow sense, he did. He was selected leader of western Roumeli by factions of notables and warlords who would not allow one of their own to be elevated and were happy to receive his money. He could speak to the Europeans. At the First National Assembly in Piada he was involved in drafting the first constitution which was widely publicized in Europe, and he was made president of the new government. He was still addressed as prince in correspondence, but in his responses he signed "The Citizen Mavrokordatos."

But he was an outsider to the Morea with no power base of his own. Soon the vacuousness of his office became obvious and in 1823 the Second National Assembly took away even the presidency. Mavrokordatos returned to the town of Missolonghi in western Roumeli. He used his money to hire local bandits and Souliots, to protect himself from other bandits and perhaps cobble together an army to pursue the war against the Ottomans. They were loyal to him while his money lasted. He financed and commanded the Philhellene Battalion of European officers, and it was he who sent it to its destruction at the Battle of Peta. He financed a first newspaper which dutifully reported what he requested. But his position was tenuous. The warlords, clans, and bandits saw him as just one more factor to consider in the larger jockeying for revenues and territories. The Greece of which he spoke was to them one of several options.

And then he met Lord Byron. Byron had recently come into his title and inheritances, still recovering from the scandal caused by his debts, the messy end to his marriage, and his active sex life. In Switzerland in 1816 he was in the company of Shelley and Godwin. The most memorable product of this period was *Frankenstein*, written by Mary Godwin—later Shelley—while another in their company wrote a vampire story that helped make the Balkan superstition into a European literary genre. Next Byron was in Italy, intermittently with the Shelleys, pondering his advancing age and grappling with his ennui. He wanted action. Causes that were both liberal and Romantic had gripped much of his generation and class. He considered joining revolutions in Italy, set his mind on South America, and commissioned a ship he named the *Bolivar*. Or perhaps it would be Spain.[20]

In the end Byron chose Greece as a cause and a destination, a place he had visited during his Classical tour and had been the subject of some of his poetry. His immensely popular *Childe Harold's Pilgrimage* (1812–18) was in part a contemplation of things Greek, enmeshed with a man's search for purpose that took him on a journey from Portugal to Greece (Byron's own itinerary in 1809 and 1810). In 1819, on the eve of the Greek Revolution, he published the first cantos of one of his most famous works, *Don Juan*. Some of it centered on his fascination with the Greece of the ancients as past civilization, as well as the Greeks of the present as compelling Oriental stereotype; or perhaps a truly free people. References to "sunsets" were as much about his own middle age as the lost glories of Greece; perhaps regeneration beckoned for both.[21]

Byron abandoned the *Bolivar* and chartered a brig which he christened the *Hercules*. In 1823 he made his way to insurgent Greece. He paused on the Ionian Islands, which were a British dominion, served his quarantine, and contemplated his next move. He intended to contribute personally to the Greek cause and referred to a figure of 20,000 pounds. In the end he probably spent more than that, on mercenaries, the Greek fleets, and one or another political faction.

Byron had also been appointed by the London Greek Committee as one of the trustees of the very large sum of gold, 308,000 pounds, and the first installments were being loaded onto ships. Between his money, the Committee's money, and his title, he was the object of multiple entreaties as he weighed the situation from Cephalonia. Alongside European adventurers and opportunists, just about all the warlords of Roumeli and quite a few from the Morea descended on him. The supplicants wanted the money. He knew some of these Greeks from his earlier travels and his agents reported back about others. Appeals came from Kolokotronis and Petrobey Mavromichalis of the Mani, and he ignored them. Invitations came from Sisinis and he was nonplussed: "I *have heard a good deal of Sisseni*, but not a *deal of good*."[22]

His encounter with Mavrokordatos was more promising. Mavrokordatos made the short trip from Missolonghi to Cephalonia, and the prince and the lord got along well. They were both aristocrats, and they were both liberals. The Shelleys were their mutual friends. Byron concluded that "he is the only civilized person (*on dit*) among the liberators."[23] In early 1824 both men were in Missolonghi, and Byron hired Souliot mercenaries as his guard. Teeming with armed men, Missolonghi was not a safe place and warriors had taken to shooting at Europeans for sport.[24] Perhaps the storied Souliots under his command would be the beginnings of a loyal and effective force to join in the conflict, though after paying them 6,000 pounds they demanded more and he sent them away.[25] He paid the Aegean fleets anchored in the region and the fleets sailed away. He outfitted the Byron Brigade of European volunteer officers and a few hundred local Christians. Ultimately he hoped to work with Mavrokordatos to launch an attack on the Ottomans. There was a bit of performance in his new calling. Along with his stunningly colorful military uniforms, Byron donned the kilts and vests for which he became famous, and prepared to become a man of action.

To a man seeking a cause to champion, Greece was a right proper mess, and quite soon Byron came to see things like Mavrokordatos. The Greeks were preventing a Greece from coming into being. With the Greeks at each other's throats, with notables and warlords carving out small autonomous fiefdoms, and with Greece still an idea without a real state or coherent territory, the moment called for a strong authority wielding a loyal military force. Rights and representation would be for another day, but not appropriate "to this society in its present combustible state." Already his friend the governor of Cephalonia, Colonel Charles Napier, had advised him to ignore the factional politics, ignore constitutional niceties, hire some mercenaries, and give all power to Mavrokordatos. In this there was a bit of the colonial mindset and indeed Napier went on to a career of colonial conquest in India. Others advising Byron referred to the Greeks as "natives" who needed to be commanded. Byron, in short, was not simply going to support Greece, but decide what was good for the Greeks and who the Greek government was. He concluded that the government should be Mavrokordatos and his allies, anyone but the Moreans.[26] It would be that kind of liberalism: a central authority that superseded the small, local, and venal interests, sponsored by a British lord and managed by a prince.

Byron died of malaria, the very stuff of a romantic life and death that spawned a cult across Europe and a new industry of statuettes, porcelain figurines, paintings, gravures, and dramatic first-hand accounts. But we know he had designated Orlandos of Hydra as recipient of the funds, at least some of them, and Orlandos was of that faction of Mavrokordatos,

Aegean Islanders, and Roumeliot politicians that was arrayed against the Moreans.[27] Two weeks later the first installments of the loan arrived in Zakynthos but there was no authority from the Committee to disburse them. Byron was dead and the other trustee had left for England.

The banker who was holding the loans in Zakynthos, Samuel Barff, decided that there was no point in sitting on the money and waiting the months required to ask for instructions from London and then receive them. The most recent massacres (Psara and Kasos) convinced him that the money was needed immediately. The money was meant for the Greeks, and Byron had already indicated which Greeks he had in mind. Before Byron's successors from the London Greek Committee could arrive and decide what to do with the funds, Barff transferred the first installments. The British authorities knew that the loan was on Zakynthos but British banking secrecy laws gave Barff wide latitude. For all their surveillance and intercepted mail the authorities were caught unawares when the loan left Zakynthos.[28] A sum was probably given directly to Mavrokordatos. The bulk went to the village of Divri in the Morean mountains, where the bankers' representatives handed it over to men representing Hydra, allied with politicians from Roumeli.[29] When the new commissioners arrived in Nafplio with another installment, they followed Barff's lead and gave a further 50,000 pounds to the same faction.[30]

A bank clerk had decided who the Greek government was: Aegean Islanders, Roumeliots, and Phanariots. What they did next was a second revolution, an overthrow of the old order of notables in the Morea and the dawn of a Greek national proto-state.

The Sack of the Morea

Roumeli for our purposes is the land directly opposite the northern Morea, across the Gulf and Isthmus of Corinth, stretching from towns like Arta and Missolonghi in the west to Athens in the east. In 1821 there were uprisings against the Ottoman authorities, but Roumeli was not like the Morea and the simple Muslim–Christian axis did not apply neatly. Here there was a larger Muslim population, and near at hand was a pool of Albanian mercenaries who could be hired on short notice to put down local rebellions. Uprisings further to the north as far as Thessaloniki failed, and the reprisals ordered by the Porte were familiar in their severity: killings, enslavement, looting, and arson.

Uprisings in Roumeli unfolded in a manner that is now familiar. Warlords entered the towns, arrested and tortured the Muslims, took what valuables they found, and very often murdered them. The murders had the effect of implicating the local Christians in the uprisings whether they had joined or not.[31] In summer 1822 a band of territory from the west coast around Missolonghi to the east coast around Athens were in the hands of the rebels. But towns changed hands with some regularity as new waves of bandits and hired mercenaries entered the fray, and as the Ottomans took back territory.[32]

The Christian warlords of Roumeli were in no way united, and when they took a territory it was often in their own names. They killed Christian notables as well as Muslims, and installed themselves in their stead.[33] Uprisings were led by hereditary bandits and mercenaries like Odysseas Androutsos, the son of a comrade of the late Lambros Katsonis, by Karaiskakis, Diakos, Gouras, Veikos and a host of warlords whose families had fought for all sides in the conflicts of the early nineteenth centuries.

Changing masters and allies was commonplace for them, and the Revolution added one more option. In 1821 very many of them were in the employ of Ali pasha of Yanena, or his enemies, or both. Androutsos was married to a woman from Ali's harem, which made him something like Ali's relative. On certain occasions in 1821 they disrupted the movement of Ottoman troops who were headed for the Morea. In these encounters the Roumeliots were not fighting on behalf of the Moreans, though the Moreans benefited; they were fighting on behalf of Ali pasha of Yanena who was making his last stand.[34]

By 1822 the Souliots had been defeated along with Ali and evicted from their strongholds, and they were in search of any homeland at all. Byron hired perhaps eight hundred of them but they demanded too much money and they fell out with each other along clan lines. A contingent of four to five hundred under a Botsaris became the guard of

Sisinis in Gastouni. Other Roumeliots who had fought for Ali pasha came to the Morea to loot.[35] They might cooperate with the politicians like Kolettis from Roumeli and with the warlords and notables of the Morea, but they could just as easily make a deal with their enemies.

In eastern Roumeli the warlords allowed the Phanariot Negris to proclaim himself leader, and in western Roumeli Mavrokordatos became the nominal leader. But in these places power had come down to raw military force. Negris lacked that power and funds and in less than a year he abandoned the region to the warlords. Mavrokordatos had his own wealth and he lasted longer. He used his own money, Byron's money, and donations from Philhellenes and Greek merchants abroad to hire his own armed forces and organize the European officers.[36] Even within the town of Missolonghi he was surrounded by potential violence, and some Roumeliot warlords attacked him. Karaiskakis for example threatened Missolonghi in 1824.

To be sure, at times the warlords acted out a Christian–Muslim divide: consider the experiences of Abazis in western Roumeli and the Athenian Muslim notables who were subjected to a totalizing nationalist rhetoric (see chapter 12). But the warlords attacked plenty of Christian notables as well, and here the language of anti-privilege was at work. The warlords could work with the Greek nationalists, they could operate on their own account, or they could just as easily cooperate with the Ottomans.

The idea of Greece had some meaning for them, but from where they stood in tumultuous Roumeli this Greece was far from secure. When the emissary of the Greek government in the Morea offered all of them commissions as colonels, they accepted—all but Markos Botsaris who thought only he deserved it, and tore up the document while swearing in Albanian.[37] When the Ottomans offered them estates, tax revenues, and cash, and when their situation became insecure, they accepted those as well. An estate was more familiar than a nation. Each defeat, such as Mavrokordatos's disaster at Peta, led to more agreements with the Ottomans. To be clear: not just a few, but almost all of the warlords of Roumeli went over to the Ottomans at some point in the 1820s.[38]

All this rests awkwardly with the place of many of these men in modern Greece, as larger-than-life national heroes. Only recently have some careful historians tried to unravel the myths and place them in their proper contexts, as mercenaries. Karaiskakis (Black Shadow in Greco-Turkish) worked with the Ottoman pashas to hunt down the Greek rebels in 1823 and the Greeks convicted him of treason. In a short time he was back in the good graces of the Greeks and in command of forces in Roumeli until his death in battle. Androutsos, who commanded Athens with murderous brutality, had rebuffed overtures from Morean Greeks and he had their emissaries murdered. He made a bid for Byron's gold and failed. He had been making overtures to the Ottomans since 1822 and in 1825 went over to the Ottoman side, and he was given a large force to recapture Athens. He was murdered by his own comrades—tortured and strung up on the walls of the Acropolis—with the blessings of the politicians in the Morea.[39] The Athenians meanwhile anxiously awaited the return of the Ottomans to put an end to the carnage.[40]

Roumeli was not a promising base for a future Greek state, but it had a vast pool of armed men who could be bought. In the summer and fall of 1824 the Greek government bought them. By this we mean that the faction that had received the English loan used the new wealth to hire them against the Morean notables and warlords. Of the first installments perhaps 20,000 pounds went to Mavrokordatos, who seems to have spent it far and wide in order to bolster his support, and also the idea of an effective government. He provided dowries for brides, salaries for government emissaries as far as the island of Santorini, and medical supplies to deal with outbreaks of disease.[41] The great bulk of the London loan of 308,000 pounds went to the Hydriots under Giorgos Kountouriotis, who claimed to be head of government. The Hydriots were allied with Ioannis Kolettis. He had served in European armies during the Napoleonic Wars and later in Ali pasha's court, and from 1822 he held a variety of positions in one or another coalition of Greek factions.

It was Kolettis who developed and implemented the plan: use the funds to hire the warlords of Roumeli, bring them to the Morea, and defeat the Morean notables and warlords. More than that: decimate the peninsula and destroy the social structures on which the notables rested. It would be "the revolutionization of the Revolution," in the words of one historian.[42] Kolettis was from Roumeli and he tapped into his networks. He turned to his uncle Yannis Gouras who had been a deputy to Androutsos (and later killed him). "Brother," wrote Kolettis to Gouras, the Morea is wealthy and the kotsabases are sitting on the booty they took from the dead Muslims, and they are behaving like pashas. He offered cash and all the booty they could take. "What else could you want?" Gouras put out the call to "all the bands" (*askeria*) from across the mainland above the Morea—from Athens in the east to Missolonghi in the west. They responded to the promise of money and loot, and announced that they would go wherever the government told them, and attack whomever the government said was the enemy. Some harbored resentments for the Moreans who had cut them out of arrangements since 1821; there had been calls to "murder the oligarchs."[43] Well-known warlords like Makriyannis responded and brought their bands, as did the Souliots under Kitzo Tzavellas and a who's who of Roumeliot warlords and bandits—Iskos, Veikos, Drakos, Zervas.

Now they pledged their loyalty to "the Greeks of the respected administration" but Drakos warned Kolettis that he needed to be paid well and promptly; they still had other options. Karaiskakis hesitated. "What government" was asking for his help and "who made it a government"? He denounced the other commanders as whores and spineless tools. He could join any cause he wanted, he wrote in his typically colorful language: "My cock has [Ottoman] war drums and it has [Christian] bugles. I'll play whichever I want." But the money was good and just about all the mercenary bosses were going, and in the end Karaiskakis joined as well.[44]

In November 1824 armed men descended on the Morea with a mission to attack the notables. More came to the seat of government in Nafplio to seek handouts, and anyone with a ship that floated arrived to proclaim their loyalty and claim their share of the money. The total number of mercenaries may have reached as high as twelve thousand. The town of Nafplio was awash in gold, flooded with ornamented weapons, gold-braided vests, and Albanian-style kilts.[45]

The mercenaries overran the north of the peninsula and fanned out to the southwest, with particular attention to Gastouni which was the home base of Sisinis. It was an exceptionally wealthy area, or at least it produced unusually large revenues. It was considered to be unusually retrograde and archaic—what with Sisinis's new Ottoman-style court, his harem, and his appointment of his sons as beys. This part of the attack was led by Makriyannis and Gouras himself, with a large band of Souliots under Tzavellas. Sisinis had hired his own Souliots as his guard and married his son into the Botsaris family to seal the alliance, but they were no match and Kolettis probably bought them off. The same happened with Deliyannis's mercenary guard. Sisinis's resplendent walled estate in the town was pillaged and burned.[46]

The peasant mobilizations that had saved men like Sisinis from the Ottomans in 1821 and 1822 did not materialize in 1824. The invaders were not Muslims but Christians, and the villagers had been waiting to do to the kotsabases what they had already done to the agas. The Hydriot leaders and Kolettis issued appeals directly to peasants and townsfolk: the kotsabases had been the handmaidens of the beys and agas, they had replaced the sultan and became pashas themselves, they continued to steal, and they were arbitrary and unjust. The peasants had spilled their blood in 1821 but the rewards went to the notables. The attack was the revolution accomplished, the taming of the "proud Peloponnesian tyrants" who lorded it over their peasantries and all outsiders. Whether peasants joined the Roumeliots is not known—some did, presumably—but the tactic probably helped ensure their passivity.[47]

Anyway, many of the peasants were also fending off attacks in what was a systematic dismantling of local society. The Roumeliot mercenaries destroyed town after town, village after village. They confronted the Morean warlords under Kolokotronis and killed his oldest son Panos. Some of the old man's allies from his Ionian days went over to the government side. Kolokotronis was emotionally defeated even before he surrendered, and he was paraded through the streets of Nafplio as locals spat on him and cursed him. He and several captured notables, including Sisinis and Deliyannis, were sent off to prison on Hydra. Also arrested was Bouboulina, Kolokotronis's in-law and ally. She was released and retreated to Spetses where she was murdered in a vendetta the following year.

Even the few notables who had collaborated with the government were overrun. These notables had agreed to host and protect the mercenaries, and in return expected protection. This mutual pledge they called, in Albanian, *besa pre besa*. As the mercenaries looted their lands and homes, the notables Lontos and Notaras wrote: "We did not know that the *besa pre besa* you gave us was a lie, because for us the *besa pre besa* among soldiers is the law, and when we say it, we have to die [before violating it]. Brother, you tricked us."[48] Instead they were encountering a pitiless power of professional mercenaries, and a cold authority that overturned the world of the spoken oath and the intimate networks of friendship and kinship upon which the old regime had been based. They were to be subordinated to an abstraction, the Greek state, and that abstraction was armed.

It was the end of a regime. It was the wanton destruction of homes, production, and people, the widespread arson of buildings and trees, the exceptionally cruel and demonstrative tortures, pillorying, and rapes, the looting and strewing about of dowries and linens—in short the dismantling of the hierarchy at the level of the family and the humiliation of the men, the women, and their children. Government forces called for the "extermination" of the Morean notables, at least as a caste. They were "apostates," a term to describe someone who betrays a religion or alliance, but now used to describe "enemies of the Greek nation."[49]

It was around this time that the government began to level the charge of treason and individuals began to denounce each other as traitors. The nation was becoming real and consequential, and the government was emboldened to police it. Karaiskakis and Androutsos were well-known examples, but many more cases were focused on the usual commerce that crisscrossed the Mediterranean and crossed lines of conflict. These were now disrupted by absolute political boundaries. Commonplace profiteering off a war would now be treason. Citizens deployed the label "traitor" against each other and as comeuppance. Townsfolk in Kalamata denounced their notable, Petrobey Mavromichalis, because he traded with "the pasha" in Alexandria, meaning Mehmed Ali. Mehmed was a collector of rare books, and Petrobey sent to Alexandria a cargo of five hundred valuable books he had received from fabulous library of Dimitsana. Petrobey was further implicated by a merchant who claimed to be acting as intermediary with Mehmed Ali in 1825, just as the Morea was being overrun by the Egyptian forces.

The intermediary was a Greek-speaking Cypriot named Nikolaos Chamoleon (an irony that no doubt escaped him). He was captured and interrogated, and he was confused and afraid. Wars had never been a reason to stop trading with anyone, since wars were for armies. He confessed without realizing it: of course he traded with Petrobey and Mehmed. Of course Mehmed was in the process of invading the Morea (see chapter 15), but what of it? He traded with anyone. He carried religious paraphernalia and relics into enemy lands. He also sold artefacts that he claimed were ancient to English "milords" in Alexandria. He carried medals of Zeus (anachronistically with a globe in his hand), Zeus with Hera, Athena with a Medusa head, and a drinker who may have been Dionysus. While in Egypt he was asked by Mehmed Ali to carry letters of friendship and offers of alliance to Petrobey, Sisinis, and Kolokotronis. When he was back in the Balkans he was given letters from Ibrahim pasha (Mehmed Ali's son) addressed to some of the same people. But what of it? He also visited Tinos and Tunisia, Missolonghi and Zakynthos. His interrogator warned him: "you need to tell the truth because things look like you're a good spy for Mehmed Ali." His interrogator concluded: "Sign here, brother, and beware."

The intermediary, an outsider with no connections and little status, was convicted of "treason to the nation" and condemned for sullying the names of patriots. Petrobey was exonerated: his services were needed. It was a new world and a new kind of politics, with a nation that was absolute but still malleable for those who had power.[50]

3+

At the start of 1825 Gouras wanted to massacre all the Morean notables but his employers would not let him. The government wanted them alive to serve the nascent state under new terms. (The most famous victim of the warfare, Panos Kolokotronis, had been killed by mercenaries who did not know who he was.) Gouras felt vulnerable. He had attacked the Morea at the government's insistence, not on his own initiative. He had no beef with them. The notables "killed neither my mama, nor my papa." But leaving them alive could invite revenge in the future, a vendetta.[51]

After the fighting the vanquished were put in prison, but very soon they were needed again. The same men continued to buy the tax farms and villagers protested when they were bought and sold without being asked. Villagers tried in vain to sell themselves under better terms. But now the government and the notables spoke in one voice, and admonished the peasants: "You do not want to recognize [Deliyannis] as the renter of the national rights to your villages."

There it was: the village was a national resource, and so was Deliyannis. Deliyannis, who had always been addressed with various cumbersome honorifics by supplicants, took to signing his correspondence "the Citizen Deliyannis." With his fellow notables he had begun and ended correspondence with "brother," a term that implied old-world intimacy and complicity. This too was replaced by "citizen." The new term was both bland in its formality and impressive in its pretense. He was performing his merger with the new national whole.[52]

But that was later. In late 1824 the Roumelian mercenaries continued to maraud and then turned on each other as they scrambled to claim loot. Skirmishes continued into 1825. The government still had enough money left from the London loan to buy their obeisance, and parts of a second London loan made their way into its hands. How responsive its Roumelian hirelings would be in a crisis was an open question.[53] They were still mercenaries and they still had other options.

This mattered because the sultan had, at long last, found an army. More accurately, he borrowed one in Egypt, and that army and fleet were already making their way to the Morea as the government savored its victory over the Morean notables.[54] The mercenaries who had been effective against the Moreans were scarce as the Egyptians disembarked in the southern Morea.

It was the time of Ibrahim, and all seemed lost.

Chapter 15

The Time of Ibrahim

Prologue

I AM DRIVING on a country road in the Peloponnese on my way to meet one of my many cousins, and I stop at a gas station owned by another cousin to ask directions. "Go straight and turn right before you enter the village." Despite the words and the waves of the hands I still do not know where to go, so I ask which village and which road to the right. "To the right" (sweep of the hand). "At Ibrahim's olive trees."

Ibrahim. It is a common enough name in many countries, and it was common in these parts until 1821. Here and now it refers to the Egyptian pasha who led an army through the Morea for a few years starting in 1825 and devastated the peninsula, as if more devastation were needed. The invasion is entrenched in local traditions across the Peloponnese, related by people who speak as if Ibrahim were still among us. The whole episode is distilled into one person's name, as is so often the case with stories of the Greek Revolution. Kolokotronis at Dervenakia refers to a mass mobilization, and Papaflessas at Maniaki refers to a battle fought by several thousand men. It is how any national history is written: Washington at Yorktown, Nelson at Trafalgar, Napoleon at Austerlitz.

So Ibrahim means "the time of Ibrahim." My cousin at the gas station is referring to the fact that the Egyptians swept through the region and burned, pillaged, murdered, raped, and enslaved, but also carefully inquired which properties had been owned by Muslims. These were preserved for the returning Muslim owners. According to local tradition the enormous, twisting, and

FIGURE 15.1. Ibrahim's Trees, Laconia, Greece, 2022. Photograph by Yanni Kotsonis. *Tradition has it that these olive trees were spared by the Egyptian army during its arson campaign of 1825–7, and were preserved for returning Muslims. The trees are indeed centuries old. My thanks to Sophie Lambroschini for providing a sense of scale.*

cragged trees on the outskirts of the village were the ones spared by the Egyptians: Ibrahim's olive trees.

As I hear the story of Ibrahim, I know there is more, a gap between what locals consider to be local, what professional historians describe as national, and what I know to be imperial as well. Ibrahim and his army traced to the encounter of France and Egypt in 1799; the arrival of a Balkan tobacco merchant in Cairo a few years later at the head of a band of Albanian mercenaries; the rise of that man to become ruler of Egypt; and the creation of

a disciplined army that would lead the way to a resurgent Egypt in the early
1820s.

The man was Mehmed Ali, and his son was the Ibrahim who gave his
name to the Peloponnesian trees. In 1825 this army was hurled at the Morea.

Mehmed Ali and the Egyptian State

Bonaparte's invasion of Egypt in 1798–9 ended in defeat. In the wake of
that campaign the sultan invited mercenaries from across his empire to
descend on Cairo and Alexandria and reestablish Ottoman authority.
In Kavala, a city that is today in northern Greece, a tobacco merchant
who was also a tax collector and general-purpose enforcer heeded the
call. He was Mehmed Ali.[1] He may have been Albanian and the armed
men he gathered around him certainly were. They were drawn from that
pool of Albanians whom we have seen repeatedly across the Balkans,
people who were poor and desperate enough to make a living by risking
their lives. They became the core of a force that arrived in Egypt, el-
bowed aside opponents, and in 1805 made Mehmed Ali ruler of all
Egypt with the blessings of the sultan. Like Ali pasha in Yanena, he had
stabilized the region.

The man was remarkable and from that time it was not clear if
Mehmed Ali really was the vassal of the sultan as he publicly asserted or
an independent force as his actions suggested. Much later he would go
to war with the Porte. In the meantime, at the Citadel of Cairo in 1811,
he carried out the slaughter of the Mamluk caste of warriors and landowners who had ruled Egypt for centuries. He turned on his Albanian
mercenaries who may have been loyal but were not much of a fighting
force, not for his purposes. He sent them to campaign in the Arabian
desert where they were consumed by hunger, thirst, and disease. Other
Albanians would come but they would be auxiliaries to a different kind
of force.

Mehmed Ali wanted a modern army, and the quest for that army
spearheaded a larger transformation of the Egyptian state. He invited
merchants and manufacturers from the Balkans and the Black Sea and
showed them with protection and privileges. He took hold of cotton

exports and the gold they fetched on the European markets. He opened workshops to produce uniforms, weapons, powder, shot, and rations. He rationalized the taxes on land which would apply to large and small landowners and farmers as well as religious institutions. He recruited Coptic Christians to collect them. This was state-building, and it was to pay for a modernized army to replace the irregulars and military castes that dominated the warfare of the eastern Mediterranean.

He was implementing his military plans in 1821 when the Greek Revolution was breaking out. Ottoman officers were recruited as the crack cavalry. Recruiters scoured the countryside for Egyptian peasants who were put into uniform and drilled to march in formation as a solid block of men that turned and straightened and advanced against enemy positions. When these forces were depleted by exposure and disease—their death rates could be as high as 60 percent—there were many more fellaheen to harvest. He sought ten thousand Druze men in Syria. Mehmed Ali sent his sons to the south to wage war in the Sudan in order to tap into that other reserve: sub-Saharan slaves. The Sudanese campaigns of 1820–24 yielded twenty thousand slaves, though only three thousand survived the forced marches, the cold, and the epidemics that swept through the camps. American physicians who were accustomed to ministering to Black slaves were hired to try to lower the death rate.[2] The transition from slave to disciplined soldier who would blindly obey an order was smooth because the modern marching soldier and the slave were so much alike. They were told to do things they would not otherwise have done, like march into a barrage of cannon or musket fire.

To help with the process Mehmed Ali tapped into one more pool of men, the European officers and NCOs who were left unemployed after 1815. This was the same pool that provided men for some European kingdoms like that of Naples, for the revolutions of Italy, Spain, and Latin America, and for the Greek uprising of the 1820s. In Egypt Frenchmen and Italians were welcome if they could advise about engineering, artillery, basic training, and medicine. Greek and Coptic veterans of the Chasseurs d'Orient—the old force of Papas-Oglou—came as well (see chapter 5). The most storied European was one Joseph Sève who converted to Islam and became Suleyman bey and an organizer of the new battalions.[3] French was to be heard at the Egyptian parade grounds and on the bridges of the new Egyptian warships. The army physicians were Italians. Whole companies of sappers were made up of Europeans. By the early 1820s their activities segued with the policy of the French government which was seeking Mediterranean influence after the defeats of the Nile and Trafalgar. Some French officers in Egypt reported on their work to the French command. French shipyards produced ships for the Egyptian fleet. The rise of Mehmed Ali as a French ally or client would be the occasion for a new French imperial assertion.[4]

By the early 1820s Egypt had men who lined up and marched when told and did what a reasonable person would never do. Ripped from their families and villages and destroyed as boys, they were reconstituted as men of the corps. They marched against enemy fire as their comrades fell dead and wounded, persisting because they and their battalion were the same thing, convinced that obeying their commanders and saving the battalion meant their own survival as well. Or if he died, his battalion would continue to exist and in a sense so would he. Mehmed Ali was accomplishing what the sultans dreamed of, tried on occasion to realize, and until then was elusive: a responsive and disciplined fighting force that followed the orders of the sultan rather than one or another caste, patron, or region, and a fiscal system to pay for it. Mehmed Ali showed the way when he slaughtered the Mamluks at the Citadel in 1811, and in 1826 the sultan would slaughter the Janissaries in order to pave the way for his own modern army.

In the meantime, the sultan could not field an army. What he had was irregulars and mercenaries recruited by the regional pashas across the empire. In the Greek War the regional pashas could gather together Albanian mercenaries and the Albanians fought when they were paid and sometimes they did not, laid sieges and then abandoned them because the promised pay was late or the promised booty never materialized. They fought Balkan-style, charging when they saw an opening and running for cover when the going got tough—a perfectly reasonable response, one should add, when facing rifle fire or a cavalry charge. The Greeks practiced the same warfare but they turned out to be better at it because they added mass mobilization and national cause to irregular warfare. The Ottoman army was decimated at Dervenakia in summer 1822 and for almost three years the Morea was secure enough to allow the Greeks the space to turn on each other.

The sultan did not have an army but the Egyptians had thirty thousand men organized in six disciplined regiments, and more were being recruited. They also had a fleet that obeyed orders. Since the outbreak of 1821 Egyptian ships had patrolled the Aegean alongside (or in place of) the Ottoman fleet, and it was this fleet that carried out the destruction of Kasos in 1824. On Crete Egyptians landed to put an end to the chaotic fighting of the clans and regions and restore authority, preventing it from forming into a revolution.[5] Crete would have its turn at revolution later in the century. The Ottoman fleet, meanwhile, avoided battle.

Egyptian actions fit into a larger strategy of making the eastern Mediterranean an Egyptian pond. The strategy very nearly succeeded. In substance Mehmed Ali was offered Crete and the Morea in return for ending the Greek rebellion, and for Egypt this would mean a land and sea hegemony that stretched from the northeast African coast to the Aegean and Ionian seas. With the Christians pacified, Mehmed intended to capitalize on Greek shipping, commerce, and industry, and he imagined enterprising Greek merchants acting as a bond in the north–south axis of his expanded sphere. Greek farmers could be moved around to occupy fallow lands.

The deal was sealed in January 1824 and took the form of a command from the sultan to his vassal and the humble submission of the pasha.[6] Just as the Greeks were busily killing each other in the second civil war, the fleet and army that had occupied Crete were turning to the Morea. More ships and battalions were gathering in Alexandria. Reports reached French and British authorities of the systematic preparations: orders for hard tack, uniforms, and powder, and new raids in the Sudan in search of more recruits for the new-style army. The Greeks knew of the Egyptian preparations as well but probably saw it as one more army, of the kind they had defeated before.

In February 1825 the Egyptian fleet sailed into the Bay of Methoni, and the Morea experienced the fruits of a political revolution in Egypt.[7] The Egyptian fleet was unopposed. The Greek island fleets were busy elsewhere and had not been paid so they would not engage. No land forces opposed the Egyptian landing. Morean forces had been defeated and dispersed by the Roumeliot mercenaries, and the Roumeliots were busy competing and fighting over the spoils of the Morea. British agents were dumbfounded when they reported that the Greek fighters, rather than rush to meet the mortal threat, were engaged in "a civil war over currants": the factions were fighting over the dried Corinthian grapes. In summer Kolokotronis had to halt operations to let his commanders and soldiers attend to the grape harvest which was promised to them as payment. The Egyptians caught on. Greek commanders approached their positions and challenged them to a battle, but the Egyptians refused to fight because they were too busy with the grapes.[8]

The Egyptians and Ottomans knew full well that the Greeks were too busy fighting each other to put up a decent resistance and expected a quick victory. Kolettis had some cash on hand but he would only pay his own guard. Kountouriotis had the balance of the London loan and he kept it at home.[9] As the size and nature of the Egyptian force became apparent, the Roumeliots gathered their pay and loot and crossed back into Roumeli, still looting along the way.[10] It was then that the government released Kolokotronis and the defeated notables from prison to organize a force to meet the Egyptians.

What the Greeks faced was probably incomprehensible to them. The force was large, to be sure, with seventeen thousand men and seven hundred cavalry, moved about by up to seventy warships and three hundred transport ships. It was exotic, with uniformed fellaheen marching alongside sub-Saharan Africans.[11] But it was just one more force, the Greeks reasoned, and they gathered what men they could.

Kolokotronis organized the usual ambushes and harassments as the Greeks searched for weaknesses and gaps to exploit. But as the Egyptian force began its march up the west coast toward the Bay of Navarino, the Greek attacks bounced off them like pebbles from a wall of stone. Attacks by the Souliots also failed, and indeed all the attacks failed. The Egyptians did not run for cover, they did not build the small stone walls from which to fire and avoid fire, and their columns turned into phalanxes that did not break apart and disperse. These blocks of men moved as if they were one person, and parts peeled off to outflank. The cavalry did not simply charge, it maneuvered in conjunction with the foot soldiers and enveloped. They kept formation, they kept marching, and new men took the place of every fallen comrade. At Maniaki in May 1825 the mad priest Papaflessas organized a heroic stand, but had problems finding enough men because "they all wanted to be paid." He was promised ten thousand men by the warlords, probably gathered two thousand in practice, and many of them began to flee when they saw Ibrahim's army maneuver. They were not suicidal, though Papaflessas was, and he died that day with all who stayed to fight. Ibrahim sent 880 pairs of ears to the sultan.[12] Again: it was hard for the Greeks to grasp what they were dealing with.

And the Egyptian navy absorbed the Ottoman fleet, coordinated with the land forces, and sailed where and when they were told by the commanders. At key moments the Egyptians coordinated their land and sea forces in attacks that were disasters for the Greeks and triumphs for the Egyptians and Ottomans. Thousands of soldiers died at Sphacteria in 1825, an island in the Bay of Navarino and the very place where the Athenians defeated the Spartans in 425 BCE. The Italian revolutionary Santarosa died here. Mavrokordatos was rescued at the last moment by ship. Back in Cairo, the cannon of the Citadel saluted the victory.[13]

The last major outpost in Roumeli was Missolonghi, which had resisted multiple attacks. In 1826 Ibrahim commanded his fleet to assist the Ottomans and he landed his troops, and the town fell in what was a military disaster and a human tragedy on a different scale. Thousands of ears reached the sultan. Thousands of women and children were sold into slavery, with perhaps 3,500 sent to Egypt alone.[14] Athens fell in June 1827. In Europe Missolonghi was the occasion for outrage and art, with Delacroix's *Greece on the Ruins of Missolonghi* capturing the imagination of generations.

Between his centralized command, logistical prowess, and disciplined army, the Greeks concluded that Ibrahim "is another Napoleon," and the comparison of the two generals who were also reformers is apt.[15] From 1825 and into the fall of 1827 the Egyptians reaped a destruction that was extreme even by the standards of the Morea in the

1820s. The main towns were taken, with Tripolitsa at its center. Christian properties were systematically burned, up to and including homes, buildings, and fruit trees that were thought to be Christian. In this the Egyptians were advised by Morean Muslims who returned with the army to reclaim their properties and stations. Some of these Moreans had been hostages ransomed off by the Greeks. Body parts flowed to Constantinople.

The other destruction was mass enslavement, which was less a strategy and more the rewards of victory as the Egyptian soldiers understood them. By one estimate the Egyptians took ten thousand slaves in the Morea. Slaves supplemented their pay and booty, and Kolokotronis narrated Ibrahim's progress by counting the slaves he took in each region: two thousand near Patras, a few hundred around Navarino, several hundred on the route from Tripolitsa to Kalavryta. He also counted the Christian heads taken by the Egyptians and the Egyptian heads taken by his own men in return for a thaler each. Ibrahim was keeping a parallel count, of pairs of ears sent to the sultan.[16]

During marches the Egyptian army enveloped regions, burned the villages, and left with columns of bound girls and women who would be sold along the coasts.[17] Men were often killed on the spot as was custom but the bustling industries in Cairo and Alexandria created a market for men as well. Those villagers who had warning fled to the mountains. Others were surprised or thought they could submit and live, which would later be true but not yet. Whole villages and valleys were surrounded and the populations rounded up.[18] The supply ships that unloaded at Navarino, mainly Austrian, left loaded with these slaves. Ionian ships carried more. Already after a year of campaigning there were three thousand Morean slaves in Alexandria and more would follow. In Alexandria enslaved men were sent to work in quarries and construction.[19]

In June 1828 groups of Greek slaves in Alexandria wrote petitions signed by 205 men who stated their names and villages of origin. The petitioners wrote that another 200 had already died. They were addressed to anyone who might have the money to ransom them, be they Greek notables and commanders or foreign diplomats and admirals.

The Egyptians delivered their petitions in hopes the ransoms would be paid. Women and children were sold around Egypt and every well-to-do Muslim household was said to have a Greek slave.[20]

Egypt meanwhile had a substantial Greek population, which took no part in the Greek War. The Alexandrian merchants and manufacturers continued to carry on their trades and the Greek colonies swelled in the 1820s as more families were drawn to the stability of Egypt and the boom of supplying the armies. This was an entirely different Greek experience. They had been brought to Egypt from across the eastern Mediterranean and the Black Sea, as tailors, builders, and gardeners. The most storied were the merchants of Hydra, Spetses, and Russia's Black Sea ports who were given privileges and protection. They thrived and stood aloof of the Revolution which they experienced when Greek pirates tried to raid the port of Alexandria in 1825. In the 1820s, as loyal Christian subjects, they petitioned the pasha to allow them to buy and free Christian slaves from the Morea. Mehmed Ali agreed as an act of benevolence, spending his own money as well.[21] Mehmed Ali was not interested in the captives: "I want to reign over men and not slaves."[22] The Greeks of Egypt, meanwhile, remained loyal to a succession of Egyptian, quasi-colonial, colonial, and post-colonial regimes into the 1950s when Nasser evicted them and they became one more wave of Greeks "returning" to a Greece they had never seen.

The desperation of the Moreans and Kolokotronis owed to the obvious fact that they were losing, badly and decisively. Perhaps more despairing was something else. With severe and demonstrative punishment meted out, the outcome was meant to be the submission of the Morea, the restoration of the *status quo ante*. The troops who ravaged the towns and villages handed to the survivors "submission papers," the patent that proved that the signatory had accepted the ruler and his own place in the hierarchy as a protected religion. He was to become a Rum and a reaya once again. And it worked in town after town. Villages stopped supplying the Greeks. Having submitted, the Greeks joined the Egyptians in the looting and capturing of slaves, and Greek bands turned on those who had yet to submit. Men from Patras went to war with men from Corinth. Pyrgos submitted and invited the surrounding regions to join them. Gastouni was followed by the powder mills of Divri.

Notables and commanders were making their peace with Ibrahim as well. The ever-adaptable Petrobey of the Mani—according to French generals serving Ibrahim—made secret agreements with the Egyptians to let the latter pass through the mountains around Kalamata, agreements secured by offering his son as a hostage and a payment in gold. It was around this time that he was accused of treason (see chapter 14). Kolokotronis turned his wrath on those who submitted and promised them "fire and axe," the destruction of their properties. That had worked in 1821 and 1822, but not at all in 1825, 1826, and 1827 when Ibrahim was more fearsome than Kolokotronis.[23] In Roumeli after the fall of Missolonghi almost all the warlords made their peace and accepted Ottoman appointments and estates.[24]

By the middle of 1827 the war was lost. But Mehmed Ali and his son had set off a chain of events in Europe that produced an independent Greece.

Chapter 16

Europe Mobilizes

Prologue

IT IS 2018 and my lecture on Greece and the European powers before and during the Greek Revolution is over. My London audience asks some questions about identity, more or less the theme of the lecture. I have described the ways in which Europeans were confounded and disappointed when they entered the region and dealt with the Balkan Christians. They turned to the forms of rule with which they were familiar from their various imperial experiences, often conditioned by aristocratic upbringing and military training. Indeed, I concluded, modern Greece was created by the decrees of European powers, at conferences to which the Greeks were not invited. They gave the Greeks an absolute monarch who was Bavarian and Catholic.

A colleague with a few more years than myself stands and delivers a comment more than a question, in a gentle tone that adds to the effect. "How else could they [the Europeans] behave?" The Greeks were corrupt, they were thieves, they were fratricidal. Worse still, they did not respect the rule of law. He might have added that they were not good at queuing up. It is a timeless trope and I suspect that the speaker is not only describing the attitudes of the time, but what he thinks to be a reality that holds true today. Most recently that truth is manifest in the bankruptcy of the country after the financial crisis of 2008 which peaked in 2015. Just about any European north of Rome and Paris will agree that Greece's financial crisis owed to its own profligacy and corruption. The punishment visited on the country took the form of austerity, massive unemployment, and a steep fall in incomes. The Greeks have earned it.

I guess I could be offended but I am used to it. And it is refreshing to hear stated what is so often implied, the heartfelt statement without the usual academic idiom that obscures the point.

But as a description of what Europeans thought at the time, the speaker is spot on, and Greeks at the time did not mind. They had won a state.

Europe Mobilizes: Public Opinion

In Russia, public support for the Greeks was constant throughout the 1820s, but it was aligned with official policy and it was not intended to shift Russia's stance. Policy was the preserve of the autocrat. Refugee relief and the redemption of slaves was permitted as the Christian thing to do, but there was no overt support for the Greek war effort (see chapter 14). In western Europe there were notes of liberalism and Greece was associated with the revolutions of Spain and Italy. This wave of Philhellene activity waned by 1825, especially in Britain. The Greeks themselves had denied any connection with liberalism, Italy, and Spain, so supporting Greece as a liberal cause made less sense. With the Ottomans gone, the fighting tended to pit Greek against Greek, using a sizable loan raised on the London exchange. There was a second loan but the London financial bubble had burst and there would be no more.[1]

A different wave of Philhellenism was centered in Geneva and Paris and it was more resoundingly a defense of Christianity than of liberalism. Liberalism in, say, Italy, was divisive, but Christianity in Greece was a cause that attracted people from a much wider political spectrum. In Switzerland the moderate liberal banker Jean-Gabriel Eynard threw himself into the cause of the Greeks with money and passion. He was a late comer to the Greek cause and his diaries scarcely mentioned Greece before 1823. But so were Byron and a whole host of Philhellene activists and the many committees that sprung up in European towns and capitals in 1825 and 1826. The timing of the new interest in Greece makes sense, for Byron and for Eynard. With the defeat of the Spanish Revolution in 1823, the Greeks were a last hope for a European revolution of any kind.[2]

Eynard set aside considerable funds of his own which he managed in separate ledgers lest the losses affect his businesses. He organized elaborate subscriptions that may not have raised impressive sums but certainly mobilized opinion. He and others made much of the fact that workers and peasants joined with a franc or two and allowed them to speak of a mass movement of Europeans. In fact most of the money came from very wealthy donors like the Duke of Orléans, who donated 10,000 francs. There was talk of putting an Orléaniste on a future Greek throne.

Eynard received a steady stream of requests for ammunition and money from the likes of Petrobey Mavromichalis of the Mani (or Sparta, as he wrote to foreigners). Kolokotronis addressed Eynard as "generous Philhellene," thanked him for sending food rations, and asked for money and ammunition. Any greeting from anyone connected with the war, and any sharing of news, was also a request for money, and these are to be found throughout Eynard's archive into the 1830s. He paid the passage to quite a few volunteer officers from Europe, Britain, and South America who were undeterred by the fate of their predecessors in Greece. He sponsored some accomplished Swiss doctors who went to the Morea in 1825. He hosted Capo d'Istria and subsidized his work.[3]

Eynard produced a massive correspondence with European royalty and nobility, officials, intellectuals, and financiers to influence the European educated public and ultimately governments. He was well positioned to do so. Eynard had been one of the bankers who converged on Vienna in 1815 to offer financial services, and he maintained good contacts with the courts and ministries.[4] But to ask conservative governments or even conservative public opinion to champion a liberal cause would not do. Whatever his thoughts about liberalism, in his letters and appeals he was careful to dissociate his activities, and the Greek Revolution itself, from the other Mediterranean movements that smacked of liberal conspiracy.

In Greece, he held, the enemy was not a Christian monarch but a Muslim tyrant. Capo d'Istria had been making the same argument since 1821 (see chapter 7), and in Geneva he and Eynard produced an enormous body of appeals and memoranda that made the case not just for the Greek cause, but for its Christian character. Byron, himself a liberal, had reached much the same conclusion: the Greeks could appeal to "honor, to justice, or even to religion," but they would get nowhere if they invoked liberalism.[5] The Greeks had also learned their lesson, and men like Mavrokordatos carefully and persistently argued to their co-nationals and to any foreigner who would listen that the Greek cause bore no relationship to the Italian and Spanish conspiracies, and that no such fraternity should be claimed. The message was distilled to Kolo-kotronis who delivered it to a visiting British officer. "Our revolution," he recalled, "did not look like any of the others in Europe today." Those were against their own governments so they were civil wars. The Greek Revolution was a war between separate nations.[6]

Men like Eynard and Capo d'Istria did not renounce their liberalism but nor did they trumpet it. The public case they made was confessional and an acceptable way for activists across the range of opinion to support the Greeks. Indeed, the French Committee for the Greeks was established under the auspices of the Society of Christian Morality. It mattered too that in promoting Christianity they avoided censorship: a bureaucrat might not object to an appeal for Christian charity on behalf of Christian victims. Eynard's appeal to a British member of parliament in 1827 was typical: "None but a few ignorant fanatics could wish that a Christian people should return to slavery and be exposed to apostasy, violation, and massacre." Affluent women in Paris were asked to send their wealth "out of religious zeal."[7]

Soldiers shared in the sentiment. The British officer Richard Church had commanded forces during the British conquest of the Ionian Islands. He had since been in command of the army of the Kingdom of Two Sicilies and in 1827 he accepted command of Greek revolutionary forces. His justification for joining the Greeks was by now familiar and formulaic, here laid out for his recent master King Francesco I: "This people, sire, has never had any rapport with the troubles of Europe," meaning the liberals who had threatened Francis's rule. This was a battle of "a Christian people" against the "horrible Turks."[8]

Here was an idiom that crossed political divides. The French Ultra-monarchist and former foreign minister Chateaubriand became a champion of the Greeks. In 1826 Chateaubriand the Ultra and Eynard the liberal were sending out joint appeals in the name of the French Committee.[9] Chateaubriand's pamphlet *Note sur la Grèce* was wildly popular. It was explicit that the cause was religious and therefore legitimate to any Christian European, anywhere on the political spectrum: "the Turks cut the throats of the Christians." It was useful in France to cast the Egyptians and Ottomans as a Muslim attack on Christians and also a Black attack on Whites: a world upside down. "The hands of negro slaves, transported from the depths of Africa, rush to achieve in Athens the work of the black eunuchs of the court."[10]

There was, to be sure, the matter of a Classical Greek heritage, and this was deployed as well. It could be awkward: the rhetoric glorified the Greeks as heirs of the ancients and ignored the fact that somewhere along the way they had all become Christians. Some wrote of "Christian Leonidases." The historian Dialla quips that the Greeks came forward as "ancient Spartans with a cross." But Eynard, for one, had no Classical education and for him the cause was loudly religious and quietly liberal. For the moment religion overwhelmed Classical Greece. All sides could converge on the defense of Christianity, the war of the cross, the new crusade, the barbarity of the crescent, and the tyranny of the Turks.[11]

Missionaries avoided the pagan past altogether and focused on martyrdom as they sent over shiploads of bibles. They were gratified that the Greeks asked for more, not realizing that the revolutionaries used the paper to make cartridges.[12] That the Greeks were neither Protestant nor Catholic was awkward for the true believer and Philhellenes offered a variety of explanations as to why the schismatic Orthodox deserved their sympathy. Their schism owed to Ottoman corruption. It was an opportunity to bring the Greeks over to the Pope. Their apostasy was not their fault, but the fault of the Enlightenment and Voltaire. It was an opportunity to save more souls and bring to them the Reformation: Swiss Germans founded the Society for the Revival of Religion and Morality among the Greeks and, like the British bible societies, called for an "interior" regeneration of the Greeks.[13] Into the 1830s and 1840s Protestant missionaries from Britain and the US entered the region to spread the true word of Christ. They were largely squashed by a Greek state that had no time for sectarians: Greek national unity depended too much on a shared Orthodoxy.[14]

The Greeks would be liberated as Christians, not citizens, and Muslims were not to be liberated at all. Philhellenism was also a civilizational movement, but it was founded on the notion that only a Christian could be civilized. Here again a liberal and a conservative could find common ground. Jeremy Bentham, that staunch defender of individual rights that superseded collective differences, concluded that the new Greece would have to be founded on its Christian populations only and endorsed the Greek insistence that Muslims could not be Greeks and would have to leave.[15] There was room for some shocking bigotry as well, though arguably the whole movement in support of the Greeks was founded on a hostility to Islam. Pouqueville, who had suffered as a prisoner of the Ottomans, was not forgiving of his captors and unleashed the popular and hateful *History of the Regeneration of Greece* in multiple imprints.[16]

The universal became particular. In its distilled form the formula that was acceptable to all was liberty, not for people, but for Christians. If there was to be a liberal outcome of rights, as some still hoped, then the rights were for Christians only.

Europe Mobilizes: Art and the Mass Market

The British had lent their money in 1824 and cooled on the Greeks.[17] Now the French lent their pens, easels, chisels, printing presses, fabrics, and pianos, and catered to the mass market. It was the apogee of the Philhellene movement, and the moment with which it is most closely associated because of the rich production of visual images that are still familiar. To this day collectors scour the flea markets of Paris, Brussels, and Waterloo in search of the remains.

Graphic works by artists who had never been to the Balkans were in high demand. Artists trying to sell their generic landscapes were told to return when they had scenes of revolutionary Greece. "Do you know," an art dealer told an artist as he rejected his works, "the Greek Revolution is going strong?"[18] The artists raced to learn more about the events and persons in question, often copying other artists who had also not seen what they were depicting. These were outputs of the European imagination mediated by the market, based on journalistic accounts which tended to be highly favorable to Greeks and blind to their excesses.

Sculptors depicted the dying moments of the heroes in full-blown statues and mass-produced plaster statuettes, with the heroes dressed as ancient Greeks. The death of Markos Botsaris was its own sub-industry, and artists copied the theme and even the symbolic detail from each other and from Classical artefacts. Engravings copied scenes from paintings and sculptures in order to make them mass-marketable as prints. On canvas it was easier to frame scenes as religion, as Christian iconography, because the canvas could accommodate the heavens above with the appropriate religious symbol; the congregations where pious or righteous priests held sermons before the believers; and the massacre or battle itself. They formed a trinity of God, righteous battle, and victimhood. A steady output of paintings was replete with skies parting to welcome the dead, heavenly light shining on advancing warriors, and plenty of clergy blessing the fighting, victorious, victimized, and expiring Greeks.[19]

It was an opportunity for the ambitious artist. The young Delacroix launched his career with *Scenes of the Massacre of Scio* (Chios) in 1822, and confirmed his reputation with *Greece on the Ruins of Missolonghi*. Both were depictions of martyrdom which Delacroix produced within weeks of the news of the events. Both were the talk of Paris when they were opened to a thronging public. *Missolonghi* offered a motif that was reusable, as the art historian Athanassoglou-Kallmyer shows. The woman at the center was Greece, violated and indignant, her chest partly exposed, beckoning to the destruction, and challenging the viewer to act. That was in 1826, the year of the massacre. In 1830, the year of the July Days and another French revolution, the woman at the center was Marianne, symbol of France, triumphant and leading insurgents against the old regime. Both were occasions to legitimize female nudity, the one violated, the other on the attack, both challenging the audience to do something.[20]

FIGURE 16.1. Ary Scheffer, *Greek Women Imploring the Virgin for Assistance*, 1826. Photograph © National Museum of Western Art, Tokyo website. *Images of victimized women in religious scenes were legion in the Philhellene repertoire. In this depiction, women sheltered in a cave pray to the Virgin Mary as a battle rages outside.*

Tailors dressed the likes of Alexander Dumas in the outfits of Greek warriors. Musicians were commissioned to produce songs and operas, and Giovanni Pacini published his "Chant de Missolonghi."[21] Ceramic mass production was coming into its own just then, with the spread of English techniques for transfer printing from copper plates onto pottery.

FIGURE 16.2. "Marcos Botzaris in the Turkish Camp," Montereau faience, France (1826–33). National Historical Museum, Athens. *Markos Botsaris spawned a veritable cult after his death in battle in 1823. The flags and banners indicate a binary fight between the cross and the crescent. This is a higher-quality ceramic, while many more were made affordable by new processes of mass production.*

French, Belgian, and German factories churned out porcelain figures of Greek warriors, platters and soup servers painted with battle scenes, salt and pepper shakers in the shape of a pair of heroes, and tea sets with whole historical sequences and specific or generic Greek men and women.

They might be paired with a generic Turk, cruel in look or given an effeminate aspect. (Hermaphrodism was thought to be an especially Turkish phenomenon.) It was quite a business, new in the sense that it embodied support for a faraway cause rather than a pasture, a myth, the distant past, or one's own monarch and history. Pricey samples still survive, but for the most part the output catered to a mass market of middle- and lower-class consumers who could place a figurine of Botsaris on the mantle, hang a decorative plate with Androutsos on the wall, salt their

FIGURE 16.3. Philhellenic teapot, Paris, Nast, approx. 1830. Philhellenism Museum, Athens. *Greek-themed ceramics of varying quality were mass produced in France, Belgium, and Germany, catering to both wealthy and modest buyers. By the time of the Greek Revolution, new English techniques such as transfer printing were being employed across the continent. This sample depicts a Greek and a Turk in battle.*

food with Miaoulis and pepper it with Bouboulina, and serve their meals from the pantheon of revolutionary heroes. They could own, touch, and handle the Greeks in daily routines. One could drink the Revolution, too: distilleries responded with new labels, such as Crème de Bobelina. Geopolitics met the mass market, mass production, and daily life.

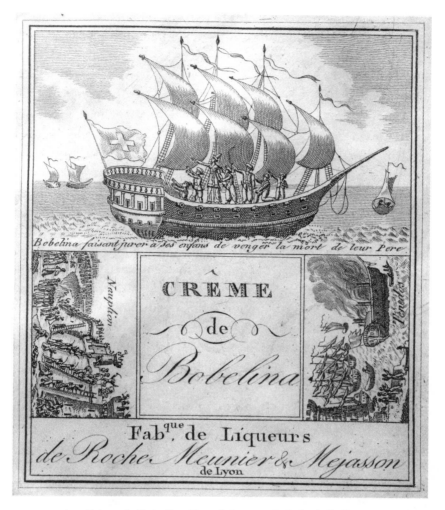

FIGURE 16.4. Crème de Bobelina. French Liqueur Label. Philhellenism Museum, Athens. *Like artists and ceramics workshops, distillers responded rapidly to events to produce new brands. This one is named after the naval hero of the Revolution, Laskarina Bouboulina, who was murdered in a vendetta in 1825.*

Europe Mobilizes: The Diplomats

The Philhellene movement was a cultural phenomenon in its own right but the ultimate measure of success was to induce European states to intervene on behalf of the Greeks. Officially the European chanceries were intransigent for the first five years of the war, or until 1826, but policy makers mingled with wealthy and titled Philhellenes to share in unofficial sentiments. Public sentiment spilled into official rhetoric though not yet policy. French consuls in the Mediterranean reported to Paris about battles and massacres in terms that were entirely religious, a historic contest between Islam and Christianity.[22] In high places too there was quite a lot of sympathy for the Greeks. The French king bought *Scenes from the Massacre of Scio* for 6,000 francs and awarded Delacroix a medal for art. Alexander of Russia continued to be outraged over the fate of his Greek coreligionists even as he refused to act. British foreign secretary Canning met with representatives of the Greeks but he too held to a policy of nonintervention.

Already from 1821 wild rumors circulated in Europe to the effect that the Ottomans planned to "wipe out Christianity" from the Earth, or, less ambitiously, "slaughter all the Christian subjects of the Ottoman Empire." Capo d'Istria, while still foreign minister, wrote to Tsar Alexander that the Porte aimed to "exterminate the Christians under their domination."[23] With the Egyptian invasion of 1825, misinformation was put out and repeated as fact in the foreign ministries and in the press. This was the Barbarization Project: Ibrahim intended to depopulate the Morea of Christians and replace them with fellaheen. This was invention but it became an article of faith in Russian diplomacy. Soon Canning was repeating it.[24]

It would be easy to surmise that policy changed in 1826 because of the influence of Philhellenism, Christianity, humanitarianism, and outrage, but this would be wrong. They were added later. The powers had strategic reasons to act, with motivations and consequences that were larger than the Greek War. But the rhetoric of religion was not entirely empty. Labeling the Greeks Christians had geopolitical implications: Christians could be equated with Europe, civilization, and full humanity. This in turn brought to the foreground the old question: Were the Ottoman Christians part of Europe? The Concert of Europe had stayed out of the Greek War because this was an Ottoman affair and outside the purview of the Congress System (see chapter 7). But since the rebels were Christian it was possible to conclude that Greece was in fact a European affair. Already in July 1821 the Russian ambassador told the Porte that "the cause that Russia is pleading is a European cause."[25] In 1823 Lord John Russell, who joined the London Greek Committee, wrote that the Greek War "affords the most cheering prospects of being able to enlarge the limit of Christianity and civilization."[26]

Still the powers stayed out of the Greek conflict, because it was outside Europe. When Russia executed a volte-face in 1826, it turned this argument on its head. Russia could intervene if it wished, without the blessings of Europe, for the same reason: Greece was outside Europe, it was outside the Congress System, and therefore Russia could act unilaterally. Britain joined Russia because it peeled Russia away from its solidarity with the other continental powers and put an end to the Congress System.[27] France joined them so as not to be left out of decisions affecting the Mediterranean. Soon the diplomats went the final distance with one more about-face: having argued that they could intervene because the rebelling regions were outside Europe, they now declared that they had to intervene because they were inside Europe; they were Christian. The three powers carried out what Russian diplomats had called "the enlargement of Europe."[28]

Three powers decided that Greece was in Europe and in 1827 they intervened.

⁍

The shift in European diplomacy was rooted in the commercial and strategic interests of France, Russia, and Britain in the eastern Mediterranean. Russia's interest in Greece as such was secondary. It had interests stretching from the Baltic to the Pacific with myriad engagements and entanglements along the way. Until 1826, as the Greek question was being debated across Europe, Russia was more concerned with its war with Persia. With regard to the Ottoman Empire, Russia was focused on matters to the north and east of the Greek lands: the Danubian Principalities that actually bordered Russia; the Caucasus where Russian expansion continued; and the Black Sea whence Russian shipping entered into the Mediterranean.[29]

Tsar Alexander repeatedly threatened to intervene but did nothing, all the way to his death in 1825. The source of Alexander's wavering was his commitment to the Congress System. Russia oversaw the system which it had created, but that system had been twisted around by Austria to become a vice. Russia would not act alone and therefore could not act at all. As early as 1823 British agents had sent out feelers to Russia about the possibility of some sort of joint policy in the Greek War, separate from the Holy Alliance, but Alexander did not commit. That same year Alexander proposed that the Greek areas be carved into three autonomous principalities but the other powers did not agree.[30] His advisors, ministers, and ambassadors found the strength to tell him in a coordinated and blunt way that he was being manipulated by Austria and ignoring Russian interests. In August 1825 foreign minister Nesselrode wrote to the European courts: "Henceforth Russia will follow only its goals and be guided by its own interests."[31]

Russian policy wavered because it depended on the whims of one man, the autocrat. Britain wavered because of the nature of the cabinet system. A change in government or foreign secretary could produce a warmer or cooler attitude to the Greeks, a greater or lesser commitment to Ottoman integrity, and a new policy. Foreign secretaries had a good deal of discretion, and Castlereagh had been firmly anti-Greek up to his suicide in 1822. When George Canning became foreign secretary in 1823 he declared British neutrality. This was new because it recognized the Greeks as a belligerent, and to that extent on par with the Ottomans. Ionian and other British ships could trade with both sides. Canning sympathized with the Greeks but he was explicit that he and his government were not motivated by sentiment. The issue "has nothing to do with Epaminondas nor (with reverence be it spoken) with St. Paul." His attitude to the Latin American revolutions was the template to understand his attitude to the Greek one. As Portugal and Spain were shut out of South America, British trade and capital would seep into the vacuum. By the same token, if the Ottomans were to lose in the southern Balkans and some sort of Greek territory created, British ships would dominate the region without the need to conquer anything. There would be none of the messiness of war and occupation—governing the Greeks of the Ionian Islands was hard enough—but a hegemony exercised from the sea by merchant ships and warships. It would be a different kind of empire.[32]

Neither power would act alone, until two developments led them to act together. The first was the death of Alexander. In 1825 Nicholas I became tsar and he was immediately confronted with a united front of advisors—princes, ministers, and ambassadors—decrying Russia's paralysis in the Congress System and the Holy Alliance. Russia needed a policy that was "national" rather than European. The advice seems to have been coordinated.[33] Nicholas agreed. He carried little of his brother's history with the Holy Alliance and the idea of a supranational Europe of consensus. Again, the issue was not humanitarian or Philhellene. Nicholas despised the Greeks, as did British officials like Wellington.[34]

More fundamental was frustration with the Porte. It had been given almost five years to restore order in its lands and seas, in the way that the Europeans had restored order in Spain and Italy. Handled right, Russian agents told Ottoman officials, "the Greek question would die of neglect." Instead the sultan had failed to retake the Morea and the Greek fleets operated with impunity. Ibrahim's conquest of the Morea could have put a final end to the land war, albeit with a good deal of scandal and outrage over the mass violence inflicted on the Christians.[35]

The enduring problem that united Britain, Russia, and later France was on sea: rampant piracy which Ibrahim had made worse. Some of it was carried out by Greeks acting formally for Greece but attacking ships under any flag whatsoever—Ottoman, Ionian, British, Russian, French, Austrian, and American. Ships from Tunis and Algiers were theoretically vassals of the sultan and they operated with the Ottoman and Egyptian fleets, but they also peeled off to attack any ship that offered booty and slaves. Still other privateers with no claims to represent a higher authority were drawn by the disorder, from France, Corsica, the Ionian Islands, Britain, and Dalmatia. Reports of murdered crews and ransomed cargoes were myriad and the consistent background to the deliberations of the European ministries.[36] Austria had lost a hundred ships by 1826. In 1827 alone Britain lost thirty-eight ships, and in the month of April 1826 Russia lost seven ships.[37] French consuls in the region thought piracy to be the main danger facing French interests and in 1826 recommended to Paris one or another intervention.[38]

Ironically one of the motivations of Mehmed Ali's invasion of the Morea was also to end the piracy that had disrupted Egyptian trade. For example, Egypt bought most of its timber in the lands of the Greek Revolution. Ending the rebellion would allow for the creation of a stable, Egyptian space in the eastern Mediterranean (see chapter 15). But Ibrahim's victories had unwittingly made matters worse, not better. Unable to withstand the Egyptians, the Greek fleet had dispersed into pirate flotillas and lone privateers who cared little about distinguishing between one flag and another, and attacked Christian islands to loot them.[39]

This swayed the European courts. Britain's naval supremacy was un-questioned but its shipping was taking heavy losses and it was not good for trade. It had been forced in practice to negotiate with one or another Greek authority to allow safe passage to its merchant vessels, and in effect recognized Mavrokordatos as the leader of Greece who could re-strain the Greek fleet; now the Greek fleet was dispersed and controlled by no one.[40]

Russia was dependent on the Black and Mediterranean seas in a more complete way. Ships carrying Russian wheat could only enter the Medi-terranean and reach its markets by passing through the Bosphorus and Dardanelles Straits, but that was only the first obstacle. From the Straits ships passed into the Aegean Sea and maneuvered though the 1,400 Aegean Islands. There was no other route. Greeks and other pirates waited concealed behind islands, islets, and rocks before they pounced. Russia's finance ministry was alarmed that Black Sea exports were de-clining and even ending altogether because of piracy, to the detriment of the trade balance, the value of the ruble, and state revenues.[41]

The new tsar agreed to negotiate with Britain and the Duke of Wel-lington sailed to St. Petersburg to congratulate the new emperor on his accession and finalize what became known as the St. Petersburg Pro-tocol of April 1826. It was an agreement to force the Porte to negotiate. Failing that, the two powers would compel the sultan, though they did not say how. A Greece of some sort would receive autonomy of some sort.[42]

The St. Petersburg Protocol was a minor revolution in diplomacy. It did away with the Congress System that required consensus before any one power altered the status quo. Now Russia could brush aside European objections. Following the St. Petersburg Protocol, Austria demanded of Russia new congresses to reach a consensus (again, in order to do nothing at all), and now Russian diplomats told the Austrians that this was not a European or Austrian affair. For Britain, inducing Russia to abandon the Congress System was a coup that disrupted the solidarity of the continental powers.[43] Now both powers could forge their own polices, act alone, or reach bilateral agreements rather than wait for Europe to hamper them. It was a defeat for Austria in particular, which had used consensus to enable itself and hamstring Russia. To be sure, Austrian commerce suffered from piracy as well but Austria insisted that the solution was to let the Porte end the Greek Revolution. In return Austrian ships received the contracts for supplying the Ottomans.[44] Now Austria was alone save for Prussia which was not a Mediterranean power at all.

France joined Russia and Britain and rethought its commitment to the Porte and to Egypt. In autumn 1825 France was still sending officers to serve under Ibrahim and French shipyards were still delivering frigates to Alexandria. When the St. Petersburg Protocol was announced French diplomats tried and failed to drag Russia back into consultations. French commanders concluded that the future of the Greeks would be decided by European powers and they were determined that France be one of them. France's strategy remained the same—a resurgence of French power in the Mediterranean—but now pursued as one of three maritime powers of the region.

Egypt would have to accommodate. Abruptly French generals sent urgent messages to Cairo urging Mehmed Ali to break with the sultan, evacuate the Morea, declare Egyptian independence from the Porte, and exercise an influence over a tiny independent Greece. "The Greeks are friends to be cultivated rather than enemies to be fought," and Greece would be Cairo's informal colony. Greeks overseen in an expanded

Egyptian space could provide Egypt with sailors, merchants, and farmers. Mediating the new arrangement would be France.

Mehmed Ali had already been thinking in similar terms. When he became convinced that the Europeans would impose Greek independence, he too envisioned an independent Greece in a wider Egyptian space. He also considered Egyptian independence from the Porte. Russia was expected to attack the Ottoman Empire in the Danube, Caucasus, and Black Sea at any moment. Egypt could use the occasion to create a stable area in the eastern Mediterranean out of the remains of the sultan's domains.[45]

It was probably too late already because the sultan was unwavering and the European powers more determined. The French command wrote to the French officers serving Mehmed Ali and urged them to leave. Some of them rediscovered their love of Europe as they packed their belongings. "What role can a civilized man play, to the detriment of humanity?" wrote General Pierre François Xavier Boyer, an advisor to Mehmed Ali. Not that Boyer was opposed to the killing of civilians, and no doubt he had advised Ibrahim and Mehmed Ali on the connection of military strategy with counterinsurgency that required attacks on a whole population. He had experience. As a volunteer for the French Republic since 1792 he likely participated in the massacres of the Vendée during the French Revolution. He was at the counterinsurgency in Spain and the shockingly brutal assault on Haiti. His problem was that he did not want to do violence "in favor of the crescent." In 1826 he returned to France. In 1830 he was at the French conquest of Algiers, part of what was widely called "a new Crusade." He was noted for his unusual brutality toward the civilian population of Oran.[46]

In the Treaty of London of July 1827, Russia, Britain, and France agreed that the Porte should be forced to negotiate with the Greeks. The allied navies would exert the pressure. Tellingly, one of the allied demands was for compensation for their losses to piracy, for which they held the Porte responsible. The outcome would be a Greece that recognized Ottoman suzerainity but not sovereignty. The diplomatic texts termed the Greek uprising "the war" or "the struggle" but not a revolt.[47] The writings and paintings and graphic art, alongside the persistent work of men like the Count and Eynard, was adopted by the chanceries to allow them to accept what they had so recently condemned: a revolution. It was not a revolution at all, they held. This was independence regained and Europe expanded.[48]

And it was now that the powers converged with the reality on the ground and the predominant public opinion in Europe: the Greece they proposed to bring into existence could only be Christian. What the Greeks had done and what Philhellenes had demanded—homogeneity— became a doctrine in diplomacy. The country could only be stable if it was uniformly Christian. It is a principle that may seem natural and obvious today in the era of nation-states where ethnicity and territory are often meant to be the same thing—Wilson's Fourteen Points toward the end the First World War is the landmark—but in the 1820s the term nation-state did not exist. In politics and diplomacy the nation was still thought to be subversive and would remain so into the Revolutions of 1848; only later would statemen like Cavour and Bismarck commandeer nationalism into the state. Meanwhile, to the multiethnic empires the nation promised division and civil conflict, and implied that sovereignty rested not with a monarch but with a people.

And yet: to solve a problem on the small tip of a small peninsula on a small continent, the powers tacitly let the nation enter their vocabulary and operate as a principle in diplomacy and a standard of statehood, where it has remained ever since. They did so by focusing on demography. The problem in Greece was the mixing of Christians and Muslims, or Greeks and Turks. The solution was to separate them and give the new land a homogeneity that had never existed before. In the leadup to the St. Petersburg Protocol of 1826 Canning instructed Wellington to pursue "the absolute separation of the Turkish and Greek populations." The final language required "a complete separation of persons from the two nations" and a transfer of Muslim properties to the Greeks.[49] Later treaties gave Ottoman Muslims the possibility of remaining in the new Greece, but hardly any did. Tiny enclaves of Muslims remained in the new country and in a few years they, too, had disappeared.[50]

The idea of two incompatible peoples penetrated military thought as well. When General Jean-Jacques Pelet reported to French military intelligence in 1826 he repeated what was becoming a commonplace: the Muslims ("the Turks") must not be allowed to stay in Europe. His reasoning was downright wrong but it was widespread and originated with Count Capo d'Istria and Stourdza. The Christians had been subjugated by the Muslims in the fifteenth century "but they did not mix. An insurmountable obstacle separates them: they are enemy religions, entirely opposed to each other, producing mores and men who are completely juxtaposed." Pelet concluded: "The Turks must be expelled from Europe."[51]

Europe Mobilizes: The Fleets

Europe's Mediterranean powers had warships in the seas around the Balkan tip because they had interests to protect and promote. All of the powers cared about shipping and commerce. Britain had the added concern for the Ionian Islands which could at any moment be drawn into the war by outside attack or internal uprising. Its fleet patrolled the Ionian and Aegean seas throughout the 1820s. France's ships protected trade and also extended French imperial interests through pockets of confessional clients—the Catholics of the Aegean Islands of Syros, Naxos, Tinos, and Andros. Very Catholic Bourbon kings claimed to be the protectors of the Catholic islanders but the islands were also a base from which warships could react quickly to unfolding events. Since the Egyptians had landed in the Morea in 1825, French ships under Admiral Henri de Rigny had been shadowing the Egyptian fleet.[52] Austria sent ships to guard its commerce, much of it dedicated to the supply of the Ottomans and Egyptians.[53] The United States sent warships that cruised between the north-African Barbary coast and the Aegean in search of pirate threats to US-flag merchant vessels. Greeks assumed (and still assume) they were acting in the Greek interest, just like the American volunteers. In fact the US government steered clear of the Greeks because it was working to sign a commercial treaty with the Porte.[54]

In October 1827, following the Treaty of London, the warships of Russia, France, and Britain converged off the western coast of the Morea and formed a single allied fleet.[55] They were commanded by Admiral

Edward Codrington of Britain, who was the most senior. He acted in consultation with Rigny of France and Ludwig Heyden (Loggin Geiden) of Russia. Their task was to force the belligerents to negotiate whether they wanted to or not. The admirals presented the Greeks with the Treaty of London and the Greeks immediately accepted because it offered some form of statehood; the Ottomans rejected it for the same reason. The task of the fleet now became to cut off Ibrahim's army from supplies and block the export of slaves, and ultimately to force the Egyptians to leave.[56] Mehmed Ali could see that Europe had changed and he proposed to the Porte that the Morean campaign be wrapped up.[57] The Porte refused. In September 1827 Ibrahim agreed with the allied admirals to suspend his military operations until he could receive instructions from Cairo, but the Greeks continued to fight and Ibrahim resumed operations.[58]

In October the allied fleet was off the west coast of the Morea while the combined Egyptian and Ottoman fleet was moored in the Bay of Navarino (today Pylos). What the allied crews saw was horrifying and incongruous. The hillsides bracketed by the intense blue sky and sea were crisscrossed by columns of smoke rising from burning villages, columns of soldiers descending the mountains, and columns of slaves being marched to the coast. The admirals warned Ibrahim to desist and Ibrahim ignored them.[59] French officers still serving with the Egyptians were advised by allied officers to become scarce, as were the whole companies of European sappers and the Italian physicians.[60] The Austrian supply ships went to the edge of the bay.

What happened next was the Battle of Navarino, and it is both a simple affair and a very complicated one. It is simple in the sense that it ended Ibrahim's campaign because he had no fleet to supply the army. Twenty-six allied ships sank some seventy Egyptian and Ottoman ships, though estimates vary. Six to eight thousand Ottoman and Egyptian sailors died that day.[61]

Since the Greek cause had been lost until that day, it was something of a miracle wrapped in a mystery because it is not clear why the allies attacked. This is where it becomes complicated. The allied fleet did not have orders to intervene in the Greek War, but its mere presence was something of an intervention. The fleet had orders not to engage unless there was cause, but the orders did not quite say what a cause might be; meanwhile Tsar Nicholas had ordered his admiral to attack to force negotiations.[62] All three admirals were probably outraged by the humanitarian disaster they were spying through their glasses. The order to enter the bay may have been meant as intimidation, or it may have been meant to provoke a reaction and a battle—which could be what happened if Ottoman or Egyptian ships in fact fired, but it is not clear that they did.

Even after the battle, the allies insisted that it was not an act of war though it is hard to see it as anything else.[63] It was all very confusing and the British government regretted the battle and launched an inquiry into Codrington's conduct. He was cleared and the king hanged the Order of Bath around his admiral's neck, allegedly whispering that it should have been a noose.[64] In Russia and France the respective admirals were received as heroes and decorated, and in Paris a new product appeared in shops: "Liqueur de Navarin."[65]

Greek independence did not follow immediately from the allied victory but made it likely. That happened in 1830 after one more Russo-Ottoman war. Greece was to be an independent state but beholden to the three powers that proclaimed Greek independence, under terms they drafted without asking the Greeks, with a king selected by them. It was to be independent, except for ample opportunities for the powers to intervene, with navies that were ever-present and sometimes sent in to enforce their will, all the while leveraging loans that could never be repaid.

And that nicely describes the arrival of modern Greece in the world. Indeed it nicely describes the modern world.

Violence, Empire, and the Nation

Prologue

WINTER 2017. I stop at a kiosk to buy cigarettes in downtown Athens. It's around midnight, still early for the Greek capital. The woman in the kiosk, perhaps in her late 60s, is pleasant and informal. She apologizes that there's a shortage of change for the 50-euro note I gave her. "Blame the foreigners," I joke, "the euros are printed in Germany."

Her voice turns metallic: "Their horn," shorthand for, roughly, "The fucking cuckolds." "It's always been this way."

I recover from grandma's authenticity and I know she is right. In the grand narratives of crisis that recur in Greek history, it is people like her who pay the price. In 2015 Greece once again could not repay its loans to foreign banks, and the crisis peaked. Government spending was slashed in return for European credits which went to repay the European banks but not to help those Greeks who were facing a calamity. In Greece it is just referred to as "the Crisis." The Crisis is human-made, and yet humans refuse to solve it no matter what the cost in poverty, suicide, infant mortality, and preventable disease. Her pension is too small to let her retire in old age. Foreign powers ("our partners") made the wrong people pay for previous excesses. Then again some Greeks invited the foreigners and their loans, as they always had; some Greeks did very well throughout the Crisis, as they often did; and some Greeks merrily implemented the austerity that would affect people other *than themselves. She may just as easily have directed her ire at smartly dressed people with 50-euro notes to spend.*

I am pleased that the woman thinks it is wrong and unjust, that she is angry. This too is a legacy of the Greek Revolution: suffering is not new, but there is an entitlement that comes with citizenship. At the very least, I can hope.

A New Whiff of Empire

Modern Greece was created by three allied powers of Europe. Together Russia, France, and the United Kingdom decided its form of government, its borders, its finances, and the disposition of the lands seized from the Ottomans. Greece was born into a new kind of empire, the traces of which are still with us.

Greek independence became a certainty because of Russian arms and diplomatic persistence. War with the Porte had been expected for some time and it was delayed by Russia's war with Persia in 1826.[1] In 1828 Russo-Ottoman relations deteriorated once again, but the ensuing war was not fought over Greece. It was fought over the Danubian Principalities, the Caucasus, and the Black Sea region, and Russia's gains were mainly here. But in the Treaty of Adrianople (today Edirne in Turkey) of 1829 the tsar inserted Article 10, which forced the sultan to accept his loss of Greece.[2] The next year, in February 1830, the allies agreed to full independence in the London Protocol.

The allies debated the location of the new border but generally agreed that Greece would encompass those lands that had rebelled in the preceding decade: the Morea, southern Roumeli, and some of the Aegean Islands. In effect they recognized a people under arms, popular sovereignty though not by name. Other Aegean Islands were given autonomy in the Ottoman Empire.[3] Areas to the north of Athens (Thessaly, Epirus, and Macedonia) remained Ottoman, and the Ionian Islands British. Capo d'Istria arrived as governor. He agitated for the creation of more Christian states to join Greece: a Dacia that resembled modern Romania, a Serbia that included Bosnia and Herzegovina, and a large Macedonia.[4] He had earlier insisted that Greece was the

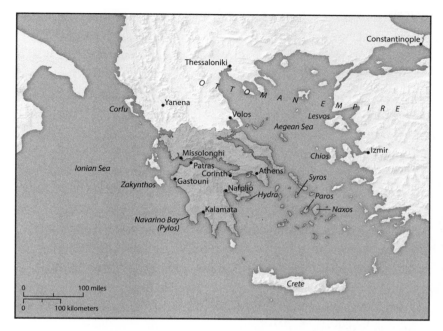

FIGURE 17.1. Independent Greece in 1833. Credit to Rob McCalebb. *Lands and seas that later became part of Greece were at that time in the Ottoman and British empires.*

exception, and now proposed that it was only the beginning. The nation was here to stay, but which state qualified as a nation in the region was up for grabs. It still is.

From the point of view of the Greeks, who had very little say in the matter, it was a start and better than nothing. Capo d'Istria as governor was a transition that ended with his assassination. Greece was then given a monarchy under a European king from a royal house, and he turned out to be Otto of Bavaria. The Greeks had asked for a constitution when they met in two more assemblies, but again their opinions mattered little to the allies because the Greeks could not govern themselves. The Greeks had murdered their governor and were once again at war with each other.[5] Parts of the fleet refused to obey commands and when cornered blew up some very expensive warships that had been bought with the second London loan. Surely, the allies concluded, absolutism was the solution for an unruly people. Their problems would be solved in Europe, and the ruler should be anything but Greek.[6]

The Greeks themselves had been open to such an outcome, or at least it could be distilled from the many things they said and did in the course of the 1820s. Monarchy was still the standard understanding of good government and the early Greek constitutions had anticipated that a king would be selected at some point in the future.[7] Foreign tutelage and rule were also possibilities. When all seemed lost in in the years 1825–7, different factions approached Russian, British, and French representatives to send a king or exercise a protectorate over Greece and save the Greeks from Ibrahim. Mavrokordatos's appeal to Britain, the Act of Submission, was the most famous and it was signed by the likes of Kolokotronis and Petrobey. But other factions petitioned France and still others Russia, and some of the same men signed those as well.[8]

Kolokotronis would take anyone, as president or king, as he explained in an exchange with a British officer before the Battle of Navarino, so long as he was a foreigner. It could save the Greeks from Ibrahim and from each other. But the Briton explained that no one power could be allowed such an influence. Anyway, with Ibrahim triumphant, it seemed to all concerned that the Greeks were doomed.

"Can't England give us a president, a king?"
"No, that can never happen."
"Can France?"
"The same."
"Russia?"
"No."
"Prussia?"
"No."
"Naples?"
"No."
"Spain?"
"No, it can't be done."

They then spoke of the Count but the Briton considered him to be a Russian. Finally he blurted out: "Take Kapodistrias or any devil you want, you're lost anyway."[9]

The Battle of Navarino changed this and the Count did arrive as governor, chosen because he was Greek but not quite Greek. He was an aristocrat, an Ionian Islander, and perhaps a Russian. Similarly, to appeal to the British and rise above their own differences, the Greeks had appointed Britons to command their forces. Thomas Cochran, a veteran of Latin American revolutions, commanded the fleet for an exceptionally good fee which he demanded in advance.[10] From 1827 the land forces were commanded by Richard Church, late of the Neapolitan army and before that a commander on the Ionian Islands.[11]

A strong executive morphing into absolutism was also put forward by the Greeks themselves. The Count had been invited to govern Greece in 1827 by a National Assembly, and he was given more or less unlimited powers at the next National Assembly of 1829. The last National Assembly, in 1832, declared a monarchy on the model of the Bourbon restoration, meaning that a legislature of grandees would have limited powers, but enough to limit the monarch. Men like Mavrokordatos were indifferent about the regime they might get, so long as it was an independent state.[12] What the allied powers decreed was an eclectic mix of these possibilities: an absolute monarchy with no legislature, and a king who was certainly above factional politics because he was Catholic and German. All this was guaranteed by the three allied powers who decreed it.

Not that this was the end of the matter: popular sovereignty was here to stay and the era of Greek absolutism lasted only a decade. In 1843 it was ended by a coup carried out by the veterans of 1821 who were not getting their wages. The constitution they secured was not an afterthought but revolutionary in its own right, drawing on pronouncements that seemed empty in the 1820s but were now brought to life as a way to limit monarchial power and negotiate differences. Every adult male could vote. The country achieved in 1843 what much of Europe would attempt by revolution five years later, in 1848.[13]

Foreign tutelage also took the form of a French force of fourteen thousand troops that landed in the Morea in August 1828, usually named for its commander, Nicolas Joseph Maison. Its mission was twofold. The first was to put an end to all warfare, be it between Greeks and Egyptians or Greeks and Greeks. The French force marched to specific locations to quash minor uprisings or bandit attacks. The French did what they could to release the slaves held by the Egyptians. Along the way the French demonstrated what a government could do by rebuilding bridges and roads. The French administered the first smallpox vaccines, though the problem by then was bubonic plague.[14] The Corfiot and now French officer Bulgari (see chapter 4) was seconded to the Count and he put to use his engineering skills to plan the reconstruction of the devastated towns. Patras today follows the scheme he laid out.

The other mission of the French force was to accept the surrender of the Egyptians and Ottomans still occupying towns and forts. Towns like Patras and Methoni that had been in Ottoman hands all along surrendered after putting up enough token resistance to satisfy the sultan who had not yet agreed to Greek independence. The resistance and surrenders were prearranged, loud but usually not lethal. The Egyptians had no fleet, so the next task was to load them on French ships and send them to Alexandria. The last Egyptians left in September 1828 when Ibrahim boarded the final evacuation ship.

The French mission was not simply military but also cultural and scientific, an opportunity to master the geography, geology, botany, and archeology of the Morea, some of Roumeli, and some of the islands. The scientists were often also former officers. This mix of military and culture made sense to a power that was reemerging as an empire: to know, name, and map was to dominate, and indeed the first accurate map of the Morea was created by the scientific expedition for the French army. The leader of the scientific expedition saw Napoleon's army in Egypt as a first example, as it took out time from the fighting to excavate the Pyramids and the Sphinx, to adore a dead civilization and attack the living one.[15]

In the Morea the French had little to say about the population in a systematic way, though the colonial contempt for people and, for example, their "barbaric and ridiculous" music and dances, made it into the memoirs.[16] They had much more to say about the ancient ruins, the towns to which they painstakingly restored ancient names, and the fauna. Soon the same force, or that part that survived disease, was sailing to Algiers as a third moment of Mediterranean conquest and scientific inquiry. It was the dawn of a new French empire.[17] With French opinion already trained in the binary of Christianity and Islam, it is little wonder that the attack on Algiers was justified, and widely supported, as a crusade.[18]

Little remarked at the time was the fact that the French army evacuated the Morean Muslims who had returned with the Egyptians in 1825, and those who had occupied a few forts throughout the decade. They numbered 2,500 and they were "repatriated" to the Ottoman Empire. In fact they were Moreans and now refugees embarking on their final exile.[19] As they left they sold their lands and buildings for whatever pittance the Christians offered them, and even Kolokotronis pitied them.[20] They arrived in their new homes, awkwardly, as Greek-speaking and Albanian-speaking Muslims. Some did well as scholars of Classical Greece.[21]

The demographic revolution, begun by the Greeks in 1821, was completed by the European powers.

Greek Debt

Independent Greece entered into a new kind of empire where small or poor states used their sovereign power to borrow and then surrender much of their sovereignty. Greece was showing the way to the newly independent states that covered the globe over the next two centuries and blanketed it with debt. Certain especially scandalous cases make the news—the work of vulture capitalists in Argentina, the financial debilitation of Haiti by French banks ever since Haitian independence—but the phenomenon is ongoing and ever-present.[22]

From the moment of independence Greece accepted the burden of debt; there was no choice.[23] The new state took responsibility for the two London loans of 1824 and 1825, and this debt—useless paper, really, since Greece had no way to repay it—would be used by speculators into the 1870s who ensured that Greece was banned from the capital markets until they were paid. Today they would be called vulture capitalists. In addition the country received a loan of 60 million gold francs, guaranteed by the three powers, which was entirely needed. For the powers this was not a lot of money, and it was well understood that Greece could not repay it. The issue was leverage. In 1838 Edmund Lyons, the ambassador to Greece, said he was "delighted" at the prospect of Greek bankruptcy because it would allow for more British intervention; "a really independent Greece is an absurdity." Spoke a French official during the Crimean crisis, his country "has the incontestable right to interfere in the affairs of Greece."[24]

Over the years gunboats visited Greek ports to seize revenues, using the debt as the pretext and forcing one or another political concession. France and Britain paid such a visit in the 1850s to ensure that Greece did not side with Russia in the Crimean War, and another in the 1890s when Greece attacked the Ottoman Empire without the permission of the powers. In the 1920s Greece was overwhelmed by a wave of refugees from republican Turkey and an international commission arrived to offer credits and control by technocrats who bypassed the Greek state altogether. And in the 2010s, loans to repay European banks came with austerity, privatization, and control over spending, a warning to any country that might object to a new economic orthodoxy. European advisors arrived with something creepier than gunboats: iPads and tablets that monitored the implementation of austerity. The German chancellor visited Athens to congratulate Greece on its success: a balanced budget, 25 percent unemployment, and a 25 percent fall in GDP.

At times it seemed that the only thing that was sovereign about Greece was its sovereign debt.

Trail of Bones

The population of what became Greece in 1830 had been much larger in 1820. One estimate holds that on the eve of the Revolution 943,000 people inhabited these lands; at independence they numbered 712,000, a loss of one in four. The Morea had a population of 450,000 in 1821 and 336,000 in 1830, also a loss of one in four. Cities fared worse. The town of Gastouni had numbered a few thousand; in 1829 it numbered ninety-two.[25]

It is worth telling of the destruction alongside the strategies, the battles, and the abstract notion that one side had won and another had lost, that the struggle was somehow clean. Most of the people who suffered were not warriors. There is no statue to commemorate the humili-

FIGURE 17.2. Skulls from the Massacre of Chios of 1822. Flioukas / Wikimedia Commons / CC BY-SA 4.0 DEED. *Monasteries gathered and still hold the remains of victims. Since Ottoman soldiers took only the ears and skins as trophies, the heads would have been left behind to be gathered by the monks.*

ated men and women, the children who succumbed to disease, and the thousands who were loaded onto slave ships. The stacks of skulls on Chios with the sword-marks still visible are only the most famous example because they are still to be seen. Many, many more bones littered the peninsula and were swept away by the rains, mixed with mortar in new buildings, ploughed under by farmers, or ground into fertilizer.[26]

The statues of a few heroes are a distraction, a suggestion that the Revolution was made by the very few rather than the very many. The Revolution succeeded because mass popular sovereignty was at its base, and popular sovereignty should be the enduring legacy of the Revolution.

࿔

In December 1830 Greek merchant ships docked at Nafplio in the Morea with loads of freed slaves who had been ransomed in Egypt by Russian officials, other governments, missionaries, merchants, Greek merchants around the Mediterranean, and Mehmed Ali himself. Nicholas I of Russia sent agents to the Ottoman Empire to ransom the Orthodox slaves they could find. The banker Eynard specialized in ransoming slaves taken at Missolonghi. King Ludwig I of Bavaria asked Eynard, "how many women, how many children might I be able to buy out of slavery?"[27] To the French and British, who were themselves owners of Black slaves, the enslavement of the Greeks was a horror because "they have our complexion."[28]

The men disembarking at Nafplio arrived in a land that was devastated. Scarcely a building was left undamaged in the new Greece. Seven hundred villages were destroyed to one extent or another and many of them were abandoned. Towns like Patras and Argos had been razed. Around Gastouni and Pyrgos nine out of every ten sheep were gone. Everywhere bridges were down, roads and paths eroded, churches and mosques torched. Trees were burned and more cut down for fuel. In the town of Leontari in the Morea, of 1,276 homes, 1,242 were torched; of 48 peasant huts, 48 were torched; of 96 workshops, 80 were torched; 5,500 fruit-bearing trees were burned.[29]

Capo d'Istria ordered a survey of the territories of the new state and he asked the regional notables to compile reports. They counted the destroyed trees and homes, markets and shops, mills and wells, and with some care recalled which aga had ruled and owned in a given locality, now dead or gone. The lists are a haunting, a final testament to a civilization that later Greeks would work so hard to scrub out of the records, the geography, and the local memory. The mosques were rubble or made into churches and warehouses. Muslim cemeteries were ploughed under. Monuments were gone. The monument to the Philhellene Santarosa on the Bay of Navarino may be fitting for the Piedmontese revolutionary who gave his life for Greek independence, but it replaced a white marble tomb of an aga—who had been revered by Christians and Muslims alike—that was smashed and thrown into the sea to join the shipwrecks.[30]

Hundreds of places with Muslim names were given Christian or Classical ones. Dervi Tselep near Gastouni became Amaliada after the new queen Amalia. Omer Tsaousi became Spathovouni. Remoustafa became

Adriani. Argos had been made up of boroughs (machalas) such as Bekir Efendi, Karamoutza, Besikler, and Rum. Slavic names would also disappear over the next century as Greek territory extended northward and bumped against new Slav-dominated states. Vostitsa became Aigio, Chorvati (think Hrvatska) became Mycenae, Agoulinitsa became Epitalion, and Levetsova became Krokeës. Frankish names from the Middle Ages were Christian, an acceptable heritage, and were retained: Gastouni (Gaston), Andravida (André Ville), and Chlemoutsi (Clermont). Then again, the port of Glarentza (Clarence) emerged nearby as Kyllini.[31]

People were dead and gone, too, and among the hundreds who were named in these reports were Mehmed Tsipoglou, Souleiman Manousos, Kiamil bey, Old Man Osman aga, and Fat Hasan. "They were sweet" (iton glykis, meaning kind and polite), local elders wrote in the reports, in defiance of the later image of blanket cruelty and barbarity. In this there was some remorse for the carnage and perhaps some bitterness because some of the writers had never wanted the mass revolution in the first place, let alone the mass destruction. "They were not religious haters and they were devoted to the Christians." Here and there were reports of the few sons and daughters of agas who had returned or never left because they were baptized. Near Leontari in the village of Hasabasa (renamed Aristodemeio) the sons of Sali Petrou and Seyndi Moutzos, both dead, appeared with their Christian names to claim the family properties. As Muslims, they no longer existed.[32]

Violence was gendered. We know well about some exceptional women who led fleets and armies, and Bouboulina is the most storied. We know better that women also mobilized in 1821 and 1822 to organize their menfolk, supply the armies, carry weapons, and gather the loot. Women managed the household economy without which there could be no military mobilization. But women were as much victims as any other category of people and they were victims of a specific kind. Any battle was the occasion for rape, and here rape was massive and came in successive waves. It will not do to sigh that armed, young, and aggressive men did such things, that it is to be expected in any war. There was much more to it and there always is. Women were the foundations of the households and the carriers of the lineage, and rape attacked the population at the molecular level. It was part of a tearing apart of resistance, from the violation of the woman to questions of family honor to doubts about who had fathered the babies born. This attack on the social foundations, down to the level of the household, was later associated with the Egyptians, but they were only the last wave. The Christians had done this to the Muslims in 1821, and the Roumeliots had done it to the Moreans in 1824.

As the French army entered towns and walked the dirt and cobbled streets, they came upon piles and piles of bones—from Methoni to Navarino, from Mystras to Monemvasia. The towns were linked by more trails of bones which the French used as markers as they moved about. The streets of Corinth were clogged with human and animal remains. The sandy beaches of Navarino were littered with the skeletons of Egyptian sailors. The French command at Navarino took over the surviving administrative buildings in the town but was overwhelmed by the stench because all the roads had been converted into cemeteries for successive waves of dead, some quite recent. The soldiers exhumed and burned them. A French scientist reminisced: "It was an operation similar to the one that happened in Algiers after the glorious conquest of that city" a year later. He was proud of the display of modern sanitation and less bothered by the slaughter that occasioned it.

Now the Egyptians were falling not to the sword or musket but to the plague. So many bodies had been left to rot over such a long period of successive massacres that the Morea became a breeding ground for epidemics, beginning with the massacre of Tripolitsa in 1821. Malaria was already endemic and afflicted newcomers, typhus was relatively new, and when the French arrived bubonic plague was rife.[33] Whenever the Greeks and the Egyptians fought or exchanged prisoners they also exchanged diseases. By one estimate the Egyptians had sent over a total of 24,000 men by the end of 1826, and only 8,000 were still alive.[34]

The French accepted the Egyptian surrenders and received the fleas. Now the French fell ill and died in large numbers.[35] French scientists escaped the "vapors" of the west coast, only to die on the east coast. French bones joined the piles already there, a last deposit in that exceptionally lethal decade.[36] Rarely mentioned in the foreign reports was the obvious fact that the Greeks had no more immunity to typhus and the plague than the Europeans. The plague became a final catastrophe to befall the Greeks in a decade of catastrophes. French observers lamented that they were losing their Greek translators.[37]

On the seas the piracy that had so afflicted the European merchant fleets and spurred some of the powers to intervene was devastating for the Christians of the islands and occasioned mass migrations. Every battle or massacre—on Crete, Samos, Psara, or Kasos—produced waves of refugees who forced themselves on islands like Kea, Naxos, Karpathos, Skopelos, Milos, and Aegina. Syros's Catholics began their uneasy cohabitation with a wave of Orthodox refugees which persists into the present day, though more amicably. Quite a few of the new arrivals had been or became pirates who looted towns, and they set off new waves of refugees.

More ships arrived at the islands in the name of the Greek government which in 1827, the time of Ibrahim, existed in name only. The ships had a mission to evict the sea bandits, which they did, and then did their own looting which they called taxation. Kea lost its wheat harvest to these liberators and Andros was relieved of 33 cows, 320 sheep, and a caïque to transport them to their new owners. Henceforth it would be the task of a more disciplined Greek navy, bolstered by the European fleets, to patrol the waters and make the towns safe.[38] They paved the way for that quick and impressive recovery of Greek shipping that lasts into the present day.

Out of the Ruins

The capacity of humans to adapt and go on is remarkable. Families survived by hiding in ancient sarcophaguses and emerged to reoccupy the villages and towns. Greek women and girls strolled about in the fashionable dresses and bonnets of New York and Paris, gifts from the many charitable collections.[39] Rubble and emptiness were filled with industry and people. Muslim villages and houses were rebuilt by their new Greek owners. The workshops of the murdered Jews of Tripolitsa reopened with Christian craftsmen.

The survivors set about planting for the next season with the slightly improved possibility of peace. Above them arrived the moneylenders and tax farmers who lived off them. Peasants would need seed, draft power, and tools, and the moneylenders went right back to work with loans at 60 to 120 percent annual interest. Kotsabases remained tax farmers for the Greek state, and transitioned into civil servants and members of parliament. In the 1890s, a Deliyannis became prime minister. The Sisinis family, whom we have treated as a case study, had a future in Greece as well. Giorgos's son Michalis was a bridge with the past: he cohabited with Aïsha, the daughter of Halil aga Hotoman zade, and they had a son together. Michalis and his brothers became officers and governors. At century's end the last of the male line wrote a brief overview of his ancestors which is sometimes candid, gathered the family archives which are rich, and bequeathed them to his only remaining heir, the nation. It rests in the basement of the building that holds the helmet of Kolokotronis.[40]

The Souliots who ended up in the new Greece likewise embraced the nation, and after decades of military service around the region became Greeks. Some traveled far from their kilts and became officers and recognizably European.

Old practices persisted but the context had changed: all of it was centered on the nation and the state. Kolokotronis returned to the business of enforcing collections and clearing out bandits, but this was not really business as usual. During his long life he had represented himself as a clan leader, a hireling, a warlord, or a friend of his allies, but henceforth he was a general of Greece following the orders of the Greek state. He forced the bandits to comply in a language they understood from the Ottoman practice: they should "submit." The Greek forces approached villages and the inhabitants responded as they always had, choosing the right flag from their collection and waving it to show that the village would not resist. Never mind that the villagers could not always tell one flag from another and waved Ottoman flags as Kolokotronis approached. The point was that they were accepting the new authority, and for once there was only one authority to accept, the Greek state. Henceforth they needed only one flag.[41]

FIGURE 17.3. *Botzaris*, unknown artist, 1835. Museum of Philhellenism. *Kostas Botsaris was the brother of Markos. Here Kostas is depicted in Albanian outfit. He served Ali pasha and was captured by the Ottomans at the fall of Yanena in 1822. He was later freed as part of the prisoner exchange and ransom for the harem of Hurşid pasha which had been captured at the massacre of Tripolitsa in fall 1821. My thanks to Constantinos Velentzas for the identification.*

FIGURE 17.4. *Kostas Botsaris*, unknown artist. National Historical Museum, Athens. *The same Kostas Botsaris years later, as a general of the Greek army.*

Cafés opened to host the French soldiers and scientists, complete with billiard tables brought by returning locals, Aegean merchants, and Greek merchants from abroad. Provençale petty traders came on the heels of the French army and set up shop. Around the Bay of Navarino new communities formed to mine the shipwrecks for timber and nails. Canteens made of planks, ropes, chains, and anchors, and held up by upright cannon, sprouted up to feed the French army and the surviving locals.[42] A major industry was the salvage of the valuable metals, the bronze, copper, and lead that attracted small traders and divers to the shipwrecks. The government got to work too and claimed 50 percent of the metals and all the cannon.[43]

There were new industries to be created. Kolokotronis, always intelligent and strategic, could see the future and he told it to Capo d'Istria.

Greece could make money from "the stones" (ancient ruins) that the foreigners loved so much. The stones should be cleaned so the foreigners would flock to Greece to see them and spend their gold. He meant what we call tourism.

On Violence

It is understandable that a talented and clear-eyed historian of the Greek Revolution was outraged when the heroic tales he had read confronted the messy historical record. Indignation mixed with sorrow. "The Turks of Greece left few traces. They disappeared suddenly and finally in the spring of 1821 unmourned by the rest of the world."[44] And yet we might ask for explanation sooner than characterization, which leaves us with the conclusion that the perpetrators were simply bad, greedy, and self-serving, as if the violence was the product of character flaws. The Greeks had other motivations and they achieved something more than revenge and their enrichment. We should not forget that 1776 and 1789 began as tax rebellions but became much more.

One can do a better job of explaining why the Greeks acted as they did in 1821, and not what they failed to be—a European fantasy about ancient Greece and Christian piety. No country subjected to such standards would come out looking pretty. This has been an aim of this book. In substance, the Greeks were Ottoman creatures who had been raised in Ottoman insecurity and violence; and they were imperial creatures who had learned of a new kind of warfare and a new kind of association. Ottoman confessional ordering met the mobilizational nation. The mix was explosive.

It should be clear by now that the empires that preceded the nation were violent places. In each case violence meant something quite different. The Greeks who rebelled in the 1820s cited the insecurity of the old regime as the explanation for what they had done. The idea that they were repressed because they were Christians was tacked on later. The issue for the Christians (and not only the Christians) was arbitrariness and unpredictability, and a violence that was random. Banditry was the symptom of a deep poverty that made banditry common and reasonable for the Morean Kolokotronis as much as the Albanian and Anatolian mercenaries he fought. The new empires in the region were also violent and systematically so, with disciplined and well-armed formations cutting their way to victory.

The violence of the nation was different. A new and total understanding of belonging, the very concept that brought together diverse and antagonistic groups into a single nation in 1821, informed a total solution to the problem of instability and survival. The Greek Revolution did not simply pit Greek against Turk; it created the categories of Greek and Turk and made the literary flourishes of the few into the reality for masses of peasants and sailors. The categories were absolute, and the violence was absolute. The carriers of the nation no longer intended to rearrange power among the actors, but to remove one of the actors altogether.

This is the demographic revolution, the quiet basis for all else that occurred here in the 1820s. This is often obscured in recitations of battles and victories that are just as easily called massacres. These were victories, to be sure, but they were also an effacement. The nature of the victory lay in that effacement, in the demographic solution to the political problem. European public opinion and the European courts confirmed that this was justified and necessary, and they agreed to the removal of the entire Muslim population. It seemed to them normal but only recently had they decided that Greece was in Europe and had no place for Muslims.

The civilian death tolls were not incidental to the victories but the form that the victory took. The mass mobilizations of 1821 and 1822 were a way to survive retribution, and the Christians acted as a collective in part because the sultan was punishing them as a collective. Greek violence in turn was directed at an entire demographic category, by another demographic category. Both categories were new and absolute. This was part of what made the Revolution revolutionary.

It did not stop in 1822. The civil war of 1824 that pitted Greek against Greek was also total. The mercenaries hired by government forces aimed to destroy a Morean way of life and a social hierarchy by attacking women, children, workshops, homes, and crops. Kolettis demanded not simply an overthrow of the Morean notables but their "extermination" as a caste. Ibrahim's campaign likewise attacked communities and attacked trees, using an army that was recognizably European in its organization and methods.

And this is the point: both the Greeks and the Egyptians learned their warfare, in part, from the Europeans. Europeans were horrified by certain practices of the 1820s and lamented that they were Oriental, but the warfare being practiced in the 1820s—its strategic goal—was on a continuum with other total campaigns waged in places like the Vendée against the Catholics, in Spain against the guerillas, and Haiti against the former slaves.[45] Contemporaries saw the connection. A French naturalist who visited the Morea likened the enraged slaughter of the Muslims in 1821 and 1822 to the carnage of the slave wars of Haiti.[46] Ibrahim's armies were advised and trained by the European veterans of those European campaigns. The Greek warlords were veterans of the European armies in the Ionian basin until 1815. We know that they learned of the nation and the French mobilizational nation from that time; they also learned how the Europeans waged national wars, culminating in the *levée en masse* in the Morea in 1821 and 1822. Soldiers had always punished and looted and civilians were killed in the process, but it was new when whole populations became the very object of attack, their destruction the strategic objective. A contained contest of armies on a battlefield or looting expeditions by irregulars exploded onto the population in new ways when driven by ideology, in this case nationalist ideology.[47]

The region had traveled quite far. In 1820 Morean notables still wrote of overthrowing a local aga or pasha and rearranging power. At the National Assembly of 1827 one of them could utter the following, which was meant to be a call for unity and affection: "Thousands of Muslims have disappeared from the sacred soil of the Fatherland. We can annihilate thousands of others if we know how to love one another."[48] In this there was a sincere duality, a promise of reconciliation in a new national whole, and a promise of utter destruction.

Greece became the new boundary of Europe against Asia. In 1830 the European border moved from the Adriatic to the Aegean, where it remains to this day. The boundary was extended northward as more Christian majorities carried out similar revolutions that reduced Islam to a few enclaves—Kosovo, Bosnia, Bulgaria—that in the 1990s and into today are under threat and declining. In Greece in western Thrace Muslims remain and account for 2 percent of the country's population. Some speak Turkish. The worst days of discrimination are over, though limits on Muslim cemeteries, mosques, and zabiha slaughterhouses outside Thrace persist for no good reason.[49]

The external borders of Europe are patrolled. The resources of the European Union are sent to prevent refugees from entering Europe, and those refugees are almost entirely Muslim. In 2020 the president of the European Commission praised the country as follows: "This border is not only a Greek border, it is a European border. I thank Greece for being our European *aspida* [shield] in these times."[50] Europe is policing a border that was established by the treaties that confirmed that Europe was Christian and Greece was in Europe.

Christianity, the foundation of Greek nationhood, functioned also as the basis for a very wide and ongoing integration. Christianity was the basis for receiving new populations into the nation, and language the instrument of assimilation. More populations were added to Greece: the Ionian Islands in the 1860s; Thessaly in the 1880s; Thessaloniki, most Aegean Islands, and Crete, after the Balkan Wars of 1912–13. (Rhodes and the Dodecanese would be added in 1947.) When the Greeks attempted to expand into Anatolia in 1922, the Greek state found its limit in the devastating defeat in Asia Minor, or what is still called the Catastrophe.

In the aftermath the powers knew what to do because they had done it before: demographic engineering. By the Treaty of Lausanne around 1.5 million Christians were evicted from the new Turkey and 1.2 million arrived in Greece. Others followed, the victims of Nasser's nationalism in the 1950s and pogroms in Istanbul in the 1960s. They came from Albania after the end of state socialism, and from the lands of the defunct USSR. It was assumed that they belonged in Greece for the simple reason that they were Orthodox Christians, with the added qualification of language which they spoke in one or another form or would soon learn. When they arrived some of the refugees spoke only Turkish, Laz, and Arabic. Others spoke dialects of Greek (Pontic) that were unintelligible in Greece itself, still others Slavic languages different from the Slavic spoken all along in the north. But they were Orthodox and therefore Greek. Whatever the cost it was understood that it had to be paid. They were part of the nation and they were coming home to a place they had never seen.

The polyglot Greeks of 1821 looked and sounded increasingly alike with each passing generation. Albanian and Vlach were the languages of whole villages in every part of Greece as late as the 1960s. They were heard less and then not at all, without even the old compromise of bilingualism (Greek in public, a different language at home). Roma may well be sharing in that outcome.[51] Dialects of Greek and even regional accents yielded to the standardized Greek of the schools, books, and newspapers. Radio, television, and the internet delivered the coup de grâce.

Destruction and empowerment; murder and liberation; effacement and entitlement; dependence and sovereignty. The nation is problematic, to be sure, and the point of this book has not been to glorify it or make excuses. But like it or not, the nation was the vessel that carried the population into an era of popular sovereignty where it could demand more and better. A nation is different from an empire: an imperial subject can supplicate; a national citizen can demand. Imperial power is far away; national sovereignty is next door and in every person.

The nation is not going away but we can certainly ask for better nation: caring for its citizens, generous to new arrivals, and defending a collective people in international affairs. Privilege for the few may become rights for all. Citizens' rights might return to where they began, as human rights.

Notes

Introduction

1. This section is gleaned from a variety of sources, including Georgios Tertsetes, *Theodorou Kolokotrone Apomnemoneumata* (Athens: Vergina, 2002); Leonidas Ch. Zoes, "O Theodoros Kolokotrones os nautikos," *Geografikon Deltion*, 2:1 (1906–7), pp. 236–41; Zoes, "Ek tou viou tou Theodorou Kolokotrone," *Messeniakon Emerologion* (1907), pp. 120–26.

2. John Mollo, *Military Fashion: A Comparative History of the Uniforms of the Great Armies from the 17th Century to the First World War* (London: Barrie and Jenkins, 1972).

3. Jane Burbank and Frederick Cooper, *Empires in World History: Power and the Politics of Difference* (Princeton: Princeton University Press, 2011).

4. Paul Werth, *The Tsar's Foreign Faiths: Toleration and the Fate of Religious Freedom in Imperial Russia* (New York: Oxford University Press, 2014); Azfar Moin, ed., "Sulh-Kull as an Oath of Peace: Mughal Political Theology in History, Theory, and Comparison," special issue of *Modern Asian Studies*, 56:3 (2022).

5. Alexis de Tocqueville, *L'Ancien Régime et la Révolution* (Paris: Gallimard, 1985).

6. Ali Yaycıoğlu, *Partners of the Empire: The Crisis of the Ottoman Order in the Age of Revolutions* (Stanford: Stanford University Press, 2016).

7. Tocqueville, *L'Ancien Régime*. Explicated for England in Steve Pincus, *1688: The First Modern Revolution* (New Haven: Yale University Press, 2009), pp. 30–45.

8. Vasiles Kremmydas, "E Oikonomike Krise ston Elladiko Choro stis Arches tou 19ou Aiona kai oi Epiptoseis tes sten Epanastase tou 1821," *Mnemon*, 6 (1977), pp. 16–33.

9. My tribute to Petros Pizanias, ed., *The Greek Revolution of 1821: A European Event* (Istanbul: Isis, 2011).

10. A very large literature is brought together in English in Paschalis M. Kitromilides, *Enlightenment and Revolution: The Making of Modern Greece* (Cambridge, MA: Harvard University Press, 2013).

11. Antonia Dialla, "The Congress of Vienna, the Russian Empire, and the Greek Revolution: Rethinking Legitimacy," *Journal of Modern Greek Studies*, 39:1 (May 2021), pp. 27–47; Dialla, *E Rosike Autokratoria kai o Ellenikos Kosmos: Topikes, Europaikes kai Pankosmies Istories sten Epoche ton Epanastaseon* (Athens: Alexandreia, 2023).

12. C. A. Bayly, *Imperial Meridian: The British Empire and the World, 1780–1830* (New York: Longman, 1989).

13. Romantic nationalism in David Ricks and Roderick Beaton, eds, *The Making of Modern Greece: Nationalism, Romanticism, and the Uses of the Past (1797–1896)* (New York: Routledge, 2016).

14. Gianfranco Poggi identifies this "certain significance" in "The Modern State and the Idea of Progress," in Gabriel A. Armond et al., eds, *Progress and Its Discontents* (Berkeley, 1977), pp. 349–52.

15. On the very creation of a category as one step toward its destruction, see Zygmund Bauman, *Modernity and the Holocaust* (Ithaca, NY: Cornell University Press, 1989); in the Balkan context, see Rok Stergar and Tamara Scheer, "Ethnic Boxes: The Unintended Consequences of Habsburg Bureaucratic Classification," *Nationalities Papers*, 46:4 (2018), pp. 575–91. On revolutionary and Napoleonic warfare, see David A. Bell, *The First Total War: Napoleon's Europe and the Birth of Warfare as We Know It* (Boston: Houghton and Mifflin, 2007).

16. Emily Greble, *Muslims and the Making of Modern Europe* (New York: Oxford University Press, 2021).

17. Alexandro García Sanjuán, "Weaponizing Historical Knowledge: The Notion of Reconquista in Spanish Nationalism," *Imago Temporis: Medium Aevum*, 14 (2020), pp. 133–62.

18. Edin Hajdarpašić, "Out of the Ruins of the Ottoman Empire: Reflections on the Ottoman Legacy in South-Eastern Europe," *Middle Eastern Studies*, 44:5 (September 2008), pp. 715–34. A smart collective of scholars is part of an effort to reinstate things Ottoman into Greek history and the Greek landscape: Panagiotes Poulos, Georgios Palles, and Elias Kolovos, eds, *Othomanika Mnemeia sten Ellada: Kleronomies ypo Diapragmateuse* (Athens: Kapon, 2023).

19. Vasilis Kremmydas, *E Ellenike Epanastasi tou 1821* (Athens: Gutenberg, 2016); Mark Mazower, *The Greek Revolution: 1821 and the Making of Modern Europe* (New York: Penguin, 2022); Chrestos Loukos, *Mia Syntome Istoria tes Ellenikes Epanastases* (Athens: Themelio, 2022).

20. An excellent example is Demetres Demetropoulos, Chrestos Loukos, and Panagiotes Michaelares, eds, *Opseis tes Epanastases tou 1821: Praktika Synedriou, Athena 12 kai 13 Iouniou 2015* (Athens: Etaireia Meletes tou Neou Ellenismou–Mnemon, 2018).

21. Avgusta M. Stanislavskaia, *Rossiia i Gretsiia v Konste XVIII–Nachale XIX Veka: Politika Rossii v Ionicheskoi Respublike, 1798–1807 gg.* (Moscow: Nauka, 1974); Grigorii Arsh, *Ioann Kapodistriia v Rossii, 1809–1822* (St. Petersburg: Aleteiia, 2003); Arsh, *Eteristskoe Dvizhenie v Rossii: Osvoboditel'naia Bor'ba Grecheskogo Naroda v Nachale XIX v. i Russko-grechskie Sviazi* (Moscow: Nauka, 1970).

22. William St. Clair, *That Greece Might Still Be Free: The Philhellenes in the War of Independence* (London: Oxford University Press, 1972), which is about more than Philhellenes; C.M. Woodhouse, *Capodistrias, the Founder of Greek Independence* (Oxford: Oxford University Press, 1973); Woodhouse, *Rhigas Velestinlis: The Protomartyr of the Greek Revolution* (Limne, Evia: Denise Harvey, 1995).

23. With particular reference to Thomas Babington Macauley: Catherine Hall, *Macauley and Son: Architects of Imperial Britain* (New Haven: Yale University Press, 2012).

24. Andreas Wimmer and Nina Glick Schiller, "Methodological Nationalism, the Social Sciences, and the Study of Migration: An Essay in Historical Epistemology," *The International Migration Review*, 37:3 (Fall 2003), pp. 576–610.

25. Zanou, *Transnational Patriotism in the Mediterranean, 1800–1850: Stammering the Nation* (New York: Oxford University Press, 2019); Dialla, *E Rosike Autokratoria*, esp. pt 1; Philliou, *Biography of an Empire: Governing Ottomans in an Age of Revolution* (Berkeley: University of California Press, 2010); Papagiorges, *Ta Kapakia: Varnakiotes, Karaïskakes, Androutsos*, 9th edi-

tion (Athens: Kastaniotis, 2014); Tzakis, "From Locality to Nation-State Loyalty," in Pizanias, ed., *The Greek Revolution of 1821: A European Event*, pp. 129–49; Beaton, *Byron's War: Romantic Rebellion, Greek Revolution* (New York: Cambridge University Press, 2013).

26. We have good studies of Catholics and Jews: Dimitris Kousouris, "The Catholic Communities of the Greek Archipelago during the Greek Revolution, 1821–1830," *Historein*, 20:1 (2021); K. E. Fleming, *Greece: A Jewish History* (Princeton: Princeton University Press, 2010); Evdoxios Doxiadis, *State, Nationalism, and the Jewish Communities of Modern Greece* (London: Bloomsbury Academic, 2018).

27. Hans Kellner, *Language and Historical Representation: Getting the Story Crooked* (Madison: University of Wisconsin Press, 1989).

28. The Russian word is *ostranenie*, translated in Viktor Shklovsky, *Theory of Prose* (Elmwood Park, IL: Dalkey Archive Press, 1993).

29. Neokles Sarres, *Proepanastatike Ellada kai Osmaniko Kratos: Apo to Cheirografo tou Souleïman Penach Efende tou Moraïte (1785)* (Athens: Erodotos, 1993), with a very useful glossary on pp. 329–407. An overview of Ottoman perceptions is Ozan Ozavci, "The Ottoman Imperial Gaze: The Greek Revolution of 1821–1832 and a New History of the Eastern Question," *Journal of Modern European History*, 21:2 (March 2020), pp. 222–37. A useful collection of documents is H. Sükrü Ilicak, ed., *"Those Infidel Greeks": The Greek War of Independence through Ottoman Archival Documents*, 2 vols (Leyden and Boston: Brill, 2021).

Chapter 1. The Ottoman Crisis in the Southern Balkans

1. His life in *Chrisallis*, 3:61 (15 July 1865), pp. 385–88, and 3:62 (30 July 1865), pp. 417–19. These are oral traditions, and other versions place him in the village of Aghia Efthimia before he took over Galaxidi.

2. In an earlier time reaya meant all agrarian populations. Michalis Sotiropoulos and Antonis Hadjikyriakou, "Patris, Ethnos, and Demos: Representation and Political Participation in the Greek World," in Joanna Innes and Mark Philip, eds, *Reimagining Democracy in the Mediterranean, 1780–1860* (New York: Oxford University Press, 2018), p. 102.

3. Papagiorges, *Ta Kapakia*, ch. 2; Sotiropoulos and Hadjikyriakou, "Patris, Ethnos, and Demos," pp. 106.

4. G.L. Arsh, "K Voprosu ob Otsenke Lambrosa Katsonisa v Istoriografii," *Voprosy Istorii*, 4 (2015), pp. 137–41; Arsh, *Eteristskoe Dvizhenie*, pp. 87–92.

5. Yaycıoğlu, *Partners of the Empire*, pp. 103ff.

6. Yaycıoğlu, *Partners of the Empire*, ch. 1 and esp. pp. 29ff; ch. 2 on local and regional negotiations with the capital.

7. Arsh, *Eteristskoe Dvizhenie*, pp. 31–41.

8. Yaycıoğlu, *Partners of the Empire*, ch. 1 and esp. pp. 37ff, 107ff.

9. Examples in Genika Archeia tou Kratous, Athens (General Archives of the State, hereafter GAK Athens), Vlachogiannes Collection, cat. 3, f.23, docs 3, 7, 52 and passim; Papagiorges, *Ta Kapakia*, pp. 87–90, 140–46, 196–205.

10. Hakan Erdem, "'Perfidious Albanians' and 'Zealous Governors': Ottomans, Albanians, and Turks in the Greek War of Independence," in Antonis Anastasopoulos and Elias Kolovos,

eds, *Ottoman Rule and the Balkans, 1760–1850: Conflict, Transformation, Adaptation* (Rethymno: University of Crete, 2007), pp. 213–33.

11. On Balkan brigandage in the Balkans and the danger to cities, see Yaycıoğlu, *Partners of the Empire*, pp. 33–4.

12. Konstantina D. Karakosta, "Moschopoliton Tychai: E Akme, Parakme, kai e Diaspora ton Moschopoliton. E Koinoteta tou *Miskolc*," doctoral dissertation, Aristotelian University of Thessaloniki, 2013.

13. GAK Athens, Vlachogiannes Collection, cat. 3, folder 36: fighters—Ionian Islands, docs 68–103.

14. Philliou, *Biography of an Empire*, pp. 49–50 and passim in ch. 1.

15. Y. Hakan Erdem, *Slavery in Ottoman Europe and Its Demise, 1800–1909* (Macmillan: Basingstoke, 1996), pp. 19–26. On Muslim slaves taken, see GAK Athens, Vlachogiannes Collection, cat. 3, f23: Armatoliks and Ionian Island corps.

16. It became more coherent in the nineteenth century. Yusuf Ziya Karabıçak, "Local Patriots and Ecumenical Ottomans: The Orthodox Patriarchate of Constantinople in the Ottoman Configuration of Power, 1768–1828," doctoral dissertation, McGill University—EHESS, 2020; Philliou, *Biography of an Empire*; Sotiropoulos and Hadjikyriakou, "Patris, Ethnos, and Demos," pp. 103–4.

17. Nikolas Vernikos, *To Schedio Autonomias tes Peloponnesou ypo Gallike Epikyriarchia* (Athens: Tolides, 1997), pp. 22–4.

18. Petros Pizanias, "From Reaya to Greek Citizen," in *The Greek Revolution of 1821: A European Event*, pp. 11–24; Kahraman Sakul, "The Ottoman Peloponnese before the Greek Revolution: 'A Republic of Ayan, Hakim, and Kocabaşı,'" *Princeton Papers*, 18 (2017), pp. 132–3.

19. Karakosta, "Moschopoliton Tychai," p. 14.

20. The enslavement of Muslims alongside Christians in GAK Athens, Vlachogiannes Collection, cat. 3, fighters 1804–10, docs 47–55; Erdem, *Slavery in Ottoman Europe*, pp. 21–3.

21. Observed for example in J.B.G.M. Bory de Saint-Vincent, *Relation du Voyage de la Commission Scientifique en Morée dans le Péloponnèse, les Cyclades et l'Attique* (Paris and Strasbourg: F.G. Levrault, 1837–8), vol.1, pp.29–30.

22. Zanou asks that we consider the "links between sea's various shores." *Transnational Patriotism*, p. 12.

23. On the Corinthian grapes, see Vasiles Panagiotopoulos, "Gastoune-Vostitsa: Dyo Antagonistika Protypa Agrotikes Anaptyxes sten Proepanastatike Ellada," in *Ametos: Ste Mneme Fote Apostolopoulou* (Athens: Kentro Mikrasiatikon Spoudon, 1984), pp. 359–75.

24. *Korinthenkacker*: someone so small-minded or stingy that even their excrement is tiny, the size of a Corinthian grape. https://www.dw.com/en/korinthenkacker/a-6615906, accessed 19 August 2023.

25. Arsh, *Eteristskoe Dvizhenie*, pp. 40–41.

26. Anna Vlachopoulou, "Like the Mafia? The Ottoman Military Presence in the Morea in the Eighteenth Century," in Anastasopoulos and Kolovos, eds, *Ottoman Rule and the Balkans*, pp. 123–36; William W. McGrew, *Land and Revolution in Modern Greece, 1800–1881: The Transition in the Tenure and Exploitation of Land from Ottoman Rule to Independence* (Kent, OH: Kent State University Press, 1985), ch. 2.

27. *Parnassos*, 2:6 (June 1878); Athanasios Photopoulos, *Oi Kotzampasedes tes Peloponnesou kata ten Deutere Tourkokratia (1715–1821)* (Athens: Irodotos, 2005), pt 1, ch. 1; Sakul, "The Ottoman Peloponnese," pp. 125–6.

28. Martha Pylia, "Leitourgies kai Autonomia ton Koinoteton tes Peloponnesou kata ten Deutere Tourkokratia (1715–1821)," *Mnemon*, 23 (2001), pp. 72–3; Michael V. Sakellariou, *E Peloponnesos kata ten Deuteran Tourkokratian (1715–1821)* (Athens: Verlag der byzantinisch-neugriechischen Jahrbücher, 1939), pp. 43–50.

29. This estimate from Bory de Saint-Vincent, *Expédition Scientifique de Morée, Section des Sciences Physiques, Géographie* (Paris and Strasbourg: F. G. Levrault, 1834), vol. 2, pt 1, p. 94. Others in *Voyage en Grèce de Xavier Scrofani, Sicilien, Fait en 1794 et 1795* (Paris: Treuttel et Wurtz, IX / 1801), vol. 1, pp. 40–43; Martha Pylia, "Les Notables Moréotes, Fin du XVIIIe Début du XIXe Siècle: Fonctions et Comportements," doctoral dissertation, University of Paris 1, 2001, ch. 2; Tasos Gritsopoulos, *Istoria tes Gastounes* (Athens: Demos Gastounes, 1998), vol. 1, pp. 445–66; Stanislavskaia, *Rossiia i Gretsiia*, p. 255; Vernikos, *To Schedio Autonomias*, p. 23.

30. McGrew, *Land and Revolution*, pp. 27–40.

31. Sakul, "The Ottoman Peloponnese," pp. 132–3.

32. On their self-perceived status, see Photopoulos, *Oi Kotzampasedes*, pt 2, ch. 1. Notables' credit operations involving peasant farmers and ayans in *Archeion Kanellou Delegianne: Ta Engrapha, 1779–1827* (Athens: Etaireia ton Philon tou Laou, 1993), docs 10–22 covering 1817–20.

33. Sakul, "The Ottoman Peloponnese," p. 129; Photopoulos, *Oi Kotzampasedes*, pt 3, ch. 1.

34. Istorike kai Ethnologike Etaireia tes Ellados (Historical and Ethnological Society of Greece, hereafter IEEE), Sisinis Archive, docs 20500 and 20501.

35. Stefanos Katsikas and Sakis Dimitriades, "Muslim Converts to Orthodox Christianity during the Greek War of Independence, 1821–1832," *European History Quarterly*, 51:3 (2021), pp. 307–8.

36. William Martin Leake, *Travels in the Morea with a Map and Plans in Three Volumes* (London: John Murray, 1830), vol. 1, pp. 398–9, 431–2.

37. Photopoulos, *Oi Kotzampasedes*, pt 2, and Tertsetes, *Theodorou Kolokotrone Apomnemoneumata*, p. 65. The comprehensive description of the lifestyles and businesses of the notables is in Pylia, "Les Notables Moréotes."

38. In 1829: Bory de Saint-Vincent, *Relation du Voyage*, vol. 1, p. 114.

39. Gritsopoulos, *Istoria tes Gastounes*, vol. 1, pp. 480–82; Stefanos Papageorgiou, "To Aarcheio Sisine," *Deltion tes Istorikes kai Ethnologikes Etaireias tes Ellados*, 23 (1980), p. 210. The financial and administrative records of the Benaki / Benacchi family from the eighteenth century are in Ottoman, Greek, and Italian: Benaki Museum, Benaki Family, 153–258.

40. Demitrios Stamatopoulos, "Constantinople in the Peloponnese: The Case of the Dragoman of the Morea Georgios Wallerianos and Some Aspects of the Revolutionary Process," in Anastasopoulos and Kolovos, eds, *Ottoman Rule and the Balkans*, pp. 149–69; Pylia, "Les Notables Moréotes," pp. 63–70; Pylia, "Leitourgies kai Autonomia," pp. 70–72; Photopoulos, *Oi Kotzampasedes*, pt 1, ch. 1, and pt 3, ch. 1. A similarly hazy electoral practice obtained in other Ottoman regions: Yaycıoğlu, *Partners of the Empire*, ch. 3.

41. Photopoulos, *Oi Kotzampasedes*, pt 1, chs 1–3.

42. Drawn from multiple sources, summarized well in Pylia, "Les Notables Moréotes," pp. 349–50 and Stamatopoulos, "Constantinople in the Peloponnese." On the agreements, see Sakul, "The Ottoman Peloponnese" and Karabıçak, "Local Patriots," pp. 345–51. A catalogue of executions is represented as revolutionary activity in Photopoulos, *Oi Kotzampasedes*, p. 226 and pt 3, ch. 3.

43. D. Stamatopoulos, "Kommatikes Phatries sten Proepanastatike Peloponneso (1807–1816): O Rolos ton 'Tourkalvanon' tou Lala os Paragontas Politikes Diaforopoiesis," *Istor*, 10 (1997), pp. 224–5; Arsh, *Eteristskoe Dvizhenie*, p. 44; Karabıçak, "Local Patriots," pp. 339–45; Pylia, "Leitourgies kai Autonomia," p. 95 n. 146; Pylia, "Les Notables Moréotes," p. 350; Gritso-poulos, *Istoria tes Gastounes*, vol. 1, pp. 479–80, 499–501.

44. Kremmydas, *E Etairia Tokoglyfias N. Tampakopoulou kai Sia, 1816–1820* (Athens: Guten-berg, 2013); GAK Athens, boxes, cat. K48a; GAK Athens, Vlachogiannes Collection, cat. 3, Palamedes Papers, file 1, subfile 8, pp. 453–6; Pylia, "Leitourgies kai Autonomia," pp. 77–80; Pylia, "Les Notables Moréotes," pp. 169–71; Sarres, *Proepanastatike Ellada*, pp. 30–47; and in the Balkan region Yaycıoğlu, *Partners of the Empire*, pp. 80 and ch. 3.

45. GAK Athens, Vlachogiannes Collection, cat. 3, Palamedes Papers, file 8, pp. 456ff; Panagi-otopoulos, "Gastoune-Vostitsa," pp. 368–9; Leake, *Travels in the Morea*, vol. 1, pp. 431–2; Ehud R. Toledano, *Slavery and Abolition in the Ottoman Middle East* (Seattle: University of Washington Press, 1998), pp. 1–17; Tertsetes, *Theodorou Kolokotrone Apomnemoneumata*, pp. 65–6.

46. Sakellariou, *E Peloponnesos*, pp. 51–2 and ch. 2; Photopoulos, *Oi Kotzampasedes*, pt 3, ch. 1; Sarres, *Proepanastatike Ellada*, pp. 63–4.

47. Photopoulos, *Oi Kotzampasedes*, pt. 3, ch. 1.

48. Sarres, *Proepanastatike Ellada*, pp. 320–22.

49. Benaki Museum, Ottoman Documents 153–258: 1765 *firman* ordering the removal of Albanian bandits for their mistreatment of the reaya; Vlachopoulou, "Like the Mafia?"

50. Tertsetes, *Theodorou Kolokotrone Apomnemoneumata*, p. 59.

51. A flurry of land purchases by notables from the turn of the century is suggestive: *Archeion Kanellou Delegianne*, docs 5–9; IEEE, Sisinis Archive, docs 28384ff.

52. Protections and privileges in Arsh, *Eteristskoe Dvizhenie*, pp. 50–51.

Chapter 2. Russia Changes the Balkans

1. Victoria Aksan, *Ottoman Wars, 1700–1870: An Empire Besieged* (London: Routledge, 2013).

2. Roger P. Bartlett, *Human Capital: The Settlement of Foreigners in Russia, 1762–1804* (Cam-bridge: Cambridge University Press, 1979), pp. 117–18; Arsh, *Eteristskoe Dvizhenie*, pp. 84–7; Dialla, *E Rosike Autokratoria*, pp. 54–5.

3. E. I. Druzhinina, *Severnoe Prichernomor'e v 1775–1800 gg.* (Moscow: Akademiia Nauk, 1959); Yaycıoğlu, *Partners of the Empire*, p. 102.

4. Stanislavskaia, *Rossiia i Gretsiia*, pp. 264–70, 310–13; Karabıçak, "Local Patriots," pp. 216–17; Nicholas Charles Pappas, *Greeks in Russian Military Service in the Late Eighteenth and Early Nineteenth Centuries* (Thessaloniki: Institute for Balkan Studies, 1991).

5. Hasan Çolak, "Amsterdam's Greek Merchants: Protegés of the Dutch, Beneficiaries of the Russians, Subjects of the Ottomans and Supporters of Greece," *Byzantine and Modern Greek Studies*, 42:1 (2018), pp. 115–33.

6. E. I. Druzhinina, *Kiuch-Kainardzhiinskii mir 1774 g. (Ego Podgotovka i Zakliuchenie)* (Moscow: Akademiia Nauk, 1955); Nikolas Pissis, "Investment in the Greek Merchant Marine (1783–1821)," in Suraiya Faroqhi and Giles Veinstein, eds, *Merchants in the Ottoman Empire* (Paris: Louvain-Dudley-Peters, 2008), pp. 152–3; Arsh, *Eteristskoe Dvizhenie*, pp. 57–8, 61–2; Stanislavskaia, *Rossiia i Gretsiia*, pp. 9ff; G. Harlaftis, "The 'Eastern Invasion': Greeks in Mediterranean Trade and Shipping in the Eighteenth and Early Nineteenth Centuries," in Maria Fusaro et al, *Trade and Cultural Exchange* (New York: Tauris, 2010), pp. 223–52.

7. On flags and immunities, see Theophilus Prousis, "Capitulations, Consulates, and the Eastern Question in the 1820s," ch. 1 of *British Consular Reports from the Ottoman Levant in an Age of Upheaval, 1815–1830* (Istanbul: Isis, 2008).

8. R. N. Mordvinov, ed., *Admiral Ushakov* (Moscow: Voenmorizdat, 1951–6), vol. 1, passim; Pissis, "Investment in the Greek Merchant Marine," p. 163; Arsh, *Eteristskoe Dvizhenie*, pp. 57–61; Kahraman Sakul, "The Ottoman Peloponnese," pp. 124–5.

9. A recent analysis of the expedition in Dialla, *E Rosike Autokratoria*, pt 1; an overview is E. B. Smilianskaia, E. M. Smilianskaia, and M. B. Belizhev, *Rossiia v Sredizemnomor'e: Arkhipelagskaia Ekspeditsiia Ekateriny Velikoi* (Moscow: Indrik, 2011).

10. Peter Hill, "Mount Lebanon and Greece: Mediterranean Crosscurrents, 1821–1841," *Historein*, 20:1 (2021); Dialla, *E Rosike Autokratoria*, pp. 45–55, 94–5.

11. Nikos V. Rotzokos, *Ethnafypnise kai ethnogenese: Orlofika kai Ellinike Istoriografia* (Athens: Vivliorama, 2007), ch. 3; Karabıçak, "Local Patriots," pp. 55, 58, 69, 71, 77.

12. Sarres, *Proepanastatike Ellada*, pp. 181–97; Arsh, *Eteristskoe Dvizhenie*, pp. 78–87.

13. Sakellariou, *E Peloponnisos kata ten Deuteran Tourkokriatian*, pp. 194–9; Gritsopoulos, *Istoria tes Gastounes*, vol. 1, pp. 497–503.

14. Benaki Museum, Benaki Family Archive, docs 28 (January 1784), 29 (January 1780); and Russian pensions to descendants in 1820s in box 111, file 1.

15. Gritsopoulos, *Istoria tes Gastounes*, vol. 1, pp. 502–6.

16. Sakellariou, *E Peloponnesos*, pp. 195–9.

17. *Archeion Kanellou Delegianne*, doc. 1, pp. 17–18; Tertsetes, *Theodorou Kolokotrone Apomnemoneumata*, pp. 30–31; Vlachopoulou, "Like the Mafia?"; Pylia, "Leitourgies kai Autonomia" ; Photopoulos, *Oi Kotzampasedes*, pt 3, ch. 3.

18. Sakellariou, *E Peloponnesos*, pp. 199–204; Tertsetes, *Theodorou Kolokotrone Apomnemoneumata*, pp. 30–35.

19. Birol Gündoğdu, "Ottoman Constructions of the Morea Rebellion, 1770s: A Comprehensive Study of Ottoman Attitudes to the Greek Rebellion," doctoral dissertation, University of Toronto, 2012; Sakul, "The Ottoman Peloponnese," pp. 132ff.

20. Sarres, *Proepanastatike Ellada*, pp. 207–31, 255, 264–5; Sotiropoulos and Hadjikyriakou, "Patris, Ethnos, and Demos," p. 109.

21. Benaki Museum, Mavrokordatos to Catherine II, 28 December 1789 (Old Style), eis.25A, p. 1.

22. Sarres, *Proepanastatike Ellada*, p. 30.

23. Arsh, *Eteristskoe Dvizhenie*, pp. 69–70.

24. Ilicak, "Introduction" in *"Those Infidel Greeks": The Greek War of Independence*, vol. 1, p. 3.

25. Dimitris Dimitropoulos, "Aspects of the Working of the Fiscal Machinery in the Areas Ruled by Ali Pasha," in Anastasopoulos and Kolovos, eds, *Ottoman Rule and the Balkans*, pp. 61–72;

K. E. Fleming, *The Muslim Bonaparte: Diplomacy and Orientalism in Ali Pasha's Greece* (Princeton: Princeton University Press, 1999), the trade on pp. 50–55; Alphonse de Beauchamp, *Vie d'Ali pacha, visir de Janina* (Paris: Villet, 1822), p. 345.

26. Yaycıoğlu, *Partners of the Empire*, ch. 4.

27. Giannes Spyropoulos, "Ventetes 'Yper Patridos kai Pisteos'? Endochristianike Via sta Sphakia stes Paramones tou 1821," in Demetropoulos, Loukos, and Michaelares, eds, *Opseis tes Ellenikes Epanastases*, pp. 111–18.

28. Euangelos Io. Savrames, "Symvolai eis ten Istorian tes Demetsanes," *Epeteris Etaireias Vyzantinon Spoudon*, 9 (1932), pp. 228–9; Pylia, "Leitourgies kai Autonomia," pp. 91–3 ; Sakellariou, *E Peloponnesos*, pp. 238–44. Karabıçak adds detail from the Ottoman archives: "Local Patriots," pp. 368–72.

29. Kolokotronis's account books (payments to his fighters) in Elleniko Logotechniko kai Istoriko Archeio, Morphotiko Idryma Ethnikes Trapezes (Greek Literary and Historical Archive, Educational Institute of the National Bank, henceforth ELIA-MIET), Kolokotronis Archive, books kept by Yannakis, 1803–6; his recollections in Tertsetes, *Theodorou Kolokotrone Apomnemoneumata*, pp. 37–50.

30. Vernikos, *To Schedio Autonomias*, pp. 34–5.

31. Martha Pylia, "Conflits Politiques et Comportements des Primats Chrétiens en Morée, avant la Guerre d'Independance," in Anastasopoulos and Kolovos, eds, *Ottoman Rule and the Balkans*, pp. 137–9.

32. Philliou, *Biography of an Empire*, pp. 44–5.

33. Sotiropoulos and Hatzikyriakou, "Patris, Ethnos, and Demos," p. 103.

34. Karabıçak, "Local Patriots," pp. 55, 77, 195. Described with insight by the Russian consul Minuaki in 1803 in Arsh, *Eteristskoe Dvizhenie*, pp. 52–3, and 69–70. On insecurity, see Pizanias, "From Reaya to Greek Citizen," pp. 31–8.

Chapter 3. Imperial Crossroads

1. Paul W. Schroeder, *The Transformation of European Politics, 1763–1848* (Oxford: Clarendon, 1994), pp. 181–2.

2. This period in very great detail in Demetres D. Arvanitakes, *E Agoge tou Polite: E Gallike Parousia sto Ionio (1797–1799) kai to Ethnos ton Ellenon* (Athens: Panepistemiakes Ekdoseis Kretes, 2020); Traian Stoianovich, *The Ionian Islands in the Time of Napoleon* (unpublished manuscript, NYU Library, 1949); Nikos E. Karapidakis, "Département de Corfu, 1798: Les Troubles," in Tassos Anastassiades and Nathalie Clayer, eds, *Society, Politics and State Formation in Southeastern Europe during the Nineteenth Century* (Athens: Alpha Bank, 2011), pp. 235–52; P.G. Rontogiannes, *Istoria tes Nesou Leukados* (Athens: Etairia Leukadikon Spoudon, 1980), vol. 2, pp. 12–63; Konstantinos Machairas, *Politiki kai Diplomatike Istoria tes Laukados (1797–1810)* (Athens: s.n., 1954), vol. 1, pp. 31ff.

3. Genika Archeia tou Kratous, Archeia Nomou Kerkyras (General Archives of the State, Archives of the Prefecture of Corfu, hereafter GAK Corfu), Republican French, box 6. The verses of the Marseillaise in Jean Savant, " Napoléon et la Libération de la Grèce," pt 1, *L'Hellenisme Contemporaine*, vol. 4 (July–October 1950), pp. 326–7.

4. Karabıçak, "Local Patriots," pp. 177ff. A typical Ottoman anti-revolutionary tract, this one penned by the Patriarch of Jerusalem, is "The Paternal Instruction" (1798), the subject of Richard Clogg, "The 'Dhidhaskalia Patriki': An Orthodox Reaction to French Revolutionary Propaganda," *Middle Eastern Studies*, 5:2 (May 1969), pp. 87–115.

5. Norman Saul, *Russia and the Mediterranean, 1797–1807* (Chicago: University of Chicago Press, 1970); Robert Holland, *Blue-Water Empire: The British in the Mediterranean since 1800* (London: Penguin, 2012).

6. The campaign in Mordvinov, ed., *Admiral Ushakov*, vol. 1, sec. 4 , passim; Stanislavskaia, *Rossiia i Gretsiia*, ch. 2.

7. Mordvinov, ed., *Admiral Ushakov*, vol.1, doc. 263, 362–3 (pp. 491–2), 372–3, 388 ("Plan for the Establishment of an Administration," May 1799). Ushakov on Bonaparte in GAK Corfu, Seven Islands Republic, box 23, doc. 1. Stanislavskaia's narration remains very good: *Rossiia i Gretsiia*, pp. 63–4.

8. Mordvinov, ed., *Admiral Ushakov*, vol. 1, doc. 252 (Cerigo / Kythira), 395 (Zante / Zakynthos); vol. 2, docs 197, 204, 244; Stanislavskaia, *Rossiia i Gretsiia*, pp. 102–21; on the general events see S.T. Lascaris, "Capodistrias avant la Révolution Grecque (sa carrière politique jusqu'en 1822)," doctoral dissertation, University of Lausanne, 1918, pp. 6–23; Woodhouse, *Capodistrias*.

9. Marie-Pierre Rey, *Alexandre Ier: Le tsar qui vainquit Napoléon* (Paris: Flammarion, 2020), chs 5–7.

10. Stanislavskaia, *Rossiia i Gretsiia*, pp. 201–3 and passim in ch. 4.

11. Mocenigo to governor of Cerigo / Kythira, September 1803: GAK Corfu, Seven Islands Republic, box 23, doc. 6.

12. GAK Corfu, Seven Islands Republic, box 7, bundle 1, doc. 1: Capo d'Istria in Argostoli to Corfu, 12 June 1801; Stanislavskaia, *Rossiia i Gretsiia*, ch. 4, ongoing noble appeals to the Porte on p. 225; the arrest and exile of the nobleman G. Cladan on pp. 220–22; the taming of the nobleman Anninos on pp. 324–5. A summary in Lascaris, "Capodistrias," pp. 21–2.

13. The passage of the constitution in Stanislavskaia, *Rossiia i Gretsiia*, pp. 192–4; the local experience in Rontogiannes, *Istoria tes Nesou Leukadas*, pp. 88–9; the postal service announced by Mocenigo in GAK Corfu, Seven Islands Republic, box 23, doc. 19.

14. Archives Nationales (Paris), Secretariat d'État Imperiale, États Dépendants: AF / IV / 1714 / B / 2, Îles Ioniennes et Corfu, 1803–1813, Talleyrand to Bonaparte, May 1802.

15. GAK Corfu, Seven Islands Republic, box 23, doc. 1; Stanislavskaia, *Rossiia i Gretsiia*, p. 326.

16. Stanislavskaia, *Rossiia i Gretsiia*, p. 331.

17. GAK Corfu, Seven Islands Republic, box 23, docs 16 (1802) and 26 (1803); Stanislavskaia, *Rossiia i Gretsiia*, pp. 355–6.

18. Tasos Anastasiades, "(An)iere Ge: Ethike kai Politike Oikonomia ton Orthodoxon Monasterion sto Sygchrono Elleniko Kratos," in Elias Kolovos, ed., *Monasteria, Oikonomia kai Politike* (Heraklion: Panepistemiakes Ekdoseis Kretes, 2011), pp. 253–85.

19. Machairas, *Politike kai Diplomatike Istoria*, pp. 423–35; Stanislavskaia, *Rossiia i Gretsiia*, pp. 356–7.

20. Zanou, *Transnational Patriotism*, p. 85.

21. 1803 in GAK Corfu, Seven Islands Republic, box 23.

22. GAK Athens, Vlachogiannes Collection, cat. 3, file 25, report of Iacovo Calanter.

23. GAK Corfu, Seven Islands Republic, box 69, file 7 on schools in Zakynthos and the en-rollment of Dionyssio Salamon. My thanks to Periklis Pangratis of the Solomos Museum for advice and for steering me to the archival source. See his "Stoicheia gia ten Pro-Italike Paideia tou Solomou," *Porphyras*, 95–6 (July–September 2000), pp. 69–84.

24. Zanou, *Transnational Patriotism*, chs 1, 3.

25. Stanislavskaia, *Rossiia i Gretsiia*, pp. 196, 254; Lascaris, "Capodistrias," p. 26.

26. Stanislavskaia, *Rossiia i Gretsiia*, pp. 173–7.

27. Service Historique de la Défense (Vincennes), Armée de Naples et Îles Ioniennes, GR 5 C 9: Chevalier Metaxas's denunciation of Cephalonian enemies, 20 October 1809, followed by extensive lists of names; more by Marino Delladecima; and still more by Metaxas. More in Archives Nationales (Paris), AF / IV / 1714 / B / 2, pp. 153–6 (May 1808), 177 (September 1810), 242 (February 1811), 287 (summer 1811).

28. Archives Nationales (Paris), AF / IV / 1714 / B / 2, 1808, pp. 47–50 (a deputation, 1808), 190–2 (the budget and the clergy), 272 (another deputation, 1811), 306 (Legion of Honor). On flattery see Savant, "Napoléon et la Libération de la Grèce," pt 1, p. 321.

29. Holland, *Blue-Water Empire*.

30. French protests to the Morean pasha in IEEE, Zygalakis Collection, docs 18774, 18780, 18784.

31. IEEE, Zygalakis Collection, docs 18796–18809, 18830: letters of Veli pasha of the Morea on exports to British forces in Portugal, Malta, and Gibraltar, 1809.

32. GAK Corfu, Imperial French, f.139, on the supply and regulation of slaughterhouses on Corfu, 1812–13; Service Historique de la Défense (Vincennes), GR 5C 10, Donzelot to Minister of War, March 1810; Archives Nationales (Paris), AF / IV / 1714 / B / 2, pp. 206 (November 1810), 262 (Donzelot to Napoleon, May 1811), and 278; Centre des Archives Diplomatiques, Nantes, hereafter Archives Diplomatiques (Nantes), 166PO / B / 46, 47, 48, 50: correspondence of am-bassador La Tour-Maubourg with Minister, 1810–11, complaining about the diversion of wheat to British merchants.

33. Service Historique de la Défense (Vincennes), GR C5 11: Napoleon and Minister of War to Donzelot, report of Lesseps, August–October 1810. Donzelot's responses in Archives Natio-nales (Paris), AF / IV / 174 / B / 2, 1803–1813, pp. 31–34 (February 1808), 52–73, 177–9, 302–3.

34. GAK Corfu, Seven Islands Republic, box 6: Paxoi, 1806–7.

35. Archives Nationales (Paris), AF / IV / 1714 / B / 2, pp. 241–2, inventory of captured British merchant ship, 1811.

36. Service Historique de la Défense (Vincennes), GR 5 C6, January 180 8; 28 June 180 8; August 1808, September 1808; C9, October 1809.

37. Sakis Gekas, *Xenocracy: State, Class and Colonialism in the Ionian Islands, 1815–1864* (New York: Berghan, 2017); Thomas Gallant, *Experiencing Dominion: Culture, Identity and Power in the British Mediterranean* (Notre Dame, IN: University of Notre Dame Press, 2002); Walter Frewen Lord, "Our Reign in the Ionian Islands," *The Nineteenth Century: A Monthly Review*, 25 (January–June 1889), pp. 558–71.

38. Arvanitakes, *E Agoge tou Polite*, pp. 526ff.

39. Mordvinov, ed., *Admiral Ushakov*, vol. 1, doc. 288 / pp. 381–5; Stanislavskaia, *Rossiia i Gretsiia*, p. 58.

40. Gekas, *Xenocracy*.

Chapter 4. The Magic Lantern of Empire

1. Service Historique de la Défense (Vincennes), GR XL 33 B: Ciolly, Georges, capitaine.

2. Will Smiley, *From Slaves to Prisoners of War: The Ottoman Empire, Russia, and International Law* (Oxford: Oxford University Press 2018).

3. Paul Henri Stahl, *Histoire de la décapitation* (Paris: Presses Universitaires de France, 1986), pp. 13, 15–47, 217; Tolga Esmer, "Economies of Violence, Banditry, and Governance in the Ottoman Empire around 1800," *Past and Present*, 224 (August 2014), pp. 191–2 and passim.

4. Matei Cazacu, "La morte Infâme: Décapitation et Exposition des Têtes à Istanbul (XV–XIX Siècles)," in Gilles Veinstein, ed., *Les Ottomans et la Morte* (Leyden: Brill, 1996), pp. 246ff; Stahl, *Histoire de la décapitation*, p. 38.

5. Service Historique de la Défense (Vincennes), GR XL 33 B, file of Psimari where the names are listed. Smiley, *From Slaves to Prisoners of War*, with reference to this episode on pp. 162–3. Also in Auguste Boppe, *L'Albanie et Napoléon (1797–1814)* (Paris: Hachette, 1914), p. 26.

6. Archives diplomatiques (Nantes), 166PO / B / 1 6: Constantinople, ambassade: Correspondance de la famille de M. Ruffin [chargé d'affaires] . . . pendant sa détention aux 7 Tours, 1799–1800.

7. See their alphabetical files in Service Historique de la Défense (Vincennes), GR XL 33B, as well as the list of reinstated officers captured on the Ionian Islands in Ciolly's file, sub-file 8 (report to Napoléon Bonaparte).

8. Service Historique de la Défense (Vincennes), GL XL 33A contains files on many of them. Christopher J. Tozzi, *Nationalizing France's Army: Foreign, Black, and Jewish Troops in the French Military* (Charlottesville: University of Virginia Press, 2016); Leonidas Kallivretakes, "Enopla Ellenika Somata ste Dine tov Napoleonteion Polemon (1798–1815)," in Vasilis Panagiotopoulos, ed., *Istoria tou Neou Ellenismou* (Athens: Ellenika Grammata, 2003), vol. 1, pp. 185–200.

9. Tozzi, *Nationalizing France's Army*, p. 27.

10. Laurent Dubois, *A Colony of Citizens: Revolution and Slave Emancipation in the French Caribbean* (Chapel Hill: University of North Carolina Press, 2004), pp. 300–303.

11. Dubois, *A Colony of Citizens*, esp. pt 2; Silvane Larcher, *L'Autre Citoyen: L'Idéal Républicain et les Antilles après l'Esclavage* (Paris: Armand Colin, 2014); John P. Walsh, *Free and French in the Caribbean: Toussaint Louverture, Aimé Césaire, and Narratives of Loyal Opposition* (Bloomington: Indiana University Press, 2013).

12. On the deportations, see Dubois, *A Colony of Citizens*, pp. 406–7; Tozzi, *Nationalizing France's Army*, pp. 175–7.

13. Service Historique de la Défense (Vincennes), XH 3: Régiments Étrangers—Pionniers Noirs.

14. Dubois, *A Colony of Citizens*, pp. 404–6.

15. Toledano, *Slavery and Abolition in the Ottoman Middle East*, pp. 6–10.

16. Ehud R. Toledano, *The Ottoman Slave Trade and its Suppression, 1840–1890* (Princeton: Princeton University Press, 2014), p. 69.

17. E. Protopsaltes, *Ignatios Metropolites Oungrovlachias (1766–1828)* (Athens: Akademia Athenon, 1961), pp. 150–51.

18. GAK Athens, Vlachogiannes Collection, Palamedes Papers, file 1, subfile 8 (notes), subfile 9 (originals). Noted but with incorrect numbers in Tasos Gritsopoulos, "Statistikai Eideseis peri Peloponnesou," *Peloponnesiaka*, 8 (1971), pp. 451 and 456. Recorded correctly in Argyrios Sakorafas, "The Presence of the African Slaves in Ottoman Greece and the Transition to the Independent Kingdom of Greece, with a Special Reference to Athens," thesis, Freie Universität Berlin, 2019, pp. 6–7.

19. Service Historique de la Défense (Vincennes), GR XL 33 B: *Souvenirs de Stamati Bulgari* (Paris: 1835); Georges Tolias, "La Lanterne Magique de Stamati Bulgari (1782–1856)", in Marie-Noëlle Bourguet, et al, eds, *Enquêtes en Méditerranée, Les Expéditions Françaises d'Égypte, de Morée et d'Algérie. Actes du Colloque Athènes—Nauplie, 8–10 Juin 1995* (Athens: Institut des Recherches Néohelléniques, 1999), pp. 57–68.

20. GAK Corfu, Imperial French, box 67, bundle 1, "Commandants des troupes," 13 October 1807.

21. Machairas, *Politiki kai Diplomatike Istoria*, vol.1, p. 677.

22. Maurice Mashaal, *Bourbaki: Une Société Secrète des Mathématiciens* (Paris: Pour la Science, 2006); Amir Aczel, *The Artist and the Mathematician: The Story of Nicolas Bourbaki, the Genius Mathematician who Never Existed* (London: High Stakes, 2007).

23. Service Historique de la Défense (Vincennes), GR XL 33 B: Psimari, Spiridion.

24. *Asma Polemisterion ton en Aigypto peri Eleutherias Machomenon Graikon* (Paris: 1800). On Korais, see Paschalis Kitromilides, "Itineraries in the World of the Enlightenment: Adamantios Korais from Smyrna via Montpellier to Paris," in Kitromilides, ed., *Adamantios Korais and the European Enlightenment* (Oxford: Voltaire Foundation, 2010), pp. 1–33.

Chapter 5. Enchanted

1. In 1828 the allied powers requested surveys of newly independent Greece in order to compensate the departed Muslims, and the multiple naming was an issue. GAK Athens, Vlachogiannes Collection, cat. 3, Palamedes Papers, f.1a-, subfile 4, doc. 245 / 34.

2. https://www.theguardian.com/uk/2005/sep/30/research.books (accessed 28 February 2024).

3. Dialla, *E Rosike Autokratoria*, pp. 60–61 on the seas, ch. 5 on the Spartans, pp. 65–6, 70 on Russian proto-Philhellenism.

4. Elizabeth Key Fowden, "Rituals of Memory at the Olympieion Precinct of Athens," in Javier Martinez Jimenez and Sam Ottewill-Soulsby, eds, *Remembering and Forgetting the Ancient City* (Oxford: Oxbow Books, 2022), pp. 297–326; and specifically Islamic inflections on Athenian sites in Fowden, "The Parthenon Mosque, King Solomon, and the Greek Sages," in Maria Georgopoulou and Konstantinos Thanasakis, eds, *Ottoman Athens: Archeology, Topography, History* (Athens: Gennadius Library, 2019), pp. 67–96. The excavations at Olympia in IEEE, Zygalakis Collection (correspondence of Veli pasha). Some artefacts made their way to the British Museum.

5. Leake, *Travels in the Morea*, vol. 1, pp. xix-x. François Pouqueville, *Voyage en Morée, à Constantinople, en Albanie, et dans Plusieurs Autres Parties de l'Empire Othoman, pendant les Anneés 1798, 1799, 1800 et 1801* (Paris: Gabon, 1805), 3 vols. See also Boppe, *L'Albanie*, pp. 170–71.

6. Service Historique de la Défense (Vincennes), military intelligence, 1 M 1619, Reconnaissances Turquie, "Memoire sur la possibilité et les moyens d'éxecution d'une invasion en Turquie par les côtes d'Épire."

7. Intimated in Dialla, *E Rosike Autokratoria*, ch. 5.

8. Service Historique de la Défense (Vincennes), GR XL 33 B: Papas-Oglou, Nicolas.

9. Aristides Chatzis, "Anazetontas ten Ellenike Tautoteta" and "O Neos Ellenas," *Kathimerini*, 3 January and 14 February 2021.

10. August Boppe, *Le Colonel Nicolas Papas Oglou et le Battallon des Chasseurs d'Orient* (Paris-Nancy: Berger-Levrault, 1900).

11. Konstantinos N. Rados, *Nikolaos Tsesmeles e Papasoglous (1758–1819). Ex Ellenikon, Gallikon kai Aravikon Pegon* (Athens: Sakellariou, 1916).

12. Tozzi, *Nationalizing France's Army*, pp. 151–2.

13. Boppe, *L'Albanie*, pp. 72–3; Boppe, *Le Colonel*, pp. 15–19; Pouqueville, *Histoire de la Régénération de la Grèce Comprenant le Précis des Événements depuis 1740 jusqu'en 1824* (Paris: Firmin Didot, 1824), vol. 1, p. 401; Stanislavskaia, *Rossiia i Gretsiia*, p. 341.

14. Boppe, *L'Albanie*, p. 56, 65–7; Pappas, *Greeks in Russian Military Service*, p. 236.

15. Printed in Rontogiannis, *Istoria tes Nesou Leukadas*, pp. 186–7.

16. Boppe, *L'Albanie*, pp. 199–215.

17. Drawn from Boppe, *Le Régiment Albanais (1807–1814)* (Paris-Nancy: Berger-Levrault, 1902); [Christophoros Perraivos], *Istoria Souliou kai Pargas Periechousa ten Chronologian kai tous Eroïkous auton Polemous, Exeretos tous ton Soulioton meta tou Ale Pasia, Egemonos tes Ellados* (Venice: Nikolaos Glykeis, 1815), 2 vols; Vaso Psimoule, "Oi Souliotes sta Eptanesa," *Ta Istorika / Historica*, 20:38 (June 2003), pp. 27–48; Pappas, *Greeks in Russian Military Service*, pp. 166–83.

18. Well studied in Vaso D. Psimoule, *Souli kai Soulites* (Athens: Kentro Neoellenikon Ereunon, 1998).

19. [Perraivos], *Istoria Souliou*, vol. 1, pp. 3–7, 53–7, 80–81; Boppe, *Le Régiment Albanais*, pp. 10–11; Boppe, *L'Albanie*, pp. 22–4, 234–43.

20. Boppe, *L'Albanie*, pp.22–6; Lord, "Our Reign in the Ionian Islands," p. 560.

21. [Perraivos], *Istoria Souliou*, vol. 2; Psimoule, "Oi Souliotes," pp. 27–9.

22. Service Historique de la Défense (Vincennes), GR 5 C2, July 1804 and April 1805; Pappas, *Greeks in Russian Military Service*, pp. 189–216; Zanou, *Transnational Patriotism*, pp. 163–5.

23. Service Historique de la Défense (Vincennes), GR 5C 10, 17 February 1810, GR C5 11, Donzelot to king of Two Sicilies, 25 March 1810; GAK Corfu, Imperial French, f.139, 1812–13; Anagnostaras and Nikitaras in Italy and Zakynthos in Konstantinos A. Konomos, "Vios Niketa Stamatelopoulou e Niketara. Katagrafe Georgiou Tertsete ek Tessaron Neon Cheirografon," in *Pragmateiai tes Akademiai Athenon*, 20:2 (1954), pp. 5–6; and Stanislavskaia, *Rossiia i Gretsiia*, p. 270.

24. Lists and payrolls in National Archives (London), WO 12–11737, Ionian Islands, 1811; WO 25 / 2289; WO 43 / 652; correspondence of British command with and about Vilaetis and Kolokotronis, in British Library, Archive and Manuscripts, add ms 36543, Church Papers, vol. 1, pp. 5–6, 22–3; Tertsetes, *Theodorou Kolokotrone Apomnemoneumata*, pp. 59–63.

25. Their service in Naples in *Vneshniaia Politika Rossii XIX i Nachala XX Veka: Dokumenty Rossiiskogo Ministerstva Inostrannykh del* (Moscow: multiple publishers, 1962–), ser. 2, vol. 2, pp. 167–8, 197–8, and n. 82–4 on pp. 763–4; and further efforts to resettle them in 1820 in vol. 3, pp. 269–70; Psimoule, "Oi Souliotes," pp. 29–31.

26. GAK Athens, Vlachogiannes Collection, cat. 6, docs 485–490; Pappas, *Greeks in Russian Military Service*, pp. 288–90.

27. Panagiotis Stathis, "From Klephts and Armatoloi to Revolutionaries," in Anastasopoulos and Kolovos, eds, *Ottoman Rule and the Balkans*, p. 175; Pappas, *Greeks in Russian Military Service*, p. 296; Stanislavskaia, *Rossiia i Gretsiia*, p. 270; Papagiorges, *Ta Kapakia*, pp. 82–3; Tzakis, "From Locality to Nation-State Loyalty," including the enlistment of the Souliots to the revolutionaries Mavrokordatos and Kolettis in the 1820s.

28. Julius Milligen, *Memoirs of the Affairs of Greece* (London: John Rodwell, 1831), pp. 68, 90.

29. GAK Athens, Vlachogiannes Collection, cat. 6, box 2, file 7, docs 503, 504.

30. Boppe, *Le Régiment Albanais*, pp. 8–9.

31. [Perraivos], *Istoria Souliou*, vol. 1, pp. 7–18, 24.

32. Printed as Titos P. Giochalas, ed., *To Elleno-Alvanikon Lexicon tou Markou Botsare (Filologike ekdoses ek tou Autografou)* (Athens: Akademia Athenon, 1980).

33. *Vneshniaia politika Rossii*, ser. 2, vol. 2, pp. 168–9, 197–8 (1819), and vol. 3, pp. 267–8 (1820); he called them Greeks in 1806: GAK Corfu, Seven Islands Republic, box 9 (Giornale Ste. Maura), report no. 10.

34. Printed in Rontogiannes, *Istoria tes Nesou Leukadas*, pp. 186–7.

35. See the full-blown transformation of Magemeno in Machairas, *Politike kai Diplomatike Istoria*, pp. 557–61. The Russian perspective in Stanislavskaia, *Rossiia i Gretsiia*, pp. 342–6.

36. Report to Senate in GAK Corfu, Seven Islands Republic, box 9 (Giornale Ste. Maura), report no. 10, with the Count's editing to "greci" on p. 3 verso. Report to Mocenigo in Stanislavskaia, *Rossiia i Gretsiia*, p. 346.

37. Protopsaltis, "Politikai Diapragmateuseis kai Synthekai Metaxy Eptanesou Politeias kai Ale Pasa, 1800–1807," in *Praktika Protou Panioniou Synedriou, 23–29 Septemvriou 1965* (Athens: s.n., 1967), pp. 333–40.

38. Zoes, " O Theodoros Kolokotrones os Nautikos," pp. 236–41; Zoes, "Ek tou Viou tou Theodorou Kolokotroni," pp. 120–26; Gerasimos Maurogiannes, *Istoria ton Ionion Neson Archomene to 1797 kai Legousa to 1815: Meta Proeisagoges en e Ektithentai e Proegoumenai Tychai Ayton* (Athens: Palligennesia, 1889), vol. 2, p. 170; some documents are in GAK Athens, Vlachogiannes Collection, cat. 3, file 15.

39. Tertsetes, *Theodorou Kolokotrone Apomnemoneumata*, pp. 50–51.

Chapter 6. Ottoman Echoes

1. Arsh, *Eteristskoe Dvizhenie*, pp. 94–102; Kitromilides, *Enlightenment and Revolution*, pp. 202–3 on language, and ch. 7 on Righas more generally.

2. Arsh, *Eteristskoe Dvizhenie*, p. 94.

3. Regas Velestinles, *Ta Epanastatika*, ed. by Demetrios A. Karamperopoulos, 5th edition (Athens: Epistemonike Etaireia Meletes Pheron-Velestinou-Riga, 2005); P. M. Kitromilides, gen.ed., *Rega Velestinle: Apanta Sozomena* (Athens: The Greek Parliament, 2000–2002). Transla-

tions and summaries in Woodhouse, *Rhigas Velestinlis*, pp. 66, 68–76; Arsh, *Eteristskoe Dvizhenie*, pp. 97–102. Overview in Kitromilides, *Enlightenment and Revolution*, pp. 224–5.

4. Arsh, *Eteristskoe Dvizhenie*, pp. 116–17.

5. Woodhouse, *Rhigas Velestinlis*, pp. 149–54.

6. Paraskeuas Kornotas, *Othomanikes Theoreseis gia to Oikoumeniko Patriarcheio, 170s-Arches 200u Aiona* (Athens: Alexandreia, 1998).

7. Philippos Eliou puts the church in this Ottoman context and explains why the hierarchy stood aloof of subversive movements: *Koinonikoi Agones kai Diaphotismos: E periptose tes Smyrnes, 1819* (Athens: Etaireia Meletes Neou Ellenismou–Mnemon, 1986). See also Kitromilides, *Enlightenment and Revolution*, ch. 10 on the Greek Counterenlightenment; Clogg, "The 'Dhidhaskalia Patriki.'"

8. Karabıçak, "Local Patriots," pp. 16–29, 104–5 and passim; Arsh, *Eteristskoe Dvizhenie*, pp. 72–3; translation with my slight modifications from Kitromilides, *Enlightenment and Revolution*, pp. 306–7.

9. Woodhouse, *Rhigas Velestinlis*, pp. 149–51; Karabıçak, "Local Patriots," pp. 219–24; Stanislavskaia, *Rossiia i Gretsiia*, pp. 290–304.

10. Archives Nationales (Paris), AF 33AP / 37, "Correspondance Pouqueville, 1806–9" and "Correspondance d'Ali Pacha"; Ali's food diplomacy in AF / IV / 1714 / B / 2, pp. 262ff (Donzelot to Minister of War, May 1811); diplomatic dealings with Russia and the Septinsular Republic in GAK Corfu, Seven Islands Republic, box 7 (May 1806).

11. See the outraged correspondence of France's ambassador to the Porte La Tour-Maubourg in Archives Diplomatiques (Nantes), 166PO / B / 46–50 (1810–12).

12. Papagiorges, *Ta Kapakia*, ch. 2, esp. p. 77.

13. Fleming, *The Muslim Bonaparte*.

14. Archives Diplomatiques (Paris), "Correspondance Consulaire, Îles Ioniennes," vol. 9: letters of Latour-Maubourg, January 1811, pp. 21ff.

15. Archives Diplomatiques (Nantes), 166PO / B / 148, Correspondence of Ministry with ambassador Latour-Maubourg, e.g. 23.01.1811, 20 March 1810; passim in 166PO / B / 46–47 (1811).

16. The British commander Richard Church: British Library, Archive and Manuscripts, add ms 36543, Church Papers, "Report on the Ionian Islands (1815)," p. 146.

17. Karabıçak, "Local Patriots," pp. 214–17; Leake, *Travels in the Morea*, pp. 79–80.

18. The excavations in IEEE, Zygalakis Collection (correspondence of Veli pasha). On suspicions that Veli was a Philhellene, see Sakellariou, *E Peloponnesos kata ten Deuteran Tourkokratian*, pp. 245–7.

19. Trade relations in IEEE, Zygalakis Collection (correspondence of Veli pasha), docs 18796–18799, 18812–18813, and Savant, "Napoléon et la Libération de la Grèce," pt 3, pp. 67–8 and 72, and pt 5, pp. 104–6; the general boom in Stanislavskaia, *Rossiia i Gretsiia*, pp. 255–60, 354–5; Arsh, *Eteristskoe Dvizhenie*, 40–41; Veli's and clan politics in Stamatopoulos, "Kommatikes Phatries."

20. Karabıçak consulted Ottoman documents and adds detail on Veli's mandate—secure against foreign empires—and his consequent raising of taxes: "Local Patriots," pp. 342–4.

21. Leake in 1805 observed this dependence on exports to Zakynthos: *Travels in the Morea*, pp. 2–3, 12–13. See also Georgios A. Chrisanthakopoulos, *E Eleia epi Tourkokratias* (Athens: s.n., 1950), pp. 19–44.

22. Archives Nationales (Paris), Fond de Secrétariat d'État Imperiale, États Dépendants: AF / IV / 1714 / B / 2, Îles Ioniennes et Corfu, 1803–1813, annex, p. 122.

23. Archives Nationales (Paris), Fond de Secrétariat d'État Imperiale, États Dépendants: AF / IV / 1714 / B / 2, Îles Ioniennes et Corfu, 1803–1813, annex, pp. 122ff. Other sources offer different details on the composition of the notable councils: Vernikos, *To Schedio Autonomias*, p. 14. Savant, "Napoléon et la Libération de la Grèce," pt 3, pp. 68–9.

24. IEEE, Archeio Zygallaki, docs 18782, 18786–91.

25. IEEE, Archeio Zygallaki, doc. 18791.

26. Recorded by a French agent: Savant, "Napoléon at la Libération de la Grèce," pt 4, p. 407.

27. Ali pasha and Veli pasha demanded that the British return Kolokotronis and Yakoub from Zakynthos: John W. Baggally, *Ali Pasha and Great Britain* (Oxford: Blackwell, 1938), pp. 40–42.

28. Pylia, "Les Notables Moréotes," pp. 351–6; Roussel (French consul in Patras) to Donzelot, 23 May 1812, in Savant, "Napoléon et la Libération de la Greece," pt 4, pp. 389–90; Sakellariou, *E Peloponnesos kata ten Deuteran Tourkokratian*, pp. 249–51; mutinies reported by the Russian consul in Arsh, *Eteristskoe Dvizhenie*, p. 44.

29. His brother Nikolaos fled to Patras around that time but the reasons are not clear. Papageorgiou, "To Archeio Sisini," pp. 210–11.

30. IEEE, Sisinis Archive, docs 20500 (repair of forts in 1818–19) and 20501 (joint payment for hiring regional doctor, 1815).

31. "Anekdota Keimena (1816–1820) (Apo to Archeio tou Sotere Charalambe)," *Peloponnesiaka*, 6 (1968), pp. 191–205.

Chapter 7. Capo d'Istria, Kapodistriia, Kapodistrias

1. These and further details in Woodhouse, *Capodistrias*, pp.17–19. More recent and with a larger source base: Chrestos Loukos, *Ioannes Kapodistrias: Mia Apopeira Istorikes Viographias* (Athens: MIET, 2022). More detail in Arsh, *Ioann Kapodistriia*; Stanislavskaia, *Rossiia i Gretsiia*, ch. 4; Lascaris, "Capodistrias," pp. 11–18, 26ff; Patricia Kennedy Grimstead, *The Foreign Ministers of Alexander I: Political Attitudes and the Conduct of Russian Diplomacy, 1801–1825* (Berkeley and Los Angeles: University of California Press, 1969), pp. 9ff; Kapodistriia, "Zapiska Grafa Ioanna Kapodistrii o ego Sluzhebnoi Deiatel'nosti," *Sbornik russkogo istoricheskogo obshchestva*, vol. 3 (St.Petersburg: Akademiia Nauk, 1868), pp. 163–7 and n. 1.

2. Konomos, "Vios Niketa Stamatelopoulou i Niketara," pp. 6–7.

3. Arsh, *Ioann Kapodistriia*, pp. 21–2, 47–8, 56; Stanislavskaia, *Rossiia i Gretsiia*, pp. 210–12, 227–47, 326–7.

4. Oleg R. Airapetov, *Istoriia Vneshnei Politiki Rossiiskoi Imperii, 1801–1914*, vol. 1 (Moscow: Kuchkovo Pole, 2017), pp. 387–8, 421.

5. Grimstead, *The Foreign Ministers of Alexander I*, p. 236 and passim in ch. 7.

6. Still good on the matter of constitutions: Marc Raeff, *Michael Speransky, Statesman of Imperial Russia* (The Hague: Martinus Nijhoff, 1957); Grimstead, *The Foreign Ministers of Alexander I*, pp. 50–55.

7. The Vienna settlement in Airapetov, *Istoriia Vneshnei Politiki*, pp. 351–83.

8. Glenda Sluga, *The Invention of the International Order: Remaking Europe after Napoleon* (Princeton: Princeton University Press, 2021), chs 11–12; Zanou, *Transnational Patriotism*, pp. 15–16.

9. Grimstead, *The Foreign Ministers of Alexander I*, pp. 9–29, 39, 46, 57.

10. Sluga, *The Invention of the International Order*, chs 5, 11–12.

11. National Archives (London), CO136 / 12, British Embassy in Constantinople to governor of Ionian Islands, 24 April 2019; Ozavci, "The Ottoman Imperial Gaze," p. 223.

12. Grimstead, *The Foreign Ministers of Alexander I*, pp. 235–6; Schroeder, *The Transformation of European Politics*, p. 559.

13. Stella Ghervas, *Réinventer la Tradition: Alexandre Stourdza et l'Europe de la Sainte-Alliance* (Paris: Honoré Champion, 2008), pp. 350ff; the Carlsbad Decrees in pp. 12–13, 79ff, 202–3. Stourdza's privileges in E. I. Druzhinina, *Iuzhnaia Ukraina v 1800–1825 gg.* (Moscow: Nauka, 1970), p. 82.

14. Ghervas, *Réinventer la Tradition*, pp. 71–5, 183ff; Dialla, *E Rosike Autokratoria*, pp. 112–13; Alexander Martin, *Romantics, Reformers, Reactionaries: Russian Conservative Thought and Politics in the Reign of Alexander I* (DeKalb: Northern Illinois University Press, 1997), pp. 150–58, 171–5.

15. As in 1814–15: Kapodistriia, "Zapiska Grafa Ioanna Kapodistrii," pp. 190ff.

16. Zanou, *Transnational Patriotism*, pp. 101–2; Grimstead, *The Foreign Ministers of Alexander I*, ch. 7.

17. National Archives (London), CO136 / 16 (1820–21), 12ff, 85–89; Maitland's reports on the uprisings in CO136 / 12, October 1819, ff.205–208; Maitland's statements in 1821 on ff.97ff, and of 1821 in CO136 / 12, ff.47–44; *Vneshniaia Politika Rossii*, ser. 2, vol. 3, pp. 228–9 and n. 106 on p. 750–51.

18. Kapodistriia, "Zapiska Grafa Ioanna Kapodistrii," pp. 239–42.

19. National Archives (London), CO136 / 13, ff.124–231, August–December 2019; Maitland's response to Bathurst in CO136 / 12, ff.209–222. The inquiries started in 1817: *Vneshiaia Politika Rossii*, ser. 2, vol. 2, pp. 73–4 (Nesselrode to Liven, Nov.–Dec. 1817).

20. National Archives (London), CO136 / 16 (1820–21), 12ff, 85–89; Maitland's certainty that the Count inspired the uprisings in CO136 / 12, ff.223–236.

21. The intercepted correspondence in National Archives (London), CO138 / 16, and Maitland's conclusion in CO136 / 12, f.237; Arsh, *Ioann Kapodistriia*, pp. 105, 108–12.

22. Zanou, *Transnational Patriotism*, pp. 89–92.

23. Sluga, *The Invention of the International Order*.

24. Arsh, *Ioann Kapodistriia*, ch. 4; Ghervas, *Réinventer la Tradition*, pp. 356ff; Grimstead, *The Foreign Ministers of Alexander I*, pp. 236–7. The exclusion of Muslims from the society in Karabıçak, "Local Patriots," p. 360 and Sakul, "The Ottoman Peloponnese," p. 135; the Count's recollections in Kapodistriia, "Zapiska Grafa Ioanna Kapodistrii," pp. 195–6.

25. Airapetov, *Istoriia Vneshnei Politiki*, vol. 1, pp. 403ff and 447–9.

26. He was approached by Galatis in 1817, Kamarinos and Xanthos in early 1820, and Ypsilantis a few months later.

27. Arsh, *Ioann Kapodistriia*, ch. 5; Ghervas, *Réinventer la Tradition*, p. 366; Airapetov, *Istoriia Vneshnei Politiki*, vol. 1, p. 423; *Vneshniaia Politika Rossii*, ser. 2, vol. 3, pp. 220–21, pp. 297–303 (Kapodistriia to Petrobey Mavromichalis and to consul in Bucharest Pini, and to ambassador

to Constantinople Stroganov, all around January 1820); the Count's recollections in Kapodistriia, "Zapiska Grafa Ioanna Kapodistrii," pp. 215–20, and repeated affirmations of his opposition to any armed action against the Porte, pp. 253–7.

28. Gregori Arš [Grigorii Arsh] and Constantin Svolopoulos, eds, *Alexandre Ypsilanti. Correspondance Inédite* (Thessaloniki: Institute for Balkan Studies, 1999), pp. 14–25; Arsh, *Eteristskoe Dvizhenie*, pp. 152ff.

29. A view perpetuated by the Porte into 1822 and beyond: reviews of Ottoman perceptions in Ozavci, "The Ottoman Imperial Gaze"; Ilicak, ed., *"Those Infidel Greeks": The Greek War of Independence*, vol. 1, pp. 256–62. Also *Vneshniaia Politika Rossii*, ser. 2, vol. 3, pp. 129–31 (Lanzheron to Nesselrode, April / May 1821); Arsh, *Eteristskoe Dvizhenie*, p. 261; Theophilus Prousis, *Russian Society and the Greek Revolution* (DeKalb: University of Northern Illinois Press, 1994), p. 20; Prousis, *British Consular Reports*, pp. 56–7.

30. *Vneshniaia Politika Rossii*, ser. 2, vol. 3, pp. 68 (Nesselrode to ambassador in Constantinople Stoganov, Kapodistriia to Ypsilantis, both in February), pp. 70–71 (Nesselrode in March); Arsh, *Ioann Kapodistriia*, ch. 5; Ghervas, *Réinventer la Tradition*, pp. 374ff; Grimstead, *The Foreign Ministers of Alexander I*, pp. 249ff; Airapetov, *Istoriia Vneshnei Politiki*, vol. 1, pp. 425ff, 451–6.

31. Airapetov, *Istoriia Vneshnei Politiki*, vol. 1, pp. 434–4; Grimstead, *The Foreign Ministers of Alexander I*, pp. 254–64; *Vneshniaia Politika Rossii*, ser. 2, vol. 3, pp. 500–503 (Kapodistriia to Alexander, May 1822); Schroeder, *The Transformation of European Politics*, pp. 559, 621.

32. *Vneshniaia Politika Rossii*, ser. 2, vol. 3, pp. 94–5 (Stourdza to Kapodistriia, April 2021); pp. 245 and 257 (Kapodistriia to Alexander, July and August 1821); pp. 327–9 (Kapodistriia pro memoria of September 1822); Ghervas, *Réinventer la Tradition*, pp. 83ff, 220–21, 370–74; Martin, *Romantics, Reformers, Reactionaries*, pp. 195–6.

33. *Vneshniaia Politika Rossii*, ser. 2, vol. 1, p. 430. Context in Dialla, *E Rosike Autokratoria*, ch. 6.

34. Maria Euthemiou, "Servike kai Ellenike Epanastase: Mia Synkrise," in Thanos Veremes and Antonis Klapses, eds, *1821: E Epanastase ton Ellenon* (Athens: Ellenika Grammata, 2021), pp. 61–84; gleaned also from Ziya Karal, "The Ottoman Empire and the Serbian Uprising, 1807–1812," in Wayne Vucinich, ed., *The First Serbian Uprising, 1804–1813* (New York: Columbia University Press, 1982), pp. 207–26.

35. The Greeks as Orthodox in Ghervas, *Réinventer la Tradition*, pp. 221–2.

36. The Greek war as revelation in Zanou, *Transnational Patriots*, chs 4 and 7, eschatology on p. 207.

37. *Vneshniaia Politika Rossii*, ser. 2, vol. 3, pp. 283–4 (Mocenigo in Turin to Nesselrode, September).

38. *Vneshniaia Politika Rossii*, ser. 2, vol. 4, pp. 203–7 (Stroganov to government of Turkey, 6 / 18 July 1821); p. 282 (appeal of the Minister of Enlightenment for charitable donations for Greek refugees, August / September 1821); the idea of nation analyzed in Anta Dialla, "Imperial Rhetoric and Revolutionary Practice: The Greek 1821," *Historein*, 20:1 (2021), pp. 12–13.

39. Arsh, *Ioann Kapodistriia*, pp. 199–215; Ghervas, *Réinventer la Tradition*, pp. 374–8; Apostolos Daskalakes, *E topikoi Organismoi tes Epanastaseos tou 1821 kai to Politeuma tes Epidavrou* (Athens: Vagionakes, 1966), pp. 116, 124, 136; Dialla, *E Rosike Autokratoria*, pp. 260–62.

40. Ghervas, *Réinventer la Tradition*, pp. 83–4; Arsh, *Ioann Kapodistriia*; Martin, *Romantics, Reformers, Reactionaries*, pp. 195–6; *Vneshniaia Politika Rossii*, ser. 2, vol. 3, p. 406 (Kapodistriia to Alexander and Nesselrode, December 1821–January 1822).

41. As related in 1827: Bibliothèque de Genève, Collection Eynard, MS SUPPL 1884, ff.392–394.

42. Bibliothèque de Genève, Collection Eynard, MS SUPPL 1884, his subsidies continuing into the 1840s when he subsidized the Count's relatives and arranged financing for the Greek state; Ghervas, *Réinventer la Tradition*, pp. 385ff; Korinna Schönhärl, *European Investment in Greece in the Nineteenth Century: A Behavioural Approach to Financial History* (London: Routledge, 2020), pp. 57ff and passim in ch. 2; some detail in Glenda Sluga, "'Who Hold the Balance of the World?': Bankers at the Congress of Vienna, and in International History," *American Historical Review*, 22:5 (December 2017), pp. 1403–30.

43. Maurizio Isabella, "Citizens or Faithful?: Religion and the Liberal Revolutions of the 1820s in Southern Europe," *Modern Intellectual History* 12 (November 2015), pp. 555–78.

44. Benaki Museum, Capodistrias Collection, box 41, doc. 23. My thanks to Konstantina Zanou for identifying the handwriting.

45. National Archives (London), CO136 / 16, entries 714–168 of 1821 and 1822; Schönhärl, *European Investment in Greece*, p. 79.

46. *Vneshniaia Politika Rossii*, ser. 2, vol. 7 (15), p. 154; Airapetov, *Istoriia Vneshnei Politiki*, vol. 2, pp. 68ff.

47. Bibliothèque de Genève, Collection Eynard, "Correspondance Relative à la Grèce," MS SUPPL.1884 / 1, f.3, Eynard to Macintosh, 10 June 1827.

48. Ghervas, *Réinventer la Tradition*, pp. 89–91.

49. *Vneshniaia Politika Rossii*, ser. 2, vol. 7 (15), p. 159 (the Russian ambassador in London, citing Canning).

50. Archives Nationales (Paris), "Fond de Secrétariat d'État Imperiale," États Dépendants: AF / IV / 1714 / B / 2, Îles Ioniennes et Corfu, 1803–1813, p. 18.

51. *Vneshniaia Politika Rossii*, ser. 2, vol. 7 (15), pp. 263–4 (Nesselrode to Admiral Heyden in the Mediterranean, his emphasis); sums of money sent by Russia to the Count in Airapetov, *Istoriia Vneshnei politiki*, vol. 2, pp. 76ff.

52. Bibliothèque de Genève, Collection Eynard, MS SUPPL.1884 / 2, f.478.

53. The finances in Bibliothèque de Genève, Collection Eynard, MS SUPPL.1888, ff.257–258, ff.260.

54. Bibliothèque de Genève, "Souvenirs: Séjour en Grèce, Dicté par Louis-André Gosse à son Fils Hyppolyte (20 Octobre 1873)," pp. 40–41.

55. John Anthony Petropulos, *Politics and Statecraft in the Kingdom of Greece, 1833–1843* (Princeton: Princeton University Press, 1986), pp. 106–17.

56. Airapetov, *Istoriia Vneshnei Politiki Rossiiskoi Imperii*, vol. 2, p. 143.

57. My reading of Dialla, *E Rosiki Autokratoria*, pt 3.

Chapter 8. The Greek Merchant Conquers, and Becomes Greek

1. My tribute to Traian Stoianovich, "The Conquering Balkan Orthodox Merchant," *Journal of Economic History*, 20:2 (June 1960), pp. 234–313.

2. Stoianovich, "The Conquering Balkan Orthodox Merchant," pp. 317–29; Vassilis Kardasis, *Diaspora Merchants in the Black Sea: The Greeks in Southern Russia, 1775–1861* (Lanham, MD: Lexington Books, 2001), appendix 2, n. 1, p. 212.

3. Deno J. Geanakoplos, "The Diaspora Greeks: The Genesis of Modern Greek National Consciousness," in Nikiforos P. Diamantopoulos, et al, eds, *Hellenism and the First Greek War of Liberation (1821–1830): Continuity and Change* (Thessaloniki: Institute for Balkan Studies, 1976), pp. 59–77.

4. A plausible etymology: Antonio de Capmany, *Nuevo Diccionario Francés-Español*, second ed. (Madrid: Imprenta de Sancha, 1817), where gringo and griego are synonyms for speaking gibberish.

5. Useful detail in Tzelina Charlaute and Katerina Papakonstantinou, eds, *E Nautilia ton Ellenon, 1700–1821: O Eonas tes Akmes prin apo ten Epanastase* (Athens: Kerdos, 2013).

6. Pissis, "Investment in the Greek Merchant Marine," pp. 152–3; Arsh, *Eteristskoe Dvizhenie*, pp. 31–7.

7. Druzhinina, *Iuzhnaia Ukraina*, ch. 7.

8. Tzelina Charlaute, *Istoria tes Ellenoktetes Nautilias, 190s–200s Aionas* (Athens: Nefele, 2011), ch. 1.

9. My thanks to Sophie Lambroschini for our discussion of volcanoes, and this reference: Wolfgang Behringer, *Tambora and the Year without a Summer: How a Volcano Plunged the World into Crisis* (Cambridge: Polity Press, 2016).

10. Some of these cycles in Kardasis, *Diaspora Merchants*, pp. 110ff. Kremmydas, "E Oikonomike Krise," focuses on the bust of the Balkans after 1815 rather than the boom that continued in Russian grain exports.

11. Druzhinina, *Iuzhnaia Ukraina*, pp. 265–8, 334–7; Airapetov, *Istoriia Vneshnei Politiki*, vol. 1, pp. 432–3.

12. Druzhinina, *Iuzhnaia Ukraina*, pp. 178–9; Arsh, *Eteristskoe Dvizhenie*, pp. 62–5, 130–50.

13. Sakul, "The Ottoman Peloponnese," p. 124; Arsh, *Eteristskoe Dvizhenie*, pp. 61–2, followed by useful information about migration to Russia's Black Sea coasts.

14. Kardasis, *Diaspora Merchants*, p. 85 and passim in ch. 5 and 7.

15. Nassia Yakovaki's overview is excellent: "Adamantios Korais's 'The Greek Library' (1805–1827): An Ingenious Publisher and the Making of a Nation," in John Spiers, ed., *The Culture of the Publisher's Series, Volume 2: Nationalisms and the National Canon* (Basingstoke: Palgrave Macmillan, 2011), pp. 72–90.

16. Philippos Eliou, "Vivlia me Syndrometes, I: Ta Chronia tou Diafotismou, 1749–1821," *O Eranistes*, 12 (1975), pp. 101–79; Kremmydas, "E Oikonomike Krise," p. 32, n. 41; St. Clair, *That Greece Might Still Be Free*, p. 20ff.

17. Orthodox Enlightenment in Zanou, *Transnational Patriotism*. Overviews of a Neohellenic Enlightenment are Anna Tabaki, "Les Lumières Néo-helléniques. Un Essai de Définition et de Périodisation", in Werner Schneiders, ed., *Les Lumières en Europe, Unité et Diversité* (Berlin: Berliner Wissenschafts-Verlag, 2003), pp. 45–56; Kitromilides, *Enlightenment and Revolution*, ch. 4.

18. Kitromilides, *Enlightenment and Revolution*, pp. 142–54 and ch. 7.

19. Evrydiki Sifneos, *Imperial Odessa: People, Spaces, Identities* (Leiden: Brill, 2018), pp. 86–7.

20. Elpida K. Vogli, "'Ellenes to Genos': Ithagenia kai Tautoteta sto Ethniko Kratos ton Ellenon," doctoral dissertation, Aristotelian University of Thessaloniki, 2003.

21. His Russian moment in *Vneshniaia Politika Rossii*, ser. 2, vol. 2, pp. 167–8 (Kapodistriia to Benaki, January 1818), pp. 763–4, n. 82–84; and pp. 197–8 (Kapodistriia to Sicilian ambassador Serra-Capriole, March 1818).

22. Rotzokos, *Ethnafypnise kai Ethnogenese*, pp. 220–22.

23. Tertsetes, *Theodorou Kolokotroni Apomnemoneumata*, pp. 65–6 and 122, as well as Konomos, "Vios Nikita Stamatelopoulou e Nikitara," where anything west of the Morea is Frankia. The Zakynthians are part of the oral tradition around Pyrgos and Gastouni, repeated to me over the years.

24. Tertsetes, *Theodorou Kolokotroni Apomnemoneumata*, pp. 50–51.

25. Tertsetes, *Theodorou Kolokotroni Apomnemoneumata*, pp. 65–6.

26. Gleaned from a variety of sources, especially Yakovaki, "Adamantios Korais's 'Hellenic Library,'" Arsh, *Eteristskoe Dvizhenie*, p.150, and Prousis, *Russian Society*, p. 14.

27. On the Greek settlements in Russia the works of Druzhinina are very useful. Good facts and numbers are gathered in vol. 2 of the Black Sea Working Papers: Evrydiki Sifneos, Valentyna Shandra, and Oksana Yorkova, eds, *Port-Cities of the Northern Shore of the Black Sea: Institutional, Economic and Social Development, 18th–Early 20th Centuries* (Rethymnon: Center for Maritime Studies, 2021). A good overview is Arsh, *Eteristskoe Dvizhenie*, ch. 4.

28. Bartlett, *Human Capital*, chs 2–3.

29. Druzhinina, *Severnoe Prichernemor'e*, pp. 58–66; Druzhinina, *Iuzhnaia Ukraina*, pp. 70–73, 119–20, 168.

30. Druzhinina, *Iuzhnaia Ukraina*, p. 179.

31. M. Podgayko, "Greky Ukrainy v Systemi Zakonodavchoi Polityky Pravliachykh Uriadiv u II Polovyni XVII-XIX st.," *Visnyk Mariupol's'kogo Derzhavnogo Universytetu, Seriia Istoriia, Politologiia*, 13–14 (2015), pp. 138–44.

32. Kardasis, *Diaspora Merchants*, appendix 2; Druzhinina, *Kiuch-Kainardzhiinskii mir*, pp. 58–9; Bartlett, *Human Capital*, pp. 18, 141–2.

33. Ioannes Karras, "Pou Pegan Oloi oi Epanastates? Oi 'Ellenes' tes Niznas sten Odysso ton Archon tou 19ou Aiona," in Kalliope Amygdalou, ed., *Kataskeues tes Patridas: Architektonike, Tautoteta kai Mneme stis Ellenikes Koinotetes tes Odyssou kai tes Massalias, 19os kai 20os Aionas* (Athens: Futura, 2022), pp. 30–45, the Melas on pp. 32–3, Xanthos on p. 34; Arsh, *Eteristskoe Dvizhenie*, p. 146.

34. Druzhinina, *Iuzhnaia Ukraina*, pp. 175, 209, 214, 313.

35. Druzhinina, *Iuzhnaia Ukraina*, p. 118; Bartlett, *Human Capital*, pp. 141–2; Kardasis, *Diaspora Merchants*, pp. 24–9.

36. Druzhinina, *Severnoe Prichernomor'e*, pp. 154–9.

37. Sifneos, *Imperial Odessa*, p. 116; Kremmydas, "E Oikonomiki Krise," p. 23; Druzhinina, *Iuzhnaia Ukraina*, p. 354; Kardasis, *Diaspora Merchants*, pp. 24–5, 55, 94–5.

38. Druzhinina, *Severnoe Prichernomor'e*, pp. 58–69; Druzhinina, *Iuzhnaia Ukraina*, pp. 110–15; Bartlett, *Human Capital*, pp. 39–40, 48–9, 124; the Serbs as "opportunity shoppers" in Karabıçak, "Local Patriots," pp. 248–87.

39. Druzhinina, *Severnoe Prichernomor'e*, pp. 58–69, 130, 159–60, 191, and ch. 1 passim; Bartlett, *Human Capital*, pp. 124, 130.

40. Sifneos, *Imperial Odessa*, pp. 86–7.

41. Karras, "Pou Pegan Oloi oi Epanastates?", pp. 31–2.

42. Druzhinina, *Iuzhnaia Ukraina*, p. 118; Bartlett, *Human Capital*, pp. 141–2; Kardasis, *Diaspora Merchants*, pp. 24–9; Arsh, *Eteristskoe Dvizhenie*, p. 144.

43. Valianos and perhaps Kallergis were in St. Petersburg if not necessarily at the school. Petropulos, *Politics and Statecraft*, p. 117.

44. Arsh, *Eteristskoe Dvizhenie*, pp. 134, 213–15, and the exceptionalism on 146–51.

45. Charles Steinwedel, *Threads of Empire: Loyalty and Tsarist Authority in Bashkiria, 1552–1917* (Bloomington: Indiana University Press, 2016), chs 2–3.

46. Stamatopoulos, "Constantinople in the Peloponnese," pp. 156–7.

Chapter 9. Greece-on-Danube

1. Kardasis, *Diaspora Merchants*, pp. 90–91.

2. Membership information from George D. Frangos, "The *Philiki Etairia*: A Premature National Coalition," in Richard Clogg, ed., *The Struggle for Greek Independence* (Hamden, CT: Archon Books, 1973), pp. 87–103.

3. Kardasis, *Diaspora Merchants*, pp. 54–5.

4. Arsh, *Eteristskoe Dvizhenie*, ch. 5, the murder of Galatis on pp. 183ff.

5. *Vneshniaia Politika Rossii*, ser. 2, vol. 3, p. 130 (Lanzheron to Nesselrode, April / May 1821); S. N. Palauzov, *Rumynskie Gosudarsva Valachiia i Moldaviia v Istoriko-Politicheskom Otnoshenii* (St. Petersburg: Kozanchikov, 1859), p. 166.

6. Arš and Svolopoulos, eds, *Alexandre Ypsilanti*, pp. 83–5, "Les Chefs des Grecs aux Armes à l'Empereur Alexandre I-er, 9 April 1821" (Old Style).

7. Olga Katsiarde-Hering, ed., *Oi Poleis ton Philikon: Oi Astikes Diadromes enos Epanastatikou Phenomenou. Praktika Emeridas, Athena, 14 Ianouariou 2015* (Athens: Voule ton Ellenon, 2018).

8. Sifneos, *Imperial Odessa*, pp. 92–3.

9. The trade routes they followed in Vasilis Panagiotopoulos, "The Filiki Etairia (Society of Friends)," in Pizanias, ed., *The Greek Revolution of 1821: A European Event*; Kremmydas, "E Oikonomike Krise," p. 33; Airapetov, *Istoriia Vneshnei Politiki*, vol. 1, pp. 414–15; membership in Dionysis Tzakes, "E Eforia tes Philikes Etaireias sten Peloponneso," *Ionios Logos*, 5 (2015), pp. 104–10; the Morean notables in Photopoulos, *Oi Kotzampasedes*, pt 3, ch. 3; Arsh, *Eteristskoe Dvizhenie*, pp. 202–13; well-off merchant support in Sifneos, *Imperial Odessa*, pp. 94–5.

10. Kremmydas, "E Oikonomike Krise," emphasizes the economic downturn as a source of discontent; heightened expectations in Gunnar Hering, "Schetika me to Provlema ton Epanastatikon Exegerseon stis Arches tou 19 Eona," *Ta Istorika*, 24–25 (1996), pp. 105–20.

11. Arsh, *Eteristskoe Dvizhenie*, pp. 71ff; Papagiorges, *Ta Kapakia*, pp. 11–23.

12. Stanislavskaia, *Rossiia i Gretsiia*, pp. 69–70.

13. *Vneshniaia Politika Rossii*, ser. 2, vol. 2, pp. 130–33 (Consul-general in Bucharest Pini to ambassador Stroganoff in Constantinople, December 1817–January 1818, on the conduct of the gospodar Caradja [Karadzha, Karatzas]); Arsh, *Eteristskoe Dvizhenie*, pp. 152ff.

14. Karabiçak, "Local Patriots," p. 280.

15. Papagiorges, *Ta Kapakia*, pp. 33–4.

16. Sifneos, *Imperial Odessa*, p. 96.

17. Airapetov, *Istoriia Vneshnei Politiki*, vol. 1, pp. 415–20; Ilicak, ed., *"Those Infidel Greeks": The Greek War of Independence*, vol. 1, p. 85; Sifneos, *Imperial Odessa*, p. 87; Keith Hitchins, *The Romanians, 1744–1866* (Oxford: Clarendon Press, 1996), p. 142.

18. Arš and Svolopoulos, eds, *Alexandre Ypsilanti*, p. 37.

19. Arsh, *Eteristskoe Dvizhenie*, pp. 301–12.

20. Nestor Camariano, "Les Relations de Tudor Vladimirescu avec l'*Hétairie*, avant la Révolution de 1821," *Balkan Studies*, 6:2 (January 1965), pp. 139–64; Aksan, *Ottoman Wars*, pp. 289–303.

21. Arš and Svolopoulos, eds, *Alexandre Ypsilanti*, p. 27; *Vneshniaia Politika Rossii*, ser. 2, vol. 3, pp. 70–71 (Nesselrode to Russian diplomatic missions); Arsh, *Eteristskoe Dvizhenie*, pp. 264–75; Palauzov, *Rumynskie Gospodarstva*, pp. 169–70.

22. Arsh, *Eteristskoe Dvizhenie*, pp. 274–5.

23. Airapetov, *Istoriia Vneshnei Politiki*, vol. 1, pp. 421–6; Arš and Svolopoulos, eds, *Alexandre Ypsilanti*, pp. 37, 76–7; *Vneshniaia Politika Rossii*, ser. 2, vol. 3, p. 39 (reports of governor I.N. Inzov of Bessarabia and consul in Jassy Pisani) and p. 701 (Nesselrode to Russian diplomatic missions).

24. Victor Taki, *Russia on the Danube: Empires, Elites, and Reform in Moldavia and Wallachia, 1812–1834* (Budapest: Central European University Press, 2021), chs 2–3; Palauzov, *Rumynskie Gospodarstva*, pp. 170–4; Hitchins, *The Romanians*, pp. 141–50.

25. *Vneshniaia Politika Rossii*, ser. 2, vol. 3, pp. 113–14 (Ambassador Stroganov to Nesselrode, April 1821); Palauzov, *Rumynskie Gospodarstva*, pp. 168–9.

26. *Vneshniaia Politika Rossii*, ser. 2, vol. 3, pp. 113–14 (Ambassador Stroganov to Nesselrode, April 1821); Arš and Svolopoulos, eds, *Alexandre Ypsilanti*, pp. 29–30.

27. Prousis, *British Consular Reports*, p. 37.

28. Arš and Svolopoulos, eds, *Alexandre Ypsilanti*, pp. 38–9 and 83, n. 47; Ş. Ilıcak, "The Revolt of Alexander Ipsilantis and the Fate of the Fanariots in Ottoman Documents," in Pizanias, ed., *The Greek Revolution of 1821: A European Event*, p. 233; pleas for forgiveness by Ypsilatis's men in Ilicak, ed., *"Those Infidel Greeks": The Greek War of Independence*, vol. 1, pp. 72–3.

29. Airapetov, *Istoriia Vneshnei Politiki*, vol. 1, pp. 428–9; Arsh, *Eteristskoe Dvizhenie*, pp. 326–46; Palauzov, *Rumynskie Gospodarstva*, pp. 186–7; Konstantinos Rados, *O Ieros Lochos kai e en Dragatsanion Mache* (Athens: Panepistemiake Epitheorisis, 1919), pp. 14–16; Hitchins, *The Romanians*, pp. 141–52.

Chapter 10. Outbreak, 1821

1. A very good reconstruction of events in the Morea in 1820 and 1821 is Photopoulos, *Oi Kotzampasedes*, pt 3, ch. 4.

2. Stamatopoulos, "Constantinople in the Peloponnese," pp. 149–68, and Dean Kostantaras, "Sources of Political and Social Unrest in the Peloponnese on the Eve of the Revolution," *Historein*, 20:1 (2022).

3. Amvrosios Phrantzes, *Epitome tes Istorias tes Anegennetheises Ellados Archomene apo tou Etous 1715, kai Legousa to 1837* (Athens: Vitoria tou Konst. Kastorche, 1839), vol. 2, pp. 146–8; Photopoulos, *Oi Kotzampasedes*, pt 3, ch. 4.

4. Phrantzes, *Epitome*, vol. 2, p. 54; Photopoulos, *Oi Kotzampasedes*, pt 3, ch. 4.

5. Gritsopoulos, *Istoria tes Gastounes*, vol. 1, pp. 581–2; Photopoulos, *Oi Kotzampasedes*, pp. 226ff.

6. *Archeion Kanellou Delegianne*, report of Spiliotopoulos, 22 February (Old Style), doc. 26.

7. Panagiotes Zepos, "Dyo Proepanastatika Schedia Apeleutheroseos tes Peloponnesou," *Peloponnesiaka*, 7 (1970), p. 457.

8. *Archeion Kanellou Delegianne*, docs 18, 21, 22, 23; Deliyannis in Karabıçak, "Local Patriots," p. 318; attitudes to the society in Photopoulos, *Oi Kotzampasedes*, pt 3, ch. 4.

9. Arsh, *Eteristskoe Dvizhenie*, pp. 264–75.

10. Photakos [Photios Chrysanthopoulos], *Vios Papa Phlesa* (Athens: S. Kalkandes, 1868), ch. 3; Vangelis Sarafis, "'. . . na nomizomen emautous apelpismenous, choris na vlemomev diorthosin tina pros oikonomian': Phovos gia ten Anapoterpte Exergese, Fevrouarios 1821," in Katerina Dede, Demetres Demetropoulos, and Tasos Sakellaropoulos, eds, *Phovoi kai Elpides sta Neotera Chronia* (Athens: Institouto Istorikon Ereunon, 2017), pp. 51–3; Gritsopoulos, *Istoria tes Gastounes*, vol. 1, pp. 571–8; Photopoulos, *Oi Kotzampasedes*, p. 226 and pt 2, chs and 4; Papaflessas in Vasislis Panagiotopoulos, "E Enarxe tou Agona tes Anexartesias sten Peloponneso: Mia Emerologiaki Proseggise," *Praktika tou 6 Diethnous Synedriou Peloponnesiakon Spoudon (Tripolis 24–29 Septemvriou 2000)*, vol. 3 (Athens: 2002), pp. 449–61.

11. Karabıçak, "Local Patriots," p. 354; Photakos, *Vios Papa Phlesa*, ch. 4.

12. Karabıçak, "Local Patriots," pp. 320, 351–2. Examples in *Vneshniaia Politika Rossii*, ser. 2, vol. 3, p. 121 (Russian vice-consul on Zakynthos, April 1821); Lucien J. Frary, "The Russian Consulate in the Morea and the Outbreak of the Greek Revolution, 1816–21," in Mika Suonpää and Owain Wright, eds, *Diplomacy and Intelligence in the Nineteenth-Century Mediterranean World* (London: Bloomsbury Academic, 2019), pp. 57–58; Palauzov, *Rumynskie Gospodarstva*, p. 175.

13. Karabıçak, "Local Patriots," pp. 351–3; *Vneshniaia Politika Rossii*, ser. 2, vol. 3, pp. 220–21 (Kapodistriia's correspondence of January 1820: Kapodistriia to Petrobey, to consul in Bucharest Pini, and to ambassador to Constantinople Stroganov); full text in "Otvetnoe pis'mo Grafa Ivana Kapodistrii Petro-Beiu, Vozhdiu Spartantsev," *Sbornik Russkogo Istoricheskogo Obshchestva*, 3 (1868), pp. 297–303.

14. Arsh, *Eteristskoe Dvizhenie*, pp. 69–70.

15. *Archeion Kanellou Delegianne*, doc. 26.

16. National Archives (London), CO136 / 18, miscellaneous correspondence, Ionian Islands, file G, Green to Maitland, 2 May 1821 (New Style).

17. Photopoulos, *Oi Kotzampasedes*, pt 3, ch. 4.

18. IEEE, Sisinis Archive, doc. 20331.

19. Phrantzes, *Epitome*, pp. 145–9.

20. ELIA-MIET, Kolokotronis Archive, 1.1.26.2, entries of 25 March 1821 (Old Style?); Giannes Vlachogiannes, *Stratiotike Diktatoria* (Athens: Bayron, 1972, offprint of 1933 journal), p. 8.

21. Konomos, "Vios Niketa Stamatelopoulou i Niketara," pp. 8–10; Tertsetes, *Theodorou Kolokotroni Apomnemoneumata*, pp. 66–8; Photakos, *Vios Papa Phlesa*, ch. 4.

22. Apostolos Vakalopoulos, *Tourkoi kai Ellenes Aichmalotoi kata ten Ellenike Epanastase, 1821–1829: Sterea Ellada, Nesia Aigaiou, Peloponnesos. Oi Aichmalosies, e Tyche e Zoe, Vaptiseis kai Ekchristianismoi, Antallages* (Athens: Ant. Stamoule, 2016), pp. 134–5.

23. Vakalopoulos, *Tourkoi kai Ellenes Aichmalotoi*, pp. 35–6.

24. An enumeration of Muslim communities that fled in https://www.settlements -peloponnese1821.eu/documents/document-3/ (accessed 20 August 2023); Ottoman reports on refugees in Ilicak, ed., *"Those Infidel Greeks": The Greek War of Independence*, vol. 1, pp. 428–9.

25. Phrantzes, *Epitome*, pp. 149–50; Gritsopoulos, *Istoria tes Gastounes*, vol. 1, pp. 588–600.

26. Sakul, "The Ottoman Peloponnese," pp. 135ff; Tertsetes, *Theodorou Kolokotroni Apomne-moneumata*, p. 69.

27. Photakos, *Vios Papa Phlesa*, ch. 4.

28. Sarafis, "'. . . na nomizomen emautous apelpismenous,'" p. 54.

29. Sakul, "The Ottoman Peloponnese," p. 135.

30. Dionyses Tzakes, "Polemos kai Schesis Exousias sten Epanastase tou 1821," in Demetro-poulos, Loukos, and Michaelares, eds, *Opseis tes Epanastases*, p. 162.

31. Konomos, "Vios Nikita Stamatelopoulou i Niketara," pp. 8–10; Tertsetes, *Theodorou Kolo-kotroni Apomnemoneumata*, pp. 69–70; Photakos, *Vios Papa Phlesa*, ch. 4.

32. IEEE, Sisinis Archive, doc. 20435 of July 1821.

33. Ilicak, "The Revolt of Alexandros Ipsilantis," pp. 227–8.

34. Examples from the Ottoman archives from summer 1821 in Ilicak, ed., *"Those Infidel Greeks": The Greek War of Independence*, vol. 1, pp. 46, 79.

35. Ilicak, "The Revolt of Alexandros Ipsilantis," pp. 233ff, 237; Karabıçak, "Local Patriots," pp. 315, 396–9; Ilicak, ed., *"Those Infidel Greeks": The Greek War of Independence*, vol. 1, pp. 7–8.

36. Hakan Erdem, "'Perfidious Albanians,'" pp. 223–4; Erdem, "'Do not Think of the Greeks as Agricultural Laborers': Ottoman Responses to the Greek War of Independence," in Thalia Dragonas and Faruk Birtek, eds, *Citizenship and the Nation-State in Greece and Turkey* (London: Routledge, 2004), pp. 67–8; Ilicak, ed., *"Those Infidel Greeks": The Greek War of Independence*, vol. 1, pp. 63, 65 (the fatwa of 1821 declaring the rebels harbi), 360, 371 (the Porte's claim of seized property around Söke and from Chios in 1822).

37. Punishments meted out in Syria in Hill, "Mount Lebanon and Greece: Mediterranean Crosscurrents"; Ilicak, ed., *"Those Infidel Greeks": The Greek War of Independence*, vol. 1, pp. 31 (grocers in Constantinople), 49 (churches and monasteries in Haifa), 52, 62 (random sniping in Constantinople), 53 (registration and deportation of artisans around Constantinople), 54 (hangings of clergy), 72–3 (refusal of offers to submit), 78 (execution of the bishop of Iraklio), 94 (forced labor), 214–15 (mob violence and looting in Izmir); Erdem, "'Do not Think of the Greeks,'" pp. 74–7.

38. National Archives (London), CO136 / 18, USII, miscellaneous correspondence, file B on 40 Ionian Island sailors stranded in London; Ilicak, ed., *"Those Infidel Greeks": The Greek War of Independence*, vol. 1, pp. 34, 37, 50 (order to the fleet), 63 (order to land forces), 75 and 77 (to kill, enslave, and loot), 138–9 (imprisonment of Greek sailors).

39. Ilicak, ed., *"Those Infidel Greeks": The Greek War of Independence*, vol. 1, pp. 103, 109, 111, 257.

40. Ilicak, ed., *"Those Infidel Greeks": The Greek War of Independence*, vol. 1, pp. 89, 103, 200 (calls for moderation), 143–4 (the conditions for amnesty), 254 (a command to grant amnesty to former rebels who submitted from February), 325 (the amnesty of Aghios Efstathios), 401–2 (the reaffirmation of the collective guilt of the whole millet).

41. On Samothrace, Giorgos Koutzakiotes, "Mia Afanes Exegerse Nesioton sten Geitonia tou Kapoudan Pasa: Archeiake Tekmeriosi ton Gegonoton tes Samothrakes," in Demetropou-los, Loukos, and Michaelares, *Opseis tes Epanastases*, pp. 59–86; Ilicak, ed., *"Those Infidel Greeks": The Greek War of Independence*, vol. 1, pp. 90–92 and n. 1 (the massacre of Ayvalik), 167 (Samo-thrace), 268, 327 (Naousa).

42. Ilicak, ed., *"Those Infidel Greeks": The Greek War of Independence*, vol. 1, pp. 103 (order to protect Christians), 297–300 and 321–2 (permission to attack whole regions and take slaves, execution of notables and church hierarchs), 332, 297.

43. Erdem, "'Do not Think of the Greeks,'" pp. 69–70.

44. Ilicak, ed., *"Those Infidel Greeks": The Greek War of Independence*, vol. 1, pp. 351–2, 375, 424–9; Prousis, *British Consular Reports*, p. 28.

45. A synthesis: Maria Christina Chatzeioannou, *Ste Dine tes Chiakes Katastrophes (1822): Diastavroumenes Istories kai Syllogike Tautoteta* (Athens: EIE / IIE, 2021), with estimates on pp. 14–15.

46. IEEE, Sisinis Archive, docs 20432 of June 1821 and 20413 of October 1821. The use of Hellas and Hellene in 1820 in Karabıçak, "Local patriots," p. 357; before 1821 in Yakovaki, "Adamantios Korais's 'Hellenic Library,'" p. 82; and the changes of 1821 in Nikos V. Rotzokos, *Epanastase kai Emphylios Polemos to Eikosiena* (Athens: Erodotos, 2016), pp. 136ff. and n. 17.

47. Tertsetes, *Theodorou Kolokotroni Apomnemoneumata*, p. 65.

48. Petropulos, *Politics and Statecraft*, pp. 72–3.

49. Sarafis, "'. . . na nomizomen emautous apelpismenous'," pp. 51–2; Photopoulos, *Oi Kotzampasedes*, p. 226 and pt 2, ch. 1.

50. Vaso Seirenidou, "O Ellenikos Kosmos stis Paramones tes Epanastases," in Veremes and Klapses, eds, *1821*, pp. 33–60; Petropulos, *Politics and Statecraft*, p. 72.

51. Sophia Laiou, "The Greek Revolution in the Morea according to the Description of an Ottoman Official," in Pizanias, ed. *The Greek Revolution of 1821: A European Event*, pp. 245–50.

52. IEEE, Sisinis Archive, Sisinis to Kalamogdartis, doc. 20510 (3), pp. 97ff.

Chapter 11. The Nation, Unbound

1. Tzakes, "Polemos kai Scheseis Exousias," pp. 155–8.

2. Phrantzes, *Epitome*, pp. 148–9; Gritsopoulos, *Istoria tes Gastounes*, vol. 1, pp. 588–600.

3. Lists of incidents in David Rodogno, *Against Massacre: Humanitarian Interventions in the Ottoman Empire, 1814–1914* (Princeton: Princeton University Press, 2011), chs 2–3; reported to the British authorities in Corfu from July 1821 and through 1822: National Archives (London), CO136 / 20, USII, pp. 47–54, 60–72ff; Evdoxios Doxiadis, "Neophotistoi and Apostates: Greece and Conversion in the Nineteenth Century," *Historein* 20:1 (2022); Vakalopoulos, *Tourkoi kai Ellenes Aichmalotoi*, pp. 39, 67–71, and passim; St. Clair, *That Greece Might Still Be Free*, ch. 4. The bishop's actions in Bory de Saint-Vincent, *Relation du Voyage*, vol. 1, pp. 211–13.

4. Kolokotronis lists his dealings with "Kyria simpethera mas Bobolina" (Our Madam in-law Bobolina) in December 1822: ELIA-MIET, Kolokotronis Archive, December 1822.

5. Phrantzes, *Epitome*, pp. 51–60; Ottoman reports of the arrangement with Kolokotronis in Ilicak, ed., *"Those Infidel Greeks": The Greek War of Independence*, vol. 1, p. 221 and n. 1.

6. Anagnostopoulos cited in Giannes Kokkonas, "Poliorkia kai Alose tes Tripolitsas: E Martyria tou Panagiote Anagnostopoulou gia tis Diapragmateuseis kai to 'Resalto,'" in Demetropoulos, Loukos, and Michaelares, *Opseis tes Epanastases*, pp. 37–8, 43; Phrantzes, *Epitome*, pp. 62–7; Tertsetes, *Theodorou Kolokotroni Apomnemoneumata*, pp. 86–92.

7. Vakalopoulos, *Tourkoi kai Ellenes Aichmalotoi*, pp. 42–3; Kokkonas, "Poliorkia," pp. 37–8; Ilicak, ed., *"Those Infidel Greeks": The Greek War of Independence*, vol. 1, p. 201 and n. 1.

8. Phrantzes, *Epitome*, pp. 53–4.

9. Phrantzes, *Epitome*, pp. 66–7 and n. 1; the fates of individual notables in Photopoulos, *Oi Kotzampasedes*, passim. Savrames, "Symvolai eis ten Istorian tes Dimitsanes," p. 296, blames these deaths on Muslims. The lone Jew, Kanon, in Kokkonas, "Poliorkia," p. 38.

10. Eirene Kalogeropoulou, "Zetemeta Anephodiasmou kai Peitharchias sto Poliorkoumeno Phrourio tes Patras (1821–1825): E Martyria tou Stratiotikou Dioikete Giousouf Mouchles Pasa," in Demetropoulos, Loukos, and Michaelaras, eds, *Opseis tes Epanastases*, pp. 45–53. The inability to mobilize forces in Erdem, "'Perfidious Albanians,'" with more archival detail in Ilicak, ed., "Introduction," in *"Those Infidel Greeks": The Greek War of Independence*, vol. 1, pp. 1–29; Aksan, *Ottoman Wars*, pp. 285, 288ff. The campaign against Ali and its relationship to the Greek uprising in Dennis Skiotis, "The Greek Revolution: Ali Pasha's Last Gamble," in Diamandouros et al, eds, *Hellenism and the First Greek War of Liberation*, pp. 97–109; decision to give priority to repressing Ali pasha rather than the Morean rebellion in Ilicak, ed., *"Those Infidel Greeks": The Greek War of Independence*, vol. 1, pp. 226–7, 249.

11. Erdem, "'Do not Think of the Greeks,'" pp. 68–71; Smiley, *From Slaves to Prisoners of War*, pp. 176–9.

12. Jan Schmidt, "The Adventures of an Ottoman Horseman," in Schmidt, ed., *The Joys of Philology: Studies in Ottoman Literature, History and Orientalism* (Istanbul: Isis, 2002), pp. 166–286.

13. ELIA-MIET, Kolokotronis Archive, 1.2.4.1-2 (1 August 1822); defeatism and desertion in Tertsetes, *Theodorou Kolokotroni Apomnemoneumata*, pp. 97–100, 105–6.

14. Photakos [Photios Chrysanthopoulos], *Apomnemoneumata* (Athens: P.D. Sakellariou, 1858), pp. 210–27.

15. Ilicak, ed., *"Those Infidel Greeks": The Greek War of Independence*, vol. 1, pp. 405, 415–16.

16. Photakos, *Apomnemoneumata*, pp. 236–7.

17. Schmidt, "The Adventures of an Ottoman Horseman," pp. 173, 237–40.

18. Tertsetes, *Theodorou Kolokotroni Apomnemoneumata*, pp. 117–21.

19. Photakos, *Apomnemoneumata*, p. 225.

20. Photakos, *Apomnemoneumata*, p. 239.

21. Tertsetes, *Theodorou Kolokotroni Apomnemoneumata*, p. 92.

22. Ozavci, "The Ottoman Imperial Gaze," pp. 222–37. Also Erdem, "'Perfidious Albanians'"; Ilicak, ed., "Introduction," in *"Those Infidel Greeks": The Greek War of Independence*, vol. 1, pp. 14–27, pp. 366–7, 430, and 650–3 (documents of 1821–6 which cite the problems of mobilizing men and supplies, and also the inactivity of the fleet in 1822 and 1823); Kalogeropoulou, "Zetemata Anephodiasmou," pp. 53–4. British agents reported on the Ottoman divisions: National Archives (London), CO136 / 27 US11, 1824, The Greek Revolution, Adams to Bathurst, 4 June 1824, pp. 18–21.

Chapter 12. The Nation, Limited

1. Koutzakiotes, "Mia Afanes Exegerse," pp. 64–5, 74; ears gathered in Photakos, *Vios Papa Phlesa*, p. 68.

2. Aksan, *Ottoman Wars*, p. 294; Erdem, "'Do not Think of the Greeks,'" pp. 69–70 describing the flood of body parts and slaves after particular campaigns and massacres; Ilicak, ed., *"Those*

Infidel Greeks": The Greek War of Independence, vol. 1, pp. 101, 102, 161, 167 and many more later examples; the heads and ears from Chios on pp. 297–300.

3. Photakos, *Apomnemoneumata*, pp. 249–50.

4. Tertsetes, *Theodorou Kolokotroni Apomnemoneumata*, pp. 59, 149, 166.

5. Nathanael Ioannou, *Euoïka* (Ermoupolis: N. Varvaresou, 1857), pp. 127–8; Ilicak, ed., *"Those Infidel Greeks": The Greek War of Independence*, vol. 1, pp. 77, 297–300, 321–2; Erdem, "'Do not Think of the Greeks,'" pp. 67–72.

6. Ilicak, ed., *"Those Infidel Greeks": The Greek War of Independence*, vol. 1, pp. 425, 611 (May 1823), 666 (November 1823), 368 and 611 (Ottoman objections to foreigners buying and selling slaves); GAK Athens, Vlachogiannes Collection, cat. 4, box 83: slaves and converts (unpaginated), copy of *Ephemeris tes Keverniseos*, 7 (1841), order of 1 / 13 March. The Ionian Senate banned the slave trade on 17 May 1823.

7. Schmidt, "Adventures of an Ottoman Horseman," pp. 237–40, 259–60.

8. Papagiorges, *Ta Kapakia*, pp. 121–2.

9. Chatzeioannou, *Ste Dine tes Chiakes Katastrofes*, pp. 45–70.

10. GAK Athens, Vlachogiannes Collection, cat. 4, box 83 (unpaginated), petition dated 10 June 1828 in Alexandria.

11. Tertsetes, *Theodorou Kolokotroni Apomnemoneumata*, p. 188.

12. Ilicak, ed., *"Those Infidel Greeks": The Greek War of Independence*, vol. 1, p. 249; the banning of the slave trade and slavery in Vakalopoulos, *Tourkoi kai Ellenes Aichmalotoi*, pp. 73–4.

13. Photakos, *Vios Papa Phlesa*, p. 38.

14. Vakalopoulos, *Tourkoi kai Ellenes Aichmalotoi*, pp. 83–5; the survey in GAK Athens, Vlachogiannes Collection, cat. 4, box 4, unpaginated list from c.1825; and another for Leonidi in 1828, box 83.

15. Bory de Saint-Vincent, *Relation du Voyage*, vol. 1, pp. 214–15.

16. As explained by the Hydriot Lazaros Kountouriotis to the Moreans in his letter of 29 March 1822: IEEE, Sisinis Archive, doc. 20422.

17. Vakalopoulos, *Tourkoi kai Ellenes Aichmalotoi*, pp. 39–45, 58–65, 65–77. The correspondence and negotiations are in ELIA-MIET, Stefanos Collection; reference in Ilicak, ed., *"Those Infidel Greeks": The Greek War of Independence*, vol. 1, p. 201.

18. Vakalopoulos, *Tourkoi kai Ellenes Aichmalotoi*, pp. 2, 29–322, 47–8 and passim.

19. Vakalopoulos, *Tourkoi kai Ellenes Aichmalotoi*, pp. 51–2; GAK Athens, Vlachogiannes Collection, cat. 4, box 83 (unpaginated), and clipping from *Chronos*, 26 September 1873.

20. Pylia, "Les Notables Moréotes," pp. 25–7; GAK Athens, Vlachogiannes Collection, cat. 3, Palamedes Papers, f.1a-, b, and g.

21. IEEE, Sisinis Archive, doc. 20510, p. 17.

22. Papageorgiou, "To Archeio Sisine," p. 213–14; Gritsopoulos, *Istoria tes Gastounes*, vol. 2, pp. 16–17.

23. Milligen, *Memoirs of the Affairs of Greece*, p. 186.

24. Vakalopoulos, *Tourkoi kai Ellenes Aichmalotoi*, p. 52 n. 1.

25. National Archives (London), CO136 / 20, eyewitness account, pp. 60–72.

26. GAK Athens, Vlachogiannes Collection, cat. 4, box 83 (unpaginated), letter of 1828 to the Temporary Commissioner of Laconia, apparently from a local elder or priest; Milligen, *Memoirs of the Affairs of Greece*, p. 217.

27. Vakalopoulos, *Tourkoi kai Ellenes Aichmalotoi*, p.49; GAK Athens, Vlachogiannes Collection, cat. 4, box 83 (unpaginated); letter of English officer of 24 June 1824, asking whether his purchase of a slave was legal.

28. Katsikas and Dimitriades, "Muslim Converts to Orthodox Christianity," pp. 307–8; Gritsopoulos, *Istoria tes Gastounes*, vol. 1, pp. 466–9.

29. Ilicak, ed., *"Those Infidel Greeks": The Greek War of Independence*, vol. 1, pp. 485 (December 1822), 751; Antones Diadakes, "Mia Pole se Kinese: Oi Plythysmiakes Metavoles sten Pole tou Mesosongiou kata ten Epanastase tou 1821," in Demeteropoulos, Loukos, and Michaelaras, eds, *Opseis tes Epanastases*, pp. 148–51.

30. Katsikas and Dimitriades, "Muslim Converts to Orthodox Christianity," pp. 309–10; Vakalopoulos, *Tourkoi kai Ellenes Aichmalotoi*, p. 21.

31. Vakalopoulos, *Tourkoi kai Ellenes Aichmalotoi*, pp. 11–13, 21, with the debate over conversion on pp. 52–8; Vogli, "'Ellenes to Genos,'" pp. 45ff.

32. GAK Athens, Vlachogiannes Collection, cat. 4, box 83 (unpaginated), with a large group of petitions dating as late as 1851, others to the 1860s; Katsikas and Dimitriades, "Muslim Converts to Orthodox Christianity," pp. 309–11; Gritsopoulos, "Statistikai Eidiseis," p. 440.

33. Anne Couderc, "Religion et Identité Nationale en Grèce pendant la Révolution d'Indépendance (1821–1832): Le Creuset Ottoman et l'Influence Occidentale," in Sylvie Gangloff, ed., *La Perception de l'Héritage Ottoman dans les Balkans* (Paris: L'Harmattan, 2005), p. 24; Vogli, "'Ellenes to Genos,'" esp. pp. 1–59.

34. Daskalakes, *E Topikoi Organismoi*, pp. 70–71.

35. See this excellent study of the constitutions: Xenofon I. Kontiades, *Oi peripetiodes Istoria ton Epanastatikon Syntagmaton tou 1821: E Themeliotike Stigme tes Ellenikes Politeias* (Athens: Kastaniotes, 2021). Overview in Spyros Vlachopoulos, "Ta Syntagmata tes Epanastases," in Veremes and Klapses, eds, *1821*, pp. 279–97.

36. Ilicak, ed., "Introduction," in *"Those Infidel Greeks": The Greek War of Independence*, vol. 1, pp. 6–7, and in very many of the documents that follow, esp. the rescript on amnesty on pp.143–4; Ayvalik on p. 833, Naousa on p. 852; Diadakes, "Mia Pole se Kinese," pp. 148–51.

37. Kokkonas, "Poliorkia kai Alose," p. 42.

38. Photakos, *Apomnemoneumata*, pp. 266–7.

39. IEEE, Sisinis Archive, doc. 20510, p. 17.

40. On Ottoman awareness of revolutions and liberalism, Karabiçak, "Ottoman Attempts to Define the Rebels during the Greek War of Independence," *Studia Islamica*, 114 (2020), pp. 68–106; on Ottoman befuddlement about the nation, Ilicak, ed. "Introduction," in *"Those Infidel Greeks": The Greek War of Independence*, vol. 1, pp. 4ff.

41. Ilicak, ed., *"Those Infidel Greeks": The Greek War of Independence*, vol. 1, pp. 34, 194, 401, 457.

42. Ilicak, in *"Those Infidel Greeks": The Greek War of Independence*, translates "Rum" as "Greek," but in some places the Turkish term is "Yunan" and confusing to the Ottomans. My thanks to Ilicak for clarifying.

43. Kokkonas, "Poliorkia kai Alosi," pp. 25–34.

44. Papagiorges, *Ta Kapakia*: the exchange on p. 239; the slaughter on p. 237, and more slaughter on pp. 240–43.

45. Vakalopoulos, *Tourkoi kai Ellenes Aichmalotoi*, pp. 46–7.

46. Sakul, "The Ottoman Peloponnese," p. 136.

47. Abazis's overtures to the Morean notables of November 1821 in IEEE, Sisinis Archive, doc. 20414; Papagiorges, *Ta Kapakia*, pp. 85–6; Vakalopoulos, *Tourkoi kai Ellenes Aichmalotoi*, pp. 26, 51–2. Kolokotronis's subsequent efforts to recruit Muslim Albanians failed: Erdem, "'Perfidious Albanians,'" pp. 224–5; more on Abazis in Ilicak, ed., *"Those Greek Infidels": The Greek War of Independence*, in "Introduction," vol. 1, pp. 16–24, and 516 (Porte to governor of Roumeli, January 1823), 751.

Chapter 13. Republics of the Privileged

1. Sarafis, "'. . . na nomizomen emautous apelpismenous,'" pp. 55–6.

2. Tzakes, "Polemos kai Scheseis Exousias," pp. 168ff; family ties among the notables in Pylia, "Les Notables Moréotes"; the localism of the eparchs in Daskalakes, *Oi Topikoi Organismoi*, pp. 20–32; McGrew, *Land and Revolution*, pp. 57ff.

3. Anast. Dimitrakopoulos, "To Epanastatiko Naftiko," in Veremes and Klapses, eds, *1821*, p. 151.

4. IEEE, Sisinis Archive, doc. 20422, 29 March 1822, Kountouriotis to the Higher Administration (the government).

5. Daskalakes, *Oi Topikoi Organismoi*, pp. 56–7.

6. Daskalakes, *Oi Topikoi Organismoi*, p. 147; and Tassos Anastassiadis, *La Réforme Orthodoxe: Église, État et Société en Grèce à l'Époque de la Confessionalisation post-Ottomane (1833–1840)* (Athens: Éditions EFA, 2021), chs 1, 3–4.

7. Philip Sherard, "Church, State, and the Greek War of Independence," in Clogg, ed., *The Struggle for Greek Independence*, pp. 182–99; Vlachopoulos, "Ta Syntagmata tes Epanastases," pp. 182–3.

8. Vlachopoulos, "Ta Syntagmata tes Epanastases," pp. 181–2; Petropulos, *Politics and Statecraft*, pp. 20–21.

9. Michalis Sotiropoulos, *Liberalism after the Revolution: The Intellectual Foundations of the Greek State, c.1830–1880* (Cambridge: Cambridge University Press, 2022). Maurizio Isabella makes constitutionalism a central framework in his comparisons of Mediterranean (plus Portuguese) revolutions: *Southern Europe in the Age of Revolutions* (Princeton: Princeton University Press, 2023).

10. Pylia makes the point that elections in 1822 were self-appointments, as they had been in Ottoman times: "Les Notables Moréotes," pp. 63–7. The self-appointment of the notables in Daskalakes, *Oi Topikoi Organismoi*, pp. 29, 41, 49, and 119. The society's promise to respect the primacy of the notables in Karabiçak, "Local Patriots," pp. 352–3.The position of Sisinis confirmed by multiple notables and would-be Greek authorities, in IEEE, Sisinis Archive, e.g., Mavromichalis in June 1823 (doc. 20388 from June 1823), Dimitris Ypsilantis in October 1821 (doc. 20413).

11. IEEE, Sisinis Archive, docs 20836 from 21 March 1823 and 20389 from 15 February 1824; and from 25 January 1824 in 20510 (6) which declares Sisinis "our leader" in charge of the "local system." Avgerinos proclaimed leader around Pyrgos in ELIA-MIET, Kolokotronis Archive, 1.3.25.1-4 (March 1824).

12. Rotzokos, *Epanastase kai Emphylios*, pp. 25ff.

13. *Archeion Kanellou Delegianne*, docs 28ff for 1822–3; promissory notes were given to Sisinis throughout the 1820s, e.g., IEEE, Sisinis Archive, docs 20422–20426, 10457–10471; Sisinis's claims of poverty in doc. 20510, pp. 97–111; collections by underlings in doc. 20476 for 1823. The 1822 tax farm agreements and the government's very notional budgets in Andreas M. Andreades, *Istoria ton Ethnikon Daneion* (Athens: Karavias, 1904), pp. 7–10.

14. IEEE, Sisinis Archive, doc. 20450 of November 1823.

15. For example, in June 1821, IEEE, Sisinis Archive, docs 20417, 20990–20391; Tertsetes, *Theodorou Kolokotroni Apomnemoneumata*, pp. 101–2, 121.

16. Kountouriotis's appeal to pay the fleet in IEEE, Sisinis Archive, doc. 20422, 29 March 1822; reports of Sisinis's men around Tripolitsa in doc. 20447; and quite a few vouchers for supplies sent to Patras and Missolonghi.

17. As did Deliyannis: *Archeion Kanellou Delegianne*, docs 28ff. The Sisinis archive is mainly about these arrangements of campaigns and supplies. He and his sons delivered final tallies in the early 1830s: IEEE, Sisinis Archive, doc. 20437 (payments and interest rates in 1822), doc. 50510, p. 154 (bill in 1824), doc. 20428 (catalogue of expenses owed to Sisinis family, April 1833), doc. 20481 (1821–8), and docs 20404–20405 on the supplying of the fleet; still others in doc. 20510 (4), pp. 145–52.

18. IEEE, Sisinis Archive, doc. 20510, Sisinis complaining of the government's extortion, pp. 107 and 111; an overview in McGrew, *Land and Revolution*, pp. 60–62.

19. E.g. Deliyannis in 1822 in *Archeion Kanellou Delegianne*, docs 35, 36, 38 and many more; Sisinis given priority in purchase of Ottoman lands and tax farms in IEEE, Sisinis Archive, doc. 20437 of March 1822; McGrew, *Land and Revolution*, pp. 60–61.

20. Tzakes, "Polemos kai Schesis Exousias," pp. 168–9; the range of taxes in *Archeion Kanellou Delegianne*, doc. 56 (August 1823); the export of Corinthian grapes and their value for 1823 and 1824 in IEEE, Sisinis Archive, doc. 20449; the purchase and revenue from Ottoman taxes and tariffs for 1824 in doc. 20454, and for 1823 in 20510 (3), p. 86. New taxes in McGrew, *Land and Revolution*, pp. 61–2, 66–7.

21. ELIA-MIET, Kolokotronis Archive, 1.3.23.1: report of Panos Kolokotronis to his father on collections around Pyrgos and Fanari (Olympia) in early 1823.

22. IEEE, Sisinis Archive, doc. 20510 (4), pp. 266ff and 20510 (7). The Deliyannis clan kept similar records: *Archeion Kanellou Delegianne*, for example doc. 56.

23. Rotzokos, *Epanastase kai Emphylios*, pp. 121–2.

24. The hagiography of Sisinis is by G. Gazi in GAK Athens, Vlachogiannes Collection, cat. 4, 73; the unflattering is George Finlay, *A History of Greece* (Oxford: Clarendon, 1877), vol. 6, pp. 335–6. Forms of address of Sisinis in IEEE, Sisinis Archive, for 1821–4, esp. doc. 20399; of Deliyannis in *Archeion Kanellou Delegianne*, docs for 1821–23, e.g. doc. 71.

25. Rotzokos, *Epanastase kai Emphylios*, pp. 97–8; Tertsetes, *Theodorou Kolokotroni Apomnemoneumata*, p. 123.

26. Daskalakes, *Oi Topikoi Organismoi*, pp. 109, 116, 136–9.

27. Daskalakes, *Oi Topikoi Organismoi*, pp. 109, 116–19; St. Clair, *That Greece Might Still Be Free*, pp. 43–5; Vlachogiannes, *Stratiotike Diktatoria*, pp. 16–18; Dialla, *E Rosike Autokratoria*, p. 262.

28. Papagiorges, *Ta Kapakia*, pp. 58–9.

29. Petropulos, *Politics and Statecraft*, p. 77; Ypsilantis's claim to be the leader of the Revolution in June 1821 in IEEE, Sisinis Archive, doc. 20409; his confirmation of Sisinis as the only representative of his province in doc. 20413 of October 1821; Kolokotronis's rescue of notables in Tertsetes, *Theodorou Kolokotroni Apomnemoneumata*, pp. 84–5, 93–4; their fear of being attacked on pp. 104–5. The appearance and disappearance of Dimitris Ypsilantis in Vakalopoulos, *Tourkoi kai Ellenes Aichmalotoi*, pp. 22, 44–5, 67–71. Ypsilantis's tensions with the notables and his appeals to "the people" in Daskalakes, *Oi Topikoi Organismoi*, pp. 19, 33–7, 102–5; more attempts to murder the notables on pp. 35–6 and 39; Ypsilantis's loss of influence on pp. 57, 124; soldiers expecting his brother Alexander on p. 202; delegates to the assemblies traveling with armed guards on p. 116. More on the clash of notables with Ypsilantis in Nikolaos Ath. Misolides, "Oi Emphylioi Polemoi ston Agona tes Anexatresias ton Ellenon, 1823–1825," in Veremes and Klapses, eds, *1821*, pp. 232–5.

30. A concise overview in English in Petropulos, *Politics and Statecraft*, pp. 83–4; in Greek in Misolides, "Oi Emphylioi Polemoi," pp. 238–44; Iakovos Michaelides, *Emphylies Diamaches ston Agona tou 1821* (Athens: Kathemerines Ekdoseis, 2019); with an emphasis on the analytic issues in Rotzokos, *Epanastase kai Emphylios*.

31. Frankly described in Tertsetes, *Theodorou Kolokotroni Apomnemoneumata*, pp. 124–36.

32. IEEE, Sisinis Archive, doc. 20510, pp. 107 (Philadelphia), 111ff, and doc. 20510 (6), p. 302 (raids by other notables).

33. *Archeion Kanellou Delegianne*, docs 56, 58–61, 64; Rotzokos, *Epanastase kai Emphylios*, pp. 48–9.

34. Petropulos, *Politics and Statecraft*, pp. 80ff.

35. Rotzokos, *Epanastase kai Emphylios*, pp. 45–6 and passim.

Chapter 14. The Second Revolution, 1824

1. Dialla, *E Rossiki Autokratoria*, p. 65.

2. Prousis, *Russian Society*; Lucien Frary, "Slaves of the Sultan: Russian Ransoming of Christian Captives during the Greek Revolution, 1821–1830," in Frary and Mara Kozelsky, eds, *Russian–Ottoman Borderlands: The Eastern Question Reconsidered* (Madison: University of Wisconsin Press, 2014), pp. 108–17.

3. Prousis, *Russian Society*, ch. 6.

4. St. Clair, *That Greece Might Still Be Free*, pp. 280ff and ch. 24.

5. Alexandre Massé, "French Consuls and Philhellenism in the 1820s: Official Positions and Personal Sentiments," *Byzantine and Modern Greek Studies*, 41:1 (April 2017), pp. 103–18; St. Clair, *That Greece Might Still Be Free*, passim.

6. Tertsetes, *Theodorou Kolokotroni Apomnemoneumata*, p. 176.

7. Massé, "French Consuls," p. 108. Detailed in St. Clair, *That Greece Might Still Be Free*, esp. ch. 10.

8. Daskalakes, *Oi Topikoi Organismoi*, pp. 161–3.

9. St. Clair, *That Greece Might Still Be Free*, chs 3, 5 and passim; the massacres as victories on p. 24.

10. John A. Levandis, *The Greek Foreign Debt and the Great Powers, 1821–1898* (New York: Columbia University Press, 1944), pp. 13–14.

11. Marc Flandreau and Juan H. Flores, "Bonds and Brands: Foundations of Sovereign Debt Markets, 1820–1830," *Journal of Economic History*, 69:3 (September 2009), pp. 646–84; in connection with Greece, Andreades, *Istoria ton Ethnikon Daneion*, pt 1, pp. 15–19 and ch. 1; Schönhärl, *European Investment in Greece*, pp. 31ff; Levandis, *The Greek Foreign Debt*, ch. 1.

12. Damian Clavel, "What's in a Fraud? The Many Worlds of Gregor MacGregor, 1817–1824," *Enterprise and Society*, 22:4 (December 2021), pp. 997–1036.

13. Lieven to Nesselrode in 1825 in *Vneshniaia Politika Rossii*, ser. 2, vol. 6 (14), pp. 241–2.

14. The calculation of the net loan in Andreades, *Istoria ton Ethnikon Daneion*, pt 1, pp. 17–19; Levandis, *The Greek Foreign Debt*, pp. 14–15, the promotion on pp. 12–13; Schönhärl, *European Investment in Greece*, pp. 31–3.

15. McGrew, *Land and Revolution*, pp. 74–5.

16. Schönhärl, *European Investment in Greece*, pp. 32–3, 60.

17. St. Clair, *That Greece Might Still Be Free*, pp. 228–32; Vlachogiannes, *Stratiotike Diktatoria*, p. 13.

18. Papagiorges, *Ta Kapakia*, pp. 37–43.

19. Beaton, *Byron's War*, p. 73.

20. Beaton, *Byron's War*, pp. 116ff.

21. An argument made very well in Beaton, *Byron's War*, e.g. on pp. 130–39, while St. Clair emphasizes the spirit of regeneration in *That Greece Might Still Be Free*.

22. Papagiorges, *Ta Kapakia*, pp. 167–8, with details on the funds in Beaton, *Byron's War*, pp. 200–201 and St. Clair, *That Greece Might Still Be Free*.

23. Beaton, *Byron's War*, pp. 177, 237.

24. National Archives (London), CO136 / 27, Humphreys to Adam, 20 February 1824.

25. National Archives (London), CO136 / 27, Adam to Horton, 15 April 1824 (on the loan); and Humphreys in Missolonghi to Adam, 20 February 1824 (on Byron); Beaton, *Byron's War*, pp. 200–201, 214–15.

26. Beaton, *Byron's War*, pp. 159–60, 194, 197–8, 221.

27. Beaton, *Byron's War*, p. 200.

28. Warnings that the money was being sent to the mainland in National Archives (London), CO136 / 22, Adam's despatches, p. 152, 15 May 1824; CO136 / 27, Adam correspondence; p. 302, copy of Barff's intercepted letter of 18 July 1824.

29. National Archives (London), CO136 / 22, p. 176, 5 June 1824; St. Clair, *That Greece Might Still Be Free*, ch. 22.

30. The details on the handovers and sums in St. Clair, *That Greece Might Still Be Free*, chs 18, 22; Beaton, *Byron's War*, pp. 268–71.

31. Diadakes, "Mia Pole se Kinesi," pp. 127–8; massacres in Vakalopoulos, *Tourkoi kai Ellenes Aichmalotoi*, pp. 17–27 and 71 n. 2.

32. The demographic mix in Diadakes, "Mia Pole se Kinese," pp. 123–8; the warlord politics in Papagiorges, *Ta Kapakia*, ch. 2.

33. Petropulos, *Politics and Statecraft*, pp. 72–3. Tzakis outlines their ever-changing alliances of the period 1821–25 in "From Locality to Nation-State Loyalty."

34. Vlachogiannes, *Stratiotike Diktatoria*, pp. 26ff; on Androutsos, pp. 18ff.

35. GAK Athens, Sisinis Archive, doc. 20.435. Varnakiotis hired some Zakynthian armed men for a looting expedition around Gastouni.

36. Levandis, *The Greek Foreign Debt*, p. 6.

37. The point, I think, of Tzakis, "From Locality to Nation-State Loyalty," and explicit in Papagiorges, *Ta Kapakia*, ch. 2 and esp. pp. 145–8.

38. National Archives (London), CO136 / 27, Adam correspondence, p. 35; aside from Karaiskakis and Androutsos, see the men working with the Ottomans catalogued in Petropulos, *Politics and Statecraft*, p. 113, and Petropulos, "Forms of Collaboration with the Enemy during the First Greek War of Liberation", in Diamandouros, et al, eds, *Hellenism and the First Greek War of Liberation*, pp.131–43; Papagiorges, *Ta Kapakia*, passim in ch. 2.

39. His arrangements with the Ottomans were extensive and elaborate, as recently published sources show: Ilicak, ed., *"Those Infidel Greeks": The Greek War of Independence*, vol. 1, pp. 489–90, 797; Petropulos, *Politics and Statecraft*, p. 93.

40. Papagiorges, *Ta Kapakia*, pp. 237, 240–3.

41. GAK Athens, Vlachogiannes Collection, cat. 6, box 2, file 5.

42. Rotzokos, *Epanastase kai Emphylios*.

43. Rotzokos, *Epanastase kai Emphylios*, pp. 145–6; Papagiorges, *Ta Kapakia*, pp. 170–71.

44. Calls to mercenaries in *Archeion Kanellou Delegianne*, doc. 89 (November 1824) and their arrival in docs 88, 90, 108; the rest in GAK Athens, Vlachogiannes Collection, cat. 6, box 2, file 7, docs 502–508; the mobilization in greater detail in Papagiorges, *Ta Kapakia*, pp. 167–76, 179–88.

45. St. Clair, *That Greece Might Still Be Free*, p. 232.

46. Petropulos, *Politics and Statecraft*, pp. 94–5; Gritsopoulos, *Istoria tes Gastounes*, vol. 1, pp. 608–10; Rotzokos, *Epanastase kai Emphylios*, p. 176. The Souliot guard in GAK Athens, Vlachogiannes Collection, cat. 6, box 2, file 6, docs 508–29, and the clash of Souliots on different sides in *Archeion Kanellou Delegianne*, doc. 108 (December 1824); the guards going over to Kolettis in Papagiorges, *Ta Kapakia*, pp. 185–6.

47. GAK Athens, Vlachogiannes Collection, cat. 6, box 2, file 4, doc. 417. Rotzokos, *Epanastase kai Emphylios*, pp. 158, 193–5.

48. GAK Athens, Vlachogiannes Collection, cat. 6, box 2, file 5, doc. 415; Rotzokos, *Epanastase kai Emphylios*, pp. 177–8.

49. Rotzokos, *Epanastase kai Emphylios*, pp. 137–44, 186–93.

50. GAK Athens, cat. 3, box 73 (treasons, bootlegging); file 2 is titled "Petrobey's Treason."

51. Vlachogiannes, *Stratiotike Diktatoria*, p. 8.

52. *Archeion Kanellou Delegianne*, docs for 1827, quote in doc. 207.

53. The second loan in Andreades, *Istoria ton Ethnikon Daneion*, pt 1, ch. 2; Schönhärl, *European Investment in Greece*, pp. 35–40, 60; Levandis, *The Greek Foreign Debt*, pp. 17ff; St. Clair, *That Greece Might Still Be Free*, ch. 22.

54. Details on the Egyptian preparations in National Archives (London), CO136 / 27, Adam despatches, pp. 89ff, 4 March 1824.

Chapter 15. The Time of Ibrahim

1. Khaled Fahmy, *All the Pasha's Men: Mehmed Ali, his Army and the Making of Modern Egypt* (Cairo: American University in Cairo, 2004), pp. 1–92.

2. Georges Douin, *Mission Militaire française auprès de Mohamed Aly (Correspondance des Generaux Belliard et Boyer)* (Cairo: Societé Royale de Géographie s'Egypte, 1923), introduction

and an extended report from Boyer in Cairo to commanders in France on pp. 68–77. Druze recruitments in National Archives (London), CO136 / 22, USII, 1824, vol. 1, Sir F. Adam papers, p. 89: report from Henry Salt in Cairo, 4 March 1824. The military reforms in Fahmy, *All the Pasha's Men*, pp. 82–90.

3. Spyros D. Loukatos, "Prospatheiai Ellenoegyptiakes Symmacheias kata ton Tourkon kata to Meson tes Ellenikes Ethnegersias," *Peloponnesiaka*, 7 (1969–70), pp. 189–90; Douin, *Mission Militaire Française*, introduction and pp. 68–9.

4. Douin, *Mission Militaire Française*, pp. x–xix, 63–4, 129.

5. Douin, *Mission Militaire Française*, p. 43; Spyridon G. Ploumidis, "E Ekstrateia tou Impraem sten Ellada, 1825–1828," in Veremes and Klapses, eds, *1821*, pp. 253–78; Cretan vendettas in Giannes Spyropoulos, "Ventetes 'Yper Pisteos kai Patridos?' Endochristianike Via kai Politike sta Sfakia tis Paramones tou 1821," Demeteropoulos, Loukos, and Michaelaras, eds, *Opseis tes Epanastases*, pp. 107–22; St. Clair, *That Greece Might Still Be Free*, ch. 23.

6. Loukatos, "Prospatheiai Ellenoegyptiakes Symmachias," pp. 193–5.

7. The landing and first month of campaigning in Michael V. Sakellariou, *E Apovase tou Impraem sten Peloponneso: Katalytes gia ten Apodiorganose tes Ellenikes Epanastases (24 Fevrouariou—23 Martiou 1825)* (Heraklion: University of Crete, 2012); the whole campaign in Konstantinos L. Kotsonis, *O Impraem sten Peloponneso* (Athens: Etaireia Peloponnesiakon Spoudon, 1999).

8. Tertsetes, *Theodorou Kolokotroni Apomnemoneumata*, pp. 164–5, 185–6.

9. Intercepted Ottoman correspondence in Bibliothèque de Genève, Collection Eynard, MS SUPPL.1884 / 2, f.303; National Archives (London), CO136 / 37, USII–Greek Revolution–1826, p. 242; Sakellariou, *E Apovase tou Impraem*, p. 129 and ch. 7 passim.

10. Sakellariou, *E Apovase tou Impraem*, ch. 8; Papagiorges, *Ta Kapakia*, pp. 188ff.

11. Photakos, *Vios Papa Phlesa*, p. 60; the army in Fahmy, *All the Pasha's Men*, pp. 55–60.

12. Photakos, *Vios Papa Phlesa*, pp. 52ff; Ilicak, ed., *"Those Infidel Greeks": The Greek War of Independence*, vol. 1, pp. 835–44.

13. Douin, *Mission Militaire Française*, pp. 43–8.

14. Aksan, *Ottoman Wars*, pp. 294, 304.

15. Photakos, *Vios Papa Phlessa*, pp. 52–3.

16. Tertsetes, *Theodorou Kolokotroni Apomnemoneumata*, pp. 137–63; Ilicak, ed., *"Those Infidel Greeks": The Greek War of Independence*, vol. 1, pp. 835–44, 869.

17. GAK Athens, Vlachogiannes Collection, cat. 4, box 83 (unpaginated).

18. Gritsopoulos, *Istoria tes Gastounes*, vol. 1, pp. 610–19.

19. British consul-general Salt in Alexandria, 12 August 1826, in Prousis, *British Consular Reports*.

20. GAK Athens, Vlachogiannes, cat. 4, box 83 (unpaginated).

21. Anastasios G. Politis, *O Ellenismos kai e Neotera Egyptos* (Alexandria and Athens: Grammata, 1928), vol. 1, pp. 166–202; Loukatos, "Prospatheiai Ellenoegyptiakes Symmachias," pp. 192–3.

22. Douin, *Mission Militaire Française*, p. 98.

23. Douin, *Mission Militaire Française*, Boyer to Belliard, 10 August 1825, pp. 53–9, 93–4, 104; Petrobey's negotiations and Kolokotronis's wrath in Tertsetes, *Theodorou Kolokotroni Apomnemoneumata*, p. 157, and many more submissions on pp. 137–8, 178–9, 186–7, 191.

24. Petropulos, "Forms of Collaboration," p. 138.

Chapter 16. Europe Mobilizes

1. Summed up in Bibliothèque de Genève, Collection Eynard, Correspondance relative à la Grèce, MS SUPPL.1884 / 1, f.3, 10 June 1827.

2. Beaton, *Byron's War*, pp. 125ff; Schönhärl, *European Investment in Greece*, pp. 70–71, 80.

3. The organization and sums in Bibliothèque de Genève, Collection Eynard, MS SUPPL.1884 / 2, ff.63–5 and passim; the Duke of Orléans in ff.331–332; Petrobey and Kolokotronis correspondence in ff.160–161, 308–309; MS SUPPL 1888, ff.388–392 for 1826, and the officers passim. Good overview in Ghervas, *Réinventer la Tradition*, pp. 385ff; details in Schönhärl, *European Investment in Greece*, pp. 61–3.

4. Bibliothèque de Genève, Collection Eynard, MS SUPPL.1870, ff.279ff.

5. Beaton, *Byron's War*, p. 224.

6. Tertsetes, *Theodorou Kolokotroni Apomnemoneumata*, pp. 173–5.

7. Bibliothèque de Genève, Collection Eynard, Correspondance relative à la Grèce, MS SUPPL.1884 / 1, f.3, Eynard to Sir James Macintosh MP, 10 June 1827; and MS SUPPL. 1884 / 2, f.161.

8. British Library, Archive and Manuscripts, add ms 36544, Church Papers, vol. II, pp. 35ff.

9. Bibliothéque de Genève, Collection Eynard, MS SUPPL.1884 / 2, f.161.

10. Le vicompte de Chateaubriand, *Note sur la Grèce* (Paris: Le Normant Père, 1825), pp. 7–8.

11. The transition to religion was accomplished by 1826 according to Frédérique Tabaki-Iona, "Philhellénisme Religieux et Mobilization des Français pendant la Révolution Grecque de 1821–1827," *Mots. Les langues du politique*, 79 (2005), pp. 52–4.

12. St. Clair, *That Greece Might Still Be Free*, p. 103.

13. Bibliothèque de Genève, Collection Eynard, MS SUPPL.1884 / 2, ff.268–269; Tabaki-Iona, "Philhellénisme Religieux"; John Hartley, *Researches in Greece and the Levant* (London: Seeley and Sons, 1831), pp. 31ff.

14. The battle against missionaries in Lucien Frary, *Russia and the Making of Modern Greek Identity, 1821–1844* (Oxford: Oxford University Press, 2015).

15. F. Rosen, *Bentham, Byron, and Greece* (Oxford: Clarendon Press, 1992), pp.85ff.

16. François Pouqueville, *Histoire de la Régénération de la Grèce, Comprenant le Précis des Évènements depuis 1740 jusqu'en 1824* (Paris: Firmin Didot, 1824), 4 vols. Cases in Dialla, *E Rosike Autrokratoria*, pt 3, ch. 2.

17. As noted by Eynard: Bibliothèque de Genève, Collection Eynard, MS SUPPL.1884 / 1, f.3, Eynard to Macinstosh, 10 June 1827.

18. Nina Athanassoglou-Kallmyer, *French Images of the Greek War of Independence, 1821–1830* (New Haven: Yale University Press, 1989), p. 13.

19. Athanassoglou-Kallmyer, *French Images*, pp. 41ff, 104.

20. Athanassoglou-Kallmyer, *French Images*, ch. 2 and pp. 88ff.

21. Bibliothèque de Genève, Collection Eynard, MS SUPPL.1884 / 2, f.254.

22. Massé, "French Consuls."

23. Athanassoglou-Kallmyer, *French Images*, p. 17; *Vneshniaia Politika Rossii*, ser. 2, vol. 4, p. 257, Capo d'Istria to Alexander, 9 / 21 August 1821.

24. Rodogno, *Against Massacre*, pp. 79ff; Canning in *Vneshniaia Politika Rossii*, ser. 2, vol. 6 (14), pp. 605ff and Russian statements throughout the same volume.

25. *Vneshniaia Politika Rossii*, ser. 2, vol. 4, p. 205, Stroganov to government of Turkey, 6 / 18 July 1821.

26. St. Clair, *That Greece Might Still Be Free*, ch. 15.

27. *Vneshniaia Politika Rossii*, ser. 2, vol. 6 (14), p. 493, Nesselrode to ambassador in Paris, May 1826.

28. Dialla, "Imperial Rhetoric and Revolutionary Practice," p. 7.

29. Airapetov, *Istoriia Vneshenei Politiki*, vol. 2.

30. A. V. Fadeev, *Rossiia i Vostochnyi Krizis 20-kh godov XIX veka* (Moscow: Nauka, 1958), ch. 2; Schroeder, *The Transformation of European Politics*, pp. 638–4.

31. Fadeev, *Rossiia i Vostochnyi Krizis*, p. 96; the advice to Alexander in 1825 is in many places in *Vneshniaia Politika Rossii*, ser. 2, vol. 6 (14).

32. St. Clair, *That Greece Might Still Be Free*, p. 316; Beaton, *Byron's War*, p. 155.

33. For example, Nesselrode and Stroganov to Nicholas in early 1826 in *Vneshniaia Politika Rossii*, ser. 2, vol. 6 (14), pp. 347–51 and 393–400.

34. Prousis, *British Consular Reports*, p. 45; Schroeder, *The Transformation of European Politics*, p. 644; Airapetov, *Istoriia Vneshnei Politiki*, vol. 2, pp. 11–12; Frary, *Russia and the Making of Modern Greek Identity*, p. 231.

35. Well summarized in Eric Weitz, *A World Divided: The Global Struggle for Human Rights in the Age of Nation-States* (Princeton: Princeton University Press, 2019), pp. 62–3; Russian and British statements in *Vneshniaia Politika Rossii*, ser. 2, vol. 6 (14), pp. 605, recounting Canning's conversations with the Russian ambassador. Quote in Ozavci, "The Ottoman Imperial Gaze," n. 66.

36. Piracy as the primary cause of allied intervention in Erik de Lange, "Navigating the Greek Revolution before Navarino: Imperial Interventions in Aegean Waters, 1821–1827," *Journal of Modern European History*, 21:2 (2023), pp. 181–98. Aksan, *Ottoman Wars*. Smiley implies the same in "War without War: The Battle of Navarino, the Ottoman Empire, and the Pacific Blockade," *Journal of the History of International Law*, 18:1 (2016), pp. 42–69.

37. Prousis, *British Consular Reports*, pp. 34–5; Airapetov, *Istoriia Vneshnei Politiki*, vol. 2, p. 67, Russian concerns on p. 66. British reports on the Ionian Islands in National Archives (London), CO136 / 23, USII, Adam correspondence, 1824, pp. 422–3.

38. Massé, "French Consuls," p. 103.

39. Douin, *Mission Militaire Française*, pp. 125–8; Egyptian motives in Fahmy, *All the Pasha's Men*, pp. 41, 49.

40. National Archives (London), CO136 / 24, Ionian Islands, Adam papers, 1824, September–December, passim, where British authorities seek agreements with one or another Greek government.

41. Finance minister Kankrin to foreign minister Nesselrode, July (August New Style) 1825, *Vneshniaia Politika Rossii*, ser. 2, vol. 6 (14), p. 221.

42. Fadeev, *Rossiia i Vostochnyi Krizis*, pp. 136–9.

43. Cf Schroeder, *The Transformation of European Politics*, pp. 647–9, where the Protocol is seen as a British defeat.

44. National Archives (London), CO136 / 37: USII, Greek Revolution, 1826, pp. 29–32, 43ff; Schroeder, *The Transformation of European Politics*, p. 638; *Vneshniaia Politika Rossii*, ser. 2, vol. 6 (14), pp. 191–2.

45. Mehmed Ali's reasoning about Greek independence in Fahmy, *All the Pasha's Men*, pp. 59–60; French communications with Mehmed Ali in Douin, *Mission Militaire Française*, pp. xxv–vi, 115–25 (Belliard in Paris to Boyer in Cairo, February–May 1826), pp. 100–107 (visions of Egyptian hegemony); unofficial French advice in Loukatos, "Prospatheiai Ellenoegyptiakis Symmachias"; French strategy in Anna Karakatsouli, "French Involvement in the Greek War of Independence," *Historein*, 20:1 (2022).

46. Douin, *Mission Militaire Française*, pp. 45 (departure of officers), 84 (French shipyards); more on Boyer in Fahmy, *All the Pasha's Men*, pp. 79–81.

47. *Vneshniaia Politika Rossii*, ser. 2, vol. 7 (15), pp. 134–6; Couderc, "Réligion et Identité Nationale," pp. 37–8.

48. Couderc, "Réligion et Identité Nationale," p. 36.

49. Weitz, *A World Divided*, pp. 70–71; *Vneshniaia Politika Rossii*, ser. 2, vol. 6 (14), pp. 449–50; Couderc, "Réligion et Identité Nationale," pp. 32–5; compensation to the Ottomans in McGrew, *Land and Revolution*, pp. 50–51 and passim in ch. 3.

50. Lambros Baltsiotes, *O Echthros entos ton Teichon: E Mousoulmanike Koinoteta tes Chalkidas (1833–1881)* (Athens: Vivliorama, 2017), pp. 28–9 and pt 8.

51. Service Historique de la Defénse (Vincennes), 1-M 1619, Reconnaissances Turquie, "Notes sur la Turquie par le Maréchal de Camp Baron Pelet," copy of 1826 original.

52. Rigny's massive file of reports and logs in Archives Diplomatiques (Nantes), 166PO / B / 84.

53. Douin, *Mission Militaire Française*, p. 111.

54. St. Clair, *That Greece Might Still Be Free*, p. 300.

55. Airapetov, *Istoriia Vneshnei Politiki*, vol. 2, p. 67.

56. First discussed in September 1826. Airapetov, *Istoriia Vneshnei Politiki*, vol. 2, pp. 69–70; Fadeev, *Rossiia i Vostochnyi Krizis*, pp. 168–2.

57. For example, in January 1826: Douin, *Mission Militaire Française*, pp. 94–5.

58. Fahmy, *All the Pasha's Men*, pp. 59–60.

59. The joint statement of the admirals in *Vneshniaia Politika Rossii*, ser. 2, vol. 7 (15), pp. 262–3, October 1827.

60. Douin, *Mission Militaire Française*, pp. 135–6; Fahmy, *All the Pasha's Men*, pp. 59–60.

61. Intercepted letter from Viaro Capodistria to his brother, 28 October 1827, in National Archives (London), CO136 / 44, Greek Revolution, Sept–Dec 1827.

62. Fadeev, *Rossiia i Vostochnyi Krizis*, pp. 171–2.

63. Smiley, "War without War."

64. Fadeev, *Rossiia i Vostochnyi Krizis*, pp. 171–2.

65. Athanassoglou-Kallmyer, *French Images*, plate 73, p. 115.

Epilogue

1. Fadeev, *Rossiia i Vostochnyi Krizis*, pp. 145–8.

2. Antones Klapses, "To Elleniko Zetema kai e Europaïki Diplomatia, 1821–1827," in Veremes and Klapses, eds, *1821*, pp. 187–8; *Vneshniaia Politika Rossii*, ser. 2, vol. 8 (16), pp. 261–65 (October 1828–July 1830).

3. Fadeev, *Rossiia i Vostochnyi Krizis*, chs 3–4.

4. Airapetov, *Istoriia Vneshnei Politiki*, vol. 2, p. 128.

5. Tertsetes, *Theodorou Kolokotroni Apomnemoneumata*, p. 222.

6. Conclusions that were already apparent in 1825: *Vneshniaia Politika Rossii*, ser. 2, vol. 6 (14), p. 194.

7. Daskalakes, *Oi Topikoi Organismoi*, pp. 201–2, 205, 223.

8. Petropulos, *Politics and Statecraft*, pp. 99–100.

9. Tertsetes, *Theodorou Kolokotroni Apomnemoneumata*, pp. 172–3.

10. St. Clair, *That Greece Might Still Be Free*, pp. 306ff; Woodhouse, *Capodistria*, chs 13–14.

11. British Library, Archive and Manuscripts, add ms 36544, Church Papers, vol. II, pp. 35ff.

12. Dialla, "The Congress of Vienna, the Russian Empire, and the Greek Revolution," pp. 27–47.

13. Sotiropoulos, *Liberalism after the Revolution*.

14. Loukia Droulia, "Reflets et Répercussions de l'Expédition Française en Grèce," in Marie-Noëlle Bourguet et al, *Enquêtes en Méditerranée: Les Expéditions Fraçaises d'Égypte, de Morée et d'Algérie* (Athens: Institut des Recherches Néohelleniques, 1999), pp. 51–2; Rodogno, *Against Massacre*, p. 87; Thanases Barlagiannes, *Iatrike Istoria tes Epanastases tou 1821: Oi Aparches tes Sygkroteses tes Ellenikes Demosias Ygeias, 1790–1831* (Athens: EAP, 2022).

15. Yannis Saïtas, ed., *To Ergo tes Gallekes Epistemonikes Apostoles tou Moria, 1829–1838*, 2 vols (Athens: Melissa, 2011–17).

16. Jean Tucoo-Chala, " La Relation de Bory de Saint-Vincent: Un 'Reportage en Direct' sur la Grèce en 1829," in Bourguet et al, eds, *Enquêtes en Méditerranée*, p. 72.

17. Bory de Saint-Vincent, *Relation du Voyage*, avant-propos, vol. 1, p. 25; Bourguet et al, eds, *Enquêtes en Méditerranée*; Marie-Noëlle Bourguet et al, eds, *L'Invention Scientifique de la Méditerranée. Égypte, Morée, Algérie* (Paris: EHESS, 1998).

18. Jennifer Sessions, *By Sword and Plow: France and the Conquest of Algeria* (Ithaca, NY: Cornell University Press, 2011), pp. 6, 28–35.

19. Archives diplomatiques (Nantes), 166PO / B / 84; Rodogno, *Against Massacre*, pp. 85–6.

20. Tertsetes, *Theodorou Kolokotroni Apomnemoneumata*, p. 203.

21. Johann Strauss, "The Greek Connection in Nineteenth-Century Ottoman Intellectual History," in Dimitris Tziovas, ed., *Greece and the Balkans: Identities, Perceptions and Cultural Encounters since the Enlightenment* (London: Routledge, 2003), pp. 47–67.

22. Matt Apuzzo et al, "The Ransom: How a French Bank Captured Haiti," *The New York Times*, 20 May 2022; Irakli Shalolashvili, "An Analysis of the Argentinian Bond Crisis," *University of Miami Inter-American Law Review*, 179 (2015), pp.180–208; Sven van Mourik, "Disciplining the World: Austerity, Europe, and the Global South since the 1970s," dissertation, New York University, 2023.

23. The following gleaned from Levandis, *The Greek Foreign Debt*, pp. 17–18; Andreades, *Istoria ton Ethnikon Daneion*; Giorgos V. Dertiles, "Diethneis Oikonomikes Scheseis kai Politike Exartese: E Ellenike Periptose, 1824–1878," *Istorika*, 1:1 (1983), pp. 145–74; Jamie Martin, *The Meddlers: Sovereignty, Empire, and the Birth of Global Economic Governance* (Cambridge, MA: Harvard University Press, 2022), chs 2–3.

24. Levandis, *The Greek Foreign Debt*, pp. 42, 45.

25. Barlagiannes, *Iatrike Istoria tes Epanastases*, p. 81; Bory de Saint-Vincent, *Relation du Voyage*, vol. 1, pp. 34–5; Gritsopoulos, *Istoria tes Gastounes*, vol. 2, p. 10.

26. Hartley, *Researches in Greece*, pp. 17–18.

27. Bibliothéque de Genève, Collection Eynard, MS SUPPL.1888, ff.126–127 and passim; 257–258.

28. Hartley, *Researches in Greece*, pp. 21–2.

29. Michael Festas, Anna Athanasouli, and Dimitris Dimitropoulos, "Mapping Deserted Villages in the Peloponnese, Eighteenth-Twentieth Centuries: Desertion Patterns at the End of the Greek Revolution," *Mediterranean Historical Review*, 37:2 (2022), pp. 179–202; Gritsopoulos, "Statistikai Eideseis," p. 419. The latter is a broad though sometimes inaccurate summary of the following reports and should be verified against the originals: GAK Athens, Vlachogiannes Collection, cat. 3, Palamedes Papers, f.1a-, b, and g.

30. Bory de Saint-Vincent, *Relation du Voyage*, vol. 1, pp. 100–101.

31. An excellent resource provides the new and old place names: *Metonomasies Oikismon tes Ellados*, https://settlement-renames.eie.gr (accessed 29 August 2022).

32. Gritsopoulos, "Statistikai Eideseis," pp. 440 and 448; GAK Athens, Vlachogiannes Collection, cat. 3, Palamedes Papers, f.1b.

33. Barlagiannes, *Iatrike Istoria tes Epanastases*, ch. 2 and passim.

34. Louis-André Gosse, *Relation de la Peste qui a Régné en Grèce en 1827 et 1828, Contenant des Vues Nouvelles sur la Marche et le Traitement de Cette Maladie* (Paris: A. Cherbuliez, 1838); Dr A.-J. Duval, " André-Louis Gosse, Docteur en Médicine," *Journal de Genève* (21 December 1873), p. 15.

35. Bibliothèque de Genève: "Souvenirs: Séjour en Grèce, Dicté par Louis-André Gosse a son Fils Hyppolyte (20 Octobre 1873)," pp. 6off; MS fr 2688 (Collection Gosse), report of Dr Georges Mavromati to governor of Greece, June 1828; MS fr 2690, lists of deceased Egyptian soldiers, year 1243 in Modon.

36. Bory de Saint-Vincent, *Relation du Voyage*, vol. 1, pp. 226–9.

37. Tucoo-Chala, "La Relation de Bory," pp. 72, 76.

38. Dimitris Dimitropoulos has written extensively on the Aegean in the 1820s, e.g., "The Capture of the Ship Ayios Ioannis Theologos in the Summer of 1825: An Investigation of Limits," *Historein*, 20:1 (2022), and "Peirates ste Steria? Prosphyges, Katadromeis kai Kathemerinoteta ton Paraktion Oikismon sta Chronia tou Agona," in Demetropoulos, Loukos, and Michaelaras, eds, *Opseis tes Eapanastases*, pp. 88–104.

39. Bory de Saint-Vincent, *Relation du Voyage*, vol. 1, pp. 256–7.

40. Papageorgiou, "To Archeio Sisine," pp. 213–5.

41. Tertsetes, *Theodorou Kolokotroni Apomnemoneumata*, pp. 204–6, 208–10, 222.

42. Bory de Saint-Vincent, *Relation du Voyage*, vol. 1, pp. 216–17, 230–31.

43. GAK Athens, Vlachogiannes Papers, cat. 4, box 83 (unpaginated), decree dated 23 March 1833; Bory de Saint-Vincent, *Relation du Voyage*, vol. 1, pp. 220–21.

44. St. Clair, *That Greece Might Still Be Free*, p. 1.

45. On revolutionary and Napoleonic warfare, see Bell, *The First Total War*.

46. Bory de Saint-Vincent, *Relation du Voyage*, vol. 1, pp. 213–15.

47. James Q. Whitman, *Verdict of Battle: The Law of Victory and the Making of Modern War* (Cambridge, MA: Harvard University Press, 2014).

48. Weitz, *A World Divided*, p. 82.

49. https://www.state.gov/reports/2022-report-on-international-religious-freedom/greece/ (accessed 22 March 2024).

50. *The Guardian*, 3 March 2020, https://amp.theguardian.com/world/2020/mar/03 /migration-eu-praises-greece-as-shield-after-turkey-opens-border (accessed 19 August 2023).

51. https://www.kathimerini.gr/opinion/interviews/562938523/leonidas-empeirikos-o -ereynitis-ton-chamenon-glosson/ (accessed 22 March 2024).

Sources and Readings

Archives

Britain

British Library, Archive and Manuscripts
National Archives, London: state and colonial collections

France

Centre des Archives Diplomatiques, Nantes: Archive of French foreign relations, including Ottoman affairs
Archives Diplomatiques, Paris–Courneuve: Formerly the main archive of the Quai d'Orsay
Archives Nationales, Paris: Archives of the French state
Service Historique de la Défense, Vincennes: French Military Archives

Greece

Benaki Museum, Historical Archives, Kifisia (Mouseio Benake, Istorika Archeia)
ELIA-MIET: Greek Literary and Historical Archive, Educational Institute of the National Bank (Elleniko Logotechniko kai Istoriko Archeio, Morphotiko Idryma Ethnikes Trapezes)
GAK Athens: General Archives of the State, Athens (Genika Archeia tou Kratous)
GAK Corfu: General Archives of the State, Archives of the Prefecture of Corfu (Genika Archeia tou Kratous, Archeia Nomou Kerkyras)
IEEE: Historical and Ethnological Society of Greece, Archive of Historical Documents (Istorike kai Ethnologike Etaireia tes Ellados, Archeio Istorikon Engrafon)

Switzerland

Bibliothèque de Genève, Manuscrits et Archives (Manuscript section of the public library of Geneva)

Guide to Select Published Sources

This guide is meant primarily for a readership that does not read Greek. I list Greek-language works that have no counterpart in Russian, French, or English.
An excellent resource that offers the multiple and changing geographic names is managed by a collective led by Dimitris Dimitropoulos: *Metonomasies Oikismon tes Elladas* (The Renaming

of the Settlements of Greece), https://settlement-renames.eie.gr/renames/ (accessed 25 September 2023).

Ottoman Empire and the Balkans

On the problem of Ottoman governance in general, see Ali Yaycıoğlu, *Partners of the Empire: The Crisis of the Ottoman Order in the Age of Revolutions* (Stanford: Stanford University Press, 2016).

The literature on the Ottoman Balkans is very good. A sampling of original research is Antonis Anastasopoulos and Elias Kolovos, eds, *Ottoman Rule and the Balkans, 1760–1850: Conflict, Transformation, Adaptation* (Rethymno: University of Crete, 2007).

On the Ottoman Morea the works of the late Martha Pylia are excellent. See "Conflits Politiques et Comportements des Primats Chrétiens en Morée, avant la Guerre de l'Indépendance," in Anastasopoulos and Kolovos, eds, *Ottoman Rule and the Balkans*, pp. 137–47. Neolkes Sarres offers a unique and persuasive view and he was among the few earlier historians to read Ottoman with its Persian and Arabic dimensions, as well as Romaic Greek: *Proepanastatike Ellada kai Osmaniko Kratos: Apo to Cheirografo tou Souleïman Penach Efende tou Moraïte (1785)* (Athens: Erodotos, 1993).

On Roumeli, there is no better work on both the prerevolution and the Revolution than Kostes Papagiorges, *Ta Kapakia: Varnakiotis, Karaïskakis, Androutsos*, 9th edition (Athens: Kastaniotis, 2014). Dionysis Tzakis's many articles are suggestive of the regional movement to a national cause, for example "From Locality to Nation-State Loyalty," in Petros Pizanias, ed., *The Greek Revolution of 1821: A European Event* (Istanbul: Isis, 2011), pp. 129–149. K. E. Fleming's is a well-written study of regional politics: *The Muslim Bonaparte: Diplomacy and Orientalism in Ali Pasha's Greece* (Princeton: Princeton University Press, 1999).

The works of Righas Velestinlis were destroyed and efforts to reconstruct them are Regas Velestinles, *Ta Epanastatika*, ed. Demetrios A. Karamperopoulos, 5th edition (Athens: Epistemonike Etaireia Meletes Pheron-Velestinou-Rega, 2005), and P. M. Kitromilides, gen. ed., *Rega Velestinle: Apanta Sozomena* (Athens: The Greek Parliament, 2000–2002).

Ionian Islands, the Mediterranean, and the Empires

The Ionian Islands in various periods are exceptionally well-covered in Konstantina Zanou, *Transnational Patriotism in the Mediterranean, 1800–1850: Stammering the Nation* (New York: Oxford University Press, 2019).

Easily the best study of the Septinsular Republic under Russian protection remains A. M. Stanislavskaia, *Rossiia i Gretsiia v Konste XVIII-Nachale XIX Veka: Politika Rossii v Ionicheskoi Respublike, 1798–1807 gg.* (Moscow: Nauka, 1974). An overview of the Russian presence is Norman Saul, *Russia and the Mediterranean, 1797–1807* (Chicago: University of Chicago Press, 1970).

Anta (Ada) Dialla treats Russia in the Mediterranean, as well as European diplomacy after 1815, in inventive and thoughtful ways: "The Congress of Vienna, the Russian Empire, and the Greek Revolution: Rethinking Legitimacy," *Journal of Modern Greek Studies*, 39:1 (May 2021), pp. 27–47.

Stella Gervais wrote a wide-ranging study of conservative thought in relation to religion, with a lot to say about the Greeks: *Réinventer la Tradition: Alexandre Stourdza et l'Europe de la Sainte-Alliance* (Paris: Honoré Champion, 2008).

August Boppe's military histories are good introductions to French rule in the region, for example: *L'Albanie et Napoléon (1797–1814)* (Paris: Hachette, 1914).

On the British period we have the comprehensive Sakis Gekas, *Xenocracy: State, Class and Colonialism in the Ionian Islands, 1815–1864* (New York: Berghan, 2017), and the anthropological approach of Thomas Gallant, *Experiencing Dominion: Culture, Identity and Power in the British Mediterranean* (Notre Dame, Indiana: University of Notre Dame Press, 2002). On British hegemony in the Mediterranean, see Robert Holland, *Blue-Water Empire: The British in the Mediterranean since 1800* (London: Penguin, 2012).

The Black Sea Region and Russia

Quite a lot of facts and data are contained in the Black Sea History Working Papers, for example Evrydiki Sifneos, Oksana Yurkova, and Valentina Shandra, eds, *Port-Cities of the Northern Shore of the Black Sea: Institutional, Economic and Social Development, Eighteenth-early Twentieth Centuries* (Rethymno: Center for Maritime Studies, 2021). Likewise two books by Druzhinina are filled with interesting and suggestive detail: E. I. Druzhinina, *Severnoe Prichernomor'e v 1775–1800 gg.* (Moscow: Akademiia Nauk, 1959), and *Iuzhnaia Ukraina v 1800–1825 gg.* (Moscow: Nauka, 1970). Also rich in detail is Vassilis Kardasis, *Diaspora Merchants in the Black Sea: The Greeks in Southern Russia, 1775–1861* (Lanham, Maryland: Lexington Books, 2001). Evrydiki Sifneos, *Imperial Odessa: People, Spaces, Identities* (Leiden: Brill, 2018), is unusual for its cosmopolitan eye.

The Greek Revolution

In the mountain of literature on the Revolution itself, there are some very good, well-written overviews, and the best combination of narrative and concision is Vasilis Kremmydas, *E Ellenike Epanastasi tou 1821* (Athens: Gutenberg, 2016). Eminently readable is Mark Mazower's synthesis, *The Greek Revolution: 1821 and the Making of Modern Europe* (New York: Penguin, 2022). Those who read Russian will be well served by Grigorii Arsh, which is based on primary sources: *Eteristskoe Dvizhenie v Rossii: Osvoboditel'naia Bor'ba Grecheskogo Naroda v Nachale XIX v. i Russko-Grechskie Sviazi* (Moscow: Nauka, 1970).

Three samplings of ways to reconsider the Revolution are Demetres Demetropoulos, Chrestos Loukos, and Panagiotes Michaelares, eds, *Opseis tes Epanastases tou 1821: Praktika Synedriou, Athena 12 kai 13 Iouniou 2015* (Athens: Etaireia Meletes tou Neou Ellenismou—Mnemon, 2018); "1821: What Made It Greek? What Made It Revolutionary?," Special Issue of *Historein*, 20:1 (2022), edited by Ada Dialla and Yannis Kotsonis; and Petros Pizanias, ed., *The Greek Revolution of 1821: A European Event* (Istanbul: Isis, 2011).

There are some good, focused studies of Ottoman responses to the Greek uprising: Ozan Ozavci, "The Ottoman Imperial Gaze: The Greek Revolution of 1821–1832 and a New History of the Eastern Question," *Journal of Modern European History*, 21:2 (March 2020), pp. 222–37, which also reviews other works on the topic on pp. 222–3. On Ottoman thought and action in the 1820s a useful course of action is to read the archival sources that are now available thanks to the translation and transcription work of a collective: H. Sükrü Ilicak, ed., "*Those Infidel Greeks*": The Greek War of Independence through Ottoman Archival Documents, 2 vols, (Leyden and Boston: Brill, 2021), vol. 1.

There is a large literature on Greek constitutionalism. Two outstanding and clear-headed works are Xenofon I. Kontiades, *Oi Peripetiodes Istoria ton Epanastatikon Syntagmaton tou 1821: E Themeliotike Stigme tes Ellenikes Politeias* (Athens: Kastaniotes, 2021), and Apostolos Daskalakes, *E Topikoi Organismoi tes Epanastaseos tou 1821 kai to Politeuma tes Epidavrou* (Athens: Vagionakes, 1966).

Maurizio Isabella makes constitutionalism the unifying issue in the Greek and other Mediterranean revolutions of the period, plus Portugal: *Southern Europe in the Age of Revolutions* (Princeton: Princeton University Press, 2023).

364   SOURCES AND READINGS

Memoirs

Among the memoirs I found two to be unusually candid, insightful, readable, and less self-serving than one might expect. The one is Kolokotronis's dictation of his memoirs which are often frank and revealing, and generally thoughtful: Georgios Tertsetes, *Theodorou Kolokotrone Apomnemoneumata* (Athens: Vergina, 2002).

The other—informative and heartfelt—is by Kolokotronis's aide: Photakos [Photios Chrysanthopoulos], *Apomnemoneumata tes Ellenikes Epanastases* (Athens: Sakellariou, 1858).

Biographies

Biographies cover the expected figures and they can be very good: C .M. Woodhouse, *Rhigas Velestinlis: The Protomartyr of the Greek Revolution*. (Limne, Evia: Denise Harvey, 1995); C. M. Woodhouse, *Capodistrias, the Founder of Greek Independence* (Oxford: Oxford University Press, 1973); Grigorii Arsh, *Ioann Kapodistriia v Rossii, 1809–1822* (St. Petersburg: Aleteiia, 2003); Chrestos Loukos, *Ioannes Kapodistrias: Mia Apopeira Istorikes Viographias* (Athens: MIET, 2022); and the still informative and well-written S. T. Lascaris, "Capodistrias avant la Révolution Grecque (Sa Carrière Politique jusqu'en 1822)," doctoral dissertation, University of Lausanne, 1918.

Philhellenes

The Philhellenes occupy an outsized space in the literature. More savvy than most is Theophilus Prousis, *Russian Society and the Greek Revolution* (DeKalb: University of Northern Illinois Press, 1994). William St. Clair is candid and graphic: *That Greece Might Still Be Free: The Philhellenes in the War of Independence* (London: Oxford University Press, 1972). The religious impulses of the movement, often neglected, are well documented in Frédérique Tabaki-Iona, "Philhellénisme Religieux et Mobilization des Français pendant la Révolution Grecque de 1821–1827," *Mots. Les Langues du Politique*, 79 (2005), pp. 52–4; and Anne Couderc, "Religion et Identité Nationale en Grèce pendant la Révolution d'Indépendence (1821–1832): Le Creuset Ottoman et l'Influence Occidentale," in Sylvie Gangloff, ed., *La Perception de l'Héritage Ottoman dans les Balkans* (Paris: L'Harmattan, 2005). Roderick Beaton, *Byron's War: Romantic Rebellion, Greek Revolution* (New York: Cambridge University Press, 2013), shows that there are new meanings to be found in a familiar phenomenon.

The art produced by the movement is on display in Nina Athanassoglou-Kallmyer, *French Images of the Greek War of Independence, 1821–1830* (New Haven: Yale University Press, 1989).

Greek Debt

This is a topic that never goes away though I wish it could, and older studies are still informative: John A. Levandis, *The Greek Foreign Debt and the Great Powers, 1821–1898* (New York: Columbia University Press, 1944). Recent and archive-based is Korinna Schönhärl, *European Investment in Greece in the Nineteenth Century: A Behavioural Approach to Financial History* (London: Routledge, 2020).

Index